MW01120206

Finding Freedom in Confinement

Finding Freedom in Confinement

The Role of Religion in Prison Life

Kent R. Kerley, Editor

PRAEGER™

An Imprint of ABC-CLIO, LLC
Santa Barbara, California • Denver, Colorado

Library of Congress Cataloging-in-Publication Data

Names: Kerley, Kent R., editor.
Title: Finding freedom in confinement : the role of religion in prison life / Kent R. Kerley, editor.
Description: Santa Barbara : Praeger, 2018. | Includes bibliographical references and index.
Identifiers: LCCN 2017042463 (print) | LCCN 2017045713 (ebook) | ISBN 9781440850325 (ebook) | ISBN 9781440850318 (hard copy : alk. paper)
Subjects: LCSH: Prisoners—Religious life. | Criminals—Rehabilitation.
Classification: LCC HV8865 (ebook) | LCC HV8865 .F56 2017 (print) | DDC 365/.665—dc23
LC record available at https://lccn.loc.gov/2017042463

ISBN: 978-1-4408-5031-8 (print)
        978-1-4408-5032-5 (ebook)

22 21 20 19 18   1 2 3 4 5

This book is also available as an eBook.

Praeger
An Imprint of ABC-CLIO, LLC

ABC-CLIO, LLC
130 Cremona Drive, P.O. Box 1911
Santa Barbara, California 93116-1911
www.abc-clio.com

This book is printed on acid-free paper ∞

Manufactured in the United States of America

To Lori, my wife, and our "Great Eight" grandchildren.

Contents

Preface

Much has changed since 2001 when I began studying the contours of religion in prison and the potential impact of faith-based prison programs. At that time the literature was quite limited, and I noted three issues. First, there were only a handful of data-driven studies, and many of those were based on small and nonrepresentative samples. Second, there was a narrow range of inquiry in that nearly all studies were of Protestant inmates and Protestant programs and nearly all were conducted in the United States. Third, and the greatest concern for me, was that most studies considered "evaluations" of faith-based programs were conducted or funded by the ministry providers themselves.

Fast forward nearly 20 years and we now have several data-driven monographs on religion in prison, dozens of data-driven research articles in respectable journals, and dozens of presentations at regional and national conferences. Those publications and presentations have been much more diverse in terms of research methodologies, faith traditions studied, and the location of studies. What is still missing, however, is an edited volume that brings together the past, present, and future of research on religion in correctional contexts. In this volume, *Finding Freedom in Confinement: The Role of Religion in Prison Life*, we provide this missing element. This volume is uniquely interdisciplinary and international in scope as it includes data-driven (quantitative and qualitative), conceptual, and policy-oriented examinations of religion in correctional contexts around the world. This volume moves the discussion of religion in prison away from popular discourse, advocacy works, and media stories that prioritize emotion over empirical verification and sensation over science. Readers will be able to move beyond a strictly emotional understanding of faith, and toward a more scientific understanding of how prisoners use faith in everyday life.

Kent R. Kerley
University of Texas at Arlington

Acknowledgments

Many important people contributed professionally to this research endeavor. I thank Alicia Merritt from Praeger/ABC-CLIO for contacting me about this project, and Jessica Gribble for being a great help and encouragement along the way. I thank our editorial board members for recruiting authors, reviewing manuscripts, and submitting their own work for this project. The board members are Harry Dammer, University of Scranton; Michael Hallett, University of North Florida; Byron Johnson, Baylor University; Jodi Lane, University of Florida; and Todd Matthews, Cabrini College. Thanks to my graduate research assistant, Illandra Denysschen, for extensive proofreading, locating resources, and making sure the manuscript format was consistent. Finally, I thank my amazing administrative assistant, Mrs. Cathy Moseley, for helping me stay organized and anticipating the time and effort needed to complete this project.

Introduction

This unique volume brings together scholars from around the world to examine the contours of religion in prison life. Religion long has been a tool for correctional treatment and inmate survival, but only since the 1980s have social scientists studied the nature, extent, practice, and impact of faith and faith-based prison programs. Although the concept of "jailhouse conversion" is common in the cultural lexicon, most fail to understand the nuances of how faith may work in prison contexts. This volume contains the most contemporary and cutting-edge research on religion in prison life, which includes data-driven (quantitative and qualitative), conceptual, and policy-oriented papers. These chapters will allow readers to move beyond a strictly emotional understanding of faith and toward a more scientific understanding of how prisoners use faith in everyday life.

Although this work stands alone as the first major edited volume specific to the study of religion in prison, it joins a literature that is increasingly well established. In the past five years, there have been five books published that focused, at least in part, on prisoners' experiences with faith and faith-based programs. Chief among those is Johnson's (2012) comprehensive and timely work, *More God, Less Crime: Why Faith Matters and How It Could Matter More*. This work is unparalleled in terms of the care taken in reviewing 273 scientific studies of religion and crime/deviance/delinquency, a large percentage of which involved prisoners. Johnson presents findings from this meta-analysis in a dispassionate and policy-oriented manner. Although there are chapters on religion in prison, the focus of the book is much broader.

Volume editor Kent Kerley's (2014) *Religious Faith in Correctional Contexts* is a data-driven monograph summarizing results from a representative sample survey of 386 inmates, as well as in-depth interviews with 203 inmates, halfway house residents, chaplains, and local parishioners. Although this work includes key insights into the religious lives of inmates, the analysis is limited to prisoners and halfway house residents in Alabama and Mississippi.

Dubler's (2014) *Down in the Chapel: Religious Life in an American Prison* is a fascinating account of religious life in Pennsylvania's maximum-security prison at Graterford. The author provides an ethnographic account of how prisoners with life sentences use faith as an identity resource and coping mechanism in a religiously pluralistic setting. Although the inmates' accounts are incredibly rich and instructive, the study is limited to prisoners with life sentences in the state of Pennsylvania.

Volume editor Kent Kerley's (2015) *Current Studies in the Sociology of Religion* is an edited volume that brings together scholars from around the world to study the impact of religion on a broad range of outcomes. It is a unique "snapshot" of current work being done in the sociology of religion, and reflects the diversity of authors, locations, topics, and faith traditions. Although this volume is comprehensive and interdisciplinary, the focus is much broader than religion in prison life; only 3 of the 18 chapters focus on religion in correctional contexts.

Most recently, Hallett and colleagues (2017) published the research monograph, *The Angola Prison Seminary: Effects of Faith-Based Ministry on Identity*. This work includes results from a groundbreaking new seminary program available to inmates at one of the largest and best-known prisons in the United States. Data collected included a survey of inmates, as well as in-depth interviews with inmates and staff. Although the results are quite interesting, they are limited to a single program in one prison facility.

About the Editor

I have over 16 years of experience conducting high-quality research on faith and faith-based programs in prisons and halfway houses in the United States. This research has culminated, to this point, in 10 peer-reviewed articles, one research monograph, one edited collection, and seven book chapters or encyclopedia entries. My research articles have appeared in well-respected outlets, including *International Journal of Offender Therapy and Comparative Criminology, Journal for the Scientific Study of Religion, Journal of Crime and Justice*, and *Social Forces*. Through this experience and professional contacts, I have recruited leading scholars from across the world that study religion in prison life from a scientific perspective.

Overview of Content

This volume is divided into three parts. Part 1 is entitled *Perspectives on Religion in Prison Settings* and includes a review of conceptual, theoretical, theological, and legal issues at the fore for those studying faith and faith-based programs in prisons. In Chapter 1, Johnson and colleagues explore the psychological and sociological underpinnings of religious identity. Far from simplistic conceptions and cultural skepticism of the validity of religious conversions, the authors provide a review of how religious faith can be used by inmates for identity creation and management, as well as for adaptive coping to difficult life circumstances. In Chapter 2, Perrin and colleagues provide an insightful summary of how faith can be used to promote crime desistance after release from prison. Although certainly this is not the first study of religion and desistance, it is among the first to focus on religion and desistance for sex offenders.

In Chapter 3, Moreno and Kerley provide an overview of legislation and case law that govern the practice of faith in U.S. prisons. Now more than ever, prisoners enjoy a broad range of religious rights, including access to religious texts, meeting space and time for worship and study, accommodation for dietary restrictions, and accommodation for most religious rituals. In Chapter 4, Hallett and Bookstaver present a fascinating case study of Prisoners of Christ (POC), which is a faith-based correctional treatment organization. The organization was under contract with the Florida Department of Corrections to provide inmate services at low cost, but was sued by the Council for Secular Humanism/Center for Inquiry for violation of Florida's "Blaine Amendment." The resulting battle served as an exemplar for the legal, political, and moral issues surrounding faith-based prison programs. In Chapter 5, Skotnicki presents a nuanced historical and theological discussion of the core philosophy and goals of criminal justice systems. He argues, rather convincingly I think, that the simultaneous goals of incapacitation and correction are largely unworkable, and certainly lacking in empirical evidence otherwise.

Part 2 is entitled *Religion in Prison in the United States*. The papers in this part include quantitative, qualitative, and legal analysis of several important issues in the practice of prisoner faith and faith-based programs. In particular, many authors explore how religiosity impacts a broad range of outcomes in the prison context. In Chapter 6, Meade and Bolin use a nationally representative sample of inmates in state and federal facilities to study the impact of religiosity on institutional misconduct. Although most studies of religion and behavioral outcomes in prisons have focused on minor- and medium-range violations, the authors here expand the analysis to consider violent crimes. In Chapter 7, the focus shifts from religion in adult prisons to religion in juvenile detention facilities. Lanza-Kaduce, Lane, and Benedini use data from the Florida Faith and Community-Based Delinquency Treatment Initiative to explore whether religion operates as a protective factor against prisonization, which has implications for positive inmate adjustment, decreases in disciplinary reports, and recidivism after release. In Chapter 8, Leary provides results from her qualitative study of an ex-offender college scholarship program created by Charles W. "Chuck" Colson, founder of Prison Fellowship Ministries. She uncovers key situational and contextual factors that influence how religious faith and college participation, experienced simultaneously, can impact former prisoners' attempts to achieve successful community reentry.

Since the groundbreaking work of William James (1902) in *The Varieties of Religious Experience*, as well as Brock's (1962) influential study, many scholars have explored the foundational issue in the study of religion: religious conversion. In Chapter 9, Rigsby revisits this issue via in-depth interviews with religious converts in a men's prison. The sample included converts to Christianity and Islam, and those interviews were supplemented with prison chaplain interviews. Leary summarizes the prisoners' accounts of the conversion process, as well as their interpretations of identity before, during, and after conversion. In Chapter 10, Hays presents findings from in-depth interviews with maximum security inmates participating in a prison seminary program. Participants were asked about their favorite scriptural stories, and Hays reports that they had a surprisingly extensive knowledge of religious texts, including not only the passages themselves but also their historical context. In many ways, these results call into question the popular culture notion that prisoners typically claim religious conversion or affiliation for special considerations and not for deeply held beliefs.

Chaplains play a critical role in the provision of faith-based programs and in the practice of faith among inmates, and yet have been the subject of few empirical studies. In Chapter 11, Denney fills this gap in the literature via his analysis of in-depth interviews with active prison chaplains. He finds rich information about the backgrounds and motivations of chaplains, including perceptions of how their occupation has changed over time. In Chapter 12, Jolicoeur and Grant discuss current restrictions on religious freedom in prison through the conceptual lens of judicial interpretation. They examine several legislative acts and key cases from the United States and other nations. They present evidence of an evolving and fluid conceptualization of inmate religious freedom, and explain how some restrictions on this freedom have been deemed acceptable, while others have not.

Part 3 is entitled *Religion in Prison outside the United States*. Although some previous chapters included international elements, the chapters here focus specifically on prisons and inmates from outside the United States. These papers also fill an important need in the literature by focusing on religious adherents from faith traditions other than Christian and Evangelical Protestant ones. In Chapter 13, Williams and Liebling provide a much-needed understanding of religion and prison life from the perspective of Muslim inmates. Drawing from fieldwork and in-depth interviews in two English high-security prisons, the authors describe the entanglements between faith recognition and provision, identity and meaning, and institutional power. In Chapter 14, Rubin provides an overview of the potential for radicalization among new Muslim converts in prison contexts. He finds that jihadist radicalization is greater in Middle East and European prisons than in U.S. prisons due to political and social conditions, and offers suggestions for how policy makers and prison officials may effectively address those issues.

In Chapter 15, Teman and Morag provide results from their study of a Jewish religious rehabilitation program, which is called the Torah Rehabilitation Program. The authors provide evidence of how adherence to Orthodox Judaism may serve as a pathway to desistance and successful reentry for men in Israeli prisons. In Chapter 16, we include the first English translation of an important article by Becci, Rhazzali, and Schiavinato, which appeared originally in *Critique Internationale*. This study involved data collection from one prison in Switzerland and one in Italy. The authors elaborate multiple ways in which religion may become significant and meaningful for prisoners identifying as Orthodox, Muslim, or Evangelical. In Chapter 17, Kewley and colleagues conducted in-depth interviews with men incarcerated for sexual crimes from one prison in England and Wales. The authors provide some preliminary explanations for how those convicted of sexual crimes who have engaged with religion or spirituality might use this affiliation to develop new nonoffending narratives and identities, to improve social status, and to reduce the effects of stigma.

The End of the Beginning

I am pleased and honored to serve as editor for this important project. This volume is interdisciplinary, interfaith, and international in scope, and will move the discussion of religion in prison away from popular discourse, advocacy works, and media stories that prioritize emotion over empirical verification and sensation over science. I am also pleased that, to our knowledge, this is the first edited volume on the topic of religion in the prison context. I trust that readers will learn a great deal from these chapters, and that they will take an interest in creating and sustaining scientific research on religion in prison life.

Kent R. Kerley
University of Texas at Arlington

References

Brock, T. C. "Implications of Conversion and Magnitude of Cognitive Dissonance." *Journal for the Scientific Study of Religion* 1 (1962): 198–203.

Dubler, Joshua. *Down in the Chapel: Religious Life in an American Prison*. New York: Farrar, Straus and Giroux, 2014.

Hallett, Michael, Joshua Hays, Byron R. Johnson, Sung Joon Jang, & Grant Duwe. *The Angola Prison Seminary: Effects of Faith-Based Ministry on Identity*. New York: Routledge, 2017.

James, William. *The Varieties of Religious Experience: A Study in Human Nature.* New York: Modern Library, 1902.

Johnson, Byron. *More God, Less Crime: Why Faith Matters and How It Could Matter More.* West Conshohocken, PA: Templeton Press, 2012.

Kerley, Kent R. *Religious Faith in Correctional Contexts.* Boulder, CO: First Forum Press/Lynne Rienner, 2014.

Kerley, Kent R. (Ed.). *Current Studies in the Sociology of Religion.* Basel, Switzerland: MDPI, 2015.

PART 1

Perspectives on Religion in Prison Settings

CHAPTER ONE

Faith and Service: Pathways to Identity Transformation and Correctional Reform

*Byron R. Johnson, Grant Duwe, Michael Hallett,
Joshua Hays, Sung Joon Jang, Matthew T. Lee,
Maria E. Pagano, and Stephen G. Post*

Over the last several decades, a significant body of evidence has emerged that consistently documents how religiosity (i.e., various measures of religious commitment) is associated with reductions in delinquent behavior among youth (Baier & Wright 2001; Johnson & Jang 2012; Johnson, Thompkins, & Webb 2006). Importantly, the salutary effect of religion remains significant even when accounting for other factors that might also prevent illegal behavior (Johnson, Jang, Larson, & Li 2001). Similarly, research has found that highly religious low-income youth from disadvantaged communities are less likely to use drugs than less religious youth from the same poverty-stricken neighborhoods (Jang & Johnson 2001).

There is also evidence that religious involvement may lower the risks of various kinds of delinquent behaviors, including both minor and serious forms of criminal behavior (Evans, Cullen, Burton, & Dunaway 1996). Additionally, one study found that religious involvement may have a cumulative effect throughout adolescence and may significantly lessen the risk of later adult criminality (Jang, Bader, & Johnson 2008; see also Jang & Johnson 2011). In other words, uninterrupted and regular church attendance may further insulate youth from crime and delinquency. Indeed, a number of studies find that religion can help prevent high-risk urban youth from engaging in delinquent behavior (Freeman 1986; Johnson, Larson, Jang, & Li 2000a, 2000b). Similarly, Wallace and Foreman (1998) found that youth who attend church frequently are less likely to engage in a variety of harmful behaviors, including drug use, skipping school, fighting, and violent and nonviolent crimes. It is not an exaggeration to state that youth exposure to religious and spiritual activities can be a powerful inhibitor of crime and youth violence. These findings are consistent with other empirical evidence linking religiosity to reductions in criminal deviance among adults and young adults (Duwe & Johnson 2013; Evans, Cullen, Dunaway, & Burton 1995; Johnson 2011; Johnson & Jang 2012; ; Kerley, Matthews, & Blanchard 2005).

The religion-crime literature has grown over the last several decades and has benefited from publication of rigorous systematic reviews and several meta-analytic studies that utilize demanding methodological tools to evaluate objectively the state of research in his area. Taken together, these review studies confirm that increasing religiosity is associated with lower rates of crime (Baier & Wright 2001; Johnson & Jang 2012; Johnson, Li, Larson, & McCullough 2000; Kelly, Polanin, Jang, & Johnson 2015). Consequently, a systematic review of the literature confirms that religion matters in consequential and beneficial ways when it comes to crime reduction (Jang, Bader, & Johnson 2008; Jang & Johnson 2005; Johnson, Jang, Li, & Larson 2001; Ulmer, Desmond, Jang, & Johnson 2010), lower rates of recidivism for ex-prisoners (Duwe & Johnson 2013; Duwe & King 2013; Johnson 2002, 2004, 2011; Johnson & Larson 2003; Johnson, Larson & Pitts 1997;), and in helping alcohol and drug abusers to desist (Johnson, Lee, Pagano, & Post 2016; Lee, Pagano, Johnson, & Post 2016). Regardless of the sample, the data set utilized, or other study differences, church attendance and religious experiences remain important factors linked to lower levels of deviant behavior and higher levels of prosocial behavior (Johnson & Jang 2012; Kerley, Matthews, & Blanchard 2005; Lee, Pagano, Johnson, & Post 2016; Lee, Poloma, & Post 2013). Simply put, we know that higher religiosity is consistently associated with less crime and delinquency.

Why Faith Matters in Crime Reduction

To know that religion is linked to less crime is obviously important, but it would be shortsighted to stop there. Research is needed to answer the more difficult question of *why* religion matters. Unfortunately, questions like the following rarely have been studied by scholars: Why are at-risk youth from disadvantaged communities who regularly attend church less likely to violate the law? Why does religiosity or religiousness help reduce the likelihood of adult criminal activity? Why do inmates who participate in Bible studies at a high level have significantly lower recidivism rates than comparable prisoners who do not participate? If graduates of faith-based prison programs outperform their secular counterparts when it comes to prisoner reentry, what is it about these programs that helps ex-prisoners successfully navigate the transition back to society?

There are several reasons for this research oversight. The main reason is that scholars for many decades have tended to overlook the study of religion. This reason is precisely why David B. Larson, the prolific health and spirituality scholar, so often referred to religion as the "forgotten factor" when it comes to research in the social and behavioral sciences. Another reason for this blind spot is that the data that would make it possible to address adequately *why* religion matters is either rarely available or has yet to be collected. Ironically, in spite of the dire need for efficacious approaches to a host of crime-related problems, coupled with published studies documenting the salutary effect of religion on crime, there often remains a reluctance to consider faith-based approaches. This reluctance points to the critical need for more thoughtful data collection and rigorous analysis of variables that would help us better identify the possible mechanisms and pathways that might accurately gauge *why* religion matters.

Faith Enhances Protective Networks of Support

Although we know that church attendance matters in positive ways, we do not have extensive research that clarifies why it is important for crime reduction. We can, however, draw upon research on church attendance across a variety of other related subjects to help us consider some possible explanations for why religion matters for crime reduction. For example, when people attend churches they tend to get connected to different social networks. Whether through classes, retreats, small groups, mission trips, church-sponsored volunteer work, or any number of related group functions, these activities connect people to multiple networks of social support that have the potential to be meaningful. Research documents that social support in congregations has been linked to better coping skills (Krause 2010), increased life expectancy (Krause 2006a), stress reduction (Krause 2006b), and better self-reported health (Krause 2009). In fact, according to Harvard scholar Robert Putnam, churches are enormous repositories of good will:

> Houses of worship build and sustain more social capital—and social capital of more varied forms—than any other type of institution in America. Churches, synagogues, mosques and other houses of worship provide a vibrant institutional base for civic good works and a training ground for civic entrepreneurs. Nearly half of America's stock of social capital is

religious or religiously affiliated, whether measured by association memberships, philanthropy, or volunteering. (Putnam & Feldstein 2004)

Houses of worship can become an effective training ground for good works and civic engagement. More recently, Putnam argues that people with religious affiliations are more satisfied with their lives mainly because they attend religious services more frequently and build social networks with people who share their faith and religious experience, thus building a strong sense of belonging to a community of religious faith (Putnam & Campbell 2010). So compelling are these faith-based networks, Putnam argues, they generate unique effects that cannot be explained in any other way. That is to say, these faith-infused networks of support—in and of themselves—are powerful independent predictors of beneficial outcomes (Lim & Putnam 2010).

Involvement in religious practices and related activities may foster the development of and integration into personal networks that provide both social and emotional support (Jang & Johnson 2004). When such personal networks overlap with other networks, it is reasonable to expect that these networks will not only constrain illegal behavior, but also protect individuals from the effects of living in disadvantaged areas (Krohn & Thornberry 1993). In other words, an individual's integration into a neighborhood-based religious network actually weakens the effects of other factors that might otherwise influence deviant behavior. Thus, religious networks can buffer or shield individuals from the harmful effects of negative structural contents.

It makes sense, therefore, that those who regularly attend church and participate in religious activities would be more likely to internalize values modeled and taught in such settings. These faith-filled networks may encourage appropriate behavior as well as emphasize concern for others' welfare. Such processes may contribute to the acquisition of positive attributes that give attendees a greater sense of empathy toward others, which in turn makes them less likely to commit acts that harm others. Perhaps this influence is why research confirms that religiosity can help people to be resilient even in the midst of poverty, unemployment, or other social ills. Churches and communities of faith provide instruction and the teaching of religious beliefs and values that, if internalized, may help individuals make good decisions.

This influence may explain why church-attending youth from disadvantaged communities are less likely to use illicit drugs than youth from suburban communities who attend church less frequently or not at all. In a similar vein, preliminary research has examined intergenerational religious influence and finds parental religious devotion is a protective factor for crime (Petts 2009; Regnerus 2003). Taken together these findings suggest that the effect of church attendance is compelling in and of itself. Either through the networks of support they provide, the learning of self-control through the teaching of religious moral beliefs, or the condemning of inappropriate behavior, regular church attendance may foster each of these possibilities.

There is additional research documenting that religion can be used as a tool to prevent at-risk populations, like those raised in poverty, from engaging in illegal behavior (Freeman 1986; Johnson, Larson, Jang, & Li 2000b). For example, youth living in poverty tracts in urban environments, or what criminologists call disadvantaged communities, are at elevated risk for a number of problem behaviors including poor school performance, drug use, and other delinquent activities. Yet youth from these same disorganized communities who participate in religious activities are significantly less likely to be involved in deviant activities. In other words, youth from "bad places" can still turn out to be good citizens if religious beliefs and practices are regular and important in their lives. In this way, religiously committed youth, on average, display resilience from the negative consequences of living in impoverished communities (Jang & Johnson 2001).

Whereas criminologists have tended to focus on the effects of living in communities with profound disadvantages that may predispose youth to delinquent behavior, we are now beginning to understand the effects that religion or religious institutions may play in providing "advantages" for those that live in these same communities. Pearce, Jones, Schwab-Stone, and Ruchkin (2003) investigated the relationship between exposure to violence and later problem behavior using the social and health assessment. They found that several measures of religiosity reduced the effect of exposure to violence and victimization on illegal acts. The authors also found that even among youth exposed to high levels of violence, those who reported higher levels of religious practices had fewer conduct problems over time. Additionally, those experiencing high levels of victimization but also indicating higher levels of religiosity were less likely to report an increase in conduct problems (Pearce et al. 2003). These findings are part of a growing body of research that has documented how "protective factors" reduce involvement in crime and delinquency (Crosnoe, Erikson, & Dornbusch 2002; Jessor, Van Den Bos, Vanderryn, Costa, & Turbin 1995; Stacy, Newcomb, & Bentler 1992; Wills, Vaccaro, & McNamara 1992).

The role of religion and religious institutions is especially critical in communities where crime and delinquency are most prevalent. For example, research has shown that the African American church likely plays a key role in reducing crime among Black youth from urban communities (Johnson, Larson, Jang, & Li 2000a). Therefore, though rarely recognized by scholars or policy experts as a provider of informal social control, the African American church likely is an important protective factor, especially in major urban environments. An important study by Evans and colleagues found that religious activities reduced the likelihood of adult criminality as measured by a broad range of criminal acts. The relationship persisted even after "secular" or nonreligious controls were included (Evans, Cullen, Dunaway, & Burton 1995). Further, the finding did not depend on social or religious contexts. It would be a mistake to continue to overlook the important role these religious congregations play in the lives of so many disadvantaged youth (Johnson

2006; Johnson, Larson, Jang, & Li 2000a). In summary, the protective effects of religiosity (i.e., most often measured by regular church attendance) tend to buffer the impact of a wide variety of risk factors that otherwise make crime, delinquency, and substance use more likely.

Faith, Crime Reduction, and Prosocial Behavior

We have made the argument that church attendance can protect individuals from crime and delinquency. Is it also possible that religious practices can help individuals already involved in deviant or illegal behavior? In other words, is it possible that participation in specific kinds of religious activity can help steer individuals back to a course of less deviant behavior and, more importantly, away from long-term criminality? Developmental and life course perspectives provide a theoretical framework for the potential role that religious experiences can play as critical "turning points" in the life course. From this expansive literature we know that turning points change behavioral trajectories from antisocial to prosocial (Petts 2009; Sampson & Laub 2005). Stated differently, can religious beliefs, practices, activities, and networks help provide effective antidotes to help offenders desist from illegal or inappropriate behavior? For example, preliminary studies addressing faith-based approaches to prison treatment have shown that inmates who regularly participate in volunteer-led Bible studies or who complete a faith-based program are less likely to commit institutional infractions (Hercik 2005) or to commit new crimes following release from prison (Duwe & Johnson 2013; Duwe & King 2013; Johnson 2004; Johnson, Larson, & Pitts 1997).

Several studies have shown that prison visitation is associated with reduced recidivism and may benefit inmates during the difficult transition back to society (Bales & Mears 2008). To understand better the connection between visitation and recidivism, a recent study examined whether visits from community volunteers—specifically clergy and mentors—had an impact on recidivism by examining 836 offenders released from Minnesota prisons (Duwe & Johnson 2016). The results indicate that visits from clergy and mentors significantly reduced all three measures of reoffending (rearrest, reconviction, and new-offense reincarceration). The salutary effect on recidivism grew as the proportion of community volunteer visits increased. The findings suggest that community volunteer visits may be consequential for prisoners during reentry and should be recognized as a programming resource, especially for high-risk offenders with low social support.

In the first major evaluation study of a faith-based prison, which was launched in 1997 in Houston, Texas, Johnson and Larson (2003) found that inmates "graduating" from the InnerChange Freedom Initiative (IFI), an 18- to 24-month-length faith-based prison program operated by Prison Fellowship Ministries, were significantly less likely to be arrested than a matched group of prisoners not receiving this religious intervention (8 percent to 20 percent, respectively) during a two-year postrelease period. There was no difference in recidivism rates when all IFI inmates were compared to all members of the matched sample. Johnson and Larson (2003) found that the presence of a faith-motivated mentor was critical in helping ex-prisoners to remain crime free following release from prison. A separate outcome evaluation reported similar results from Minnesota's InnerChange Freedom Initiative, a faith-based prisoner reentry program that has operated within Minnesota's prison system since 2002 (modeled after the InnerChange Freedom Initiative in Texas). Duwe and King (2013) examined recidivism outcomes among a total of 732 offenders released from Minnesota prisons between 2003 and 2009. Results from the Cox regression analyses revealed that participating in the faith-based program significantly reduced the likelihood of rearrest, reconviction, and reincarceration.

These "positive criminology" approaches can draw on secular as well as faith-based models. In the Minnesota Department of Corrections, mentors who visit offenders in prison are associated not only with faith-based programs such as the InnerChange Freedom Initiative but also with community service agencies that are not necessarily faith-based. For example, in the Twin Cities (i.e., Minneapolis and St. Paul) metropolitan area, organizations like Amicus—which recently merged with Volunteers of America–Minnesota—have provided volunteers with opportunities to mentor offenders in prison since the 1960s (Duwe & Johnson 2016). Programs like IFI, Amicus, and the Salvation Army are doing important positive criminology work. Decision makers interested in cost-effective approaches to crime desistance among offender populations should give careful consideration to these promising approaches.

Hallett, Hays, Johnson, Jang, and Duwe (2017) found evidence of a link between religiosity and identity transformation for prisoners at the Louisiana State Penitentiary, also known as "Angola," which is America's largest maximum security prison. But how does religiously motivated self-change happen? What are the causes and pathways for this change? Drawing on data from recent studies and in-depth interviews with prisoners at Angola, the authors described how and why faith matters in identity transformation for prisoners and how this transformation subsequently influences prosocial behavior. Indeed, criminologists have spent far less time studying prosocial behavior than antisocial behavior. This relative neglect is unfortunate because when it comes to prosocial behavior, there is much more encompassed than merely obeying the law and desisting from criminal behavior. We need to know why people do commendable things such as supporting charities, doing volunteer work, and intentionally serving others.

Recent scholarship has examined the relationship between increasing religiosity and higher levels of prosocial behavior. On average, these studies find that religiosity is a source for promoting or enhancing beneficial outcomes like well-being (Blazer & Palmore 1976; Graney 1975; Markides 1983; Musick 1996; Tix & Frazier 1997; Willits & Crider 1988), hope, meaning, and purpose (Sethi & Seligman 1993), self-esteem (Bradley 1995; Ellison & George 1994; Koenig, Hays, Larson, George, Cohen, McCullough, Meador, & Blazer 1999), and educational attainment (Jeynes 2007; Regnerus 2001). For example, the more actively religious are more likely to give to charities (both religious and nonreligious) and to volunteer time for civic purposes (Brooks 2006). A national survey revealed that religious experience was consistently associated with benevolence directed toward the "near and dear" (friends and family), as well as at the level of the community and beyond (Lee, Poloma, & Post 2013). A metareview of a very large number of published studies utilizing diverse samples and methodologies leads to the consistent conclusion that the effect of religion on physical and mental health is remarkably positive (Koenig, Larson, & McCullough 2001).

Studies also suggest that being involved in or exposed to altruistic or prosocial activities and attitudes—something that is central to the mission of many churches and other faith-based organizations—appears to reduce the risk of youth violence. Based on an objective assessment of the research literature, we know that participation in religious congregations and other measures of religiousness can have a significant buffering or protective effect that lessens the likelihood of delinquent or criminal behavior among youth as well as adults. Additionally, we know that increasing measures of religiosity are associated with an array of prosocial outcomes. In this way, religion not only protects from deleterious outcomes like crime and delinquency, but also promotes prosocial or beneficial outcomes that are considered normative and necessary for a productive society. If congregations can be viewed as institutions dedicated to improving the plight of at-risk populations, it may be that faith- and community-based organizations represent key factors in helping ex-prisoners transition to society.

Faith and Service: Keys to Rehabilitation and Recidivism Reduction

As noted previously, the emerging subfield of "positive criminology" (Elisha, Idisis, & Ronel 2012; Ronel, Frid, & Timor 2013; Ronel & Segev 2014) has generated research findings suggesting that positive and restorative practices may be more efficacious than the predominantly punitive approaches currently in use. Such positive and restorative programs may include efforts to foster social support and connectedness, enhance meaningful service to others, promote transformative spiritual experience, and develop noncriminal identity change. Both traditional and more contemporary restorative justice practices attempt to shift the self-centered lifestyle of irresponsibility that is often characteristic of those involved in crime and drug abuse toward a stance of *active responsibility* in all aspects of living (Braithwaite 2005).

Correctional practices can be explicitly designed to promote such a virtuous orientation (Cullen, Sundt, & Wozniak 2001). It is unlikely, however, that one could find very many correctional facilities that openly embrace and prioritize the goal of virtue. By establishing a Bible College in 1995 and encouraging the formation of inmate-led congregations, however, Angola provides a concrete example of a prison designed to promote virtue. John Robson, former director of the Bible College at Angola, argues that this faith-based program is helpful because it:

> . . . de-institutionalizes the dehumanization of punitive justice [because it gives a person] the responsibility of making the *right choices* for the *right reasons*. Whereas dehumanization within a punitive system demands simply making choices for the wrong reasons—because they fear punishment. (Quoted in Hallett, Hays, Johnson, Jang, & Duwe 2017, 13; emphasis in the original)

Robson's observation appears consistent with Braithwaite's (2005, 291) crucial distinction between the *passive* responsibility inherent in the phrase "serving time," and the *active* responsibility central to restorative justice processes that focus on "taking responsibility for putting things right into the future." In other words, when the state "warehouses" an offender this may not directly engage an experience of active responsibility linked to a "redemption script" (Maruna 2001, 85–87). Such scripts support a "coherent and convincing" narrative and related identity transformation that mark the transition from a selfish offender to a responsible and prosocial "new person." From this vantage point, those convicted of crimes are not simply a set of *risks* to be managed or a bundle of *needs* to be met, but a holder of *strengths* to be deployed in mutually beneficial relationships (Maruna & LeBel 2004). The "wounded healer" (e.g., a former addict whose "dark past" with addiction provides the shared experience and credibility needed to help other addicts) is perhaps the most powerful monitor to others.

We now review recent findings on youth recovery that support recent work in positive criminology. Positive criminology highlights traditional rehabilitative and restorative practices, but it also draws attention to a topic that has been somewhat neglected in the literature, which is "cultivating spirituality as a pathway for challenging self-centeredness" (Hallett et al. 2017, 4; see also Ronel & Elisha 2011; Ronel, Frid, & Timor 2013; Ronel & Segev 2014). We begin with a discussion of spirituality and then turn to other factors that are important for adolescent recovery.

Lee, Pagano, Veta, & Johnson (2014) explored changes in belief orientation during treatment and the impact of increased daily spiritual experiences (DSE) on adolescent treatment response. A sample of 195 adolescents referred by the courts to a two-month residential treatment program were assessed at intake and discharge. Forty percent of youth who entered treatment as agnostic or atheist identified themselves as spiritual or religious at discharge. Increased daily spiritual experiences was associated with greater likelihood of abstinence, increased prosocial behaviors, and reduced narcissistic behaviors. This study was the first to include detailed measures of spirituality and religiosity as independent variables at baseline and over the course of treatment for a sample of adolescents following the Alcoholics Anonymous (AA) program, and was the first to determine which aspects of religiosity/spirituality help teens stay sober and engage in service to others (Lee et al. 2014). This study is consistent with recent research attempting to disentangle the effects of religion and spirituality in a 12-step context on care-for-self (e.g., sobriety) and care-for-others (e.g., prosocial behaviors). Indeed, it has been suggested that AA's effectiveness depends on the extent to which those working the 12 steps become more spiritual or religious during the treatment process (Zemore 2007). Increased DSE was associated with greater likelihood of abstinence during treatment and increased care for others. The findings indicate a link between sobriety, spirituality, and service to others and suggest the utility of incorporating spiritual approaches to treatment modalities for young people.

Social anxiety disorder (SAD) affects millions of youth in the United States and is the most common co-occurring anxiety disorder with alcohol and other drug (AOD) use disorders (Buckner et al. 2008; Zimmerman et al. 2003). This fact is especially important because treatment for those struggling with AOD use disorders tends to take place in group settings rather than one-on-one counseling sessions. As might be expected, addicted youth with SAD are less likely to participate in therapeutic activities that carry the risk of negative peer appraisal. Peer helping, however, is a low-intensity, social activity in the 12-step program that has been found to be associated with greater abstinence among those seeking treatment (Pagano, Friend, Tonigan, & Stout 2004; Pagano, Kelly, Scur, Ionescu, Stout, & Post 2013; Pagano, White, Kelly, Stout, & Tonigan 2013).

In another recent study focusing on this very issue, Pagano, Wang, Rowles, Lee, and Johnson (2015) examined the influence of SAD on clinical severity at intake, peer helping during treatment, and outcomes in a large sample of adolescents court-referred to residential treatment. Pagano et al. (2015) found that 42 percent of youths reported a persistent fear of being humiliated or scrutinized in social situations, and 15 percent met current diagnostic criteria for SAD. This study found evidence of an association between SAD and earlier age of first use, greater lifetime use of heroin, incarceration history, and lifetime trauma. SAD, however, was associated with higher service participation during treatment, which was associated with reduced risk of relapse and incarceration in the six-month period posttreatment. Findings confirm the benefits of service participation for juveniles with SAD, which provides a nonjudgmental, task-focused venue for developing sober networks in the transition back into the community.

Another recent study examined the relationships among a specific combination of "spiritual virtues" (helping others and the experience of divine love) and outcomes related to criminal involvement, sobriety, and character development among adolescents (Lee, Pagano, Johnson, & Post 2016). One hundred ninety-five adolescents with substance dependency court-referred to residential treatment were assessed at intake, discharge, and six months following treatment. Lee et al. (2016) found evidence that higher service to others predicted reduced recidivism, reduced relapse, and greater character development. Moreover, experiencing divine love enhanced the effect of service on recidivism. The results suggest that inclusion of the twin spiritual virtues (love and service) might improve treatment for youth involved with alcohol, drugs, and certain forms of self-centered crime such as theft, burglary, and vandalism (Lee et al. 2016). Perhaps treatment approaches focusing on love and service provide a prosocial setting that is necessary for improving character development, reducing AOD use, and decreasing crime.

Social support has long been recognized as vital in bringing patients out of social isolation as well as enhancing sobriety. Recognizing that few individuals, if any, recover from addiction on their own, recovery supports have been a dimension of treatment planning in the American Society of Addiction Medicine's guidelines since its inception in the 1950s. Current alcoholism treatment approaches focus on providing help to clients (e.g., skill acquisition, social support, or pharmacological treatments), and the benefits from receiving social support have been well documented, especially for youth (Nicholson, Collins, & Homer 2004). Moreover, because addiction is a socially isolating disease, social support for recovery is an important element of treatment planning, especially for youth struggling with AOD disorders. A supportive social network that includes members from AA appears especially important for sustained periods of abstinence (Rynes & Tonigan 2012).

A study by Johnson, Pagano, Lee, and Post (2015) examines the relationship between social isolation, giving and receiving social support in Alcoholics Anonymous during treatment, and posttreatment outcomes among youth court-referred to addiction treatment. Based on prior research, Johnson et al. (2015) hypothesized that social isolation would be associated with greater likelihood of relapse and return to criminal activity. Because of the emphasis on service in the 12-step program and associated long-term benefits on abstinence (Pagano, White, Kelly, Stout, & Tonigan 2013), they also hypothesized that giving help would alter AOD use and criminal activity more than receiving help from others in AA. Adolescents (N = 195) aged 14 to 18 were prospectively assessed at treatment admission, treatment discharge, 6 months, and 12 months after treatment discharge. The influence of social isolation variables on relapse and severe criminal activity in the 12 months posttreatment was examined using negative binomial logistic regressions and event history methods. As expected, juveniles entering treatment with social estrangement were significantly more likely to relapse, be incarcerated, and commit a violent crime in the 12-month period following treatment. Giving help to others in AA during treatment significantly reduced the risk of relapse, incarceration, and violent crime in the 12 months after treatment, whereas receiving help did not (Johnson et al. 2015).

In sum, these recent studies of youth struggling with addiction point to the significance of faith and service to others in maintaining sobriety as well as reducing the likelihood of recidivism for other kinds of criminal behavior. These studies confirm that these twin virtues of faith and service may combat narcissism and social isolation, which are factors known to be highly predictive of drug and alcohol abuse among adolescents and young adults. Faith and service also enhance social connectivity, which also enhances responsible behavior and accountability.

Finding Positive Criminology at Angola

In the previous sections of this chapter, we have shown how and why religion matters in consequential ways for juveniles, drug and alcohol addicts, adults, prisoners, and ex-prisoners. In this last section, we connect the mounting body of empirical evidence documenting the positive impact of religion on a variety of outcomes to the research we have conducted on prisoners at the Louisiana State Penitentiary. Just as empirical evidence shows that church attendance is a significant protective factor that insulates individuals from a host of harmful outcomes for the general population, our findings suggest that church attendance in one of 29 different inmate-led churches at Angola is also protective for prisoners. The overlapping networks of social support found within these churches and the Bible College have helped to build much-needed social capital within the prison. Additionally, just as research consistently shows that church attendance is associated with crime reduction and prosocial behavior, we have found that church attendance at Angola has similar effects. Our surveys, as well as in-depth interviews, with prisoners at Angola confirm that participation in the Bible College and attendance at churches within the prison generate many prosocial impacts. For example, the following excerpt from an in-depth interview with one prisoner reflects the tendency towards prosocial behavior:

> How can I meet the needs of the people? Because that's why Jesus came. He came healing. He came feeding the hungry. He came meeting the needs of the people because he's in the people business. And so my ministry is centered on meeting people's needs.

Interviews with prisoners and numerous observations during our fieldwork confirm that faith and service to others within the prison provide a powerful combination that helps to reform prisoners, many of whom are serving life sentences with no hope for parole. Many prisoners we interviewed now view their criminal past recast as a gift and an opportunity to serve others. The time wasted on crime, deviance, addiction, and other self-centered behavior is now reformulated as a valuable experience to help others avoid the same missteps. The following quote is indicative of the prevalent attitude of service, which involves a cognitive process Paternoster and Bushway (2009) called "crystallization of discontent," among Bible College students, graduates, and members of churches:

> A lot of things that I've done or been a part of in the past, I'm not proud of, but I know I can't change it. A lot of people that I've hurt, I wish that I could change it, and I know that I can't. So the man that I used to be and the man that I am now, it's like Clark Kent and Superman, you know? But I know that everything that I've done then has been a testimony to everything that God is doing now. So I'm okay with that. . . . So now, the thing that I try to do now, is try to help other guys from maybe making the same mistakes that I've made.

Like addicts who through faith and service are able successfully to recover and maintain sobriety by experiencing an identity transformation, we find this transformation to be the case with many prisoners at Angola that have been influenced by the Angola church, the Bible College, or a combination of both. The following excerpt from an inmate interview points to identity transformation (Farrall 2005; Giordano, Cernkovich, & Rudolph 2002; Jang & Johnson in press):

> Once you go through the Bible college, it gives you that, it gives you something sort of to grope, to latch onto, so you can be able to start . . . it's a ladder, like, it's a process. So now you put yourself in a position, you are in a position now, the Spirit of God will work with you one way or another at some point going through the four years of college. I've got a purpose, you know? I may not be going home, but I got a purpose. I still have a purpose. I still can serve a purpose while I'm here. I can still serve a purpose for my family, you know? I still communicate with my family and let them know who I am, the different me, the new me. That's when the transition starts.

We also found that participation in both the Bible College as well as involvement in one of Angola's 29 churches has helped inmates develop responsibility and accountability within the prison. The following quotes from two different inmates reflect this prosocial development:

> We have such a higher level of accountability living in this fishbowl. Everything is seen. In here we live in a glass house. If something goes on, everyone

knows about it in no time's sake. So if you confess to be a Christian . . . you have to walk what you talk, because if you don't, everybody knows you're just faking change. So you have to walk what you talk about, and that's a difficult thing to do in here.

Conclusion

Research is beginning to help us understand the importance of religious influences in not only protecting people from harmful outcomes, but in how faith promotes salutary and prosocial outcomes. This beneficial relationship is not simply a function of religion's constraining function or what it discourages—opposing drug use or criminal behavior—but also through what it encourages—promoting behaviors that can enhance purpose, well-being, or educational attainment. Research is beginning to confirm that religious institutions can play an important role in promoting the health and well-being of those they serve, even in prison. And new research will allow us more fully to understand the ways in which religion directly and indirectly impacts crime, delinquency, prisoner rehabilitation, as well as provide insights for rethinking prison reform.

As policy makers consider strategies to reduce crime and drug addiction and to reform our correctional system, it is essential for such deliberations to consider seriously and intentionally the role of religion and religious institutions in implementing, developing, and sustaining multifaceted approaches. From after-school programs for disadvantaged youth to public/private partnerships that bring together secular and sacred groups to tackle social problems like mentoring offenders and the prisoner reentry crisis, it is apparent that any effective strategy will be needlessly incomplete unless the power of religion and religious communities, and the networks of social support found within them, are integrally involved. Indeed, a better understanding of the mechanisms associated with prosocial behavior will assist in the development of future prevention and intervention strategies. Unraveling the role of religiosity, religious institutions and congregations, and the ways in which they promote prosocial behavior should be a priority for academic researchers as well as federal and private sources of funding.

To that end, our research on young offenders struggling with alcohol and drug addiction and prisoners at Angola is helping us to understand the contours of correctional programs seeking to counter the harmful effects of self-centered behavior and social isolation. We also explore whether those programs promote self-control, desistance from crime, identify transformation, and pro-social behavior.

Bibliography

Baier, C. J., & Wright, B. E. " 'If You Love Me, Keep My Commandments:' A Meta-Analysis of the Effect of Religion on Crime." *Journal of Research in Crime and Delinquency* 38 (2001): 3–21.

Bales, W. D., & Mears, D. P. "Inmates Social Ties and the Transition to Society: Does Visitation Reduce Recidivism," *Journal of Research in Crime and Delinquency* 45 (2008): 287–321.

Blazer, D. G., & Palmore, E. "Religion and Aging in a Longitudinal Panel." *Gerontologist* 16 (1976): 82–85.

Bradley, D. E. "Religious Involvement and Social Resources: Evidence from the Data Set 'Americans' Changing Lives." *Journal for the Scientific Study of Religion* 34 (1995): 259–267.

Braithwaite, J. "Between Proportionality & Impunity: Confrontation, Truth, Prevention." *Criminology* 43 (2005): 283–305.

Brooks, A. E. *Who Really Cares: The Surprising Truth about Compassionate Conservatism—Who Gives, Who Doesn't, and Why It Matters.* New York: Basic Books, 2006.

Buckner, J. D., Schmidt. N. B., Lang, A. R., Small, J. W., Schlauch, R. C., & Lewinsohn, P. M. "Specificity of Social Anxiety Disorder as a Risk Factor for Alcohol and Cannabis Dependence." *American Journal of Psychiatric Research* 42 (2008): 230–239.

Crosnoe, R., Erickson, K. G., & Dornbusch, S. M. "Protective Functions of Family Relationships and School Factors on the Deviant Behavior of Adolescent Boys and Girls: Reducing the Impact of Risky Friendships." *Youth and Society* 33 (2002): 515–544.

Cullen, F. T., Sundt, J. L., & Wozniak, J. F. *"Virtuous Prison: Toward a Restorative Rehabilitation."* In H. N. Pontell & D. Shichor (Eds.), *Contemporary Issues in Crime and Criminal Justice: Essays in Honor of Gilbert Geis* (pp. 265–286). Upper Saddle River, NJ: Prentice Hall, 2001.

Duwe, G., & Johnson, B. R. "Estimating the Benefits of a Faith-Based Correctional Program." *International Journal of Criminology and Sociology* 2 (2013): 227–239.

Duwe, G., & Johnson, B. R. "The Effects of Prison Visits from Community Volunteers on Offender Recidivism." *The Prison Journal* 96, no. 2 (2016): 279–303.

Duwe, G., & King, M. "Can Faith-Based Correctional Programs Work? An Outcome Evaluation of the InnerChange Freedom Initiative in Minnesota." *International Journal of Offender Therapy and Comparative Criminology* 57, no.7 (2013): 813–841.

Elisha, E., Idisis, Y., & Ronel, N. "Window of Opportunity: Social Acceptance and Life Transformation in the Rehabilitation of Imprisoned Sex Offenders." *Aggression and Violent Behavior* 17, no.4 (2012): 323–332.

Ellison, C., & George, L. K. "Religious Involvement, Social Ties, and Social Support in a Southeastern Community." *Journal for the Scientific Study of Religion* 33 (1994): 46–61.

Evans, T. D., Cullen, F. T., Burton, V. S., Dunaway, R. G., Payne, G.L., & Kethineni, S. R. "Religion, Social Bonds, and Delinquency." *Deviant Behavior: An Interdisciplinary Journal* 16 (1996): 169–175.

Evans, D. T., Cullen, F. T., Dunaway, R. G., & Burton, V. S. "Religion and Crime Reexamined: The Impact of Religion, Secular Controls, and Social Ecology on Adult Criminality." *Criminology* 33 (1995): 195–224.

Farrall, S. "On the Existential Aspects of Desistance from Crime." *Symbolic Interaction* 28 (2005): 367–386.

Freeman, R. B. "Who Escapes? The Relation of Churchgoing and Other Background Factors to the Socioeconomic Performance of Black Male Youths from Inner-City Tracts." In R. B. Freeman and H. J. Holzer (Eds.), *The Black Youth Employment Crisis*. Chicago: University of Chicago Press, 1986.

Giordano, P. C., Cernkovich, S. A., & Rudolph, J. L. "Gender, Crime, and Desistance: Toward a Theory of Cognitive Transformation." *American Journal of Sociology* 107 (2002): 990–1064.

Graney, M. J. "Happiness and Social Participation in Aging." *Journal of Gerontology* 30 (1975): 701–706.

Hallett, M., Hays, J., Johnson, B. R., Jang, S. J., & Duwe, G. "First Stop Dying: Angola's Christian Seminary as Positive Criminology." *International Journal of Offender Therapy and Comparative Criminology* 61, no. 4 (2017): 445–463.

Hercik, J. M. *Rediscovering Compassion: An Evaluation of Kairos Horizon Communities in Prison*. Caliber Associates, 2005.

Jang, S. J., Bader, C., & Johnson, B. R. "The Cumulative Advantage of Religiosity in Preventing Drug Use." *Journal of Drug Issues* 38, no. 3 (2008): 771–798.

Jang, S. J., & Johnson, B. R. "Neighborhood Disorder, Individual Religiosity, and Adolescent Drug Use: A Test of Multilevel Hypotheses," *Criminology* 39 (2001): 501–535.

Jang, S. J., & Johnson, B. R. "Strain, Negative Emotions, and Deviant Coping among African Americans: A Test of General Strain Theory." *Journal of Quantitative Criminology* 19, no.1 (2003): 79–105.

Jang, S., & Johnson, B. "Explaining Religious Effects on Distress among African Americans." *Journal for the Scientific Study of Religion* 43, no. 2 (2004): 239–260.

Jang, S. J., & Johnson, B. R. "Gender, Religiosity, and Reactions to Strain among African Americans." *Sociological Quarterly* 46, no. 2 (2005): 323–358.

Jang, S. J., & Johnson, B. R. "The Effects of Childhood Exposure to Drug Users and Religion on Drug Use in Adolescence and Young Adulthood." *Youth & Society* 43, no. 4 (2011): 1220–1245.

Jang, S. J., & Johnson, B. R. "Religion, Spirituality, and Desistance from Crime." In A. Blokland & V. van der Geest (Eds.), *International Handbook of Criminal Careers and Life-Course Criminology* (in press). New York: Routledge.

Jessor, R., Van Den Bos, J., Vanderryn, J., Costa, F. M., & Turbin, M. "Protective Factors in Adolescent Problem Behavior: Moderator Effects and Developmental Change." *Developmental Psychology* 31 (1995): 923–933.

Jeynes, W. "Religion, Intact Families, and the Achievement Gap." *Interdisciplinary Journal of Research on Religion* 3 (2007): 1–22.

Johnson, B. R. "Assessing the Impact of Religious Programs and Prison Industry on Recidivism: An Exploratory Study." *The Journal of Corrections* 28 (2002): 7–11.

Johnson, B. R. "Religious Program and Recidivism among Former Inmates in Prison Fellowship Programs: A Long-Term Follow-Up Study." *Justice Quarterly* 21 (2004): 329–354.

Johnson, B. R. *The Role of African American Churches in Reducing Crime among Black Youth.* Institute for Studies of Religion (ISR Research Report), Baylor University, www.isreligion.org/publications/reports. 2006.

Johnson, B. R. (2008). A tale of two religious effects: Evidence for the protective and prosocial impact of organic religion. In K. K. Kline (Ed.), *Authoritative communities: The Search Institute series on developmentally attentive community and society* (Vol. 5). New York: Springer.

Johnson, B. R. "The Role of Religious Institutions in Responding to Crime and Delinquency." In Peter B. Clarke (Ed.), *The Oxford Handbook of the Sociology of Religion.* New York: Oxford University Press, 2009.

Johnson, B. R. *More God, Less Crime: Why Religion Matters and How It Could Matter More.* Conshohocken, PA: Templeton Press, 2011.

Johnson, B. R., & Jang, S. J. "Religion and Crime: Assessing the Role of the Faith Factor." In R. Rosenfeld, K. Quinet, & C. Garcia (Eds.), *Contemporary Issues in Criminological Theory and Research: The Role of Social Institutions* (pp. 117–150). Collected Papers from the American Society of Criminology 2010 Conference, 2012.

Johnson, B. R., & Larson, D. B. *The InnerChange Freedom Initiative: A Preliminary Evaluation of a Faith-Based Prison Program.* Baylor University, Institute for Studies of Religion, ISR Report, 2003.

Johnson, B. R., Larson, D. B., & Pitts, T. "Religious Programming, Institutional Adjustment and Recidivism among Former Inmates in Prison Fellowship Programs." *Justice Quarterly* 14 (1997): 145–166.

Johnson, B. R., Jang, S. J., Larson, D. B., & Li, S. D. "Does Adolescent Religious Commitment Matter? A Reexamination of the Effects of Religiosity on Delinquency." *Journal of Research in Crime and Delinquency* 38 (2001): 22–44.

Johnson, B. R., Larson, D. B., Jang, S. J., & Li, S. D. "The 'Invisible Institution' and Black Youth Crime: The Church as an Agency of Local Social Control." *Journal of Youth and Adolescence* 29 (2000a): 479–498.

Johnson, B. R., Larson, D. B., Jang, S. J., & Li, S. "Who Escapes the Crime of Inner-Cities: Church Attendance and Religious Salience among Disadvantaged Youth." *Justice Quarterly* 17 (2000b): 701–715.

Johnson, B. R., Lee, M. T., Pagano, M. E., & Post, S. G. "Positive Criminology and Rethinking the Response to Adolescent Addiction: Evidence on the Role of Social Support, Religiosity, and Service to Others." *International Journal of Criminology and Sociology* 5 (2016): 75–85.

Johnson, B. R., Li, S. D., Larson, D. B., & McCullough, M. E. "Religion and Delinquency: A Systematic Review of the Literature." *Journal of Contemporary Criminal Justice* 16, no.1 (2000): 32–52.

Johnson, B. R., Pagano, M. E., Lee, M. T., & Post, S. G. "Alone on the Inside: The Impact of Social Isolation and Helping Others on AOD Use and Criminal Activity." *Youth and Society* 47 (2015): 1–22.

Johnson, B. R., Thompkins, R. B., & Webb, D. *Objective Hope—Assessing the Effectiveness of Faith-Based Organizations: A Review of the Literature.* ISR Report, Baylor Institute for Studies of Religion, Baylor University, 2006.

Johnson, E., & Waldfogel, J. *Children of Incarcerated Parents: Cumulative Risk and Children's Living Arrangements.* JCPR Working Paper #306. Chicago: Joint Center for Poverty Research, Northwestern University/University of Chicago, 2002.

Kelly, J. F., Pagano, M. E., Stout, R. L., & Johnson, S. M. "Influence of Religiosity on 12-Step Participation and Treatment Response among Substance-Dependent Adolescents." *Journal of Studies on Alcohol and Drugs* 72 (2011): 1000–1011.

Kelly, P. E., Polanin, J. R., Jang, S. J., & Johnson, B. R. "Religion, Delinquency, and Drug Use: A Meta-Analysis." *Criminal Justice Review* 40, no. 4 (2015): 502–523.

Kerley, K. R., Matthews, T. L., & Blanchard, T. C. "Religiosity, Religious Participation, and Negative Prison Behaviors." *Journal for the Scientific Study of Religion* 44 (2005): 443–457.

Koenig, H. J., Hays, D., Larson, D. B., George, L. K., Cohen, H., McCullough, M., Meador, K., & Blazer, D. "Does Religious Attendance Prolong Survival? A Six Year Follow-Up Study of 3,968 Older Adults." *Journal of Gerontology* 54 (1999): 370–376.

Koenig, H. J., Larson, D. B., & McCullough, M. *Handbook of Religion and Health.* New York: Oxford University Press, 2001.

Krause, N. "Church-Based Social Support and Mortality." *Journal of Gerontology: Social Sciences* 61, no. 3 (2006a): S140–S146.

Krause, N. "Exploring the Stress-Buffering Effects of Church-Based Social Support and Secular Social Support on Health in Late Life." *Journal of Gerontology: Social Sciences* 61, no.1 (2006b): S35–S43.

Krause, N. "Church-Based Volunteering, Providing Informal Support at Church, and Self-Rated Health in Late Life." *Journal of Aging and Health* 21, no.1 (2009): 63–84.

Krause, N. "The Social Milieu of the Church and Religious Coping Responses: A Longitudinal Investigation of Older Whites and Older Blacks." *International Journal for the Psychology of Religion* 20 (2010): 109–129.

Krohn, M. D., & Thornberry, T. P. "Network Theory: A Model for Understanding Drug Abuse among African-American and Hispanic Youth." In M. R. De

La Rosa & J. R. Adrados (Eds.), *Drug Abuse among Minority Youth: Advances in Research and Methodology.* NIDA Research Monograph 130. U.S. Department of Health and Human Services, 1993.

Lee, M. T., Pagano, M. E., Johnson, B. R., & Post, S. G. "Love and Service in Adolescent Addiction Recovery." *Alcohol Treatment Quarterly* 34, no. 2 (2016): 197–222.

Lee, M. T., Pagano, M. E., Veta, P. S., & Johnson, B. R. "Daily Spiritual Experiences and Adolescent Treatment Response." *Alcohol Treatment Quarterly* 32, no. 2 (2014): 290–317.

Lee, M. T., Poloma, M. P., & Post, S. G. *The Heart of Religion: Spiritual Empowerment, Benevolence, and the Experience of God's Love.* New York: Oxford University Press, 2013.

Lim, C., & Putnam, R. D. "Religion, Social Networks, and Life Satisfaction." *American Sociological Review* 75, no. 6 (2010): 914–933.

Maruna, S. *Making Good: How Ex-Convicts Reform and Rebuild Their Lives.* Washington, DC: American Psychological Association, 2001.

Maruna, S., & LeBel, T. "A Strengths-Based Reentry Court." *Offender Programs Report* 8, no. 1 (2004): 1–12.

Markides, K. S. "Aging, Religiosity, and Adjustment: A Longitudinal Analysis." *Journal of Gerontology* 38 (1983): 621–625.

Musick, M. A. "Religion and Subjective Health among Black and White Elders." *Journal of Health and Social Behavior* 37 (1996): 221–237.

Nicholson, H. J., Collins, C., & Holmer, H. "Youth as People: The Protective Aspects of Youth Development in After-School Settings." *The ANNALS of the American Academy of Political and Social Science* 591 (2004): 55–71.

Pagano, M. E., Friend, K. B., Tonigan, J. S., & Stout, R. L. "Helping Other Alcoholics in Alcoholics Anonymous and Drinking Outcomes: Findings from Project MATCH." *Journal of Studies on Alcohol* 65 (2004): 766–773.

Pagano, M. E., Krentzman, A. R., Onder, C. C., Baryak, J. L., Murphy, J. L., Zywiak, W. H., & Stout, R. L. "Service to Others in Sobriety (SOS)." *Alcoholism Treatment Quarterly* 28 (2010): 111–127.

Pagano, M. E., Wang, A. R., Rowles, B. M., Lee. M. T., & Johnson, B. R. "Social Anxiety and Peer-Helping in Adolescent Addiction Treatment." *Alcoholism: Clinical and Experimental Research* 39, no. 5 (2015): 887–895.

Pagano, M. E., White, W. L., Kelly, J. F., Stout, R. L., & Tonigan, J. S. "10-Year Course of Alcoholics Anonymous Participation and Long-Term Outcomes: A Follow-Up Study of Outpatient Subjects in Project MATCH." *Substance Abuse* 34 (2013): 51–59.

Pagano, M. E., Zeltner, B. B., Jaber, J., Post, S. G., Zywiak, W. H., & Stout, R. L. "Helping Others and Long-Term Sobriety: Who Should I Help to Stay Sober?" *Alcoholism Treatment Quarterly* 27 (2009): 38–50.

Pagano, M. E., Zemore, S. E., Onder, C. C., & Stout, R. L. "Predictors of Initial AA-Related Helping: Findings from Project MATCH." *Journal of Studies on Alcohol and Drugs* 70 (2009): 117–125.

Paternoster, R., & Bushway, S. D. "Desistance and the 'Feared Self': Toward an Identity Theory of Criminal Desistance." *Journal of Criminal Law and Criminology* 99 (2009): 1103–1156.

Pearce, M. J., Jones, S. M., Schwab-Stone, M. E., & Ruchkin, V. "The Protective Effects of Religiousness and Parent Involvement on the Development of Conduct Problems among Youth Exposed to Violence." *Child Development* 74, no.6 (2003): 1682–1696.

Petts, R. "Trajectories of Religious Participation from Adolescence to Young Adulthood." *Journal for the Scientific Study of Religion* 48 (2009): 552–571.

Putnam, R. D., & Campbell, D. *American Grace: How Religion Divides and Unites Us.* New York: Simon & Schuster, 2010.

Putnam, R. D., & Feldstein, L. *Better Together: Restoring the American Community.* New York: Simon & Schuster, 2004.

Regnerus, M. D. *Making the Grade: The Influence of Religion upon the Academic Performance of Youth in Disadvantaged Communities.* Research Report, Institute for Studies of Religion. Baylor University, 2001.

Regnerus, M. D. "Linked Lives, Faith, and Behavior: An Intergenerational Model of Religious Influence on Adolescent Delinquency." *Journal for the Scientific Study of Religion* 42 (2003): 189–203.

Ronel, N., & Elisha, E. "A Different Perspective: Introducing Positive Criminology." *International Journal of Offender Therapy and Comparative Criminology* 55, no.2 (2011): 305–325.

Ronel, N., Frid, N., & Timor, U. "The Practice of Positive Criminology: A Vipassana Course in Prison." *International Journal of Offender Therapy and Comparative Criminology* 57, no. 2 (2013): 133–153.

Ronel, N., & Segev, D. "Positive Criminology in Practice." *International Journal of Offender Therapy and Comparative Criminology* 58, no. 11 (2014): 1389–1407.

Rynes, K. N., & Tonigan, J. S. "Do Social Networks Explain 12-Step Sponsorship Effects? A Prospective Lagged Mediation Analysis." *Psychology of Addictive Behaviors* 26, no. 3 (2012): 432–439.

Sampson, R. J., & Laub, J. H. "A Life-Course View of the Development of Crime." *The ANNALS of the American Academy of Political and Social Science* 602 (2005): 12–45.

Sethi, S., & Seligman, M. E. P. "The Hope of Fundamentalists." *Psychological Science* 5 (1993): 58.

Stacy, A. W., Newcomb, M. D., & Bentler, P. M. "Interactive and Higher-Order Effects of Social Influences on Drug Use." *Journal of Health and Social Behavior* 33 (1992): 226–241.

Stephanie L., Randolph, M. N, Vinokur, A. D., & Smith, M. L. (2003). "Providing Social Support May Be More Beneficial Than Receiving It: Results from a Prospective Study of Mortality." *Psychological Science* 14 (1992): 320–327.

Tix, A. P., & Frazier, P. A. "The Use of Religious Coping during Stressful Life Events: Main Effects, Moderation, and Medication." *Journal of Consulting and Clinical Psychology* 66 (1997): 411–422.

Ulmer, J. T., Desmond, S., & Jang, S. J. "Religiosity and Dynamics of Marijuana Use: Initiation, Persistence, and Desistence." *Deviant Behavior* 33 (2012): 448–468.

Ulmer, J. T., Desmond, S., Jang, S. J., & Johnson, B. R. "Teenage Religiosity and Changes in Marijuana Use during the Transition to Adulthood." *Interdisciplinary Journal of Research on Religion* 6 (2010): 1–19.

Wallace, J. M., & Forman T. "Religion's Role in Promoting Health and Reducing Risk among American Youth." *Health Education and Behavior* 25 (1998): 721–741.

Willits, F. K., & Crider, D. M. "Religion and Well-Being: Men and Women in the Middle Years." *Review of Religious Research* 29 (1988): 281–294.

Wills, T. A., Vaccaro, D., & McNamara, G. "The Role of Life Events, Family Support, and Competence in Adolescent Substance Use: A Test of Vulnerability and Protective Factors." *American Journal of Community Psychology* 20 (1992): 349–374.

Zemore, S. E. "A Role for Spiritual Change in the Benefits of 12-Step Involvement." *Alcoholism: Clinical and Experimental Research* 31 (2007): 76–79.

Zimmerman, P., Wittchen, H. U., Hofler, M., Pfister, H., Kessler, R. C., & Lieb, R. "Primary Anxiety Disorders and the Development of Subsequent Alcohol Use Disorders: A 4-Year Community Study of Adolescents and Young Adults." *Psychological Medicine* 33 (2003): 1211–1222.

CHAPTER TWO

Religion and Desistance: Working with Sexual and Violent Offenders

Christian Perrin, Nicholas Blagden, Belinda Winder, and Christine Norman

The place of religion in prisons has received little attention in the context of offender rehabilitation and desistance. Instead, criminological explorations of religion and offending have largely focused on the apparent subversive or criminogenic influence of religion. This is evident across the growing body of research exploring the link between sexual offending and religious authority figures, that is, priests (Eshuys & Smallbone 2006). Scholars have perhaps resisted exploring the impact of religion on rehabilitation and change due to the growing demands for what can be considered robust scientific research; as researchers, we are concerned with observable, measurable constructs, and religion to much an extent is shrouded in mystery and characterized by the personal and subjective experiences of the spirit (Clear, Hardyman, Stout, Lucken, & Dammer 2000). This of course places a limit on any implications that can be drawn from research exploring how religion might impact behavioral change. Nevertheless, some encouraging findings from research that has looked generally at religion in prison can help shed light on why religiosity might warrant discussion in the context of criminal desistance. This chapter explores some of the most prominent arguments for and against religion as a "hook for change," and in doing so, illuminates the present status of this research topic. The authors of this chapter have narrowed focus on the theoretical perspectives that have been most applicable and poignant for the offenders they have worked with throughout recent investigations into religion and criminal activity.

Religion as a Generally Constructive Input: Key Arguments

Thus far, research has demonstrated a relationship between religiosity in prison and reduced frequency and severity of depressive symptoms (Eytan 2011), enhanced ability to cope with feelings of guilt, imprisonment, and social rejection (Aydin, Fischer, & Frey 2010), improved adjustment to the prison environment (Clear & Sumter 2002), and the capacity to establish less stressful and more mutually beneficial inmate relationships (Clear et al. 2000). Although these outputs do not necessarily represent direct links to rehabilitation and desistance, it has been argued that feeling safe, having constructive social inputs, and being able to manage stress while serving time affords prisoners the headspace they need to take stock of their position and make the most of the resources available to them in prison (Blagden & Perrin 2016; Perrin & Blagden 2014). Indeed, the apparent protective elements that religiosity appears to offer prisoners is akin to those discussed in rehabilitative climate studies (Blagden, Perrin, Smith, Gleeson, & Gillies 2017), and in good practice reports disseminated by organizations such as the National Offender Management Service (NOMS) (NOMS 2015). Ellison (1991) has written extensively on the mechanisms via which religiosity may be linked with coping in prison. It has been argued that religious individuals are more likely to engage in religious role taking that is based on prosocial scriptural behaviors such as treating others with respect, kindness, and empathy. Individuals who routinely behave in these ways are more likely to internalize such behaviors and actualize more positive selves (Ellison 1991; Ellison & Levin 1998; Pargament, Tarakeshwar, Ellison, & Wulff 2001).

Along with the claimed protective elements associated with finding religion in prison, the shift in desistance research especially over the last two decades may go some way to explaining how religion can be constructive for inmates. The body of desistance research concerned with offending narratives—the way in which offenders begin to make sense of "going straight" (Laub & Sampson 2001; Maruna 2001; Vaughan 2007)—can be used to explore why the narratives associated with being religious might enable offenders to move away from criminality. Such research depicts desistance as a personal and subjective process, not characterized by a swift and abrupt "knifing off" of a criminal past (Laub & Sampson 2001; Maruna & Roy 2007), or solely a set of reconstructed social bonds (Gottfredson & Hirschi 1990), but a complex journey that involves myriad social and subjective changes (Maruna 2001).

Vaughan (2007), for example, emphasized the importance of reintegrating offenders building subjective desistance narratives around their lives to help them understand why crime may no longer fit into their life story. Maruna (2001) posited that two main forms of such narratives can either see a person locked into a life of persistent offending or on the journey to "going straight" and "making good." Persistent offenders, for instance, are more likely to engage "condemnation scripts," which are characterized by helplessness, low locus of control, and a feeling of being condemned to a life of criminality. Conversely, desisting offenders construct much more optimistic "redemption scripts," which afford individuals a sense of control over their futures and an opportunity to make sense of how and why such a big change (leaving behind a life of criminality) is happening. These latter narratives, Maruna argues, can provide offenders with hope, optimism, and the drive to continue striving for positive change when things get tough (Maruna 2001).

Although research exploring religion and rehabilitation is scarce, there are some encouraging findings that suggest those who adopt religious values and principles "behind bars" may be able to galvanize redemption scripts, cultivate hope, and begin to make sense of going straight. Clear et al. (2000), for example, found that via observing the practices of a specific religion, participants were better able to take responsibility for their "mistakes," deal with consequent guilt from such acknowledgment, and establish a new way of life that appeared to mark a shift away from feeling "doomed to deviance." Perrin and Blagden (2014), in research exploring volunteer work in prisons, found that the establishment of a "new me" through doing good things and giving back was crucial in enabling prisoners to move on with their lives. Whether it be via meaningful activity in prison, religion, education, or the discovery of new constructive inputs, there is congruence across the literature that discusses the importance of offenders' having something meaningful in their lives that they can use to make sense of why offending no longer fits into their life story (Maruna 2001; Vaughan 2007).

Along with the importance attached to desistance narratives, scholars have highlighted the role of subjective as well as social changes in the desistance process (LeBel, Burnett, Maruna, & Bushway 2008). "Turning points" such as marriage, a new job, relocation, or becoming a father (Laub & Sampson 1993) are often categorized as social changes. Much of the research surrounding turning points cites the discovery of religion behind bars. Conversely, subjective changes may take the form of shifts in personality and self-concept, and feature phrases from offenders such as "new person" or a "new outlook on life." Subjective changes have been described alongside words such as "cognitive," "internal," and "identity," and refer commonly to personally meaningful goals, value systems, beliefs, and motivations (LeBel, Burnett, Maruna, & Bushway 2008, 133). The distinction between these two forms of change is important, and promulgates the more contemporary and sophisticated definition of desistance as a long journey that can begin long before the cessation of criminal activity can be truly claimed. This definition highlights the need to understand an individual's mindset before they may begin to consciously rationalize "going straight" or "making good," and before they may have lasted a sustained period of time without offending (Maruna 2001). Put simply, exploring movements *toward* desistance is crucial in understanding and encouraging actual desistance—the cessation of criminal activity over a sustained period of time (Perrin & Blagden 2016). Moreover, understanding the influence of value changes in an individual's life may go some way to explaining how the onset of desistance can be triggered. If religion can indeed be viewed as a turning point that results in changes in an otherwise offending trajectory, it should warrant continued exploration.

There has been some suspicion surrounding cases of religious conversion in prison, with researchers such as Thomas and Zaitzow (2006) raising questions relating to "conning or conversion." Nevertheless, research on religiosity within the general population boasts many positive effects. For example, religion outside of prison has been associated with enhanced mood (Hicks & King 2008), lower rates of substance abuse, lower rates of depression and suicide (Koenig 2008), an increased ability to cope with stressful events (Gall, Malette, & Guirguis-Younger 2011), and increased life expectancy (George, Ellison, & Larson 2002). For those already imprisoned, religiosity has also been demonstrated as reducing general prison deviance, including violence and arguments (Kerley, Copes, Tewksbury, & Dabney 2011) and the number of imposed disciplinary sanctions (O'Connor & Perreyclear 2002). Furthermore, there is large body of research evidence outlining the deterrent effect that religion has (Baier & Wright 2001; Johnson & Jang 2012) and thus its utility in reducing criminal behavior. Indeed, for those who are successful at desisting from crime, religiosity is often attributed as a source of their desistance (Hallett & McCoy 2014). Although there is skepticism within the media apropos prisoners "finding" religion as a means of "faking good" (Tan & Grace 2008), religion may provide a protective factor for some (Johnson & Jang 2012). Religious conversion may also trigger a pathway out of offending (Eshuys & Smallbone 2006), enabling individuals to achieve positive self-change, and provide an adaptive coping and shame management mechanism that allows the replacement of negative labels with a new social identity (Maruna, Wilson, & Curran 2006). Alongside the development of a positive self-identity, scholars have highlighted the importance of a working narrative identity that enables offenders to maintain forward momentum and keep the hope of change alive (Perrin, Blagden, Winder, & Dillon 2017).

Religion and Narrative Identity

A narrative identity can be understood as "an active information-processing structure, a cognitive schema, or a construct system that is both shaped by and later mediates social interaction. People construct stories to account for what they do and why they do it" (Maruna & Copes 2005, 33). In this way, when individuals especially with sexual offense convictions espouse religious identities or actively use religious narratives in the construction of self, the accounts are not impassive or value-neutral but are attempts to construct and convey a positive and stable narrative identity. Religious converts, for example, routinely construct a "prosocial narrative identity" that can account for why their prior actions are not true reflections of their core selves and why their present and future actions have new meaning and significance (Kerley & Copes 2009). This narrative shift is an important aspect in the creation of a prosocial identity and also for the desistance process. Indeed, religious narratives allow for a new lens through which people can view their lives, and an opportunity to reinterpret their current situation into something more positive and manageable (Kerley & Copes 2009; Maruna et al. 2006).

As has been noted, religious conversion in offenders undergoing some form of identity shift can aid in the maintenance of a viable identity (Maruna, Wilson, & Curran 2006). In a study from Blagden et al. (2011) that investigated overcoming denial, one theme from participants' narratives was that at the time of their offending, arrest and conviction were especially a time of identity crisis, with the fear of going to prison and the fear of being found out as a "sex offender" especially damaging. However, overcoming denial for most participants was based on a narrative characterized by "moral reform," via which individuals who had offended could return to "being good" through "getting right with God" (Presser & Kurth 2009). Through such narratives, offenders can portray "good selves" and assert that the person who offended is not really who they are (ibid). This reference to religion occurred in several other interviews, and may suggest that religions or other "appeals to higher loyalties" can influence/change/transform one's narrative identity. Changes in narrative identities and the subscription of redemptive scripts represent important mechanisms for self-change and afford individuals the belief that change is possible and that they are not "doomed to deviance"—that is, forever stuck in a deviant life with no hope of escape (Maruna & Copes 2005). This links with Sykes and Matza's (1957) neutralization technique that links to the "appeal to higher loyalties." However, instead of the technique facilitating offending, as in the original conception, it appears it is being used to help participants to re-story life in a positive manner. Thus, believing that a higher power is "behind" you and protecting you may make the journey toward redemption appear more achievable.

Personal change, identity transformation, and assigning oneself new core roles and beliefs is not an easy thing for someone to do; such transformations can be uncomfortable and liable to cause feelings of anxiety and fear. Transformations in one's identity require substantial and at times global shifts in one's self-understandings, as well as requiring significant effort in renegotiating interpersonal interactions (Veysey, Martinez, & Christian 2009). Goffman

(1963) emphasized this struggle particularly with regard to stigma and stigmatized individuals. He contends that the issue for stigmatized individuals is how they manage the spoiled identity in interactional and interpersonal contexts. One possible way could be to deny or disavow that identity and present oneself in a different light. Another way, as described up to this point, is to attach to new and "clean" value system (e.g., Christianity), which can provide validation that change has either occurred or is occurring. In this sense, changes in narrative identities strike at the heart of the Good Lives Model (GLM) of offender rehabilitation (see Ward & Marshall 2007; Ward & Stewart 2003). The GLM aims to help offenders construct more adaptive narrative identities while also giving the offender the tools to enable them to attain those goods that are important to them postrelease. This parallels Vaughan's (2007) argument that change in one's internal narrative identity comes from a reconsolidation of their ultimate concerns. There is evidence to suggest that religion can represent the core from which many of these mechanisms can flourish and assist the desistance process in offenders.

Redemption and Resurrection

The redemptive self is a powerful motivator of change because one's identity becomes invested in this narrative of change (McAdams 2006). In essence, redemption is the deliverance from suffering to a positive affective state. In cultural narratives, common redemptive narratives incorporate forms of Christian atonement with redemption being one of the strongest themes in Western culture (McAdams 2006). A negative emotional event becomes the opening act in a transformative and redemptive sequence. The positive ending, here, being a "new" person and being redeemed by God, can become an enduring sense of positive self-transformation within the identity-defining life story (McAdams 2006). The "redemption script," for example, is characterized by wanting to "give something back" and a recognition that, although individuals cannot change the past, they are aware that no one but themselves can control their present and future (Maruna 2001). There are, however, limits to this narrative and to "God's forgiveness."

Across the research, the themes relating to redemption have links to the Christian concept of resurrection, which comprises of death, descent into hell, and finally the resurrection (Geary 2010). The "resurrected self" is a form of identity metamorphosis (see Robinson & Smith 2009). In narrative storytelling terms, we can understand the religious narrative effects on sexual offenders as potentially akin to a "rebirth" plot, whereby the individual begins in an aversive setting and through various plots twists and turns becomes a "new" person. This transformative episode (or rebirth) has been found to occur during and after traumatic events and related to identity transitions (Robinson & Smith 2009). This identity metamorphosis has been linked to redemptive episodes, where the negative past is reconstructed as a positive and leads to the transformation of that person (McAdams 2006). This narrative construction has been noted in individuals with sexual offenses who have overcome their offense denial. For example, Blagden et al. (2011) found the reflection of the "me now" was a product of the recognition of the failings of the "old self," with some participants ascribing religious beliefs as a facilitator of this identity shift (Blagden et al. 2011). Research has been consistent in revealing how offenders crave to be redeemed in the eyes of loved ones and by wider society (Maruna 2001; Perrin & Blagden 2014; Vaughan 2007), and the creation of a new, religious viable identity, at its most primitive, can galvanize a framework whereby one becomes their "resurrected" good self.

Forgiveness is a core Christian value, and it is thought that forgiveness enhances one's relationship with God and is part of carrying out "God's plan" (Macaskill 2007; Rye et al. 2001). Forgiving the self appears important in the self-change process, as forgiveness narratives are future-orientated and important for the process of "moving on." In research by Perrin, Blagden, Winder, & Dillon (2017), there was some reluctance from participants to "fully" forgive themselves, but there was a consistent theme that self-forgiveness was important for a positive future. Being able to forgive the "self" appeared a form of "active responsibility-taking" (Ware & Mann 2012). A belief in God, that is, having God on your side, supported this form of adaptive responsibility-taking.

Is Religion Protective or Subversive for Offenders?

Ultimately, the research concerning religion and offending since the emergence of desistance theory has centered on its influence as either positive or negative. This section presents some of the core viewpoints from each standpoint. First, despite the varieties of beliefs and practices across religions, there are commonalties in the research on religion and rehabilitation that highlight several protective mechanisms available to those who belong to a particular faith. For example, research has revealed that all varieties of religion involve (1) some form of reflective practice (which may be prayer, meditation, mindfulness, and ritual) that involves an individual undertaking personal and direct communion with a higher figure (Brown & Ryan 2003; Tremmel 1993); (2) a moral code or tenets by which an individual should live his or her life, and there is typically some sense of punishment for transgressors or reward for loyal followers (Stavrova & Siegers 2014); (3) a sense of community and belonging, characterized by feeling like part of an "in-group" (Ysseldyk, Matheson, & Anisman 2010); (4) a sense of purpose and meaning in life, often derived from the social groups and activities that come with practicing a specific faith (Emmons 2005). All of these core tenets of religion have in some way been linked with better outcomes for offenders both in and after prison. For example, the research on therapeutic communities (TCs) mostly in the context of violent and sexual offenders has consistently revealed that reflective practice, self-reflection in groups and alone, and opportunities for learning, practice, rehearsal, and modeling are key for positive outcomes (Ware, Frost, & Hoy 2010). Through involvement in religious practices and social groups, individuals incarcerated for crimes are better equipped to engage in such activities, which may in fact compliment treatment interventions. There is also some evidence that religion itself can underpin therapeutic intervention entirely, with some research highlighting that religious people are more likely to believe that therapy should include coping style training, greater collaborative and less self-directed problem solving, and a focus on self-reflection and openness (Stanley, Bush, Camp, Jameson et al. 2011). Indeed, such principles are considered crucially important in effective TC or rehabilitative climate environments (Blagden & Perrin 2016; Ware, Frost, & Hoy 2010).

Other research has condoned activity that represents opportunity for meaning making and positivity gathering in prison. Perrin, Blagden, Winder, and Dillon (2017), for example, found that sexual offenders who engaged in volunteer social groups while serving time were able to cultivate more meaningful lives in prison, carve out a personally constructive purpose, and share problems and concerns with fellow volunteers. Involvement in such groups also appears to bring similarly positive outputs for prisoners with varying offense types (Perrin & Blagden 2014, 2016). Whether or not religious practice itself is constructive for offender rehabilitation, there is a wealth of evidence that supports prison-based interventions that enable inmates to engage in active citizenship, form prosocial networks, and invest in something legitimate and challenging (Blagden et al. 2017; Edgar, Jacobson, & Biggar 2011). On this pragmatic basis alone, religious groups in prison can be protective for those who engage. More intricately, religion can represent a turning point from which offenders can embrace change and away from crime; provide offenders with hope and a belief that they can desist; galvanize a narrative that enables them to make sense of turning away from crime; enable identity reconstruction; afford offenders the chance to re-story guilt and shame and forgive themselves; and help offenders cultivate meaningful inputs in their lives from which they can generate "goods" that they wish not to lose by reoffending (Geary 2010; Maruna 2001; Robinson & Smith 2009; Ward & Stewart 2003).

Up until this point the discussion of religious narratives has been broadly positive, with theoretical links highlighting how religious narratives may facilitate prosocial identity and potentially crime desistance. However, perhaps more commonly cited is a "darker" side to religion in that "God" can be used, in narrative terms, to rationalize and justify offending behavior. In particular, some have delineated criminogenic effects of religion, arguing that it can contribute to cognitive distortions that facilitate crime (Knabb, Welsh, & Graham-Howard 2012; Saradjian & Nobus 2003; Topalli, Brezina, & Bernhardt 2013) or the creation of an "excuse syntax" (Pollock & Hashmall 1991). Others have portrayed religion in offending contexts as a mode of defensiveness (Rogers & Dickey 1991), an external rationalization of harmful behavior (Neidigh & Krop 1992), or a tool for outright denial (Blagden, Winder, Thorne, & Gregson 2011). In encapsulating many of these "darker" sides to God, one study exploring serious street crime offenders (Topalli, Brezina, & Bernhardt 2013, 49) reported a criminogenic effect of religiosity, highlighting that religion can be used in selfish and self-serving ways by offenders who "exploit the absolvitory tenets of religious doctrine." Essentially, these offenders were found to interpret the religious doctrine in such a way that allowed them to justify their offending, with the authors arguing that this not only allowed but could also maintain and encourage offending (Topalli et al. 2013).

With the exception of some studies (e.g., Topalli et al. 2013), most research on religion and narratives of change is conducted ex post facto, that is, after their offending when they are actively trying to portray good or moral selves. However, it is interesting to consider the narratives of those who were religious and who also offended. In such studies, participants have discussed "falling away from God" or that what they were doing could not be that bad "if God allowed it." These narratives are inherently criminogenic—self-serving biases are frequently linked to criminal behavior—and can ultimately encourage persistence in offending (Tyler & Devinitz 1981). As such, the research agenda concerning individuals' experiences of offending and desisting should include the impact of religious narratives. There are also important implications for practice that need to be considered here, especially those that relate to the efficacy of prison programs and treatment interventions.

There are other ways in which religious subscription may be harmful and encourage persistence in offending. Some research in this regard has pointed to experiences of shame and guilt. Feelings of shame and guilt are quintessential aspects of being human and play a crucial role in how people relate to others (Clark 2012). Shame and guilt have been broadly regarded as "moral emotions" because of their presumed role in inhibiting socially undesirable behavior and in fostering prosocial behavior (Tangney, Stuewig, & Hafez 2011). There is now a large body of data derived from a variety of methodologies that attests to the separateness of shame and guilt as affective experiences (Clark 2012). Shame has been described as representing an important mechanism in crime, justice, and rehabilitation (McAlinden 2007). Harder and Lewis (1987) argue that when experiencing shame, the self is pictured as unable to cope and viewed as a rejected object of scorn and/or disgust. The experience of shame engenders feelings of being worthless and "often motivates denial, defensive anger and aggression" (Tangney & Dearing 2003, 2). When clients experience shame, the self becomes an object of self-scrutiny and the motivation is to externalize blame (Bumby, Marshall, & Langton 1999).

Some research has asserted that religion can lock people into cycles of destructive behavior as a consequence of the high moral and behavioral expectations that religiosity comes with (Graham & Haidt 2010; Heaton 2006). When people fail to live up to the expectations demanded from their God or "higher power," they can experience feelings of worthlessness and a sense of having nothing to lose. This in turn can bring about problematic behaviors that can either be subsequently rationalized by absolvitory practices or ruminated on in terms of shame and personal disheartenment (Tangney 1992; Topalli et al. 2013). In terms of the latter, shame has been associated with rational choice decisions to commit crime and thus deviancy amplification (Tibbetts 1997). Shame can also bring about crises in self-identity that can lead to offending. Shame is a discrepancy between what the person wants to be and the way that person is being identified socially. At its core the experience of shame is concerned with one's ideal identity (Lazarus 2006). Maruna, Wilson, and Curran (2006) found that religious "conversion" helped prisoners maintain a viable identity in a time typified by identity crisis. Such conversions were seen as adaptive mechanisms in shame management and allowed negative labels to be replaced with a new identity. However, those who fail to live up to religious conversions or view themselves as "bad believers" can experience opposing religiosity outcomes, such as feelings of failure and low self-worth that subsequently increase the likelihood of offending, especially for sexual offenders (Bumby, Marshall, & Langton 1999; Proeve & Howells 2002).

Conclusion

This chapter has provided an overview of the prominent theoretical contributions and perspectives pertaining to the status of religion in the context of offender change and desistance. Across the growing body of literature exploring this area, there is convergence on several features of a variety of religious doctrines. Many of these features make religiosity potentially valuable in assisting offenders' journeys away from crime. For example, there is a general consensus that religion is one of the major resources used to generate meaning in life. That is, religion often creates attachments to one or more social groups and is associated with involvement in a variety of routine activities (such as prayer) (Fletcher 2004). It has also been robustly argued that people can effectively utilize their religiosity as a coping mechanism, especially during incarceration (Kerley & Copes 2009; Stringer 2009). The structured nature of religious adherence can help individuals take stock of their lives and to come to terms with internal and external stressors (Heilman & Witzkum 2000).

Other research findings have suggested that religious people generally experience enhanced life satisfaction as a consequence of regularly attending religious services, thus building positive and meaningful social networks (Lim & Putnam 2010; Rambo 1993). All of these outputs are synonymous with those often described as critically important in the literature surrounding risk and protective factors, adequate rehabilitative climate, and desistance (Blagden et al. 2017; Lösel & Farrington 2012; Mann, Hanson, & Thornton 2010). As such, at the very least, it is conceivable to think of religion as a platform from which offenders can build prosocial networks, cultivate meaning and purpose during imprisonment, and carve out the headspace needed to make sense of 'going straight' (Blagden & Perrin 2016; Maruna 2001).

Religion may also support desistance in even more intricate and meaningful ways. Göbbels, Ward, and Willis (2012), for example, have emphasized the importance of positive practical identities in the desistance process and the importance of "turning points" that provide the opportunities for the momentum of change in which the self is constructed in a positive light. This chapter has illuminated how offenders can move toward desirable "possible selves" and live up to positive practical identities by subscribing to religious tenets underpinned by moral codes of conduct and prosocial routine activities. Religious individuals may experience turning points from their faith, but may also experience it as a collection of guiding principles that keep them "on track." Indeed, research on violent and sexual offenders has revealed that it is crucial for desisting ex-offenders to have "something to believe in," "something to lose," and positive inputs in life that allow for the construction of positive and desired selves (Abrams & Aguilar 2005; Perrin & Blagden 2014; Perrin et al. 2017). This cannot be underestimated, as research has found that self-identification and positive self-image are significant predictors of postprison outcomes (LeBel, Burnett, Maruna, & Bushway 2008). In contrast, feelings of stigmatization and a fear of being "doomed to deviance" are associated with increased rates of recidivism (McCulloch & McNeill 2008).

In addition to the growing research highlighting religion as a potentially protective influence, there is also optimism of its utility in treatment contexts. Heilman and Witzkum (2000), for example, found that participants suffering with mental illnesses were equipped, via religious beliefs and practices, with a means of destigmatizing their illnesses. This in turn meant that they were better able to engage in therapy. It was argued that for participants, redefining "mental illness" and the prospect of undergoing therapy within religious or spiritual terms made treatment personally and culturally acceptable. Given the intensive treatment programs often involved in prison contexts and the stigma they attract (especially in violent and sexual offending populations)

(Blagden, Winder, Gregson, & Thorne 2013; Ware & Mann 2012), there may be some value in further exploring religious adherence in the context of treatment uptake and their associated gains.

At the very least, with widespread research highlighting problems such as treatment refusal, dropout, and "program anxiety," religion might represent a buffer for some individuals. At present, however, there are large gaps in research surrounding the influence of religion in the context of offender rehabilitation. There are also reasons to exercise caution, with some recent research findings revealing potentially subversive effects from religious subscription such as increased suicide ideation (Azorin, Kaladjian, Fakra, Adida, Belzeaux, Hantouche, & Lancrenon 2013) and therapeutic conflict (Touchet, Youman, Pierce, & Yates 2012). Therefore, whether positive or negative, with 48 percent of UK prisoners classifying themselves as Christian alone (Field 2014), the influence of religion in the context of offending behavior should continue to be allotted space within the sphere of criminological research.

Bibliography

Abrams, L. S., & Aguilar, J. P. "Negative trends, possible selves, and behavior change: A qualitative study of juvenile offenders in residential treatment." *Qualitative Social Work* 4, no. 2 (2005): 175–196.

Aydin, N., Fischer, P., & Frey, D. "Turning to God in the face of ostracism: Effects of social exclusion on religiousness." *Personality and Social Psychology Bulletin* 36, no. 6 (2010), 742–753.

Azorin, J. M., Kaladjian, A., Fakra, E., Adida, M., Belzeaux, R., Hantouche, E., & Lancrenon, S. "Religious involvement in major depression: Protective or risky behavior? The relevance of bipolar spectrum." *Journal of Affective Disorders* 150, no. 3 (2013): 753–759.

Baier, C., & Wright, B. R. E. "'If you love me, keep my commandments': A meta-analysis of the effect of religion on crime." *Journal of Research in Crime and Delinquency* 38, no. 1 (2001): 3–21.

Blagden, N., & Perrin, C. "'Relax lads, you're in safe hands here': Experiences of a sexual offender treatment prison." In C. Reeves (Ed.), *Experiencing imprisonment: Research on the experience of living and working in carceral institutions* (pp. 27–45). New York: Routledge, 2016.

Blagden, N., Perrin, C., Smith, S., Gleeson, F., & Gillies, L. "'A different world' exploring and understanding the climate of a recently re-rolled sexual offender prison." *Journal of Sexual Aggression* 23, no. 2 (2017): 151–166.

Blagden, N., Winder, B., Gregson, M., & Thorne, K. "Working with denial in convicted sexual offenders: A qualitative analysis of treatment professionals' views and experiences and their implications for practice." *International Journal of Offender Therapy and Comparative Criminology* 57, no. 3 (2013): 332–356.

Blagden, N. J., Winder, B., Thorne, K., & Gregson, M. "'No-one in the world would ever wanna speak to me again': An interpretative phenomenological analysis into convicted sexual offenders' accounts and experiences of maintaining and leaving denial." *Psychology Crime and Law* 17, no. 7 (2011): 563–585.

Brown, K. W., & Ryan, R. M. "The benefits of being present: Mindfulness and its role in psychological well-being." *Journal of Personality and Social Psychology* 84, no. 4 (2003): 822.

Bumby, K. M., Marshall, W. L., & Langton, C. M. "A theoretical formulation of the influences of shame and guilt on sexual offending." *The Sex Offender* 3 (1999).

Clark, A. "Working with guilt and shame." *Advances in Psychiatric Treatment* 18, no. 2 (2012): 137–143.

Clear, T. R., Hardyman, P. L., Stout, B., Lucken, K., & Dammer, H. R. "The value of religion in prison: An inmate perspective. *Journal of Contemporary Criminal Justice* 16, no. 1 (2000): 53–74.

Clear, T. R., & Sumter, M. T. "Prisoners, prison, and religion: Religion and adjustment to prison." *Journal of Offender Rehabilitation* 35, no. 3–4 (2002): 125–156.

Edgar, K., Jacobson, J., & Biggar, K. *Time well spent: A practical guide to active citizenship and volunteering in prison.* London: Prison Reform Trust, 2011.

Ellison, C. G. "Religious involvement and subjective well-being." *Journal of Health and Social Behavior* (1991): 80–99.

Ellison, C. G., & Levin, J. S. "The religion-health connection: Evidence, theory, and future directions." *Health Education & Behavior* 25, no. 6 (1998): 700–720.

Emmons, R. A. "Striving for the sacred: Personal goals, life meaning, and religion." *Journal of Social Issues* 61, no. 4 (2005): 731–745.

Eshuys, D., & Smallbone, S. "Religious affiliations among adult sexual offenders." *Sexual Abuse: A Journal of Research and Treatment* 18, no. 3 (2006): 279–288.

Eytan, A. "Religion and mental health during incarceration: A systematic literature review." *Psychiatric Quarterly* 82 (2011): 287–295.

Field, C. D. "Measuring religious affiliation in Great Britain: The 2011 census in historical and methodological context." *Religion* 44, no. 3 (2014): 357–382.

Fletcher, S. K. "Religion and life meaning: Differentiating between religious beliefs and religious community in constructing life meaning." *Journal of Aging Studies* 18 (2004): 171–185.

Gall, T. L., Malette, J., & Guirguis-Younger, M. "Spirituality and religiousness: A diversity of definitions." *Journal of Spirituality in Mental Health* 13, no. 3 (2011): 158–181.

Geary, B. "Resurrection themes in the care of sex offenders." *Practical Theology* 3, no.1 (2010): 9–22.

George, L. K., Ellison, C. G., & Larson, D. B. "Explaining the relationships between religious involvement and health psychological inquiry." *Religion and Psychology* 13, no. 3 (2002), 190–200.

Göbbels, S., Ward, T., & Willis, G. "An integrative theory of desistance from sex offending." *Aggression and Violent Behavior* 17, no. 5 (2012): 453–462.

Goffman, E. *Behavior in public place.* New York: Glencoe, Free Press, 1963.

Gottfredson, M. R., & Hirschi, T. *A general theory of crime.* Redwood City, CA: Stanford University Press, 1990.

Graham, J., & Haidt, J. "Beyond beliefs: Religions bind individuals into moral communities." *Personality and Social Psychology Review* 14, no. 1 (2010): 140–150.

Hallett, J. M., & McCoy, S. "Religiously motivated desistance: An exploratory study." *International Journal of Offender Therapy and Comparative Criminology* 59 (2014): 855–872.

Harder, D.W., & Lewis, S. J. "The assessment of shame and guilt." *Advances in Personality Assessment* 6 (1987): 89–114.

Heaton, P. "Does religion really reduce crime?" *The Journal of Law and Economics* 49, no. 1 (2006): 147–172.

Heilman, S. C., & Witzkum, E. "All in faith: Religion as the idiom and means of coping with distress." *Mental Health, Religion and Culture* 3 (2000): 115–124. doi:10.1080/713685606

Hicks, J. A., & King, L.A. "Religious commitment and positive mood as information about meaning in life." *Journal of Research in Personality* 42 (2008): 43–57.

Johnson, B. R., & Jang, S. J. "Religion and crime: Assessing the role of the faith factor." In R. Rosenfeld, K. Quinet, & C. Garcia (Eds.), *Contemporary issues in criminological theory and research: The role of social institutions* (pp. 117–150). Collected papers from the American Society of Criminology 2010 Conference, 2012.

Kerley, K. R., & Copes, H. "'Keepin' my mind right': Identity maintenance and religious social support in the prison context." *International Journal of Offender Therapy and Comparative Criminology* 53, no. 2 (2009): 228–244.

Kerley, K. R., Copes. H., Tewksbury, R., & Dabney. D. A. "Examining the relationship between religiosity and self-control as predictors of prison deviance." *International Journal of Offender Therapy and Comparative Criminology* 55, no. 8 (2011): 1251–1271.

Knabb, J. J., Welsh, R. K., & Graham-Howard, M. L. "Religious delusions and filicide: A psychodynamic model." *Mental Health, Religion & Culture* 15, no. 5 (2012): 529–549.

Koenig, H. G. "Religion and mental health: What should psychiatrists do?" *Psychiatric Bulletin* 32 (2008): 201–203.

Laub, J. H., & Sampson, R. J. "Turning points in the life course: Why change matters to the study of crime." *Criminology* 31, no. 3 (1993): 301–325.

Laub, J. H., & Sampson, R. J. "Understanding desistance from crime." *Crime and Justice* 28 (2001): 1–69.

Lazarus, R. S. "Emotions and interpersonal relationships: Toward a person-centered conceptualization of emotions and coping." *Journal of Personality* 74, no. 1 (2006): 9–46.

LeBel, T., Burnett, R., Maruna, S., & Bushway, S. "'The chicken and egg' of subjective and social factors in desistance from crime." *European Journal of Criminology* 5, no. 2 (2008): 131–159.

Lim, C., & Putnam, R. D. "Religion, social networks, and life satisfaction." *American Sociological Review* 75, no. 6 (2010): 914–933.

Lösel, F., & Farrington, D. P. "Direct protective and buffering protective factors in the development of youth violence." *American Journal of Preventive Medicine* 43, no. 2 (2012): S8–S23.

Macaskill, A. "Exploring religious involvement, forgiveness, trust, and cynicism." *Mental Health, Religion and Culture* 10, no. 3 (2007): 203–218.

Mann, R. E., Hanson, K., & Thornton, D. "Assessing risk for sexual recidivism: Some proposals on the nature of psychologically meaningful risk factors." *Sexual Abuse: A Journal of Research and Treatment* 22, no. 2 (2010), 191–217.

Maruna, S. *Making good: How ex-convicts reform and rebuild their lives.* Washington, DC: American Psychological Association, 2001.

Maruna, S., & Copes, H. "What have we learned from five decades of neutralization research?" *Crime and Justice* 32 (2005): 221–320.

Maruna, S., & Roy, K. "Amputation or reconstruction? Notes on the concept of 'knifing off' and desistance from crime." *Journal of Contemporary Criminal Justice* 23, no. 1 (2007): 104–124.

Maruna, S., Wilson, L., & Curran K. "Why God is often found behind bars: Prison conversions and the crisis of self-narrative. *Research in Human Development* 3, no. 2–3 (2006): 161–184.

McAdams, D. P. "The redemptive self: Generativity and the stories Americans live by." *Research in Human Development* 3, no. 2–3 (2006): 81–100.

McAlinden, A. M. (Ed.). *The shaming of sexual offenders: Risk, retribution and reintegration.* Chawley Park, Cumnor, Oxford, UK: Hart, 2007.

McCulloch, T., & McNeill, F. "Desistance-focused approaches." In S. Green, E. Lancaster, & S. Feasey (Eds.), *Addressing offending behaviour: Context, practice and values* (pp. 154–171). Cullompton, UK: Willan, 2008.

National Offender Management Service. (2015). *Annual report and accounts 2014–2015.* Retrieved December 1, 2016, from https://www.gov.uk/government/uploads/system/uploads/attachment_data/file/434548/NOMS_AR14_15_report_accounts_Final_WEB.pdf

Neidigh, L., & Krop, H. "Cognitive distortions among child sexual offenders." *Journal of Sex Education and Therapy* 18, no. 3 (1992): 208–215.

O'Connor, T. P., & Perreyclear, M. "Prison religion in action and its influence on offender rehabilitation." *Journal of Offender Rehabilitation* 35, no. 3–4 (2002): 11–33.

Pargament, K. I., Tarakeshwar, N., Ellison, C. G., & Wulff, K. M. "Religious coping among the religious: The relationships between religious coping and well-being in a national sample of Presbyterian clergy, elders, and members." *Journal for the Scientific Study of Religion* 40, no. 3 (2001): 497–513.

Perrin, C., & Blagden, N. "Accumulating meaning, purpose and opportunities to change 'drip by drip': The impact of being a listener in prison. *Psychology, Crime & Law* 20, no. 9 (2014): 1–19.

Perrin, C., & Blagden, N. "Movements towards desistance via peer-support roles in prison." In L. Abrams, E. Hughes, M. Inderbitzin, & R. Meek (Eds.), *Palgrave Studies in Prisons and Penology. The voluntary sector in prisons: Encouraging personal and institutional change* (pp. 99–128). New York: Palgrave Macmillan, 2016.

Perrin, C., Blagden, N., Winder, B., & Dillon, G. "'It's sort of reaffirmed to me that I'm not a monster, I'm not a terrible person': Sex offenders' movements toward desistance via peer-support roles in prison." *Sexual Abuse: A Journal of Research and Treatment.* Published online (2017, March 13), https://doi.org/10.1177/1079063217697133

Pollock, N. L., & Hashmall, J. M. "The excuses of child molesters." *Behavioral Sciences & the Law* 9, no. 1 (1991): 53–59.

Presser, L., & Kurth, S. "'I got a quick tongue': Negotiating ex-convict identity in mixed company." In B. Veysey, J. Christian, & D. J. Martinez (Eds.), *How offenders transform their lives* (pp. 72–86). Portland, OR: Willan Publishing, 2009.

Proeve, M., & Howells, K. "Shame and guilt in child sexual offenders." *International Journal of Offender Therapy and Comparative Criminology* 59 (2002): 855–872.

Rambo, L. *Understanding religious conversion.* New Haven, CT: Yale University Press, 1993.

Robinson, O., & Smith, J. "Metaphors and metamorphoses: Narratives of identity during times of crisis." In *Narrative, memory and identities* (pp. 85–94). Huddersfield, UK: University of Huddersfield, 2009.

Rogers, R., & Dickey, R. "Denial and minimization among sex offenders." *Annals of Sex Research* 4, no. 1 (1991): 49–63.

Rye, M. S., Loiacono, D. M., Folck, C. D., Olszewski, B. T., Heim, T. A., & Madia, B. P. "Evaluation of the psychometric properties of two forgiveness scales." *Current Psychology* 20, no. 3 (2001): 260–277.

Saradjian, A., & Nobus, D. "Cognitive distortions of religious professionals who sexually abuse children." *Journal of Interpersonal Violence* 18, no. 8 (2003): 905–923.

Stanley, M. A., Bush, A. L., Camp, M. E., Jameson, J. P., Phillips, L. L., Barber, C. R., . . . & Cully, J. A. "Older adults' preferences for religion/spirituality in treatment for anxiety and depression." *Aging & Mental Health* 15, no. 3 (2011): 334–343.

Stavrova, O., & Siegers, P. "Religious prosociality and morality across cultures: How social enforcement of religion shapes the effects of personal religiosity on prosocial and moral attitudes and behaviors." *Personality and Social Psychology Bulletin* 40, no. 3 (2014): 315–333.

Stringer, E. C. "Keeping the faith: How incarcerated African American mothers use religion and spirituality to cope with imprisonment." *Journal of African American Studies* 13 (2009): 325–347.

Sykes, G. M., & Matza, D. "Techniques of neutralization: A theory of delinquency." *American Sociological Review* 22, no. 6 (1957): 664–670.

Tan, L., & Grace, R. C. "Social desirability and sexual offenders: A review." *Sexual Abuse: A Journal of Research and Treatment* 20 (2008): 61–87.

Tangney, J. P. "Situational detenninants of shame and guilt in young adulthood." *Personality and Social Psychology Bulletin* 18, no. 2 (1992): 199–206.

Tangney, J. P., & Dearing, R. L. *Shame and Guilt.* New York, NY: Guilford Press, 2003.

Tangney, J. P., Stuewig, J., & Hafez, L. "Shame, guilt, and remorse: Implications for offender populations." *Journal of Forensic Psychiatry & Psychology* 22, no. 5 (2011): 706–723.

Thomas, J., & Zaitzow, B. H. "Conning or conversion? The role of religion in prison coping." *The Prison Journal* 86, no. 2 (2006): 242–259.

Tibbetts, S. G. "Shame and rational choice in offending decisions." *Criminal Justice and Behavior* 24 (1997): 234–255.

Topalli, V., Brezina, T., & Bernhardt, M. "With God on my side: The paradoxical relationship between religious belief and criminality among hardcore street offenders." *Theoretical Criminology* 17, no. 1 (2013): 49–69.

Touchet, B., Youman, K., Pierce, A., & Yates, W. "The impact of spirituality on psychiatric treatment adherence." *Journal of Spirituality in Mental Health* 14 (2012): 259–267.

Tremmel, R. "Zen and the art of reflective practice in teacher education." *Harvard Educational Review* 63, no. 4 (1993): 434–459.

Tyler, T. R., & Devinitz, V. "Self-serving bias in the attribution of responsibility: Cognitive versus motivational explanations." *Journal of Experimental Social Psychology* 17, no. 4 (1981): 408–416.

Ward, T., & Marshall, B. "Narrative identity and offender rehabilitation." *International Journal of Offender Therapy and Comparative Criminology* 51, no. 3 (2007): 279–297.

Ward, T., & Stewart, C. A. "The treatment of sex offenders: Risk management and good lives." *Professional Psychology: Research and Practice* 34, no. 4 (2003): 353.

Ware, J., Frost, A., & Hoy, A. "A review of the use of therapeutic communities with sexual offenders." *International Journal of Offender Therapy and Comparative Criminology* 54, no. 5 (2010): 721–742.

Ware, J., & Mann, R. E. "How should 'acceptance of responsibility' be addressed in sexual offending treatment programs?" *Aggression and Violent Behavior* 17, no. 4 (2012): 279–288.

Vaughan, B. "The internal narrative of desistance." *British Journal of Criminology* 47 (2007): 390–404.

Veysey, B. M., Martinez, D. J., & Christian, J. *"Identity transformation and offender change."* In B. M. Veysey, J. Christian, & D. J. Martinez (Eds.), *How offenders transform their lives.* Devon, UK: Willan, 2009.

Ysseldyk, R., Matheson, K., & Anisman, H. "Religiosity as identity: Toward an understanding of religion from a social identity perspective." *Personality and Social Psychology Review* 14, no. 1 (2010): 60–71.

CHAPTER THREE

Religious Rites and Rights of Prisoners in the United States

Janet Moreno and Kent R. Kerley

The criminal justice system in the United States has been rooted in a variety of punishment philosophies over time. The primary goal of punishment in early prisons was to rehabilitate offenders. Rehabilitation was seen as a way to integrate offenders back into society as productive citizens, but quickly gave way to more punitive approaches, such as incapacitation, just deserts, and retribution. Correctional philosophies would shift many times between rehabilitation and punishment, often in dramatic ways based on various economic, social, and cultural changes. The punitive approach—often called "getting tough on crime"—has predominated since the late 1960s. Regardless of the correctional philosophy used, most criminologists have concluded that the impact of the criminal justice system on crime has been moderate at best (Austin & Irwin 2012).

The role of religion in U.S. prisons currently is a matter of much debate, but it can be argued that the first prisons were faith-based facilities. In fact, the first attempts to establish a correctional system in the U.S. were made by the Religious Society of Friends, a group more commonly known as the Quakers. Their methods were meant to rehabilitate offenders by providing an environment that allowed for reflection, remorse, and communication with God (Kerley 2014; Newbold 1999).

In this chapter we summarize legislation that has significantly influenced religious practice in U.S. prisons. First, we describe the correctional methods of the Quakers that promoted compassionate principles and hard work as essential to rehabilitation. Second, we discuss the First Amendment's religious clauses, which include the Establishment Clause and the Free Exercise Clause. Third, we explain how religious accommodations are examined under an undue hardship standard. Fourth, we describe the role of the Religious Freedom Restoration Act of 1993 in religious rights cases. Fifth, we examine the Religious Land Use and Institutionalized Persons Act (RLUIPA) of 2000, including its constitutionality and application to six religious accommodations in prisons: religious diet, religious services and rituals, Sabbath observance, religious objects, religious literature, and religious grooming and dress. Sixth, we conclude with comments on the effectiveness of RLUIPA and potential applications in future cases.

Early Prisons in the Quaker Era

In 1679, Nantucket, Massachusetts, became home to the first prison in the Massachusetts Bay Colony. Incarceration practices at this facility tended to be quite brutal, as they emphasized physical abuse, including whippings, stocks, and hangings. In 1682, however, William Penn came to the United States and brought with him a different perspective on crime and punishment (Newbold 1999). In addition to founding the Province of Pennsylvania, he created the Quaker code, which highlighted compassionate principles, along with hard work, as essential for the treatment of most offenders (Esperian 2010). The Quaker code's establishment in Pennsylvania, a refuge for the Quakers, was not by chance. The Quakers did not agree with common violent methods like capital punishment because of their religious beliefs. In fact, the Quakers were victims of persecution in other colonies, which resulted in their death or incarceration. Consequently, their own personal experiences with harsh treatment led to their efforts to reform the correctional system.

The Quakers believed that quiet reflection on one's actions was a way to attain Inner Light, which they conceived as a personal revelation resulting in enlightenment. The hope was that prisoners might attain that Inner Light via solitary confinement and hard work (Rubin 2017). By 1718, however, the established Quaker code was removed and harsh English methods became predominant. The new Anglican code reduced the criteria necessary to receive the death penalty and added 13 new capital offenses, which included murder, manslaughter, rape, treason, witchcraft, and sodomy (Esperian 2010).

In 1787, Philadelphia became home to America's first prison reform society called the Society for Alleviating the Miseries of Public Prisons. This group had grave concerns about the harsh treatment of offenders. They wanted to construct a new penitentiary, one that would stir true repentance among offenders (Pizarro, Stenius, & Pratt 2016). In 1790, a milestone for the Quakers was the creation of the first penitentiary in the newly minted United States, which was called the Walnut Street Jail. The penitentiary was created via a law enacted by the Pennsylvania legislature to house offenders separately from homeless and unruly individuals in local communities (Newbold 1999; Rubin 2017). This approach stands in stark contrast to contemporary confinement modalities, where the goal is to separate offenders from members of society, and thus to place all of the "negative influences" in one place.

Soon after the creation of the Walnut Street Jail, the legislature in 1794 changed the penal code once again to eliminate executions for all offenses with the exception of first-degree murder and allowed violent criminals to be placed in solitary confinement. After that change, every felon was incarcerated at the Walnut Street Jail. The penitentiary became a place where offenders were separated from society's negative influences. The goal was for individuals to reflect on their offenses while performing hard work, with reflection and work as pathways to reformation (Rubin 2017). In many ways, the Walnut Street Jail never met expectations. The building had only 16 cells for solitary confinement, and those were used to house the most violent offenders.

To make matters worse, in 1794 the City of Philadelphia forced the Walnut Street Jail to accept offenders from all over the state, which resulted in mass overcrowding (Rubin 2017). Eventually, as the post–Civil War era came to an end, reformers were disappointed with the outcomes of the penitentiary system due to the lack of deterrence and reform. The reformatory movement, which surfaced at the end of the 19th century, highlighted the importance of general education and training. The likelihood of release depended on an offender's achievement and behavior. After this period ended, the progressive movement developed in the early 1900s. People believed that states would be able to manage social problems. Furthermore, they believed that an offender's history was of great importance in tailoring treatment programs to individual needs instead of punishment based on offense severity. This is another stark contrast to the current primary goal of corrections being the incapacitation of the offender (Esperian 2010).

First Amendment Clauses: Establishment and Free Exercise of Religion

The failed attempts to reform offenders through a separate system of inmate confinement—one that placed religious faith and practice as its core goals—solidified the importance of the Establishment Clause in the United States. The First Amendment to the U.S. Constitution contains two clauses pertaining to religion. The first states that Congress will not create a law that establishes a specific religion. This clause not only forbids the appointment of an official religion, but also forbids laws that favor a particular religion over others. The Establishment Clause constructs a boundary between religious institutions' purpose and government interests. This is done to prevent the violence and persecution that have become common consequences of the comingling of government and religion (First Amendment Center 2011). During the first 150 or so years since the founding of the United States, there was not ample opportunity for a clear interpretation of the Establishment Clause due to the First Amendment's lack of application to the states. The First Amendment originally dictated only the actions of Congress and the federal government. However, immediately following the Civil War, the Fourteenth Amendment (1868) was passed. This amendment declares that no state has the authority to deny someone the right to life, liberty, or property without due process. The Establishment Clause is deemed a liberty that is protected by due process. Consequently, the government at all levels must now follow the limitations set forth by the Establishment Clause (First Amendment Center 2011). There is widespread disagreement about the meaning of the phrase "establishment of religion." Some believe that the phrase was meant to prevent the establishment of a national religion, as well as to prevent one religion from being preferred over another. Others believe that establishment of religion means that government should not be influenced at all by religion, including favoring one religion over another.

The second clause pertaining to religion under the First Amendment is the Free Exercise Clause, which stipulates that the government cannot create a law that forbids the free expression of religion. Although this clause could be interpreted very broadly, the U.S. Supreme Court has understood the Free Exercise Clause to mean that individuals have the absolute right to belief systems, yet the freedom to act on those beliefs is not absolute. Problems surface when citizens' duty to follow the law clashes with their religious beliefs or practices, and thus the law would be in violation of the First Amendment if it targeted a certain religion. Issues arise also when a law is neutral to religion, yet manages to unintentionally interfere with a certain religion (Mullally 2011).

Reynolds v. U.S. (1878) was the first case brought to the U.S. Supreme Court in need of an interpretation of the Free Exercise Clause. The Court upheld the legitimacy of a federal law that prohibited polygamy despite the protests of many Mormons. They claimed that polygamy was a necessary part of their religion. In this case, the Court made a strong distinction between religious beliefs and actions. The religious beliefs of individuals cannot be prohibited by the government, but the actions related to their religion can be limited if there is a rational basis for regulation. From this case, the rational basis test was implemented to determine if a law that negatively impacted a religiously motivated action infringed on the Free Exercise Clause (Mullally 2011).

The next significant case was *Lemon v. Kurtzman* (1971). In 1968, Pennsylvania's Nonpublic Elementary and Secondary Education Act was passed, which allowed school district superintendents to compensate teachers at private schools for teaching secular subjects and utilizing resources the superintendent authorized. They key issue in Lemon was whether states could provide funding for nonpublic, nonsecular schools without violating the Establishment Clause. As a result of the act, in many private schools in Pennsylvania, teachers could be paid by the state if they taught classes also available in public schools, used materials available in public schools, and abstained from teaching classes related to religion. The Court found that approximately 25 percent of elementary-aged children in the state attended private schools, and approximately 95 percent of those children attended a Roman Catholic school. The Court held that the act benefited only Roman Catholic schools and thus was unconstitutional. State funding of private schools in this case led the government and religion to intertwine, thus resulting in a violation of the Establishment Clause (First Amendment Center 2011).

From this landmark decision in 1971, the Lemon test was created to determine whether the government action under examination has a genuine secular motive, such as education, public safety, or social welfare. This goal is grounded in the idea that government should not become involved in religious matters. Next, the Court would determine whether state action would essentially result in promoting or hindering religion. Lastly, the action needs to be examined to determine if it would cause government and religion to intertwine (First Amendment Center 2011).

The next major decision was in *Employment Division v. Smith* (1990). In this case, two Oregon residents lost their jobs at a drug rehabilitation organization due to their use of peyote, a hallucinogenic drug, which was taken during a ceremony in their Native American congregation. As a result of this case, the rational basis test was replaced. Now any law that infringes on a religious practice is not required to prove a rational basis, so long as the law applies to everyone and does not aim to burden a certain religion or religious practice (Mullally 2011).

Religious Accommodations and the "Undue Hardship Standard"

An important issue to examine when it comes to legal restrictions on religious practice is the number of accommodations to which individuals are entitled. The U.S. Supreme Court has interpreted cases concerning the First Amendment clauses in which it determined that the government cannot accommodate individual religious practices if they cause a burden to others. The Court held that individuals, under the First Amendment, are not to have others conform their behavior in accordance with religious practice. The government cannot compel some individuals to sacrifice for the sake of other people's religious practices. However, it is necessary to view religious accommodations under an "undue hardship standard" (Schragger, Schwartzman, & Tebbe 2017). This standard means that for religious accommodations to be granted, they should be reasonable to provide without creating significant difficulties or harm to government agents and citizens.

It should be noted that there are some situations in which religious accommodations do not affect third parties (Schragger, Schwartzman, & Tebbe 2017). For instance, in *Protos v. Volkswagen of America* (1986), Angeline Protos worked for a company that granted days off based on seniority and she lacked the seniority necessary to take off every Saturday for Sabbath. However, the company employed a group of individuals that covered absences. There were enough employees to cover for the absence of Protos, and they were not paid an extra amount. The district court held that her observance of the Sabbath would not result in extra costs for Volkswagen or other employees, and thus did not create an undue hardship.

In other instances, accommodating individuals' religious practices would result in undue hardship for others when considering financial and nonfinancial burdens (Schragger, Schwartzman, & Tebbe 2017). For example, in *TWA v. Hardison* (1977), Larry Hardison was an employee of Trans World Airlines. Hardison was part of the Worldwide Church of God, which instructed him to use Saturdays as a day dedicated to his faith and abstinence from work. However, the airline would not accommodate him. The company gave Saturdays off based on employees' seniority, and Hardison did not have the seniority necessary to take off Saturdays. Furthermore, TWA was not able to place him in another position or to find employees willing to exchange days off. He was eventually released by TWA and later sued. The Court determined that giving Hardison Saturdays off would deprive other employees of the benefits of their seniority. Other employees could not be deprived of a benefit because they did not follow a religion that required them to observe the Sabbath on Saturdays.

There are other religious accommodations that fall between no costs and undue hardship (Schragger, Schwartzman, & Tebbe 2017). In *Tooley v. Martin-Marietta Corp.* (1981), Tooley was part of the Seventh Day Adventists that viewed monetary contributions to organized labor as sins. His work, nevertheless, made it mandatory for all employees to pay union dues. Tooley proposed that he would donate an equal percentage to a charity agreed on by both parties. The court held that his religious accommodation was reasonable. Although the union would not receive any dues, the absence of that amount would not stop them from functioning.

Although the previous three cases were important illustrations of the varying degrees of burdens that religious accommodations can have on third parties, they were general cases rooted in workplace relations. This has also been applied to inmates. Inmates are a special population in the United States for whom rights have been a controversial topic. In *Turner v. Safley* (1987), a Missouri inmate named Leonard Safley began a relationship with a female inmate. Eventually, Safley was moved to a different prison. He attempted to send her several letters, and they wanted to be married. However, the prison had a policy in place that forbade inmates from sending letters to other inmates at different prisons, except for family members. Furthermore, another policy made it difficult for inmates to marry each other. The letters were not handed over to the female prisoner because prison officials concluded they would be acting against her best interest. The Court determined that the first policy that banned mail was related to legitimate correctional interests involving the prison's security. On the other hand, the marriage policy was not reasonably related to correctional interests, which consequently violated the inmates' rights.

If a prison policy restricts an inmate's rights, it is necessary to examine several factors to determine if it is reasonably related to correctional interests. First, there needs to be a determination of whether there is a valid relationship between prison rules and the government justification provided. There should be a legitimate and neutral government reason. Second, there must be an examination of whether the inmates can take advantage of their rights via alternative means. Third, it is important to consider whether accommodations provided to inmates will restrict the rights of prison officials or other inmates and affect the prison's resources. Fourth, it is important to determine if there are alternative means of accommodating inmates at minimal costs to correctional interests (Hudson 2008).

Another case that involved inmates' rights, specifically religious rights, was *O'Lone v. Estate of Shabazz* (1987). The Court used the standard set forth by the Safley case. The case involved Muslim inmates who challenged the legitimacy of several New Jersey prison policies. The policies served as barriers for inmates' Friday faith services. The first required outside labor on Friday afternoons, and the second forbade inmates from returning to their housing units during daytime. The Court determined the policies to be in accordance with reasonable correctional interests; consequently, no violation of their free exercise of religion occurred. The state argued that the established policies reduced overcrowding in the prison, resulting in heightened security, and the Court agreed. The Court also determined that the policies in place allowed inmates alternative means of exercising their religious freedom. Although the inmates could not attend Friday afternoon services, the Court determined that they still had the opportunity to attend several other religious gatherings. As stated by the Court, alternative means should provide methods of expressing religious rights, but the alternatives do not have to be the inmate's first choice of expression.

Religious Freedom Restoration Act of 1993

The Religious Freedom Restoration Act of 1993 was the first important legislation that resulted from religious rights cases in the United States. The act was passed as a response to the controversial case, *Employment Division v. Smith* (1990). In this case, two members of the Native American Church were fired from their jobs as drug rehabilitation counselors for participating in a religious ritual where peyote was consumed. The individuals were not able to obtain unemployment benefits due to their misconduct. The U.S. Supreme Court ruled that illegal drug use as part of a religious ritual was not protected. According to Justice Scalia, a religious exclusion that clashes with existing law would have negative and wide-ranging impacts.

The RFRA was enacted in 1993 to reverse this decision (FRFRA Overview 2016). RFRA stated that the government should not significantly restrict free exercise of religion unless it had a "compelling interest" (Bomboy 2014). The standard of compelling interest arose originally in *Sherbert v. Verner* (1963). Adell Sherbert was a part of the Seventh Day Adventists, which instructed believers to practice their Sabbath on Saturdays. She was fired because of her need to be absent from work on Saturdays. She was unable to find other positions that gave her Saturday off. So she applied for unemployment but was rejected because she did not accept appropriate employment and lacked good reason.

During the process of the case, the Sherbert test was created. First, it asks if the state policy placed a significant burden on the individual's religious exercise. Second, it asks if there is a justification that involves compelling state interest and if this is the least restrictive way to carry out this interest. The Court used the test to conclude that Sherbert's religious expression was restricted. She was essentially forced to stray from her religious practice to obtain unemployment compensation. The ruling held that there were other ways to achieve the state's interest to hinder fraudulent unemployment requests. The Court created the opportunity for individuals to request religious exemptions from laws that apply to the general public.

Interestingly, however, in 1997, the U.S. Supreme Court held that the act could not be enforced in states (Bomboy 2014). The case that precipitated this decision was *City of Boerne v. Flores* (1997). In this case, a Catholic archbishop requested a permit to expand his church in Boerne, Texas. Zoning authorities did not grant the permit, citing that the church was part of a historic zone and had to be preserved. The permit was challenged under RFRA. It was concluded that Congress had overstepped its authority when it wanted to implement RFRA to state laws that burdened people's religious exercise. The U.S. Supreme Court deemed that clause unconstitutional. Therefore, RFRA could not override the states' historic preservation ordinances. RFRA is currently a federal law, but various states have passed their own version of RFRA that specifies protections similar to those in the federal version (FRFRA Overview 2016).

Religious Land Use and Institutionalized Persons Act (RLUIPA) of 2000

Following the Court's conclusion that it was unconstitutional to apply RFRA to the states, Congress tried to supplement the missing legislation with passage of the Religious Land Use and Institutionalized Persons Act of 2000. Under the act, the government cannot place a *significant burden* on an individual's free exercise of religion, except if the burden furthers a government interest and it is the *least restrictive method* of advancing that interest. However, this portion applies to certain situations. First, the burden must be placed on a program or activity that obtains federal assistance. Second, the burden itself or the removal of the burden must influence the exchange of products and services across states. Third, the burden must be placed through a land use regulation in which the government can make case-by-case evaluations on how the land is intended to be used. Government must enforce a land use regulation in a way that places a religious institution and a secular institution on equal terms. Government cannot enforce a land use regulation that results in the discrimination of a specific religion. Government cannot enforce a land use regulation that completely denies religious institutions access to a territory or significantly restricts religious institutions in a particular territory.

Besides protecting religious land use, the act protects inmates in exercising their religious rights. The government cannot place a significant burden on the free exercise rights of an institutionalized person, as specified in the Civil Rights of Institutionalized Persons Act (1980). An exception arises if the burden is necessary for the advancement of a compelling government interest and no other less restrictive method of advancing the governmental interest is available. This portion applies in certain cases. In the first potential scenario, the burden is placed on a program or activity benefiting from federal funds. Second, the burden itself or its removal influences the exchange of products and services. RLUIPA's influence originates from three forms of congressional power. Under the Constitution's Spending Clause, the act mandates that all people who receive federal assistance agree to act in accordance with RLUIPA's substantial burden requirement pertaining to land use regulation. Furthermore, the act relies on the Commerce Clause to manage interstate commerce. Finally, Congress strengthens RLUIPA through the Fourteenth Amendment by allowing the act to ratify legislation that enforces people's civil rights. The restrictions were implemented to maintain RLUIPA within Congress's authority (American Center for Law and Justice 2011).

It is important to examine in more detail how the Religious Land Use and Institutionalized Persons Act of 2000 affects inmates. The act holds that any action by the state that places a substantial burden on an inmate's free exercise of religion is illegitimate, unless prison authorities prove that placing a burden on free exercise is the least restrictive method of reaching a compelling correctional interest. Furthermore, it is necessary to mention that lower courts did not recognize the protections afforded to inmates under RFRA. This point is illustrated through the 90 percent of cases that inmates lost. Due to the narrow definition placed on RFRA, the lower courts protected a very limited amount of free exercise. Consequently, in creating RLUIPA, Congress made sure to define the act using an inclusive definition (Gaubatz 2005).

If inmates choose to file a suit, the RLUIPA has three requirements. First, inmates must prove that prison authorities have placed a significant burden on their free exercise of religion. Second, inmates must prove that the burden was placed in a program or activity that obtains federal assistance or that influences the exchange of goods and services. Third, inmates must prove that they have utilized all administrative options available to them. If they are successful in making this claim, then the responsibility shifts to the prison authorities to show that their actions resulting in a significant burden meet strict scrutiny. If officials cannot successfully meet the standard, then inmates have the right to receive appropriate relief, including attorney costs (Gaubatz 2005).

The RLUIPA does not restrict the types of religious exercise that are afforded protection. In fact, its inclusive definition perhaps means that "any" distinct case of religious exercise is protected under the act. This inclusion is beneficial because it resolves the manner in which the courts used the Turner and O'Lone standards. The courts typically strike down suits claiming that a prison has significantly limited a specific religious practice by concluding only that alternative means of religious expression were available to inmates. Such a standard makes it easier for prisons to limit the amount of religious accommodations they provide. This may be particularly true in cases of less common and nonmainstream religions. In general, however, the RLUIPA broadens the availability of religious accommodations (Gaubatz 2005).

RLUIPA only affords protection to acts that are part of religious expression. To obtain protection under the act, plaintiffs must demonstrate two things. First, individuals must show that the burdened action is part of a religious belief, and not based on secular motives. The term "religious belief" refers to beliefs that are founded on a higher power or being on whom everyone else depends. Second, individuals must show that they sincerely hold the religious belief under examination. It is important to weed out false claims because the act will only accommodate truly held religious convictions (Gaubatz 2005). When an individual has satisfied the two requirements, there is a high likelihood that the appropriate accommodations will be made available. At this point there are six important areas of religious accommodations within prisons: diet, religious services, Sabbath observance, religious objects, religious literature, and grooming and dress (Boston & Manville 2011).

Religious Diet

The foods available to prisoners can have an important impact on the exercise of their faith, or even be an aspect of their faith. If inmates must eat a diet inconsistent with their religious teachings, it could adversely impact their level of religious commitment. On the other hand, some inmates may choose not to eat because they want to follow their religious teachings, and their health may suffer (RLUIPA 2015).

One recent case that illustrates RLUIPA's protection of religious diet in prison settings is *Stavenjord v. Schmidt* (2015). Stavenjord, an inmate who practiced Buddhism, asked for a kosher diet and to be allowed to buy a prayer shawl. The Alaska Department of Corrections did not grant his requests; consequently, he filed a claim under RLUIPA. The superior court initially sided with the Department of Corrections claiming that the plaintiff failed to show that his religion required a kosher diet and a prayer shawl, that he held sincere religious beliefs, and that the absence of accommodations significantly burdened his free exercise. The U.S. Supreme Court, however, reversed the lower court's decision, and held that the department of corrections did not demonstrate how granting the accommodation created a burden on prison staff or that there were no other means of granting the request. The Court also held that the RLUIPA does not require a religion to mandate a particular practice for that practice to be accommodated. Thus, in this case the act does not require individuals to prove that their religion deems certain dietary practices as necessary or forbidden. Overall, courts have ruled that faith-based dietary requests should be granted so long as they do not cause an undue burden on prison staff (American Civil Liberties Union 2016).

Religious Services and Rituals

Courts typically rule in favor of inmates' rights to attend religious services; nevertheless, there are exceptions. Prisons are not forced to establish religious services for all religions in an institution, although frequently they work with local faith congregations to offer them (Kerley, Bartkowski, Matthews, & Emond 2010; Kerley, Matthews, & Shoemaker 2009). If there are no religious clergy available for certain religious services, those services will not be offered and no violation of RLUIPA has occurred in those cases (American Civil Liberties Union 2016).

One case illustrating the protection provided for inmates' religious services under RLUIPA was *Mayweathers v. Newland* (2002). Several Muslim inmates sued the California prison system because prison policies punished them for attending religious services on Fridays. The inmates claimed initially a violation of the First Amendment, but after RLUIPA was passed in 2000 they claimed a violation under the new act. The state of California argued that RLUIPA had overstepped the power held by Congress under the Spending and Establishment Clauses. In the end, the U.S. Supreme Court held that the RLUIPA was constitutional and that prison authorities could not punish inmates for attending religious services. The Court found the act to meet all four requirements necessary for laws enacted under the Spending Clause. The act also included the tripartite Lemon test, which meant that it was not a violation of the Establishment Clause.

In the case of *Charles v. Verhagen* (2002), a Muslim inmate filed suit against the Wisconsin Department of Corrections claiming his religious exercise was violated, in addition to RLUIPA. Jerry Charles's prayer rituals called for the use of prayer oil. The Department of Correction, however, implemented guidelines that specified the types of religious items that inmates could possess. The oil needed for the Muslim prayer was not among the listed items. The district court concluded that RLUIPA was within Congress's authority under the Spending and Establishment Clause. The U.S. Supreme Court then ruled in favor of Charles that the accommodation should be made.

Sabbath Observance

Courts have held that limitations forcing inmates to forgo the Sabbath is a violation of the First Amendment (American Civil Liberties Union 2016). A case that illustrated this point was *Murphy v. Carroll* (2002). Murphy, an inmate at the Maryland Correctional Training Center, asked correctional officer Carroll to provide cleaning materials to clean his cell on another day besides the Sabbath. They did not grant his request because prison policy dictated that cleaning materials be provided only on Saturdays. He filed an administrative complaint but was ignored. Murphy eventually sent his grievance to the Inmate Grievance Office. An administrative law judge mandated that prison authorities provide the inmate with cleaning materials on another day besides Saturday. Murphy was accommodated and given cleaning materials on Sundays instead.

Religious Objects

Courts have held frequently that prison authorities can prohibit religious objects that pose security threats. However, they must prove that the prohibitions are based on responses to genuine security threats. Furthermore, prison authorities cannot arbitrarily ban certain religious objects and allow others. Prison authorities are also not compelled to provide the religious objects if the inmates can obtain them on their own (American Civil Liberties Union 2016). The accommodations made for inmates cannot surpass the safety of the correctional officers and other inmates. In *Mark v. Nix* (1993), Kim Mark was an inmate at the Iowa State Penitentiary held in a section of the prison designated for security risk individuals. Mark's rosary with a plastic crucifix attachment was removed from his possession. Prison policy banned metal and plastic crucifixes in the section of the prison where he was housed. A potential security threat would involve the inmates using the crucifixes as keys to remove their handcuffs. However, they could possess plain rosaries. The district court concluded that although the plaintiff had a sincere religious belief, removal of the crucifix was reasonably connected to legitimate security interests.

Religious Literature

Courts have held that prison authorities can restrict the amount of literature that inmates have in their cells, but they cannot ban religious literature if other reading material is allowed. Furthermore, inmates are usually allowed to have the primary literature of their religion (American Civil Liberties Union 2016). Nevertheless, some cases deem it necessary for prisons to ban some religious literature. In *Borzych v. Frank* (2006), Garry Borzych claimed that prison authorities had violated RLUIPA because they denied him three books he described as a necessary part of his free exercise of religion. He was part of the Odinism religion that involves worshipping Norse gods. The Wisconsin prison system, however, claimed the books were not religious literature and that they simply encouraged white-supremacist violence. The prison system agreed that Odinism was a religion, and the district court initially held that the denial of the books significantly burdened his free exercise. Eventually, the judge held that the prison's correctional interest in maintaining safety was compelling because the books promoted violence. The court concluded that the ban on the books was the least restrictive method of furthering the correctional interest.

In a similar case, *Cutter v. Wilkinson* (2005), inmates held in an Ohio prison filed suit under RLUIPA claiming they were not allowed to hold religious services or to obtain religious literature. The religious groups included Odinism, the white supremacist Church of Jesus Christ, Wicca, and Satanism. Prison authorities claimed that RLUIPA promoted religion and therefore was a violation to the Establishment Clause. A district court had initially dismissed the suit. However, the Sixth Circuit Court of Appeals held that since the act reinforced religious exercise, there was a violation of the Establishment Clause. The U.S. Supreme Court eventually examined the case, and found RLUIPA to be constitutional and thus reversed the Court of Appeals's decision. The Court also ruled in favor of the inmates, which meant they were to be afforded protection under RLUIPA, and that their religious accommodations should be granted.

Religious Grooming and Dress

Inmates have been largely unsuccessful in pursuing accommodations for grooming and dress. Courts typically rule against inmates in these cases, especially when they involve haircuts. The same lack of success can be found in cases involving headgear and other religious clothing. A challenge against a prison policy about grooming and attire may be more easily won if it is not applied the same to all religions (American Civil Liberties Union 2016). In *Holt v. Hobbs* (2015), an inmate held at the Arkansas Department of Corrections requested to keep a half-inch beard because his Muslim faith required it. The department's grooming policy bans beards, with the exception of inmates with dermatological issues. The department did not grant Holt's request, and he filed suit against several correctional officers, including the director. The prison authorities contended that the grooming policy was a safety measure because beards can conceal contraband. The U.S. Supreme Court decided that the Arkansas Department of Corrections cannot enforce a beard length restriction under RLUIPA (Boston & Manville 2011).

Conclusion

The Religious Land Use and Institutionalized Persons Act of 2000 is unique among similarly broad legislative acts in that it has had only minimal legal challenges. This is due in large part to challenges to the Religious Freedom Restoration Act of 1993 being addressed in the drafting of the RLUIPA of 2000. Most observers consider the RLUIPA to be very open and inclusive for inmates of most faith traditions, including ones considered nonmainstream or even "fringe" traditions. The RLUIPA appears to include the necessary limits needed to prevent the same mistakes as its predecessor. Chief among those is the "undue hardship standard" for correctional facilities (American Center for Law and Justice 2011; Schragger, Schwartzman, & Tebbe 2017).

Most observers contend that the act is not too broad because it has restrictions in place to prevent it from overstepping Congress's power. Under RLUIPA, the government cannot place a significant burden on an individual's free exercise of religion, except if the burden furthers a government interest and is the least restrictive method of advancing that interest. However, this prohibition is valid only under certain circumstances. First, if an institution receives federal assistance, then they must abide by the act's limitations on burdening the free exercise of inmates. Second, the burden itself or its removal must affect interstate commerce. Third, the burden must be placed utilizing a land use regulation in which the government makes case-by-case decisions on the land's intended use.

The most likely applications of RLUIPA in the future are twofold. First, the act creates the potential for frivolous lawsuits filed by inmates claiming religious accommodations for the use of drugs, alcohol, or other contraband in their religious services. Additionally, various hate groups in prisons might claim that religious accommodations are required for the circulation of violent literature, objects, and paraphernalia. Second, the act could be used by inmates in cases where correctional officers or other employees demonstrate a clear bias against a particular religious group or practice (Gaubatz 2005).

Bibliography

American Center for Law and Justice. "ACLJ Memorandum: An Overview of the Religious and Use and Institutionalized Persons Act ('RLUIPA')—2004." Technical Report. 2011.

American Civil Liberties Union. "Know Your Rights: Freedom of Religion in Prison." Technical Report. https://www.aclu.org/know-your-rights/freedom -religion-prison. Accessed on November 11, 2016.

Austin, James, & John Irwin. *It's about Time: America's Imprisonment Binge,* 4th ed. Belmont, CA: Cengage, 2012.

Bomboy, Scott. "What Is RFRA and Why Do We Care?" *Constitution Daily.* June 30, 2014.

Boston, John, & Daniel E. Manville. *Prisoner's Self-Help Litigation Manual,* 4th ed. New York: Oxford University Press, 2011.

Esperian, John H. "The Effect of Prison Education Programs on Recidivism." *Journal of Correctional Education* 61, no. 4 (2010): 316–334.

Federal Religious Freedom Restoration Act Overview." FindLaw.com. 2016. http:// civilrights.findlaw.com/discrimination/federal-religious-freedom-restora tion-act-overview.html.

First Amendment Center. "First Amendment Center." September 16, 2011.

Gaubatz, Derek L. "RLUIPA at Four: Evaluating the Success and Constitutionality of RLUIPA's Prisoner Provisions." *Harvard Journal of Law and Public Policy* 28, no. 2 (2005): 501–607.

Hudson, David L. "First Amendment Center." First Amendment Center. 2008. http://www.firstamendmentcenter.org/prisoners-rights.

Hudson, David L. "First Amendment Center." First Amendment Center. May 1, 2008. http://www.firstamendmentcenter.org/turner-v-safley-high-drama -enduring-precedent.

Kerley, Kent R. *Religious Faith in Correctional Contexts.* Boulder, CO: First Forum Press/Lynne Rienner, 2014.

Kerley, Kent R., John P. Bartkowski, Todd L. Matthews, & Tracy L. Emond. "From the Sanctuary to the Slammer: Exploring the Narratives of Evangelical Prison Ministry Workers." *Sociological Spectrum* 30 (2010): 504–525.

Kerley, Kent R., Todd L. Matthews, & Jessica Shoemaker. "A Simple Plan, a Simple Faith: Chaplains and Lay Ministers in Mississippi Prisons." *Review of Religious Research* 51 (2009): 87–103.

Mullally, Claire. "First Amendment Center." First Amendment Center. September 16, 2011. http://www.firstamendmentcenter.org/free-exercise-clause.

Newbold, Greg. "A Chronology of Correctional History." *Journal of Criminal Justice Education* 10, no. 1 (1999): 87–100.

Pizarro, Jesenia M., Vanja M. K. Stenius, & Travis C. Pratt. "Supermax Prisons: Myths, Realities, and the Politics of Punishment in American Society." *Criminal Justice Policy Review* 17 (2016): 6–21.

Religious Land Use and Institutionalized Persons Act of 2000. U.S. Department of Justice. https://www.justice.gov/crt/religious-land-use-and-institutionalized -persons-act. Accessed on August 17, 2015.

Rubin, Ashley. "Pennsylvania Prison System." In Kent R. Kerley (Ed.), *The Encyclopedia of Corrections*. Hoboken, NJ: Wiley-Blackwell, 2017.

Schragger, Chard, Micah Schwartzman, & Nelson Tebbe. "How Much May Religious Accommodations Burden Others." In Elizabeth Sepper, Holly Fernandez Lynch, & I. Glenn Cohen (Eds.), *Law, Religion, and Health in the United States*. New York: Cambridge University Press, 2017.

Court Cases

Borzych v. Frank, 439 F.3d 388 (2006).

Charles v. Verhagen, 220 F. Supp. 2d 955 (2002).

City of Boerne v. Flores, 521 US507 (1997).

Cutter v. Wilkinson, 544 US709 (2005).

Employment Division v. Smith, 494 US872 (1990).

Holt v. Hobbs, 574 US (2015).

Lemon v. Kurtzman, 403 US602 (1971).

Mark v. Nix, 983 F.2d 138 (1993).

Mayweathers v. Newland, 314 F.3d 1062 (2002).

Murphy v. Carroll, 202 F. Supp. 2d 421 (2002).

O'Lone v. Estate of Shabazz, 482 US342 (1987).

Protos v. Volkswagen of America, 615 F. Supp. 1513 (1986).

Reynolds v. U.S., 98 US145 (1878).

Sherbert v. Verner, 374 US398 (1963).

Stavenjord v. Schmidt, S-14917 (2015).

Tooley v. Martin-Marietta Corp., 648 F. 2d 1239 (1981).

Trans World Airlines, Inc. v. Hardison, 432 US63 (1977).

Turner v. Safley, 482 US78 (1987).

CHAPTER FOUR

"We Serve Forgotten Men": Structural Charity versus Religious Freedom in Serving Ex-Offenders

Michael Hallett and Megan R. Bookstaver

The Resurgence of Religion in American Corrections

Despite widespread reliance by correctional officials in the United States on faith-based programs for delivering "cost-effective" services to prisoners and ex-offenders, religious volunteers often find themselves unwelcome participants in correctional programming (Abrams et al. 2016; Sullivan 2009). Faith-based volunteers have become an increasingly important staple of correctional services in the United States, especially in jurisdictions striving to "shrink government" through expanded privatization and direct outreach to volunteer service organizations (Hallett 2006; Willison et al. 2010; Hallett 2006). As a result of an emphasis on lowering costs, legislation for faith-based programming in several states has explicitly identified the fiscal and human capital resources made available from religious volunteer organizations as a proxy resource for strategic reductions in correctional spending (Dagan & Teles 2012, 2014; Hallett 2006).

State and local governments' desire to shrink correctional budgets through the use of faith-based organizations, however, may sometimes trample over the rights of incarcerated citizens left with few alternatives while serving their time in underresourced prisons (Hallett et al. 2016; Sullivan 2009). Indigent prisoners and otherwise homeless ex-offenders may effectively be coerced into participation in faith-based programs by virtue of a comparative lack of available secular alternatives for rehabilitation (Fields 2005; Hallett et al. 2016). Alternatively, religious volunteers themselves, long concerned about the deleterious and neglectful state of prisons and who genuinely seek to assist inmates through voluntary service, may find themselves in legal jeopardy for violating "religious establishment" strictures under both the U.S. Constitution and individual state constitutions (Graber 2011; Sullivan 2009). Caught in the middle are prisoners and ex-offenders—required by courts to demonstrate personal transformation and a track record of prosocial behavior, while often being denied meaningful opportunities for doing so.

In this chapter we offer a case study of a "religious freedom" lawsuit filed against a volunteer faith-based correctional services provider in Jacksonville, Florida. In this case, Prisoners of Christ (POC) was sued for violation of Florida's "Blaine Amendment" while working under contract with the Florida Department of Corrections (FL DOC) and providing services at low cost to the state. POC works to assist released state prisoners who would otherwise be homeless by providing a broad range of services including transitional housing, emergency medical care, transportation, food, 12-step substance abuse treatment, and employment services. Although the contract between POC and the FL DOC provides only minimal support for transitional housing and anti-addiction-related programming (12-step meetings), numerous additional services are provided at no cost to FL DOC or the state of Florida. According to POC leaders, program participants are not required to attend religious services, are not required to have a particular religious affiliation, and are not asked to pursue religion as a condition of receiving assistance.

Although the religious volunteers won the lawsuit against them, their experience is instructive regarding the structural contradictions of late-modern American corrections (Garland 2001). This chapter is constructed largely by way of indirect participant observation, since the lead author served on the board of directors of POC as the case was resolved in the courts. The voluntary sector is an increasingly important facet of correctional programming, and private citizens increasingly find themselves indirectly involved in policy disputes surrounding correctional policy (Abrams et al. 2016).

State-Based "Religious Freedom" Litigation: Blaine Amendments

Currently in 38 states, so-called Blaine Amendments limit governmental contracting with religious organizations on grounds that such partnerships violate state constitutional prohibitions against "religious establishment" (see Adams 2011). In 1875, President Ulysses S. Grant supported the call for a constitutional amendment mandating free public education and prohibiting state use of public funds in "sectarian" schools. Congressman James G. Blaine, who was then Speaker of the House and had presidential aspirations, authored the amendment to the U.S. Constitution, which passed the House of Representatives 180 to 7, but failed by four votes to receive the two-thirds majority required for passage in the US Senate. "After Blaine's proposed amendment failed to become part of the US Constitution, 38 states passed their own constitutional amendments barring state funding of religious organizations, including religious schools" (Pew Research Center 2008, 1). The context of Blaine's amendment passing in the various states was arguably less driven by a desire to guarantee citizens "freedom of religion" than by an attempt to limit further "establishment" of religious practice already widespread in public schools. Due to increases in Catholic immigration to the United States in the mid-to-late 1800s, Protestant citizens began to worry about the "Catholicization" of American public education. Although recitation of Protestant prayers in public schools was commonplace at the time, the growing population of Catholic immigrants in America "began to resent" the lack of equivalent religious opportunities for their children in public schools (Pew Research Center 2008, 2).

> So they decided to start their own schools, where Catholic children could recite their own prayers and read from their own version of the Bible. The creation of these schools made many Protestants worry about whether the government would start funding Catholic schools. The Blaine Amendments arose from this concern about the "Catholicization" of American public education. (Pew Research Center 2008, 2)

These so-called "state Blaines," many dating back to the 1800s, are viewed today as increasingly relevant to national religious freedom jurisprudence in the states since, by some interpretations, the U.S. Supreme Court "has progressively softened federal constitutional barriers to religious access of public funds" (Duncan 2003, 493). This chapter tells the story of a Christian volunteer organization sued for alleged violations of Florida's religious freedom statute while working under contract with the Florida Department of Corrections.

"Big Government" versus "Structural Charity": The Neoliberal Context of Faith-Based Corrections

According to the Urban Institute (Willison et al. 2010, 2), "resource-strapped policymakers and criminal justice practitioners are increasingly turning to the faith community to help meet the multiple needs of the roughly 700,000 individuals released annually from the nation's prisons." A little-recognized facet of increased faith-based programming in corrections has been its corresponding emergence with efforts to privatize government services and lower overall spending in criminal justice (see Hackworth 2012; Hallett 2006). Insofar as "crackdowns" on crime have long been a safe issue for those seeking political office, such efforts have also funneled massive amounts of taxpayer money into federal, state, and local coffers for prison construction, justice personnel, and longer prison sentences (Beckett & Sasson 2004; Petersilia 2000). The vast majority of dollars spent in the "war on crime," of course, have gone to public and governmental agencies, thus expanding the size of government and imposing a massive fiscal burden on taxpayers. Numerous directives regarding faith-based programming, however, have explicitly sought to redirect government responsibility for crime away from public agencies by allowing religious volunteer organizations to access public funds, with the goal of supplanting the "governmental monopoly" in the delivery of services and reducing overall costs (Hackworth 2012, 45–46). Legislation for "faith-based" programming, in fact, frequently identifies religious volunteers as a fiscal and human capital resource available for "cost-effective" programming by states.

Although underrecognized as a central part of the rationale for expanding use of faith-based programming in corrections, this strategic vesting of "structural charity" as an established bulwark for the delivery of services in corrections has been a central part of the justification for increased promotion of "faith" in prisons (Cooper 2015, 65). The Florida legislature in 2000, for example, established a Task Force on Ex-Offenders charged with finding remedies to the causes of high recidivism, ultimately amending 15 Florida statutes and passing a law authorizing private religious organizations to contract with the state to help lower rates of reoffending. With Jeb Bush serving as governor of Florida, much of the state's new emphasis on faith-based programming was modeled off that initiated under President George W. Bush's "faith-based initiative." President Bush's faith-based initiative used federal authority to expand governmental access to funding for religious nonprofit organizations. The preamble to Florida's enabling legislation authorizing the state's use of faith-based programs, including the state's first entirely faith-based prison dormitory (at Lawtey Correctional Institution), demonstrates an emphasis on private spirituality as a resource for fiscal conservatism. The preamble to the legislation reads in part:

> Whereas state government should not and cannot bear the sole burden of treating and helping those suffering from addictions and self-injurious behaviors, and, Whereas, faith-based organizations are "armies of compassion" devoted to changing individuals' hearts and lives and can offer cost-effective substance abuse treatment through the use of volunteers and other cost saving measures, and Whereas research has proven that "one-on-one" private and faith-based programming is often more effective than government programs in shaping and reclaiming lives because they are free to assert the essential connection between responsibility and human dignity;

their approach is personal, not bureaucratic; their service is not primarily a function of professional background, but of individual commitment; and they inject an element of moral challenge and spiritual renewal that government cannot duplicate and, Whereas, in an effort to transform lives and break the personally destructive and expensive recidivism cycle, Florida should increase the number of chaplains who strengthen volunteer participation and expand the pilot [faith-based] dormitory program that includes a voluntary faith component that supports inmates as they reenter communities . . . Be It Enacted by the Legislature of the State of Florida (see FL Statutes 944.4731(3)(a)(b)).

In short, as a case in point illustrating the centrality of structural charity in deploying faith-based programming in American prisons, Florida's "faith-based" legislation removes the state from full responsibility over crime and rehabilitation, while leveling "private cost-effective armies of compassion that will change hearts" in the fight against crime and addiction.

Ending Big Government Corrections

In a speech given on July, 22, 1999, Texas governor George W. Bush, who in 2002 would be elected U.S. president, made these observations:

I visit churches and charities serving their neighbors nearly everywhere I go in this country. And nothing is more exciting or encouraging. Every day they prove that our worst problems are not hopeless or endless. Every day they perform miracles of renewal. Wherever we can, we must expand their role and reach, without changing them or corrupting them. It is the next, bold step of welfare reform. We must apply our conservative and free-market ideas to the job of helping real human beings. (Olasky 2003)

The strong bipartisan support won by President George W. Bush's "faith-based initiative" was aided in part by its appeal to diverse audiences on opposite sides of the political spectrum (Dagan & Teles 2014; Hackworth 2012). Prison reformers on the left highlighted the importance of community-based rehabilitation programs for reducing offender recidivism. Reformers on the right focused on criminal justice spending, with the costs of high recidivism being a central focus. Over time, a growing segment of political leadership from both parties came to see criminal justice spending as wasteful and ineffective. As conservative criminal justice reform advocate Grover Norquist recently noted, "Spending more on education doesn't necessarily get you more education. That's also true about national defense. It turns out it's also true about criminal justice and fighting crime" (Dagan & Teles 2014, 274). In that context, failing prisons came to be viewed as suffering from similar fiscal dysfunctions as failing public schools, with correctional officer employee unions being cast as equivalent to public education unions, who allegedly resisted attempts to measure their performance:

> Once you believe that prisons are like any other agency, then it becomes natural to suspect that wardens and prison guards, like other suppliers of government services, might submit to the temptations of monopoly, inflating costs and providing shoddy service. And, of course, conservatives have long made such arguments to justify their pet project of bidding out incarceration to for-profit businesses. (Dagan & Teles 2012, 31)

Prisoners of Christ

Prisoners of Christ (POC) is a faith-based nonprofit volunteer organization serving ex-offenders through providing transitional housing, substance abuse treatment, health care, food subsidies, and employment assistance. Founded in 1995 and based in Jacksonville, Florida, the organization has served thousands of former prisoners in various capacities over two decades, sometimes with the help of small government grants but always primarily through private monies obtained through ecumenical church-based outreach. Private resources have always comprised the majority of POC's operating budget, with governmental contracts reaching an apex of roughly 30 percent of the organizational budget in 2015.

With a primary focus of serving released prisoners who have completed long sentences, most clients served by POC have been incarcerated for 10 years or more and typically suffer from pronounced effects of prison institutionalization on release. With limited means of supporting themselves in the free world, POC's clients frequently describe themselves as being disoriented by and fearful of routine public interactions such as standing in a grocery store checkout line, using computers or cell phones, using the Internet, and interviewing for jobs. Most POC clients have limited literacy and have never produced a written résumé.

Ninety percent of POC clients report problematic histories with addiction and substance abuse, while suffering as well from familial dissociation and social isolation. Most POC clients report that they would be homeless but for the services of POC. The program has served roughly 2,500 released prisoners since its inception in 1995, providing basic needs such as transitional housing, food subsidies, medical assistance, clothing, substance abuse treatment, direct employment services, and a wide range of other services.

In 2000, Florida's Task Force on Ex-Offenders recommended a series of modifications to state law, which included passage of a "statute allowing private organizations, including faith-based organizations, to bid on contracts for providing substance abuse treatment and transitional housing services" for released prisoners (*Council for Secular Humanism, Inc. v. McNeil*, 44 So. 3d 112 (Fla. 1st DCA 2010) (Case No.: 2007-CA-1358, 5). The legislation authorized expanded volunteer faith-based programming inside prisons as well as new state contracts for delivery of services to ex-offenders. After a competitive bidding process in 2004, POC was awarded a contract by the Florida Department of Corrections to provide ex-offender transitional housing and related services. The second "religious" awardee was a separate faith-based organization, Lamb of God Ministries (LOG). Of the 15 awardees that year, only 2 were given to explicitly "faith-based" organizations, POC and LOG. Since this initial award, POC has successfully maintained the original service contract and has received small increases to the award amount over time.

Under the auspices of Florida DOC's "faith-based" correctional service contracts, client enrollment is entirely voluntary and must be available to citizens of all faith traditions or no faith background at all. Religious service attendance is not a criterion of acceptance into the program, nor is any religious programming required of participants. POC considers itself to be a "faith-based" organization in that the majority of its operating budget is provided through religiously oriented outreach across a broad range of ecumenical sources. The all-volunteer board of directors membership describes itself as "motivated by faith" to serve ex-offenders and prisoners. Both LOG and POC are thus "faith-based" in their conceptualization; however, neither organization depends on governmental funding for the services they provide, nor do they maintain congregations or hold services open to the general public. Although POC does provide optional religious materials for those who want to integrate their faith into their recovery process, such materials are not required elements of program delivery.

Under the service contract with the Florida Department of Corrections, POC is provided $14.28 per day for each released prisoner served with transitional housing and related programming, and this lasts typically for 10 months. This sum of $14.28 per day/per client fails to meet even half the cost of services provided, which amounts to roughly $39 per day/per client. POC pays the difference of the cost entirely through private donations and private fundraising. Drawing on what one board member describes as its "open door/open heart culture," POC has purchased five small "transition houses" over its 23 years of existence, today serving roughly 35 men per year. In addition, POC serves roughly four hundred additional "walk-in clients" per year, providing clothing, food, emergency shelter, food stamps, transportation, resources for medical assistance, dental services, and assistance for obtaining driver's licenses and social security cards. Eighty percent of POC's transitional housing clients successfully complete the program within 10 months after release from prison, which is defined as becoming self-sustaining and remaining arrest free.

The Lawsuit

This case involves payments by the State of Florida, Department of Corrections, to Prisoners of Christ, Inc. and Lamb of God Ministries, Inc. The payments are for substance abuse and transitional housing services offered pursuant to contracts authorized by Section 944.4731, Florida statutes. The question before this court is does the statute and the payments violate Article I, Section 3 of the Florida Constitution, known as the "no aid" provision based on the religious nature of the two faith-based programs (*Center for Inquiry, Inc. v. Jones,* 2007-CA-1358, 2).

As described above, the litigation in question against Prisoners of Christ was filed pursuant to a "religious freedom" claim under Florida constitutional law, specifically Florida's Blaine Amendment, rather than a claim under the U.S. Constitution's First Amendment "Establishment Clause." The lawsuit in this case proceeded on state constitutional grounds specifically targeting the "no aid" provision of Florida's so-called Blaine Amendment, which restricts use of state monies by religious organizations. In this case, the plaintiff's counsel alleged that the new service contracts issued by the Florida Department of Corrections to faith-based providers violated the "religious freedom" statute articulated in Florida's Blaine Amendment, which was adopted by the state in 1885 (Adams 2011, 7). The Religious Freedom clause of the Florida Constitution reads as follows:

Article 1, Section 3.

Religious freedom.

There shall be no law respecting the establishment of religion or prohibiting or penalizing the free exercise thereof. Religious freedom shall not justify practices inconsistent with public morals, peace or safety. No revenue of the state or any political subdivision or agency thereof shall ever be taken from the public treasury directly or indirectly in aid of any church, sect, or religious denomination or in aid of any sectarian institution. (Article 1, Section 3, Florida's Blaine Amendment)

First filing against POC in 2007 under the name Council for Secular Humanism (CSH), and subsequently as *Center for Inquiry, Inc. v. Jones* [(FL Cir. Ct., Jan. 20, 2016)], the plaintiffs sued for revocation of the FL DOC service contracts with both POC and LOG, specifically citing the "no aid" provision of Florida's "religious freedom" statute and alleging the contracts violated Florida's Constitution. The "no aid" clause of the statute reads:

No revenue of the state or any political subdivision or agency thereof shall ever be taken from the public treasury directly or indirectly in aid of any church, sect, or religious denomination or in aid of any sectarian institution.

Results of the Case

Despite several iterations in the case over many years, the Council for Secular Humanism/Center for Inquiry (CSH/CFI) persisted through nearly a decade-long series of appeals and revisions in their effort to terminate the FL DOC contracts with both POC and LOG. Defining itself as a public interest advocacy group with a mission statement that reads in part, "We vigorously object to government support of religion and the use of religious dogma to justify public policy," the CSH/CFI expressed concern about Florida's expanded justification for use of faith-based programming in delivery of correctional services (Center for Inquiry 2016). Despite an ultimate legal finding to the contrary, CSH/CFI stated in their initial petition that "Prisoners of Christ and Lamb of God are churches, sects, religious denominations or sectarian institutions, and the State's payments are being used to fund sectarian services" (Council for Secular Humanism 2007, 4). Although stating emphatically that "we do not oppose the free exercise of religion," CSH/CFI felt strongly that the decision of the Florida Department of Corrections to expand faith-based programming improperly mixed religious activity into public policy:

CSH's complaint is based on the Florida Constitution, not the Establishment Clause of the United States Constitution. CSH made a deliberate decision to seek relief under the Florida Constitution, because it has a very broad prohibition on aid to religious institutions. Specifically, the "No-Aid" provision of the Florida Constitution, Article I, Section 3, expressly mandates that *no* revenue of the state can be provided "directly or indirectly in aid of any church, sect, or religious denomination or in aid of any sectarian institution." (Council for Secular Humanism 2016, 4)

In the end, the Council for Secular Humanism/Center for Inquiry lost the case, with the District Court in Leon County issuing its final opinion in January 2016. The court found that, particularly because the contracts between FL DOC and POC/LOG covered only a fraction of the costs of services provided, that no religious activity was required of participants, that monies provided were not spent on religious activities, and that no violation of the Florida Constitution had taken place. An excerpt from the final ruling follows:

The No-Aid provision permits government contracts with religious organizations if the funds are not spent "in aid of" religion but rather to further the state's secular goals. See *Council for Secular Humanism, Inc v. McNeil*, 44 so. 3d 112 (Fla. 1st DCA 2010) ("CSH"). Applying CSH factors to the record in this case, the payments from DOC to the Contractors are not being made "in aid of religion." The Program exists to promote the State's anti-recidivism and anti-addiction interests, not religion. The Program is not "significantly sectarian": it permits some religious content only to the extent the content is offered in a nondiscriminatory and wholly optional and voluntary fashion. Further, the record shows that the Program does not indoctrinate, require participation in religious ritual, or favor any one religion over another. Instead, the record demonstrates that the Program provides social services purchased from the Defendant Contractors at or below market prices, which the State could have purchased from nonreligious private entities. Therefore the Court grants the Defendant's motions for Summary Judgement and denies the Plaintiff's motion for Summary Judgement. (*Center for Inquiry, Inc. v. Jones*, FINAL JUDGEMENT, 3–4)

Hollow Victory: "We Serve Forgotten Men"

While by the end of the case emotions were running high among POC staff and volunteers, especially among those that considered themselves victims of "malicious persecution," by the next week a more reflective pall of sadness fell over the group. One POC board member said in a follow-up meeting: "Here we are, fighting and struggling to give services to men who otherwise have nothing—in a state that genuinely wants to cut resources to the point where these men literally have nothing—all while having to fight for our own right to practice our faith providing services that the state itself says actually work! Who is driving the ship?" After a moment of silent reflection the board member stated: "We serve forgotten men. No one actually cares what happens to released prisoners in the state of Florida. The Florida Department of Corrections' top priority seems to be to simply cut costs. The [pausing-for-emphasis] *intellectuals'* fighting us top priority seems to be to make sure that the 'right people' are spending the money. And meanwhile fewer resources are available for more and more prisoners being released every year. We serve forgotten men."

Bad Faith: Shrinking Budgets or Saving Souls?

Although many ex-offenders find it impossible to overcome society's dogged and often totalizing definition of them as irredeemable, successful desisters frequently espouse spirituality and religion as a source of positive behavior change and reconceptualized self-identity (Adorjan & Chui 2012; Giordano et al. 2002; Giordano, Longmore, Schroeder, & Seffrin 2008; Maruna 2001; Paternoster & Bushway 2009; Schroeder & Frana 2009). Religious spirituality has been found to be a highly salient resource for many successful desisters, especially under conditions of low emotional support and weak informal social control (Giordano et al. 2002; Kerley, Copes, Tewksbury, & Dabney 2011). Phenomenological analyses of the desistance process reveal that religion and spirituality frequently help offenders construct stories of change that become vital to an altered sense of self (Giordano et al. 2002, 1018; Maruna 2001; Paternoster & Bushway 2009). More importantly, religiosity seems to help desisters undertake preliminary agentic moves that, while often not outwardly visible to family members or justice officials, are the beginnings of an evolving self-narrative that is both prosocial and provides a redemptive path (Giordano et al. 2002; Jang & Johnson 2005; Maruna & Ramsden 2004; Schroeder & Frana 2009).

Specifically, life-history narratives highlight agentic moves that draw on stories of change emphasizing the ways religious practice and spirituality provide emotional, cognitive, and linguistic resources utilized by desisters in their daily lives (Adorjan & Chui 2012; Giordano et al. 2002; Schroeder & Frana 2009; Shover & Thompson 1992; for the centrality of narratives, see also Denzin 1987). As Giordano et al. (2002) summarize the issue: Thus, in addition to its relative accessibility, religion seems to have potential as a mechanism for desistance because many core concerns within religious communities and the Bible relate directly to offenders' problem areas. Even more importantly, religious teachings can provide a clear blueprint for how to proceed as a changed individual (Giordano et al. 2008, 116; see also Goodwin 2001).

The extent to which Florida's and the nation's "faith-based" efforts in corrections demonstrate a hyperfixation on cost cutting rather than adequate provision of services to released prisoners, who as a group suffer from weak levels of overall habilitation, arguably compromises rather than effectuates the availability of effective rehabilitation services overall. Although faith-based providers may offer services that help ex-offenders succeed, they should not become an excuse to cut resources and further limit public responsibility for offender rehabilitation. Were more programming options available, as POC volunteers themselves recognized, it is possible that some clients of POC would choose nonreligious options for assistance after release from prison.

Religious Freedom and Corrections on the Cheap

For most of the history of the lawsuit against POC, religious volunteers working daily with former prisoners genuinely believed they would lose the case. Litigants from the Council for Secular Humanism/Center for Inquiry were obviously very determined to fight. They had persisted for nearly 10 long years in fighting POC's miniscule service contract with the Department of Corrections. But who, POC volunteers wondered, is actually looking out for the interests of Florida's released prisoners? FL DOC has continued to make dramatic cuts to spending on ex-offender services budgets. Florida prisons themselves were among the most violent in the country and getting worse (Brown 2015). And bedspace for transitional housing for older and long-institutionalized inmates was almost nonexistent. "And yet here we are fighting a 10-year mega battle with people we've never met and who probably know none of the facts that we do."

Shortly after POC's victory, the Center for Inquiry (CFI) posted a lengthy missive to their website. CFI expressed a desire to appeal the case, although at this writing it has been more than one year since the ruling:

> CFI, an organization that promotes science, reason, and secular humanism, plans to appeal this decision, characterizing the ruling as legally flawed and, at its core, illogical. . . . We are taken aback by this indefensible ruling. According to this trial judge, Floridians have no recourse if the government chooses to fund faith-based services provided by explicitly Christian ministries, provided no one is coerced into using these services. (Center for Inquiry 2016).

Ultimately the court disagreed with CSH/CFI, supporting POC's contention that state money was not in fact used for "religious activity" but for providing basic services that are in the state's and inmates' best interests. POC volunteers were motivated by their faith to provide these services, but religious activity was not a requirement of clients receiving them. "That would be the ultimate hypocrisy," stated one board member. "We offer these services with no strings attached. That's how it has to be if we're going to be effective at all." As court documents from the case showed, clothing, heat and air, bus passes, print paper for résumés, and food for hot meals were the items on which POC disproportionately spent its money. One particular facet of the lawsuit that became a genuine sore spot among POC volunteers, however, was its tendency to problematize not the services POC provided but what one court document called the "Nature of the Defendant Contractors." "What the heck does that mean?!" asked one POC board member. "In other words—they're not mad that we're actually providing these services—they're mad that it's Christians providing them! In fact, they seem to agree that these services should be provided because they left everyone else alone."

Of ultimate concern to POC volunteers, however, was the conspicuously absent expression of concern from CSH/CFI about the well-being and success of Florida's released prisoners. Their materials expressed no awareness of the troubled context of prisoner reentry in Florida nor the deteriorating condition of Florida's prisons. In defense of its contracting with POC and LOG, moreover, the Florida Department of Corrections asserted the value of cost savings, noting that: "The state is aware that it could not purchase these services this cheaply from other sources. With the small amount of state funds that are paid into this contract, there's no way that they would come close to covering the light bills and the gasoline bills, or just the upkeep on the houses. I don't think state funding would come close to completing all their expenses" (Case No. 2007-CA-1358, 5).

Having endured the "religious freedom" lawsuit on behalf of their work, at the end of their years-long legal battle, POC volunteers ultimately identified new concerns about the braided logics of faith-based programming and "cost cutting" in American corrections. The extent to which emphasis is placed on the value of faith-based programs as a cost-cutting structural charity rather than as an asset for mending citizens after serving their sentence, is the extent to which the integrity of state support for faith-based initiatives arguably compromises the overall goal of successful rehabilitation.

Bibliography

Abrams, L. S., Hughes, E., Inderbitzen, M., & Meek, R. (Eds.). *The Voluntary Sector in Prisons: Encouraging Personal and Institutional Change.* New York: Palgrave Macmillan, 2016.

Adams, N. A. "Florida's Blaine Amendment: Goldilocks and the Separate but Equal Doctrine." *Saint Thomas Law Review,* Fall 2011.

Adorjan, M., & Chui, W. H. (2012). "Going Straight in Hong Kong: Personal Accounts of Male Ex-Prisoners in Hong Kong." *British Journal of Criminology* 52: 577–590.

Bakken, N. W., Gunter, W., & Visher, C. "Spirituality and Desistance from Substance Abuse among Reentering Offenders." *International Journal of Offender Therapy and Comparative Criminology* 58, no. 11 (November 2014): 1321–39.

Beckett, K., & Sasson, T. *The Politics of Injustice: Crime and Punishment in America,* 2nd ed. Thousand Oaks, CA: Sage, 2004.

Brown, J. "The Inmate Who Exposed Florida Prisons' Culture of Cruelty." *The Miami Herald.* 2015. Available at http://www.miamiherald.com/news/special -reports/florida-prisons/article30490770.html

Center for Inquiry. "Religious Rehab Ruling Defies Logic, Violates Florida Constitution, Says Center for Inquiry." 2016. Available at http://www.centerforin quiry.net/newsroom/religious_rehab_ruling

Cooper, M. "The Theology of Emergency: Welfare Reform, US Foreign Aid and the Faith-based Initiative." *Theory, Culture & Society* 32, no. 2 (2015): 53–77.

Council for Secular Humanism. "Petition for Declaratory Judgement, 2007." Available at http://www.centerforinquiry.net/uploads/attachments/complaint -CSH%20v.%20McDonough.pdf

Council for Secular Humanism. "CASE SUMMARY." Council for Secular Humanism v. Jones, Case No. 2007-CA-1358 (Leon County Circuit Court). Available at http://www.centerforinquiry.net/advocacy/council_for_secular _humanism_v._jones

Dagan, D., & Teles, S. "The Conservative War on Prisons." *Washington Monthly,* November/December 2012. Available at http://washingtonmonthly.com /magazine/novdec-2012/the-conservative-war-on-prisons

Dagan, D., & Teles, S. "Locked In? Conservative Reform and the Future of Mass Incarceration." *Annals of the American Academy of Political and Social Science* 651, no. 1 (January 2014): 266–276.

Denzin, N. K. *The Recovering Alcoholic.* Thousand Oaks, CA: Sage, 1987.

Duncan, K. "Secularism's Law: State Blaine Amendments and Religious Persecution." *Fordham Law Review* 72, no. 3 (2003): 493–593.

Duwe, G., Hallett, M., Hays, J., Jang, S. J., & Johnson, B. R. "Bible College Participation and Prison Misconduct: A Preliminary Analysis." *Journal of Offender Rehabilitation* 54, no. 5 (2015): 371–390.

Fields, R. R. W. *"Perks for Prisoners Who Pray: Using the Coercion Test to Decide Establishment Clause Challenges to Faith-Based Prison Units."* University of Chicago *Legal Forum* no. 1 (2005): 541–567.

Florida Criminal Rehabilitation Act of 2001. Preamble, 2001 Florida Criminal Rehabilitation Act 2001 Fl. ALS 110; 2001–110 Fla. Laws ch. 110; 2001 Fla. SB 912.

Giordano, P. C., Cernkovich, S. A., & Rudolph, J. "Gender, Crime, and Desistance: Toward a Theory of Cognitive Transformation." *American Journal of Sociology* 107 (2002): 990–1064.

Giordano, P. C., Longmore, M. A., Schroeder, R., & Seffrin, P. A. "Life-Course Perspective on Spirituality and Desistance from Crime." *Criminology* 46 (2008): 99–132.

Goodwin, L. "Time for Change: A Study of Religious Conversion and Self-Identity in Prison." PhD dissertation, University of Sheffield, 2001.

Graber, J. *The Furnace of Affliction: Prisons and Religion in Antebellum America.* Chapel Hill: University of North Carolina Press, 2011.

Hackworth, J. *Faith Based: Religious Neoliberalism and the Politics of Welfare in the United States.* Atlanta: University of Georgia Press, 2012.

Hallett, M. *Private Prisons in America: A Critical Race Perspective.* Chicago: University of Illinois Press, 2006.

Hallett, M., Hays, J., Johnson, B., Jang, S. J., & Duwe, G. *The Angola Prison Seminary: Effects of Faith-Based Ministry on Identity Transformation, Desistance, and Rehabilitation.* New York: Routledge, 2016.

Jang, S. J., & Johnson, B. "Gender, Religiosity, and Reactions to Strain among African Americans." *Sociological Quarterly* 46 (2005): 323–357.

Kerley, K. R., Copes, H., Tewksbury, R., & Dabney, D. A. "Examining the Relationship between Religiosity and Self-Control as Predictors of Prison Deviance." *International Journal of Offender Therapy and Comparative Criminology* 55 (2011): 1251–1271.

Maruna, S. *Making Good: How Ex-Convicts Reform and Rebuild Their Lives.* Washington, DC: American Psychological Association Books, 2001.

Maruna, S., & Ramsden, D. "Living to Tell the Tale: Redemption Narratives, Shame Management, and Offender Rehabilitation." In A. Lieblich, D. McAdams, &

R. Josselson (Eds.), *Healing Plots: The Narrative Basis of Psychotherapy* (pp. 129–142). Washington, DC: American Psychological Association, 2004.

Olasky, M. *Compassionate Conservatism: What It Is, What It Does, and How It Can Transform America.* New York: Free Press, 2003.

Paternoster, R., & Bushway, S. "Desistance and the Feared Self: Toward an Identity Theory of Criminal Desistance." *Journal of Criminal Law and Criminology* 99, no. 4 (2009): 1103–1156.

Petersilia, J. "When Prisoners Return to the Community: Political, Economic, and Social Consequences." *Sentencing and Corrections: Issues for the 21st Century* no. 9 (November 2000): 1–6.

Pew Research Center. *The Blaine Game: Controversy over Blaine Amendments and Public Funding of Religion.* Washington, DC: Pew Research Center on Religion & Public Life, 2008.

Schroeder, R., & Frana, J. "Spirituality and Religion, Emotional Coping and Desistance: A Qualitative Study of Men Undergoing Change." *Sociological Spectrum* 2 (2009): 718–741.

Shover, N., & Thompson, C. Y. "Age, Differential Expectations, and Crime Desistance." *Criminology* 30 (1992): 89–104.

Sullivan, W. F. *Prison Religion: Faith-Based Reform and the Constitution.* Princeton, NJ: Princeton University Press, 2009.

Willison, J. B., Brazzell, D., & Kim, K. *Faith-Based Corrections and Reentry Programs: Advancing a Conceptual Framework for Research and Evaluation.* Washington, DC: Urban Institute, 2010.

CHAPTER FIVE

A Theological Critique of the "Correctional" System

Andrew Skotnicki

In this chapter I will argue that contemporary systems of criminal justice have, for the most part, committed what T. S. Elliot (1938) calls "the greatest treason." They do "the right thing for the wrong reason." What they rightly do is to incapacitate those men and women who are intentionally harmful to themselves and to the natural and social worlds. What they do wrongly is fail to "correct" in any consistently verifiable way the people forced to dwell within places of detention. This is largely due to the fact that they operate under various expressions of the normative banners of retribution, deterrence, and rehabilitation. It will be my contention that these latter terms, as they are typically discussed in the literature and put into practice in the correctional milieu, can do nothing other than resort to coercion and violence due to a morally ambiguous and dualist approach to social and psychological analysis that is in service to a conservative ideology of social control and selective prosecution. Thus, they surrender any pretense to moral authority. This is particularly true when viewed from a lens derived from the dominant biblical paradigm for treating the offender as well as from the way such persons were treated in the early Christian church.

The chapter will first present an overview of the sociology of the contemporary American correctional experience and the ideological tensions between competing paradigmatic organizational principles that have rendered the entire system incoherent and, at least according to the desire to amend the behavior of its captives, ineffective. It will then survey the dominant approach to sin, penance, and excommunication in the New Testament and primitive Christian sources, revealing the belief in the ontological sacredness of the human person, the inevitability of willful alienation from social participation, the harmful consequences of this alienation, and a methodology of conversion wherein offenders are restored to wholeness without the need to punish, "treat," or use them as examples to others. Lastly, this chapter will suggest that the way to address the correctional conundrum is through a dialogue between past and present approaches. Such a dialogue offers the promise of overcoming not only the inherent dualism in systemic philosophies, but also the dualism of the division between science—including social science—and religion into competing networks of meaning and knowledge rather than essential and necessary partners in preserving the integrity and unity of nature and the human community.

The Crisis in the Meaning of Correction

A great amount of "truly depressing" literature has been written in recent years on the problems involved in criminal justice (Murphy 2014, 73). These studies point to a method of prosecution that disproportionately punishes members of racial minorities, the poor, and those with mental problems (Alexander 2010; Muhammad 2010; Murakawa 2014; Travis, Western, & Redburn 2014). The correctional complex contains over five thousand penal facilities that resemble "nothing so much as the Soviet Gulag" (Garland 2001, 178) and operate on a system-wide principle of "degradation" and "the intoxication that comes with treating people as inferiors" (Whitman 2003, 23). The system is largely governed by a neoliberal, market-driven approach that has awarded corporations inspired by the profit motive the right to oversee the health and well-being of tens of thousands of their fellow citizens in airrtight facilities that muffle the cries of neglect (Burkhart 2014; Gottschalk 2015). The internal culture of many of these institutions is marred by rape, murder, and the tyranny of street gangs (Haney 2006; Murphy 2014); and the hundreds of thousands of people who are released from confinement each year are confronted by a reentry system that is so hindered by legislative restrictions, social prejudice, and limited opportunities that even those earnestly seeking to improve their social and economic lot through licit channels find it virtually impossible and must either live a hand to mouth existence or return to illegal activity (Becket & Herbert 2010; Petersilia 2009; Travis 2005).

Most readers are familiar with this abbreviated litany of both critical and shameful institutional ills, and it is not my intention to repeat the thorough analysis that has been done by gifted scholars about the administration of justice in the United States and elsewhere. What I would like to focus on is the rupture in continuity between the original ethos for confinement—conversion—and the institutional configuration designed to foster and sustain it, and the various ideologies that currently intersect and ultimately conflict in the penal sphere: retribution, deterrence, and rehabilitation, although I will argue that all three, despite different aims and moral emphases, are driven by the default values of power and social control. These principles are not only inherently unable to function independently or jointly under the same institutional rubric, as the history of the modern prison repeatedly reveals (Foucault 1979; Ignatieff 1978; McKelvey 1977; Rothman 1980), but they also are predicated on two fundamental errors that are at the heart of the catalogue of problems outlined above: the inability to espouse a set of transcendent moral norms and an overarching stance of dualism.

Concerning the issue of conceptual incompatibility and power, I call the reader's attention to David Rothman's (1980) volume on the origins of the Progressive penal ideology in the later decades of the 19th century. The 1870 Penal Congress in Cincinnati was a turning point in the history of corrections. It came at a time of buoyant social optimism: the end of the Civil War, the emergence of the social sciences, the Darwinian revolution, and the fusion of the Second Great Awakening's focus on the thousand years of peace prior to the second coming of Christ with a belief in steady, limitless progress under the aegis of the American political and economic order (Hofstadter 1959; Lasch 1991; Smith 1957). The conveners and distinguished conference attendees were animated by the belief that solutions to the problem of crime and improvements in the "conceded failure" (Brockway 1912, 165) of the penitentiary system in which the prisoner "breathes . . . a religious atmosphere" (De Beaumont & De Tocqueville 1833, 94) were within reach given the measureable variables provided by scientific investigation, "rational educational correction," and "individual, industrial efficiency" (Brockway 1912, 163, 173).

Rothman emphasizes the undeniable good will of the reformers, especially their desire to turn from vengeance to treatment (Rothman 1980, 31). However, he details both the philosophical and programmatic failures that doomed the Progressive agenda, its institutional innovation—the reformatory—and, indeed, virtually all subsequent attempts to "correct" those under penal supervision. His main contention is that all efforts to fit the offender into the moral horizon of penal planners and administrators involved the expansion of state power; and this antinomy between "correction" and coercion is not only irresolvable, it always splits the difference on the side of the latter: "They were convinced that their innovations could satisfy all goals, that the same . . . institution could at once guard and help, protect and rehabilitate, maintain custody and deliver treatment. . . . The Progressive effort to link them failed. In the end, when conscience and convenience met, convenience won. When treatment and coercion met, coercion won" (Rothman 1980, 10).

Rothman's sober analysis alludes to the hermeneutical constraints that so often shield reformers and policy planners from the internal contradictions

involved in their efforts: "Failures, they believed, reflected faulty implementation, not underlying problems with theory" (1980, 9). And, while one could
argue that we have learned much since the late 19th century, particularly given
the new developments in rehabilitative theory such as the Risk-Needs-
Responsivity (RNR) and Good Lives models (Andrews & Bonta 2010; Maruna
2001; Ward & Maruna 2007), the limitations of moral agnosticism and dualism, accompanied by the default reliance on power, will continue to trouble
strategies meant to address human malfeasance, whether driven by the principles of treatment, just deserts, or deterrence.

The first major weakness in contemporary correctional literature is the lack
of a moral ontology. The philosophical and moral parameters of criminal justice discourse are direct descendants of the Enlightenment and, later, the
positivist social scientific search for a rational and individualist foundation
for ethics without accountability to a community, save in a contractual relation wherein failure to conform to the law merits a punitive response. This
"view from nowhere" (Nagel 1986) in which only the subjective calculations
of the ego have moral authority must, by definition, yield an emotivist ethical
vocabulary of multiple and competing conceptions of the good with no external standard to adjudicate one from another (MacIntyre 1981; Taylor 2007).
The result is a massive legal bureaucracy in which the courts are saddled with
the role of arbitrators between claimants and in which settlements, that by
definition cannot be resolved morally, must be settled either by quiet submission or forceful execution.

The various philosophical foundations for current penal administration all
rely on versions of this subjective and "rootless" understanding of morality
and, inevitably, the power of the state as the decisive tool to bring about compliance. From Beccaria (1963) and Bentham (1970, Chs. 12–14) and the host
of utilitarian theorists that descend from them come the principal ideas concerning deterrence: punishment is for the purpose of teaching a lesson to
potential lawbreakers in terms of a "spoonful of pain" (Christie 1981, 11). The
one punished is, by definition, not an end in himself or herself but a peda-
gogical object whose suffering instructs not in terms of morality but "from a
sharpened awareness of the penalties attached to wrongdoing" (Sykes 2007, 10).
Although the humanitarian innovations of the theory cannot be gainsaid, relative to the callous mistreatment to which reformers such as John Howard (1973)
nobly drew attention, the most reliable and coherent values in this and all other
contemporary penal theories are still the threat and exercise of coercion: "[Pun-
ishment] must involve pain . . . for an offense against legal rules . . . imposed
and administered by an authority constituted by a legal system against which
the offense is committed" (Hart 1968, 4–5).

Retributive theorists similarly seek to inflict suffering on the wrongdoer,
whether in service to universal, rationally deducible principles of ethics (Kant
1996, 6.331–6.333) or the moral values of the community (Durkheim 1984,

42–43; Morris 1968) that are irreparably tarnished when lawbreakers are not punished; or from a sense of moral outrage and "noble and generous resentment" that the "impartial" inner self wishes on those who willfully bring harm on others (Smith 1966, II, 2). Despite the objective, rational overtones of the Kantian discourse, Adam Smith and Emile Durkheim rightly locate the desire to inflict suffering in the passions. Garland (1990, 32) argues similarly: "The essence of punishment is not rationality . . . the essence of punishment is irrational, unthinking emotion fixed by a sense of the sacred and its violation. Passion lies at the heart of punishment." And despite the sensibilities of the "modern" era with its horror of the brutal administration of justice in the past (Foucault 1979; Spierenberg 1984), retributive theory turns on the willful infliction of violence on the guilty; a violence immeasurable in the pain it delivers under the guise of rational judicial procedure and custodial formality that safely shroud its victims from public view (Cover 1986; Garland 1990, 243; Scarry 1985, 11–19).

Rehabilitative theories are, in most circumstances, similarly unable to formulate a definition of the moral life rooted in a source beyond individual preference or social conformity. There is frequently an implied sense of behavioral or cognitive change or, in the case of criminologists, at least a commitment to refrain from lawbreaking, but lacking any foundational ethical commitments beyond what is termed being "prosocial," they invariably view the offender as a dependent variable whose "desistance" or "reform" is typically measured in terms of legal compliance, not moral transformation. This approach is what Edward Shils (1980, 35–36) referred to as "technological sociology." It is based on a positivist conception of knowledge and human endeavor, serving as "a tool for technocrats to rule the human race." Society in this view is populated by objects of "rational-empirical knowledge." Gibson Winter (1966, 41) terms this method "physical sociology." Its credo is the dogma "that scientific investigation requires understanding, prediction, and control." The language of most reports on rehabilitation echoes this view of the offender as a problem to be solved, or a moral deviant needing to be socialized into the standards of conduct approved by the privileged and dominant classes. Even longtime rehabilitative theorists like Francis Cullen, who decry retributivism and believe in a "virtuous prison," cannot escape the trap spoken of by Rothman in which the desire to treat inevitably leads to judgment and coercion. After affirming that rehabilitation is a "moral enterprise," Cullen and his colleagues then state: "Inmates should be seen as having the obligation to become virtuous people and to manifest moral goodness . . . There are standards of right and wrong . . . offenders must conform to them" (Cullen et al. 2014, 65).

The barrenness of the moral language in contemporary sociological reports and institutional discourse is accompanied by a dualism, once again rooted in philosophical conceptions of the human person and the acquisition of knowledge—a dualism that despite the good intentions of most penal reformers, is trapped in a conception of reality that divides the world between those in need of help and those qualified to help them, or, worse, between the morally deficient and those who have in some sense overcome their moral failures. The very objectivity that is sought belies what the traditions of religious wisdom, phenomenology, and "consensual" or "intentional" sociologists assert is the sine qua non of understanding: a compassionate consciousness and the development of an "I-Thou" or "we-relation" in which all immediate reflexivity and judgments are suspended (Buber 1958; Husserl 1931, 264–265; Schutz 1962).

Dualism is not only the driving force behind much contemporary penal analysis and practice; theological systems are also often constructed and justified by a divisive view of the world that is quick to condemn and isolate those outside of their narrow understanding of redemption and salvation. Harold Berman traces the full emergence of dualism in the West to a significant strain of medieval thought, especially in the theology of St. Anselm, and later to the philosophy of Descartes and the scientific revolution. He terms this the era of the ego, one in which the "mind stands outside of the objective reality it perceives. . . . This is the era of the radical separation of subject from object, of essence from existence, of person from act, of spiritual from secular. . . . Indeed, the dualistic character of traditional Western thought has penetrated almost every kind of analysis" (Berman 1974, 111). In such a perspective, "objective" judgments are rendered, labels are created, the concept of the deviant is formulated (Bauman 2000, 205–06; Lofland 1969, 9–10), and interventions aimed at deterring, punishing, treating, or eliminating him or her are justified.

Conversion as Correction

Institutions cannot endure without being nourished by, and in conversation with their past. Organizational theorists across the disciplinary continuum point to the fact that the ideals that motivate a given social organization or tradition must be both constantly renewed and must serve to renew the contemporary life experience of the group as it faces the significant social and epistemological challenges that history unfailingly provides (Baum 1987; Habermas 1974; McCoy 1983; Wittberg 1994). Group identity, no less than individual identity, is solidified and unified only as present challenges and future plans are placed in active conversation with the past (Bruner 2002; Maruna, Wilson, & Curran 2006). The prison is not only no exception to this truth, it is also a poignant and painful example of what happens when an institution loses sight of its founding vision, indeed, the very reason it came into existence.

It is correct to state that the idea of confining people in penal facilities as the normative societal response to illegal behavior did not begin until the late 18th century in England and the early 19th century in the United States. What is incorrect is to assume that there was no lengthy prehistory of the prison, a prehistory that established the architectural and moral template for the various institutional models in use throughout much of the world (Peters 1995; Sellin 1927).

The first centuries of the Christian experience saw, among other things, the need to create an internal "correctional" network. This was for two reasons: The Scriptures mandated that believers settle their differences among themselves rather than relying on a legal judgment, let alone a non-Christian one (Mt 5: 25; I Cor 6: 6); and the experience of the brutal Roman criminal justice system that had made martyrs of most of the early Christian saints and untold numbers of their coreligionists (Bauman 1996; Musurillo 1972).

Furthermore, the New Testament provided the divinely sanctioned example for resolving intergroup conflicts (1 Cor: 5; Mt 18: 15–17; Lk 17: 3–4). Believers were enjoined always to seek to settle differences privately; if unresolved, a group intervention with the troubled person was to be attempted, again in private; failing that, the offender was to be brought before the entire church community. If the offender still remained recalcitrant, he or she was to be, in the words of Jesus, "treated like a pagan or a tax collector" (Mt 18: 17) or, in the words of St. Paul, "handed over to Satan for the destruction of the flesh that the spirit might be saved" (I Cor 5: 5). Both terms are ironic: Jesus repeatedly stated that it was precisely the sinners and tax collectors who were far closer to "the reign of God" than the upstanding members of society (Mt 21: 31; Mk 2: 15; Lk 7:29; 15: 1; 18: 9–14; 19: 1–9); St. Paul, as numerous commentators have affirmed, was solicitous and deeply compassionate toward those who had failed morally. His "excommunication" was a desperate attempt to coax the sinner to face his or her alienation and isolation ("handed over to Satan") and allow contrition and conversion to enable the "spirit" to be "saved" that the person may be restored to a full life within the community (1 Cor 5; II Cor 2: 5–8; Favazza 1988, 70–71; Johnson 1997, 185–90; Sanders 1983).

The development of the sacrament of penance not only reaffirmed this biblical method, but it established the moral and the systematic foundation for the penitentiary as it developed in Catholic monastic communities and ecclesiastical jurisdictions and, later, through their influence, in the prototypical American institutions at Philadelphia (Eastern State Penitentiary) and Auburn, New York.

Although the history of penance is quite complex, the overarching themes are the ontological goodness of the human person despite the unavoidability of sin—understood throughout the first millennium of Christianity as a relational failure (Favazza 1988, 238–39). Although the great majority of sins were absolved through private acts of prayer and penance, the church inherited from its Jewish heritage the understanding that certain sins were of a public nature and, as such, required a public confession and the imposition of a penitential discipline (McNeill & Gamer 1938, 4–7; Tertullian 1959; Vogel 1968,

179–93). What is unique about the evolution of this process is the imposition of a time sentence: the priest or bishop would require a period of time for acts of remittance and, especially in the Eastern Christian churches, penitents were not only required to follow ascetic practices such as fasting and sexual abstinence, but were assigned specific places when the assembly gathered for weekly mass. The "weepers" were to spend a specific period of time at the entrance to the church, humbly asking for prayerful intercession as the congregation gathered for worship. At the conclusion of the designated time, they joined the hearers who were stationed in the vestibule or entrance to the worship space. After completion of this time sequence, they became "prostrators" or "kneelers" who gathered around the ambo or lectern where the Scriptures were proclaimed. Both hearers and prostrators were dismissed after the priest peached the homily and the petitions were offered. Finally, the penitent became a "costander," joining the congregation throughout the mass but still unable to receive the Eucharist (McNeill & Gamer 1938, 7–8; Poschmann 1964, 88–91).

Implicit always in the historical progression of the sacrament was the belief that all sin could be remitted through the internal dynamic of confronting one's alienation, being "bound" by a penance (Mt 8: 18; 16: 19), symbolically enacting that alienation through various forms of excommunication, and finally being formally received back into the community with full rights restored after the completion of the exculpatory process (Favazza 1988, 243–45).

The entire methodology was based on the belief that there was no intentional or manifest need to make the penitent suffer, or serve as a deterrent to others, or undergo "therapeutic" intervention, although all three could be seen as latent functions of the penitential process. The idea of "treatment" was implied in the practice of assuring that members of the congregation accompanied the penitent in the period of isolation or at least made sure that he or she was maintaining the ascetic discipline, but the firm belief was that the process of solitude, fasting, and prayer was sufficient in itself to unmask the false attitudes that led to antisocial comportment, to bring about contrition and amendment, and to restore natural sociability with God and with the community (Favazza 1988, 70–71; Poschmann 1964, 86–87; Vogel 1968, 229–32).

The idea underlying the whole approach was not only that the human person is relational by nature but also that the restoration of sociability required a conversion: a widening of the moral and spiritual horizon to embrace God, the social world, and, indeed, one's very self. This is the concept that best expresses what Jesus refers to as being "born again" (Jn 3: 3). Conversion, in other words, was neither akin to what modern sociologists of religion refer to as denominational "switching" or to the facile way that it has been associated with a single emotional experience of being "saved." In this it verifies the observation of many sociologists who recognize the lacunae in the common portrayals of conversion and acknowledge the need for a deeper phenomenology of the process (Giordano et al. 2002, 27–28; Johnson 2011, 158; Snow & Machalek 1984, 175).

With these rudiments in place throughout the Christian world in the first centuries after the death of Jesus, the final evolution of the penal model took place in the monasteries that began to flourish in the fourth century and took on a singular role in both social stability and educational and cultural innovation after the fall of the Roman Empire. In fact, the monastery was the first prison as we have come to know it. Monks entered an enclosed space and were bound to remain there until death. This voluntary incarceration was the incarnation in the monastic lifeworld of the penitential methodology practiced throughout the church (Johnston 2000, 17–18; Peters 1995; Skotnicki 2008, 81–87): a person approached spiritual perfection by following the penitential path of silence, solitude, fasting, prayer, and work.

The institutional innovation that occurred formally in the monastery concerned the process of discipline for those who committed serious relational offenses. The idea of a time sentence and of a specific place in which to carry out the needed reflective and ascetic practices was understood but, within the monastery, the excommunication could not ordinarily lead to expulsion since the monk was bound to the monastic community for life. Hence, in all of the monastic constitutions, most importantly in that of the largest of the orders, the Benedictines, provisions were made to remand the monk to a special place of confinement, normally a cell, to conduct the needed penitential measures. Eventually, the cells were grouped together either adjoining the chapel, or in a specific location within the enclosure, or, in some instances, as noted by St. John Climacus in sixth century Egypt, in a specific facility built adjacent to the monastery. In these early developments the idea of the prison as we know it today was born (Johnston 2000, 19–23; St. John Climacus 1959, Steps 4–5).

Monks undergoing penance were regularly visited by wise older members of the community ("senpectae") whose task was, according to St. Benedict, to accompany and encourage the erring brother, lest "he be devoured by too much sorrow" (St. Benedict 1996, Ch. 27). Meanwhile, all of the community were enjoined to pray for the imprisoned brother, and it was the specific role of the abbot to "imitate the role of the Good Shepherd who left the flock of ninety-nine sheep to find the one who was lost and, upon finding it, placed it upon his sacred shoulders and carried it back to the flock" (St. Benedict 1996, Ch. 27).

In all of this we see, once again, the refusal to inflict suffering, to manipulate the suffering of the penitent as a warning to others, or to believe that any form of direct intervention was necessary for the work of healing or to facilitate the return to cooperative sociability. The foundation for the prison was the monastery and the correctional methodology of the sacrament of penance: people are fundamentally good since each carries the divine within himself or herself; each loses his or her "birthright" due to selfish preoccupation and disregard for the well-being of others; each is naturally led to inner peace, wholeness, and resocialization by immersion in an experience that provides what St. Thomas Aquinas referred to as the "medicine" necessary for conversion to occur (St. Thomas Aquinas 1949, II–II, Q. 108, a. 4).

Not only were there prisons in each of the many thousands of monasteries throughout the Catholic world up to and, in many instances, after the Reformation, but also, in 1298, Pope Boniface VIII instituted the decree that all dioceses were to build at least one prison for the incarceration of members of the clergy who had committed serious violations of ecclesiastical and public morality (Peters 1995, 29; Pugh 1970, 135). These prisons became the focus of secular magistrates, particularly with the decline of feudalism and the growth of cities (Dunbabin 2002; Geltner 2008). Although, as noted, the full institutionalization of the prison into the role it serves today only took place in the last 200 years, the ideological foundation for its emergence came through secular attention to the monastic model (in the case of the separate system of the Eastern State Penitentiary), and the ecclesiastical model (in the case of the silent system of Auburn) (Cajani 1990; Sellin 1927).

It is the contention of this chapter not only that any reflection on the justification, meaning, and goal of imprisonment must be attentive to and in conversation with the foundational motivation for incarceration provided in the history of the church, but also that the dominant justifications for the existence and meaning of detention—retribution, deterrence, and rehabilitation—fail to honor the historical and moral roots of confinement and, as a result, their efforts at correction or desistance have withered accordingly.

Facing the Crisis in Corrections

Criminal justice is a tradition, an extended socially embodied argument concerning how a specific institution is to confront disruptive and uncooperative members. I have argued that an essential, perhaps the essential, interlocutor in the philosophical and procedural questions that arise as a result of delinquent behavior has been left out of the conversation due to inattentiveness to or disregard for its ancient and continuing role in addressing the issue (Johnson 2011, Ch. 1; Stark, Kent, & Doyle 1982, 22).

Contributing to the problem are the constraints of methodology, particularly the positivist, "technocratic" methodology, still dominant in most graduate sociology programs, whose roots are based in a belief in epistemological and social evolution in which religion ceded its priority in matters of truth first to reason and, finally, to the surest intellectual resource: science. Here, in concert with the Enlightenment belief in "disinterested" reason, research is protected by the "objective" procedural coordinates of categorization, theoretical formulation, definition of problems, and procedures for testing hypothetical propositions (Winter 1966, 73). As Stanley Cohen phrases the evolution of the discipline: "the Holy Grail of causation" has been replaced by "the Holy Grail of evaluation" (Cohen 1985, 176–77). I have suggested that such a dualist stance is implicated in the elevation of an approach to social analysis that places the researcher in the service of a conservative ideology that measures "correction" in terms of the regnant social order and trades in the currency of guiding systemic principles (retribution, deterrence, and rehabilitation) that eschew foundational moral commitments in favor of various expressions of social control, the justification for coercion, and invasive behavioral technologies (Garland 1985, 93–94).

In the same vein, such an "agnostic" approach not only fails to appreciate the time-honored method of creating the conditions for a conversion based on a widening of the scope of human compassion, it also, ironically, demonstrates what Gibson Winter (1966, 108) terms "bad faith." Winter believes that a science of the social world must be founded on a phenomenological starting point that he refers to as "intentional." This approach shares common ground with the original Christian vision of "corrections" in terms of a moral ontology based on the primacy of relationality and the creation of the environmental conditions seen as necessary for its restoration among those whose who justified a selfish turn toward the self and its interests rather than the common good. Winter, echoing the thought of Alfred Schutz, writes that the "ultimate horizon" of the self is an "infinite concern . . . for integrity." The latter is understood in terms of "intentionality toward the social and cultural world" based on "the essential unity of self and other" (Winter 1966, 108–09). From this perspective, in the state of bad faith "the harmony of self and other to which the 'I' belongs is sacrificed for a lesser reality of the 'I's' choice and the basic relatedness of self and other is denied" (Winter 1966, 108).

It has been the argument of this chapter that the methodological constraints created and sustained by objective, impersonal approaches to understanding the phenomenon of "crime," and the dismissive attitude regarding the early Christian involvement in shaping the ethos of confinement, provide the foundation for the default principles of retribution, deterrence, and rehabilitation that are inexorably linked to the instrumental use of state power and, worse, contribute, however unwittingly, to the "depressing" circumstances that make the current state of corrections, in the words of Jeffrie Murphy, "a disgrace to the ideals of the United States" (Murphy 2014, 75).

The criminological discipline has a vast corpus of analytical studies, many of them impeccably researched that seek to understand the phenomenon of human alienation and the way that social disaffection often leads to willful violence and exaggerated disregard for the welfare of others. Moreover, there is a prescriptive tone that dominates the discipline in a manner that is not strictly sociological. Sociology seeks to understand present human interaction in light of antecedent processes, yet many social scientific studies of the criminal justice system are committed to addressing the systemic issues that were touched on in the beginning of this chapter and seek to bring about, if not a more compassionate, at least a more unbiased system of justice and, indeed, a more harmonious and equitable social order. The eminent criminologist, Edwin Sutherland, stated that since criminology often implies such a prescriptive dimension, it is not strictly scientific (Sutherland 1978, 22).

On the other hand, theological systems, particularly Christianity, whose traditional approach to human malfeasance has been summarized in this chapter, are ultimately future oriented: they interpret the present in terms of revealed sources that summon a trust in divine providence that inevitably guides history toward a glorious union of all life with its Creator (Yoder 1971, 55–90). Yet they, too, are theologically bound to address the social question and, in the present case, the way to respond to human relational failures utilizing the moral and spiritual resources bequeathed to them.

One cannot, in other words, construct a theology without, at the same time, developing a sociology (Milbank 1990). At the same time, it seems to me that a sociology that is any way consensual or intentional cannot function without a set of moral principles and a commitment to human solidarity that ultimately draw their content and authority from theological sources. Without this necessary cooperative dynamic, theology resorts to Manichaean or Gnostic conceptions of the human experience that abandon efforts to shape human experience in light of God's compassionate love for all and, instead, withdraws either in "pious" despair or in cynical rejection of all who do not subscribe to their parochial and judgmental interpretation of history. Sociology often loses sight of what Schutz and other "intentional" members of the discipline call the "we-relation," predicated on a belief that human sociability and the innate yearning for transcendence make apparent that the self only comes to full actualization in relations of care with others (Schutz 1962, I, 174ff). The latter is not only a moral statement; it is an epistemological and systemic one. The objective distance of the detached observer not only fails to heed the "consensual" claim that the everyday world is accessible to us only by participation (Schutz 1962, I, 207ff; Shils 1980), but it also yields to the pitfall of power to resolve social problems that Christian history and the elements of sociological theory just spoken of state can only be resolved morally.

The roots of criminal justice are steeped in theological commitments to human goodness, to the relentless hunger for human transcendence, to the necessary pain brought about by human alienation, and to a restorative correctional methodology based on creating the conditions for conversion, a process whereby natural sociability and the desire for integrity and unity in ever widening levels are fostered through ascetic discipline and attentive care. There can be no justification or, for that matter, need for the sort of judgment that would bring harm on the culpable for any reason or force them to conform to a set of behavioral expectations that, lacking a moral ontology, reveal a congruence with the will of the dominant classes and conformity with the current state of economic and political affairs.

David Garland calls our attention to the fact that the system of criminal justice is always mediated by cultural codes: languages, discourses, and sentiments. Until we can begin to have a different language and different sentiments with which to envision the future other than those of the current penal regime and its diffuse moral ideology, there will be no change in the culture of punishment (Garland 1990, 198). Similarly, Byron Johnson writes that "it is increasingly apparent that any crime-fighting strategy will be needlessly incomplete unless communities of faith and their vast networks of social and spiritual support are integrally involved" (Johnson 2014, 3).

This chapter has argued that penal theorists seeking to address the problem of human destructiveness are often compromised not so much by a lack of intellectual resources internal to their disciplines, but by a faulty reliance on methods of analysis predicated on a dualist view of reality and by investigative procedures shorn of a moral ontology. They are further diminished by a lack of attention to the initial correctional ethos of the primitive Christian church. These lacunae have led to the elevation of conceptual guides for the system of criminal law that are at once incoherent, given the initial foundations of the system, and are inevitably tied to the expansion of state power and the use of violence to address a problem that can only be resolved by creating the conditions for conversion and self-transcendence.

Bibliography

Alexander, Michelle. *The New Jim Crow.* New York: New Press, 2010.

Andrews, D. A., & P. Bonta. *The Psychology of Criminal Conduct* (5th ed.). New Providence, NJ: Matthew Bender, 2010.

Aquinas, St. Thomas. *Summa Theologica.* Trans. Fathers of the English Dominican Province. New York: Benziger, 1949.

Baum, Gregory. *Compassion and Solidarity.* Concord, Ontario: House of Anansi, 1987.

Bauman, Richard. *Crime and Punishment in Ancient Rome.* London and New York: Routledge, 1996.

Bauman, Zygmunt. "Social Issues of Law and Order." *British Journal of Criminology* 40 (2000): 205–221.

Beccaria, Cesare. *On Crimes and Punishments.* Trans. Henry Paolucci. Indianapolis: Bobbs-Merrill, 1963.

Becket, Katherine, & Stephen Kelly Herbert. *Banished: The New Social Control in Urban America.* New York: Oxford University Press, 2010.

Benedict, St. *Benedict's Rule.* Trans. Terrence G. Kardong. Collegeville, MN: Liturgical Press, 1996.

Bentham, Jeremy. *Introduction to the Principles of Morals and Legislation.* London: Athlone, 1970.

Berman, Harold J. *The Interaction of Law and Religion.* Nashville: Abingdon, 1974.

Brockway, Zebulon. *Fifty Years of Prison Service.* New York: Charities Publication Committee, 1912.

Bruner, Jerome. *Making Stories: Law, Literature, Life.* New York: Farrar, Straus, & Giroux, 2002.

Buber, Martin. *I and Thou.* New York: Scribner, 1958.

Burkhardt, Brett C. *Private Corrections and Public Discourse.* Madison: University of Wisconsin Press, 2011.

Burkhardt, Brett C. "Private Prisons in Public Discourse: Measuring Moral Legitimacy." *Sociological Focus* 47 (2014): 279–298.

Cajani, Luigi. "Surveillance and Redemption: The Casa di Correzoine of San Michele a Ripa In Rome." In Norbert Finzsch & Robert Jutte (Eds.), *Institutions of Confinement.* Washington, DC: German Historical Institute, 1990: 301–324.

Christie, Nils. *Limits to Pain.* New York: Martin Robinson, 1981.

Climacus, St. John. *The Ladder of Divine Ascent.* Trans. Lazarus Moore. London: Faber & Faber, 1959.

Cohen, Stanley. *Visions of Social Control.* New York: Cambridge University Press, 1985.

Cover, Robert. "Violence and the Word." *Yale Law Journal* 95 (1986): 1601–1639.

Cullen, Francis, Jody Sundt, & John Wozniak. "The Virtuous Prison." In Francis Cullen, Cheryl Leo Jonson, & Mary Stohr (Eds.), *The American Prison: Imagining a Different Future.* Los Angeles: Sage, 2014: 62–84.

De Beaumont, Gustave, & Alexis De Tocqueville. *On the Penitentiary System in the United States and Its Application to France.* Philadelphia: Carey, Lea & Blanchard, 1833.

Dunbabin, Jean. *Captivity and Imprisonment in Medieval Europe, 1000–1300.* Houndmills, UK: Palgrave Macmillan, 2002.

Durkheim, Emile. *The Division of Labor in Society.* Trans. W. D. Halls. New York: Free Press, 1984.

Eliot, T. S. *Murder in the Cathedral.* New York: Faber and Faber, 1938.

Foucault, Michel. *Discipline and Punish.* Trans. Alan Sheridan. New York: Vintage, 1979.

Favazza, Joseph. *The Order of Penitents.* Collegeville, MN: Liturgical Press, 1988.

Garland, David. *Punishment and Welfare.* Tallahassee, FL: Florida Parole Commission, 1985.

Garland, David. *Punishment and Modern Society.* Chicago: University of Chicago Press, 1990.

Garland, David. *The Culture of Control.* Chicago: University of Chicago Press, 2001.

Geltner, Guy. *The Medieval Prison.* Princeton, NJ: Princeton University Press, 2008.

Giordano, Peggy, Monica A. Longmore, Ryan Schroeder, & Patrick M. Seffrin. "A Life Course Perspective on Spirituality and Desistance from Crime." *Criminology* 46, no.1 (2002): 99–132.

Gottschalk, Marie. *Caught: The Prison State and the Lockdown of American Politics.* Princeton, NJ: Princeton University Press, 2015.

Habermas, Jurgen. *Legitimation Crisis.* Trans. Thomas McCarthy. Boston: Beacon, 1974.

Haney, Craig. *Reforming Punishment.* Washington, DC: American Psychological Association, 2006.

Hart, H. L. A. *Punishment and Responsibility.* New York: Clarendon, 1968.

Heidegger, Martin. *Being and Time.* Trans. John Macquarie & Edward Robinson. New York: Herder and Herder, 1962.

Hofstadter, Richard. *Social Darwinism in American Thought.* New York: G. Braziller, 1959.

Howard, John. *Prisons and Lazarettos*, Montclair, NJ: Patterson Smith, 1973.

Husserl, Edmund. *Ideas: General Introduction to Pure Phenomenology.* Trans. W. R. Boyce Gibson. London: George Allen & Unwin, 1931.

Ignatieff, Michael. *A Just Measure of Pain.* New York: Columbia University Press, 1978.

Johnson, Byron R. *More God, Less Crime.* West Conshohocken, PA: Templeton Press, 2011.

Johnson, Byron R. "Religious Participation in Criminal Behavior." In J. A. Humphrey & P. Cordella (Eds.), *Effective Intervention in the Lives of Criminal Offenders.* New York: Springer, 2014: 3–18.

Johnson, Luke Timothy. *Reading Romans.* New York: Crossroad, 1997.

Johnston, Norman. *Forms of Constraint.* Champagne: University of Illinois Press, 2000.

Kant, Immanuel. *Groundwork for the Metaphysics of Morals.* Trans. Mary Gregor. New York: Cambridge University Press, 1996.

Lasch, Christopher. *The True and Only Heaven.* New York: Norton, 1991.

Lofland, John. *Deviance and Identity.* Englewood Cliffs, NJ: Prentice-Hall, 1969.

MacIntyre, Alasdair. *After Virtue.* South Bend, IN: University of Notre Dame Press, 1981.

Maruna, Shadd. *Making Good.* Washington, DC: American Psychological Association, 2001.

Maruna, Shadd, Louise Wilson, & Kathryn Curran. "Why God Is Often Found Behind Bars." *Research in Human Development* 3 (2006): 161–184.

McCoy, Bowen H. "The Parable of the Sadhu." *Harvard Business Review* (September–October 1983): 103–108.

McKelvey, Blake. *American Prisons: A History of Good Intentions.* Montclair, NJ: Patterson Smith, 1977.

McNeill, John T., & Helena Gamer. *Medieval Handbooks of Penance.* New York: Columbia University Press, 1938.

Milbank, John. *Theology and Social Theory.* New York: Blackwell, 1990.

Morris, Herbert. "Persons and Punishment." *The Monist* 52 (1968): 475–501.

Muhammad, Kahlil Gibran. *The Condemnation of Blackness*. Cambridge, MA: Harvard University Press, 2010.

Murakawa, Naomi. *The First Civil Right*. New York: Oxford University Press, 2014.

Murphy, Jeffrie. "'In the Penal Colony' and Why I Am Now Reluctant to Teach Criminal Law." *Criminal Justice Ethics* 33 (2014): 72–82.

Musurillo, Herbert (Ed. & Trans.). *The Acts of the Christian Martyrs*. New York: Clarendon, 1972.

Nagel, Thomas. *The View from Nowhere*. New York: Oxford University Press, 1986.

Peters, Edward. "Prison before the Prison." In Norval Morris & David Rothman (Eds.), *The Oxford History of the Prison*. New York: Oxford University Press, 1995: 3–47.

Petersilia, Joan. *When Prisoners Come Home: Parole and Prisoner Reentry*. New York: Oxford University Press, 2009.

Poschmann, Bernhard. *Penance and the Anointing of the Sick*. Trans. Francis Courtney, S. J. New York: Herder & Herder, 1964.

Pugh, Ralph. *Imprisonment in Medieval England*. New York: Cambridge University Press, 1970.

Rothman, David. *Conscience and Convenience*. Boston: Little Brown, 1980.

Sanders, E. P. *Paul, the Law, and the Jewish People*. Philadelphia: Fortress, 1983.

Schutz, Alfred. *Collected Papers* (2 Vols.). Ed. Arvid Brodersen. The Hague, Netherlands: Martinus Nijhoff, 1962.

Scarry, Elaine. *The Body in Pain*. New York: Oxford University Press, 1985.

Sellin, Thorsten. "Dom Jean Mabillon: A Prison Reformer of the Seventeenth Century." *Journal of the American Institute of Criminal Law and Criminology* 17 (1927): 581–602.

Shils, Edward. "The Calling of Sociology." In *The Calling of Sociology and Other Essays on the Pursuit of Learning*. Chicago: University of Chicago Press, 1980: 3–92.

Skotnicki, Andrew. *Criminal Justice and the Catholic Church*. Lanham, MD: Rowman & Littlefield, 2008.

Smith, Adam. *The Theory of Moral Sentiments*. New York: Augustus M. Kelley, 1966.

Smith, Timothy L. *Revivalism and Social Reform*. New York: Abingdon Press, 1957.

Snow, David A., & Richard Machalek. "The Sociology of Conversion." *Annual Review of Sociology* 10 (1984): 167–190.

Spierenberg, Pieter. *The Spectacle of Suffering*. New York: Cambridge University Press, 1984.

Stark, Rodney, Lori Kent, & Daniel Doyle. "Religion and Delinquency: The Ecology of a Lost Relationship." *Journal of Research in Crime and Delinquency* 19 (1982): 4–24.

Sutherland, Edward, & Donald R. Cressey. *Criminology* (10th ed.). New York: J. P. Lippincott, 1978.

Sykes, Gresham. *The Society of Captives*. Princeton, NJ: Princeton University Press, 2007.

Taylor, Charles. *A Secular Age*. Cambridge, MA: Belknap Press, 2007.

Tertullian, "On Penitence." In *Treatises on Penance*. Trans. William P. Le Saint, S. J. Westminster, MD: Newman Press, 1959.

Travis, Jeremy. *But They All Come Back*. Washington, DC: Urban Institute Press, 2005.

Travis, Jeremy, Bruce Western, & Steve Redburn (Eds.). *Incarceration in the United States*. Washington, DC: National Academies Press, 2014.

Vogel, Cyril. "Sin and Penance." In Philippe Delhaye et al. (Eds.)., *Pastoral Treatment of Sin*. New York: Desclee, 1968: 177–282.

Ward, Tony, & Shadd Maruna. *Rehabilitation: Beyond the Risk Paradigm*. London and New York: Routledge, 2007.

Whitman, James. *Harsh Justice*. New York: Oxford University Press, 2003.

Winter, G. *Elements for a Social Ethic: Scientific and Ethical Perspectives on Social Process*. Ann Arbor, MI: Macmillan, 1966.

Wittberg, Patricia. *The Rise and Fall of Catholic Religious Orders*. Albany: State University of New York Press, 1994.

Yoder, John Howard. *The Original Revolution*. Scottdale, PA: Herald Press, 1971.

PART 2

Religion in Prison in the United States

CHAPTER SIX

Religion and Prison Violence

Benjamin Meade and Riane M. Bolin

Religion has played an influential role in prisons for centuries, with its first introduction likely occurring with the incarceration of religious men during biblical times (Dammer 2000). In the United States, religion was central to the development of its penal system, with the two early prison systems, the Pennsylvania system and the Auburn system, both emphasizing religious principles (Clear & Myhre 1995; Rothman 1995; Skotnicki 2000). Both systems enforced hard labor and solitary confinement, believing that this would lead offenders to repent of their sins and refrain from engaging in further criminal acts; thus, the early penal institutions were aptly named penitentiaries (Dammer 2000; Johnston 2009; O'Connor 2002).

Following the American Civil War, the public became dissatisfied with penitentiaries and a call was made for the reformation of the penal system. Specifically, many policy makers and citizens alike advocated for the implementation of indeterminate sentencing and a focus on rehabilitation (Clear, Cole, & Reisig 2006). This ultimately resulted in the transformation of the penitentiary into a reformatory, where the focus was on reforming inmates through treatment as opposed to harsh labor and solitary confinement (Pisciotta 1994). Although this new penal era relied heavily on social science as the official guiding approach to the treatment of offenders (Clear et al. 2006; Rothman 1980), religion remained influential as chaplains were often used to administer treatment to prisoners (Dammer 2002; Sundt & Cullen 1998; Sundt, Dammer, & Cullen 2002). The influence of religion on the penal system waned during most of the 20th century, but in recent years, a renewed emphasis has emerged with the introduction of faith-based programming (DiIulio 2009; Dodson, Cabage, & Klenowski 2011).

Due to the influence that religion has had on the development of prisons, as well as the programming available in prisons, studies have explored the various ways in which religion and/or religiosity may impact prisoners, including, but not limited to, emotional and behavioral coping (Kerley, Allison, & Graham 2006; Thomas & Zaitzow 2006), institutional adjustment (Clear et al. 1992; Clear & Sumter 2002; Johnson, Larson, & Pitts 1997), and offender rehabilitation/criminal desistance (O'Connor & Perreyclear 2002; Schroeder & Frana 2009). One area that has been of particular interest to researchers is the link between religiosity and prisoner misconduct (Clear et al. 1992; Clear & Myhre 1995; Clear & Sumter 2002; Kerley et al. 2011; O'Connor & Perreyclear 2002; Steiner & Wooldredge 2008; Sturgis 2010). The research that has been conducted exploring this relationship has produced mixed findings. A number of studies have found that religiosity is negatively related to prisoner misconduct (Camp et al. 2008; Clear et al. 1992; Clear & Sumter 2002; Kerley et al. 2005; LaVigne, Brazzell, & Small 2007; Young et al. 1995), while other studies have found that no relationship exists (Johnson 1987; Johnson & Larson 2003; Johnson et al. 1997; Koenig 1995; Sturgis 2010). Of the most recent studies that have identified a significant relationship, religiosity has been found to be more consistently related to lower odds of serious and violent misconduct (Kerley et al. 2006; Steiner & Wooldredge 2008; Sturgis 2010). This finding runs counter to research on religiosity and deviance in the general population where studies have revealed that religiosity is more strongly related to lower odds of less serious deviance, such as substance use (Baier & Wright 2001; Cochran & Akers 1989; Hadaway, Elifson, & Peterson 1984; Hoffman & Bahr 2005; Reisig, Wolfe, & Pratt 2012; Ulmer et al. 2012).

Based on these findings, additional research is needed to further explore the relationship between religiosity and misconduct and to explain why religion may impact types of deviance differently based on the environment: prison versus general population. The present study attempted to address this gap in the literature. Through the use of a national data set of state prisoners, the relationship between religiosity and violence in prison was explored.

Literature Review

Religiosity and Misconduct in Prison

One of the primary outcomes explored by penologists has been inmate misconduct (Flanagan 1983; Gendreau, Goggin, & Law 1997; Goetting & Howsen 1986; Steiner, Butler, & Ellison 2014). Misconduct, according to the literature, is defined as the violation of institutional rules by a prisoner. Violations can range from relatively minor incidents, such as failure to obey staff instructions, to serious incidents such as assault on another inmate/staff member or even murder (Steiner & Wooldredge 2013). A number of factors have been found to be predictive of inmate misconduct (see Steiner, Butler, & Ellison 2014 for systematic review). These factors stem from three different sources including institutional, such as prison crowding, facility security level, and perceived level of control of one's environment (Camp et al. 2003; Gendreau et al. 1997; Gover, Perez, & Jennings 2008; MacKenzie, Layton, Goodstein, & Blouin 1987; Meade & Steiner 2013; Steiner et al. 2014; Steiner & Wooldredge 2013; Wright 1985, 1993); individual, such as age, race, criminal history, sentence length, offense type, and gang affiliation (Cunningham & Sorensen 2007, Gendreau et al. 1997; Griffin & Hepburn 2006; Steiner et al. 2014); and management, such as prison governance and consistency and integrity of policies and procedures by staff (Bottoms 1999; DiIulio 1987; Huebner 2003).

Another factor that has been thought to affect inmate misconduct is religiosity. For many inmates, religion is an important aspect of their incarceration, with approximately 32 percent of inmates regularly participating in worship services, and nearly 50 percent reporting experiencing a spiritual conversion while incarcerated (Dammer 2002; Johnson & Larson 1997; O'Connor and Perreyclear 2002). Research has sought to explore the reasons that inmates seek out religion while incarcerated and have identified both intrinsic and extrinsic motivations (Clear et al. 2000; Dammer 2002; Johnson & Larson 2003). In regards to intrinsic motivations, research has found that religiosity helps inmates to cope with the loss of autonomy and freedom (Clear et al. 2000; Dammer 2002) and to accept responsibility for their crimes, deal with their guilt, and find forgiveness (Clear et al. 2000; Johnson & Larson 2003). Extrinsic motivations have also been identified in the research, including safety and access to goods, materials, and outside visitors. All of these reasons have led researchers to speculate that participation in religious activities helps facilitate adjustment to prison, thus lowering the likelihood of involvement in misconduct.

Studies examining the relationship between religion or religiosity and inmate misconduct have produced mixed findings (Camp et al. 2008; Clear et al. 1992; Clear & Myhre 1995; Clear & Sumter 2002; Johnson 1987; Johnson & Larson 2003; Johnson et al. 1997; Kerley, Matthews, & Blanchard 2005; Koenig 1995; LaVigne et al. 2007; Sturgis 2010; Young et al. 1995). Consistent with findings from studies examining the impact of religiosity on deviance/crime, numerous studies have found a significant inverse relationship between religiosity and crime, indicating that those who are more religious or participate in more religious activities tend to have lower odds and/or rates of misconduct (Clear et al. 1992; Clear & Myhre 1995; Clear & Sumter 2002; Kerley et al. 2011; O'Connor & Perreyclear 2002; Steiner & Wooldredge 2008; Sturgis 2010). Clear et al. (1992), for example, found that religiosity significantly predicted a lower number of infractions, after controlling for a number of other variables. Similarly, Kerley et al. (2011) found that participation in religious services significantly reduced the incidence of prison deviance.

Not all studies, however, have found religion to be significantly related to inmate misconduct (Johnson 1987; Johnson & Larson 2003; Johnson et al. 1997; Koenig 1995; Sturgis 2010). Interestingly, in the study mentioned above conducted by Kerley et al. (2011), two other measures of religious participation, praying privately and watching religious television, were not found to be significantly related to prison deviance. Steiner and Wooldredge (2008) and Sturgis (2010) found similar mixed results in their study, with some religious indicators being inversely related to misconduct, while other indicators were not found to be significantly associated with infractions.

To further explore the relationship between religiosity and inmate misconduct, Meade (2014) conducted a systematic review of studies examining the effect of religiosity on inmate misconduct during the time frame of 2000 to 2013. Focusing only on studies that had utilized multivariate models, he discovered that approximately 68 percent of the models found a significant, inverse relationship between religiosity and misconduct. However, he also noted that the other 32 percent of studies found no significant relationship between the two variables.

Unlike the studies on religion and crime/deviance, which explored multiple types of deviant and criminal behavior, most studies of religiosity and inmate misconduct have used a composite measure of rule infractions (e.g., Clear & Myhre 1995; Clear & Sumter 2002; Johnson 1987; O'Connor & Perreyclear 2002; Pass 1999), thereby removing the ability to determine whether the strength of the relationship varies by types of misconduct (i.e., violent, nonviolent, substance use, etc.). However, of the recent studies that have focused on specific types of misconduct, it has been found that religiosity in prison is more consistently related to lower odds of serious and violent misconduct (Camp et al. 2008; Kerley et al. 2005; Steiner & Wooldredge 2008; Sturgis 2010).

Kerley et al. (2005), for example, using a random sample of inmates at a large prison facility in Mississippi, explored the relationship between religiosity and self-reports of the frequency of arguing and fighting with other inmates. Five measures of religiosity were included: religious conversion, belief in a higher power, belief that right and wrong should be based on God's laws, attendance at religious services, and attendance at Operation Starting Line (a national prison ministry event). It was found that four of the five religiosity variables (belief in a higher power, belief that right and wrong should be based on God's laws, attendance at religious services, and attendance at Operation Starting Line) were significant predictors of the likelihood of arguing with other inmates, with religiosity reducing the likelihood of arguing. In regard to fighting with other inmates, only one religiosity variable, belief that right and wrong should be based on God's laws, was found to be a significant predictor, with those inmates who strongly agreed with the statement that right and wrong should be based on God's laws being less likely to fight one or more times per month. Although direct effects were not found between most of the religiosity variables and fighting, indirect effects were found. Specifically, inmates believing in a higher power and attending the Operation Starting Line event were even less likely to engage in fighting because they participated in fewer arguments. Based on these findings, the researchers concluded that religion can help to reduce the incidence of negative behaviors in prison facilities.

Steiner and Wooldredge (2008) also explored whether religiosity had an impact on inmate misconduct. In contrast to Kerley et al. (2005), however, Steiner and Wooldredge (2008) were not specifically focused on the relationship between religiosity and misconduct, but were instead interested in identifying both individual and environmental effects on prison rule violations. To assess the impact of individual and environmental effects on inmate misconduct, self-reported data were collected in 1991 and 1997 from male inmates housed in 204 facilities. Three dichotomous measures of misconduct were explored: assaults, drug and alcohol offenses, and other nonviolent rule infractions. Participation in religious activities was included as an individual level measure. It was found that participation in religious activities was a significant predictor of assaults (1997 only) and drug/alcohol offenses, but not other nonviolent types of misconduct. The researchers concluded that further research was needed to explore the role that religiosity played in inmate misconduct.

Unlike the previous two studies, Camp et al. (2008) used official records of inmate misconduct to explore whether participation in faith-based programming reduced the likelihood of prisoner misconduct. Participants enrolled in the Life Connections Program (LCP) at five different facilities were compared to non-LCP participants from 13 different prisons. The comparison subjects were matched based on sex of the inmate and security level of the prison. Three types of misconduct were explored: all types, serious (e.g., homicide or an escape) and less serious (e.g., violating rules such as where to smoke and when to move between buildings). Camp and colleagues (2008) found that participation in the Life Connections Program lowered the probability of engaging in serious forms of misconduct, but no effect was found when examining less serious forms of misconduct or the combined measure of misconduct.

More recently, Sturgis (2010) found similar results when exploring the relationship between religiosity and institutional misconduct using data from the 1997 Survey of Inmates in State and Federal Correctional Facilities. Three dependent variables were explored: total number of violations, substance use (drug violations and alcohol violations), and assault (physical assault of another inmate, verbal assault of another inmate, physical assault of a staff member, and verbal assault of a staff member). When examining the total number of violations, religiosity was not found to be related to institutional misconduct. However, when examining minor misconduct (substance use) and serious misconduct (assault) individually, it was found that religiosity was a significant predictor of serious misconduct, but not of minor misconduct.

Different patterns emerge from studies on religion and crime in the community outside of prison. Studies examining the relationship in the general population have tended to find evidence supportive of the antiascetic hypothesis, which states that religiosity is more effective at deterring minor forms of crime/deviance than more serious forms (Middleton & Putney 1962; Sturgis 2010). Specifically, numerous studies have found religion/religiosity to have a stronger effect on minor forms of deviance, such as substance use (Baier & Wright 2001; Cochran & Akers 1989; Hadaway et al. 1984; Hoffman & Bahr 2005; Reisig et al. 2012; Ulmer et al. 2012).

Theoretical Explanations of Religiosity and Prison Violence

Several theories can be used to explain why religiosity may have an impact on institutional misconduct including social control theory and life course theory. According to social control theory, individuals are naturally self-interested; therefore, there is no need to explain why individuals engage in deviant behavior (Kornhauser 1978; Hirschi 1969). Instead, what must be explained is why all individuals do not commit deviant acts (Hirschi 1969). The theory argues that social control is what helps individuals refrain from deviant behavior. It can be argued that religion can serve as a form of social control restraining individuals from deviance. Hirschi's (1969) social bond theory can be used to explain why religious prisoners may be less likely to engage in misconduct.

According to Hirschi (1969), there are four elements that make up the social bond: attachment, commitment, involvement, and belief. Religion can help to develop each of these bonds. Attachment refers to relationships with positive influences that help to control behavior. It is argued that when individuals care about the wishes and expectations of others, they will abstain from engaging in behavior with which those individuals disapprove. Thus, in prison, religious inmates may abide by institutional rules and avoid misconduct so that they do not disappoint or alienate religious affiliates and leaders. Commitment refers to the degree to which individuals invest themselves and their energy in conventional behaviors. Hirschi (1969) argues that the more time and energy that inmates devote to a particular activity, the more they feel they have to lose by engaging in deviant acts. Thus, inmates who have committed themselves to having a spiritual relationship with God may refrain from misconduct so as not to jeopardize the feeling of closeness with Him. Involvement restrains one's ability to engage in deviant acts. Inmates who are more involved in religious activities will naturally have less time to engage in misconduct. Finally, beliefs represent the extent to which one holds normative values. It can be argued that religious inmates will engage in fewer acts of misconduct because their religious beliefs have instilled conventional morals along with respect for authority and the law.

Life course theories may also be used to explain the link between religiosity and misconduct by viewing spiritual conversion while in prison as a turning point in one's life (Sampson & Laub 1993). Spiritual conversions tend to serve an important function for prisoners. According to Maruna, Wilson, and Curran (2006) who examined a number of narratives on religious conversions, such conversions serve five main functions for prisoners: (1) it allows the inmate to create a new social identity; (2) it provides purpose and meaning to imprisonment; (3) it empowers inmates by turning them into an agent of God; (4) it provides the prisoner with the possibility of forgiveness; and (5) it provides a sense of control over an unknown future (174–175). All of these elements serve to help the inmate refrain from engaging in misconduct.

Similarly, Dammer (2002) explored the reasons for religious involvement in the correctional environment. He found that inmates who were sincere in their motivations for involvement in religion commonly stated that religious practice offered them "motivation, direction and meaning for life, hope for the future, peace of mind, positive self-esteem, and change in lifestyle" (39). Many inmates often cited feeling hopeless about their future prior to their religious involvement. However, religion gave them the opportunity to change their situation by providing them with rules to live by. According to Giordano and colleagues (2002), this internal change within the individual can be referred to as a cognitive shift/transformation. Spiritual conversion, Giordano et al. (2002) argue, represents a hook for change, which allows for a cognitive shift to take place. This hook for change motivates inmates to recognize the new environmental situation in a positive light and to redefine themselves based on the new environment. Once they have discarded their criminal self, the final step in the cognitive transformation is when the actor no longer sees deviant behavior as acceptable or desirable. Ultimately, the religious conversion changes the thinking process that allows inmates to work through and overcome their past circumstances.

Present Study

In sum, the state of the literature regarding religiosity and prisoner misconduct remains mixed in regards to the efficacy of religion to reduce inmate deviance. On the other hand, recent studies have seemingly reached a consensus in findings that religiosity has the potential to reduce serious forms of inmate misconduct, particularly violence, but may have little impact on less serious forms of institutional rule violations. As of yet, researchers have largely failed to note this trend in study findings, let alone conduct studies to further examine the potential religiosity may have for reducing institutional violence.

One potential reason for this oversight may be related to the findings regarding religiosity in the general population. Consistent with the antiascetic hypothesis, many scholars may generalize findings from community samples to institutional samples with the assumption that religiosity may have stronger effects on minor forms of deviance, particularly substance use. In addition, most studies, as cited above, have not measured misconduct as separate conceptual categories (e.g., violent, nonviolent), but rather have analyzed misconduct as a singular phenomenon. In the present study, we attempt a preliminary investigation into the trend in studies that religiosity has a more pronounced effect on serious forms of institutional deviance, especially violence.

Through this study, we contribute to the literature in several ways. First, using a large, national sample of inmates housed in state prisons, we examine the effect that religiosity has on several different conceptual categories of misconduct. We also include two outcome measures of prison assaults. Findings from this study indicating (or failing to find) a consistent relationship between religiosity and prison assaults would contribute additional evidence to (or contradict) the recent body of literature discovering religiosity is more important in curtailing serious and violent misconduct in prison. Finally, we use multilevel modeling to correct for problems associated with nested data structures (inmates housed in prisons) to provide a more rigorous estimate of the relationship between religiosity and inmate misconduct.

Methods

Data and Sample

The data used for this study were culled from the 2004 Survey of Inmates in State and Federal Correctional Facilities (ICPSR 4572), with the target population being all inmates housed in secure confinement facilities at the state level across the United States. The Survey of Inmates is a nationally representative sample of inmates in state and federal facilities and provides data on inmates' current offense and sentence, criminal history, demographic and personal characteristics, family background, substance use and abuse, and experiences and activities while incarcerated. The analyses reported in this study were restricted to inmates in state facilities and inmates held in secure confinement facilities. In other words, federal facilities and community-based facilities, such as work release camps, were deleted from the data. Federal facilities and community-based facilities may be significantly different from state confinement facilities in unmeasured ways in terms of differences, for example, in inmate populations and facility culture and structure.

The sample of state inmates was selected in a two-stage process. The 2000 Census of State and Adult Correctional Facilities served as the sampling frame for stage one selection. The facilities were stratified by inmate sex, and the largest facilities were selected with certainty. The remaining facilities were substratified by region of the country, ordered by size of the inmate population, and then randomly selected based on probabilities proportionate to size. Based on this design, 283 facilities were selected. The second stage of sampling selected a random sample of inmates housed in the facilities sampled at stage one, resulting in the selection of 14,499 offenders. The deletion of community-based facilities left a sample size of 12,332 inmates housed in 242 facilities. Following this, 292 cases were deleted due to missing data on the measures selected to be modeled in the analyses for this study. This left a final sample size of 12,040 inmates housed in 242 state-operated, secure confinement facilities. After the deletion of missing data, descriptive statistics were compared between the samples with and without missing data. Analyses revealed no significant differences in the demographic characteristics of inmates between the two samples. We concluded that the deletion of missing data did not affect the means or distributions of the measures to be used in this study. Finally, a sampling weight was provided in the data based on the inverse of each participant's odds of selection; these weights were normalized based on the new sample size and applied to all analyses reported in this study.

Measures

All measures used in the study are listed in Table 6.1, along with their descriptive statistics. The outcomes for this study include the prevalence and incidence of various forms of inmate misconduct. The prevalence of misconduct measures, which are dichotomous, indicate whether or not inmates ever reported being written up or found guilty for a violation of institutional rules. The incidence of misconduct measures are counted outcomes indicating the number of times offenders reported being written up or found guilty for violating institutional rules. Steiner and Wooldredge (2013) uncovered that analyzing different conceptual categories of misconduct is important, as they reveal different findings in regards to the important predictors. In addition, in this study, we are interested in whether religiosity has different effects on different forms of misconduct, with special focus on the relationship between religiosity and violence in prison. Our misconduct measures, then, are categorized into assaults, physical assaults, drug/alcohol, and all other forms of misconduct.

The distinction between the assault and physical assault measures of misconduct pertains to the inclusion of verbal assaults. The assault measures include inmates' responses to questions regarding being written up or found guilty of a physical or verbal assault against a staff member or another inmate.

Table 6.1   Description of Measures

Variable	Mean	SD
Prevalence of assault	.20	.40
Prevalence of physical assault	.15	.36
Prevalence of drug/alcohol violation	.07	.26
Prevalence of other misconduct	.48	.50
Incidence of assault	.68	2.20
Incidence of physical assault	.39	1.68
Incidence of drug/alcohol violation	.15	.75
Incidence of other misconduct	2.29	5.96
Religiosity	.57	.50
Age	35.60	10.44
Female	.20	.40
African American	.39	.49
Hispanic	.17	.38
Other race/ethnicity	.06	.24
Child(ren)	.69	.46
Conventional behaviors	1.13	.80
Incarcerated for violent offense	.51	.50
Used drugs in month before arrest	.56	.50
Antisocial peers growing up	.56	.50
Mental health diagnosis	.29	.46
Prior incarceration	.56	.50
LN time served	3.20	1.45
LN hours worked in past week	1.82	1.59
N=12,040		

The physical assault measures include only responses regarding a physical assault on a staff member or another inmate. The drug/alcohol misconduct measures include inmates' responses to questions regarding use or possession of drugs or alcohol while incarcerated. The measure of other misconduct includes any other questions about inmates' rule violations, including, for example, possessing contraband, stealing from another inmate, being out of place, or failing to follow directions of staff. It is important to note that the misconduct outcomes are technically self-reports of official detection, thus making the measures susceptible to the limitations of both self-report and official data. Self-reported data is limited because of the potential for poor recall and the possible hesitancy of subjects to admit deviant acts. Official measures of misconduct have been criticized for underestimating the prevalence/incidence of misconduct due to officer discretion and inability to detect all instances of misconduct (Steiner & Wooldredge 2014). A number of studies have compared official and self-reported misconduct and found them to be generally valid and reliable (Hewitt, Poole, & Regoli 1984; Van Voorhis 1994). More recently, Steiner and Wooldredge (2013) compared the effects of a number of covariates of both official and self-reported misconduct and found much more consistency than difference between the two approaches to measurement.

Religiosity was measured based on inmates' response to the item in the survey "in the past week, have you engaged in any religious activities, such as religious services, private prayer or meditation, or Bible reading or study?" This measure captures several different dimensions of religiosity that researchers have used in previous studies. The measure includes attendance at religious services and individual, private activities such as prayer, meditation, and scripture reading/study (Evans et al. 1995; Johnson et al. 2000; Kerley et al. 2011; Stark 1996). Although the item contains these important dimensions, it is impossible to decompose these individual aspects of religiosity because of the wording of the question.

Additional controls were selected based on their theoretical relevance to misconduct, as well as importance in past studies of inmate misconduct. *Age* represents the age in years of participants at the time of the survey. Sex was measured through a dichotomous indicator of whether the inmate was *female*. Race/ethnicity was measured through a series of dichotomous variables indicating whether the inmate was *African American, Hispanic,* or of *other race/ethnicity.* White inmates were used as the reference category. We also controlled for whether the inmate had a child or *child(ren)* or was involved in *conventional behaviors.* The measure of conventional behaviors is a three-item additive scale comprised of inmates' responses to questions about whether they were currently married, had a high school diploma, or had a job or business in the month before their arrest (see Wooldredge, Griffin, & Pratt 2001).

We also controlled for whether the inmate was *incarcerated for a violent offense* or had *used drugs in the month before arrest.* The measure of *antisocial peers growing up* was a dichotomous question that asked inmates if they participated in illegal activities with friends while growing up. *Mental health diagnosis* is a dichotomous measure of whether inmates reported *ever* being diagnosed with any of the following mental health disorders: depressive disorder, manic-depressive or bipolar disorder, schizophrenia or another psychotic disorder, posttraumatic stress disorder (PTSD), an anxiety disorder, a personality disorder, or any other mental or emotional condition. *Prior incarceration* is a dichotomous indicator of whether inmates reported being previously incarcerated. The variables *time served* in months and *hours worked in past week* were both skewed, so we modeled the natural log of each measure.

Analytical Plan

Given that the data involved a hierarchal structure (inmates nested within prisons), multilevel modeling was used to adjust for potential problems created by hierarchical data. The software HLM 7 was used to adjust for problems of correlated error among inmates housed in the same facility and allowed us to control for unmeasured differences across facilities that might impact the prevalence and incidence of misconduct. It is important to note that although multilevel modeling was used to address issues of correlated error and other problems of nested data, our models are technically single-level models since we do not examine any facility-level predictors.

The first step in the analyses was to estimate unconditional models for each outcome. These models determine whether there is significant variation in the outcome across facilities. Next, Bernoulli models were used to estimate the effect of the predictor variables on the dichotomous misconduct outcomes, and Poisson regression with correction for overdispersion was used for the incidence of misconduct measures (see Table 6.1 for descriptive statistics of the count outcomes). Fixed effects models were estimated for all outcomes. All predictors, with the exception of sex, were group-mean centered, which adjusts for unmeasured facility-level effects that may influence variation on the outcomes included in the analyses. Finally, prior to estimating the final models, we examined the predictors for multicollinearity and determined that it was not present among our selected covariates.

Results

Before discussing the results of the models estimating the effect of religiosity on inmate misconduct, it is important to underscore the distribution of the covariates of religiosity and misconduct. Fifty-seven percent of inmates in the sample reported engaging in religious activities in the week prior to the administration of the survey. In terms of violence, 20 percent of respondents reported being written up or found guilty of a verbal or physical assault on a staff member or an inmate, while 15 percent reported committing only a physical assault. The average number of assaults inmates reported committing was .68, while physical assaults reported averaged .39.

Table 6.2 presents the results of the multivariate, multilevel models of the association between religiosity and the prevalence of misconduct. Among the four outcomes, religiosity was only significantly associated with lower odds of physical assaults. According to the odds ratio, religiosity was associated with a .13 decrease in the odds of committing a physical assault. In other words, inmates who did not report engaging in religious activities had almost 15 percent higher odds of reporting a physical assault on a staff member or another inmate. Religiosity was not significantly related to the odds of assaults, drug/alcohol violations, or other forms of misconduct.

Turning to the effects of the covariates, age was inversely associated with the odds of all forms of misconduct. Younger inmates were more likely to report engaging in misconduct of all types. Being female was associated with lower odds of assaults, physical assaults, and drug/alcohol misconduct, but sex was not associated with the odds of other forms of misconduct. African American inmates were more likely to report being written up for assaults, but there were no significant racial/ethnic differences in the odds of any other type of prison rule violation.

Inmates with children, those who were married, those who were educated, and those who were employed prior to coming to prison had lower odds of most forms of misconduct. Those incarcerated for a violent offense were more likely to report engaging in assaults, physical assaults, and drug/alcohol misconducts, but not other forms of misconduct. Inmates who used drugs in the month before arrest, inmates who had antisocial peers, inmates who had been in prison before, and inmates who had ever been diagnosed with a mental health disorder had higher odds of nearly all types of misconduct than those who did not use drugs, did not have antisocial peers, had never been to prison before, and had not been diagnosed with a mental health disorder. Longer time served in prison was associated with higher odds of all forms of misconduct, while working more hours in prison was associated with lower odds of all forms of misconduct.

Table 6.3 depicts the models of the association between religiosity and the incidence of misconduct. Once again, religiosity was not a significant predictor of nonviolent forms of misconduct. There was no statistically significant difference between religious and nonreligious inmates in the number of drug/alcohol violations or other forms of nonviolent misconduct. On the other hand, and in contrast to the models regarding the prevalence of misconduct, religiosity was associated with lower incidence of assaults, but not with lower incidence of physical assaults. Nonreligious inmates were more likely to report committing a greater number of physical and verbal assaults on staff members or other inmates; however, there was no statistically significant difference between religious and nonreligious inmates in the number of strictly physical assaults on staff members or other inmates. Based on the event rate ratio, religiosity was associated with a 15 percent reduction in the incidence of assaults.

The effects of the covariates on the incidence of misconduct are similar to the results from the models on the prevalence of misconduct, with a few differences. Again, age was related to lower incidence of misconduct, with

Table 6.2 Religiosity and the Prevalence of Misconduct

	Assaults		Physical assaults		Drug/alcohol violation		Other misconduct	
	b Exp(b)	(se)	b Exp(b)	se	b Exp(b)	se	b Exp(b)	se
Intercept	-1.63** .20	(.05)	-2.07** .13	(.06)	-3.18** .04	(.08)	-.09** .91	(.05)
Religiosity	-.09 .91	(.05)	-.14* .87	(.06)	-.02 .98	(.08)	.02 1.02	(.05)
Age	-.05** .95	(.01)	-.05** .95	(.01)	-.03** .97	(.01)	-.03** .97	(.01)
Female	-.45** .64	(.11)	-.55** .58	(.12)	-1.11** .33	(.21)	.07 1.07	(.15)
African American	.24** 1.27	(.06)	.17 1.19	(.07)	-.20 .82	(.09)	.05 1.05	(.05)
Hispanic	.07 1.07	(.08)	.11 1.12	(.09)	-.16 .85	(.11)	-.12 .89	(.06)
Other race/ethnicity	-.01 .99	(.11)	.06 .94	(.10)	-.02 .98	(.13)	.13 1.14	(.09)
Child(ren)	-.17* .85	(.05)	-.15* .86	(.06)	.12 1.12	(.08)	-.15** .86	(.04)
Conventional behaviors	-.09* .92	(.03)	-.09* .92	(.04)	-.05 .95	(.05)	-.08* .92	(.03)

	Model 1		Model 2		Model 3		Model 4	
Incarcerated for violent offense	.21**	(.06)	.28**	(.07)	.24*	(.08)	.12	(.05)
	1.24		1.33		1.27		1.13	
Used drugs in month before arrest	.17**	(.06)	.12	(.06)	.84**	(.09)	.16**	(.05)
	1.19		1.13		2.33		1.17	
Antisocial peers growing up	.34**	(.06)	.34**	(.07)	.38**	(.08)	.39**	(.05)
	1.40		1.40		1.46		1.48	
Prior incarceration	.26**	(.06)	.25**	(.06)	.37**	(.07)	.21**	(.04)
	1.29		1.28		1.45		1.23	
Mental health diagnosis	.42**	(.06)	.36**	(.06)	.14	(.08)	.31**	(.05)
	1.52		1.43		1.15		1.36	
LN time served	.68**	(.03)	.72**	(.04)	1.02**	(.05)	.61**	(.03)
	1.97		2.06		2.78		1.83	
LN hours worked in past week	-.12**	(.02)	-.11**	(.02)	-.07*	(.02)	-.05**	(.01)
	.89		.89		.93		.95	
N = 12,040								
χ^2	1,264.85		1,283.43		1,110.57		1,686.53	

Note: Maximum likelihood coefficients reported with robust standard errors in parentheses.

* $p \leq .01$; ** $p \leq .001$

Table 6.3 Religiosity and the Incidence of Misconduct

	Assaults		Physical assaults		Drug/alcohol violation		Other misconduct	
	b Exp(b)	(se)	b Exp(b)	se	b Exp(b)	se	b Exp(b)	se
Intercept	−.94** .39	(.06)	−1.59** .20	(.07)	−2.87** .06	(.09)	.38** 1.46	(.05)
Religiosity	−.16* .85	(.06)	−.17 .84	(.08)	−.10 .90	(.06)	.05 .95	(.04)
Age	−.05** .95	(.01)	−.06** .94	(.01)	−.03** .97	(.01)	−.05** .95	(.01)
Female	−.50** .60	(.09)	−.84** .43	(.12)	−1.29** .28	(.21)	−.10 .91	(.08)
African American	.25** 1.28	(.05)	.20* 1.22	(.08)	−.30** .74	(.08)	.02 1.02	(.04)
Hispanic	−.06 .95	(.08)	−.01 .99	(.12)	−.04 .96	(.10)	−.21** .81	(.06)
Other race/ethnicity	.13 1.14	(.10)	.20 1.22	(.13)	.05 1.05	(.14)	−.03 .97	(.08)
Child(ren)	−.22** .80	(.05)	−.25** .78	(.07)	.07 1.07	(.07)	−.17** .84	(.04)

	Model 1		Model 2		Model 3		Model 4	
Conventional behaviors	−.04	(.03)	−.02	(.05)	−.10	(.04)	−.05	(.03)
	.96		.98		.91		.95	
Incarcerated for violent offense	.09	(.06)	.12	(.09)	.17	(.07)	.09	(.04)
	1.10		1.13		1.18		1.09	
Used drugs in month before arrest	.08	(.06)	.01	(.08)	.81**	(.08)	.14*	(.05)
	1.09		1.01		2.25		1.15	
Antisocial peers growing up	.37**	(.06)	.40**	(.08)	.58**	(.08)	.34**	(.04)
	1.45		1.50		1.79		1.40	
Prior incarceration	.21**	(.05)	.17	(.08)	.33**	(.07)	.18**	(.04)
	1.23		1.19		1.39		1.20	
Mental health diagnosis	.54**	(.06)	.40**	(.07)	.17	(.08)	.39**	(.04)
	1.72		1.50		1.19		1.48	
LN time served	.89**	(.02)	.95**	(.03)	1.21**	(.04)	.81**	(.02)
	2.43		2.60		3.34		2.26	
LN hours worked in past week	−.12**	(.02)	−.14**	(.02)	−.06*	(.02)	−.09**	(.02)
	.88		.87		.94		.92	
N = 12,040								
χ^2	2,349.49		2,248.66		1,873.42		4,110.42	

Note: Maximum likelihood coefficients reported with robust standard errors in parentheses.

*$p \le .01$; ** $p \le .001$

109

younger inmates more likely to have higher rates of all forms of misconduct. Females had lower rates of assaults, physical assaults, and drug/alcohol violations, but sex was not associated with the incidence of other misconduct. African Americans were more likely to have higher rates of violent misconduct compared to other races/ethnicities, but significantly lower rates of drug or alcohol violations. Hispanic inmates had significantly lower rates of other nonviolent misconduct, but there were no other statistically significant racial or ethnic differences in the incidence of misconduct.

Having children was associated with lower rates of violent and other nonviolent misconduct, but there were no statistically significant differences in the incidence of drug/alcohol violations between offenders with children and without children. Conventional behaviors were not significantly associated with the incidence of any form of misconduct. Being incarcerated for a violent offense also was not significantly related to the incidence of any type of misconduct. Using drugs in the month before arrest was related to higher rates of nonviolent misconduct, particularly drug/alcohol violations, but was not associated with violent forms of misconduct. Having antisocial peers, a prior incarceration, or a mental health diagnosis was associated with higher rates of most forms of misconduct, with a few exceptions. Finally, inmates who had served more time and inmates who worked fewer hours were significantly more likely to report committing a greater number of all types of misconduct.

Discussion and Conclusion

The results of this study contribute additional confirmation to the body of research findings revealing that religiosity, particularly in the prison context, has a more significant, stronger effect on serious forms of misconduct, especially violence. We used a national data set of prisoners housed in state secure confinement facilities, and discovered that inmates who reported involvement in religious activities were less likely to be written up or found guilty of a verbal or physical assault on a staff member or a fellow inmate. The findings regarding the control variables in our models are largely consistent with prior research on inmate misconduct (see Steiner et al. 2014).

Across our models, specifically, we found that religiosity was significantly associated with a reduction in the odds of physical assaults, as well as being associated with a lower incidence of all assaults (including physical and verbal). It seems that religious inmates in general are less likely to commit a physical assault overall, and that religious inmates are likely to commit fewer verbal/physical assaults than nonreligious inmates. To further explain, religiosity is significantly related to lower odds (i.e., prevalence) of physical assaults, but not lower odds of all assaults (verbal and physical). Conversely, in the incidence models of misconduct, religiosity is related to a greater likelihood to commit fewer assaults (verbal and physical), but religiosity is nonsignificant in terms of only physical assaults. It could be that religious inmates are less likely overall to commit physical violence, but religiosity may not have as much of a deterrent effect on verbal altercations. For example, in a tense, crowded environment, such as prison, it is easy to imagine the potential for verbal arguments with either staff members or fellow inmates, regardless of whether one is religious or not. The salient effect of religiosity, then, may be the power to prevent verbal altercations from becoming physical. This is seemingly consistent with the findings from Kerley et al. (2005). If this is the case, and religiosity is efficacious for keeping inmate disagreements from becoming physically violent, then it would stand to reason that religiosity would not be strongly related to the incidence of physical violence. Even though religiosity may not totally prevent inmates from becoming involved in verbal assaults, it appears, from our results in Table 6.3, that it does result in fewer verbal assaults than nonreligiosity.

It is important to make readers aware at this point that because of the nature of the analyses and limitations of the data and measures (which will be discussed in more detail below), our models are not causal, and findings should be interpreted with caution. However, given the results of this study, and in light of the fact that researchers have yet to explore reasons why religiosity appears to have stronger effects on serious forms of deviance in prison, it is important to speculate as to why this might be the case. Again, our data, for a number of reasons, do not allow us to test the following suppositions; that is a task that future researchers will want to undertake.

As noted on multiple occasions in this chapter, and confirmed in the findings of this study, religiosity seems to be particularly salient at reducing inmate involvement in serious and violent behavior while incarcerated. Religiosity, then, may be a way for inmates to reject the violence in their past histories, as well as the violence associated with prison culture. Research has long documented that a culture of violence exists in prison (Johnson 2002; Sykes 1958). Violence is used by inmates to establish social status and standing, and force and violence are the subtext of interactions among staff and inmates. Many religions endorse nonviolence and encourage love and kindness, and Christianity, in particular, exhorts adherents to obey civil authorities, even in the face of adversity. Religious teaching and practice could encourage inmates to find alternatives to violence as a means to settle disputes and disagreements, and, more broadly, provide a framework for prison life and interactions that is not based on violence or the threat of violence.

Several qualitative studies have uncovered themes in offenders' narratives regarding the potential for religiosity to provide a "road map" for a new or different way of life (Clear et al. 2000; Dammer 2002). Religion provides a set of rules and guidelines, and essentially establishes a total, systematic worldview for adherents. Prisoners have noted that religion provides direction and gives them a separate set of norms to abide by in contrast to the prison code

(Johnson & Larson 2003). Religion also helps offenders deal with guilt stemming from their past offenses. The criminal justice process is a direct condemnation of offenders and their behavior, and incarceration may be seen as a form of symbolic banishment (Clear at al. 2000). As a result of this process and the stigma associated with it, many offenders certainly feel a great deal of guilt (Dammer 2002). Religion provides forgiveness for offenders. It also helps offenders to explain their past criminality, and a spiritual or religious conversion allows them to replace the old deviant identity with a new, meaningful, and conforming self. In other words, religion may allow offenders to reject and condemn their criminal behaviors while maintaining self-worth, while, at the same time, providing a framework for how to move forward and live life as a different, law-abiding individual (Clear at al. 2000; Dammer 2002; Johnson & Larson 2003). This narrative of guilt, redemption, and living a new life may be most salient for individuals with a violent past. Violent offenses are legally and morally considered the most serious, and offenders with violent histories may have more guilt to deal with. For example, using the same data, Meade (2015) examined factors that were associated with religiosity. He discovered that being incarcerated for a violent offense was significantly associated with religiosity. In light of the results of this study, this seems to indicate a general pattern that inmates with a violent history who engage in religious activity in prison then go on to have significantly reduced odds of involvement in violent behavior. This may provide support for the preceding explanation that religiosity is a way for inmates to reject their violent pasts, and religion provides a means of moving forward in a nonviolent lifestyle amid a violent culture.

Given the discussion regarding religion and religiosity as a means for offenders to live a life of conformity, it is interesting to note that religiosity seems to have little effect and no significance across studies for less serious forms of rule infractions. One potential explanation for this pattern is that many forms of nonserious misconduct have little, if any, moral implications. For example, many of the items comprising the *other misconduct* category would not be criminal violations in general society. Being out of place, failing to follow the directions of staff, etc. may be violations that could even occur by accident. It is entirely plausible that inmates could be written up for failing to make their beds or not keeping their cells tidy. Religion would provide little restraint in terms of these types of violations.

On the other hand, the antiascetic hypothesis argues that religiosity will have a stronger effect on minor forms of deviance, and findings from the religiosity and crime literature seem to support this conclusion (see Baier & Wright 2001). The theoretical argument underlying the antiascetic hypothesis argues that religion will have the most effect on deviant outcomes when religious norms and controls are unique in contrast to secular controls. Religious ascetic norms emphasize self-control over "worldly" desires, such as sexual activity, alcohol and drug use, and gambling (Middleton & Putney 1962). There is a great deal of moral ambiguity in society regarding these behaviors; however, most religions take a firm stance regarding their immorality. The antiascetic hypothesis argues, then, that since the church opposes these behaviors while many in society do not, religiosity will prevent adherents from being involved in antiascetic behaviors (Middleton & Putney 1962). On the other hand, since both the church and society condemn violence and theft, religion will have little effect on these deviant behaviors because the efforts of the church to control these behaviors are "duplicated by a great many secular influences" (Burkett & White 1974, 461).

On their face, it may seem as if the findings regarding religiosity and violence in prison contradict the pattern prescribed by the antiascetic hypothesis. It is possible, however, that the inverse relationship between religiosity and prison violence is consistent with the theoretical assumptions underlying the antiascetic hypothesis. In the prison culture of violence, religion may provide *unique* norms/controls over violent behavior. In society, both religious and secular norms condemn violence; however, in prison, violence is explicitly and/or tacitly endorsed by the predominant cultural and structural values (Johnson 2002; Sykes 1958). Thus, religious inmates are faced with a conflict between the norms of the prison culture and religious norms that condemn violence. Given the violent context of prisons, religious staff and volunteers may deliver messages and sermons condemning violence, and substance use may not be seen as a priority for religious instruction in prison. For example, only 7 percent of inmates in the sample reported being written up for a drug or alcohol violation, compared to 20 percent for assaults. It is also more difficult to get access to drugs and alcohol in prison; thus, chaplains and volunteers may concentrate their teachings on problems they perceive to be more directly related to the challenges and temptations inmates face in prison. Given the theoretical assumptions of the antiascetic hypothesis, religion in the prison context, then, may have stronger effects on violent behavior, as the religious norms regarding violent behavior, rather than antiascetic behavior, are unique, although the same underlying process may be at work.

Although the above discussion attempts to make sense of the findings regarding religiosity and serious inmate deviance, the results of our study may be largely influenced by the limitations of the measurement of religiosity provided in the inmate data used. In our study, religiosity is measured with a single-item question. Research has uncovered, however, that religiosity is a multidimensional concept. For example, religiosity includes attendance at services, frequency of private expressions of religiosity such as prayer and study of religious texts, religious/denominational affiliation, and the self-reported importance of religion in the daily lives and decision making of adherents (Larson & Johnson 1998). Although our measure captures some of these dimensions, it does not include, for example, affiliation or religious salience (importance of religion in daily life/decisions). Also, our measure is a dichotomous composite of several dimensions of religiosity, which limits the variation among those reporting involvement in religious activities. Larson and Johnson (1998) suggest the best measures of religiosity would involve multiple items that tap most of the dimensions of religiosity mentioned above, and their systematic review found that studies using items measuring a greater number of dimensions of religiosity were much more likely to find that religiosity was inversely associated with deviant outcomes. Thus, much of the null findings in our models could be a result of the measurement of religiosity.

There is also a temporal ordering concern in our measures. The misconduct outcomes are derived from questions asking about infractions since admission to prison, while the religiosity measure only asks about religious activities in the past week. Many inmates may have committed misconduct prior to becoming involved in religious activities or experiencing a conversion, but there is no way, given the limitations of the data, to detect whether inmates may have committed misconduct either before or after they became involved in religion. These issues may have confounded the results regarding the relationship between religiosity and misconduct, and the temporal-ordering limitation may explain why religiosity was largely unrelated to some types of misconduct.

After careful considerations of the limitations of the study, our results seem to contribute to the trend in research findings that religiosity is more consistently and strongly associated with serious and violent forms of misconduct. We have attempted to provide some potential insight into the explanations for this trend, which seems to be somewhat inconsistent with the body of literature regarding religiosity and deviance among the general population. Future research should continue to study this question using better data sources and measures of religiosity to examine the potential causal links between religiosity and prison violence and misconduct more broadly. Religion is an integral social and, certainly, spiritual phenomenon in American prisons and the lives of many incarcerated therein. Continued study of this relationship will provide a better understanding of the role of religion in prisons and prisoners' lives.

Bibliography

Baier, Colin J., & Bradley R. E. Wright. "'If You Love Me, Keep My Commandments': A Meta-Analysis of the Effect of Religion on Crime." *Journal of Research in Crime and Delinquency* 38, no. 1 (2001): 3–21.

Bottoms, Anthony E. "Interpersonal Violence and Social Order in Prisons." *Crime and Justice* 26 (1999): 205–281.

Burkett, Steven R., & Mervin White. "Hellfire and Delinquency: Another Look." *Journal for the Scientific Study of Religion* 13, no. 4 (1974): 455–462.

Camp, Scott D., Dawn M. Dagget, Okyun Kwon, & Jody Klein-Saffran. "The Effect of Faith Program Participation on Prison Misconduct: The Life Connections Program." *Journal of Criminal Justice* 36 (2008): 389–395.

Camp, Scott D., Gerald G. Gaes, Neal P. Langan, & William G. Saylor. "The Influence of Prisons on Inmate Misconduct: A Multilevel Investigation." *Justice Quarterly* 20, no. 3 (2003): 501–533.

Clear, Todd R., George F. Cole, & Michael Reisig. *American Corrections* (7th ed.). Belmont, CA: Thomson-Wadsworth, 2006.

Clear, Todd R., Patricia L. Hardyman, Bruce Stout, Karol Lucken, & Harry R. Dammer. "The Value of Religion in Prison." *Journal of Contemporary Criminal Justice* 16, no. 1 (2000): 53–74.

Clear, Todd R., & Marina Myhre. "A Study of Religion in Prison." *IARCA Journal on Community Corrections* 6 (1995): 20–25.

Clear, Todd R., Bruce D. Stout, Harry R. Dammer, Linda Kelly, Patricia L. Hardyman, & Carol Shapiro. "Does Involvement in Religion Help Prisoners to Adjust to Prison?" *National Council on Crime and Delinquency Focus* 11 (1992): 1–7.

Clear, Todd R., & Melvina T. Sumter. "Prisoners, Prison, and Religion: Religion and Adjustment to Prison." *Journal of Offender Rehabilitation* 35, no. 3–4 (2002): 125–156.

Cochran, John K., & Ronald L. Akers. "Beyond Hellfire: An Exploration of the Variable Effects of Religiosity on Adolescent Marijuana and Alcohol Use." *Journal of Research in Crime and Delinquency* 26, no. 3 (1989): 198–225.

Cunningham, Mark D., & Jon R. Sorensen. "Predictive Factors for Violent Misconduct in Close Custody." *The Prison Journal* 87, no. 2 (2007): 241–253.

Dammer, Harry R. *Religion in Corrections.* Lanham, MD: American Correctional Association, 2000.

Dammer, Harry R. "The Reasons for Religious Involvement in the Correctional Environment." *Journal of Offender Rehabilitation* 35, no. 3–4 (2002): 35–58.

Dilulio, John. *Governing Prisons: A Comparative Study of Correctional Management.* New York: Free Press, 1987.

Dilulio, John. *Godly Republic: A Centrist's Blueprint for America's Faith-Based Future.* Berkeley, CA: University of California Press, 2009.

Dodson, Kimberly D., Leann N. Cabage, & Paul M. Klenowski. "An Evidence-Based Assessment of Faith-Based Programs: Do Faith-Based Programs "Work" to Reduce Recidivism?" *Journal of Offender Rehabilitation* 50, no. 6 (2011): 367–383.

Evans, T. David, Francis T. Cullen, R. Gregory Dunaway, & Velmer S. Burton, Jr. "Religion and Crime Reexamined: The Impact of Religion, Secular Controls, and Social Ecology on Adult Criminality." *Criminology* 33, no. 2 (1995): 195–224.

Flanagan, Timothy J. "Correlates of Institutional Misconduct among State Prisoners." *Criminology* 21, no.1 (1983): 29–40.

Gendreau, Paul, Claire E. Goggin, & Moira A. Law. "Predicting Prison Misconducts." *Criminal Justice and Behavior* 24, no. 4 (1997): 414–431.

Giordano, Peggy C., Stephen A. Cernkovich, & Jennifer L. Rudolph. "Gender, Crime, and Desistance: Toward a Theory of Cognitive Transformation." *American Journal of Sociology* 107, no. 4 (2002): 990–1064.

Goetting, Ann, & Roy Michael Howsen. "Correlates of Prisoner Misconduct." *Journal of Quantitative Criminology* 2, no. 1 (1986): 49–67.

Gover, Angela R., Deanna M. Perez, & Wesley Jennings. "Gender Differences in Factors Contributing to Institutional Misconduct." *The Prison Journal* 88, no. 3 (2008): 378–403.

Griffin, Marie L., & John R. Hepburn. "The Effect of Gang Affiliation on Violent Misconduct among Inmates during the Early Years of Confinement." *Criminal Justice and Behavior* 33, no. 4 (2006): 419–448.

Hadaway, C. Kirk, Kirk W. Elifson, & David M. Peterson. "Religious Involvement and Drug Use among Urban Adolescents." *Journal for the Scientific Study of Religion* 23, no. 2 (1984): 109–128.

Hewitt, John D., Eric D. Poole, & Robert M. Regoli. "Self-Reported and Observed Rule-Breaking in Prison: A Look at Disciplinary Response." *Justice Quarterly* 1 (1984): 437–447.

Hirschi, Travis. *Causes of Delinquency.* Berkeley: University of California Press, 1969.

Hoffman, John P., & Stephen J. Bahr. "Crime/Deviance." In Helen R. Ebaugh (Ed.), *Handbook of Religion and Social Institutions* (pp. 241–263). New York: Springer, 2005.

Huebner, Beth. M. "Administrative Determinants of Inmate Violence: A Multilevel Analysis." *Journal of Criminal Justice* 31 (2003): 107–117.

Johnson, Byron. R. "Religiosity and Institutional Deviance." *Criminal Justice Review* 12 (1987): 21–30.

Johnson, Byron R., Spencer De Li, David B. Larson, & Michael McCullough. "A Systematic Review of the Religiosity and Delinquency Literature." *Journal of Contemporary Criminal Justice* 16, no. 1 (2000): 32–52.

Johnson, Byron R., & David Larson. "Linking Religion to the Mental and Physical Health of Inmates: A Literature Review and Research Note." *American Jails* 11, no. 4 (1997): 28–36.

Johnson, Byron R., & David Larson. *The InnerChange Freedom Initiative: A Preliminary Evaluation of a Faith-Based Prison Program.* Philadelphia, PA: Center for Research on Religion and Urban Civil Society, 2003.

Johnson, Byron R., David B. Larson, & Timothy C. Pitts. "Religious Programs, Institutional Adjustment, and Recidivism among Former Inmates in Prison Fellowship Programs." *Justice Quarterly* 14, no. 1 (1997): 377–391.

Johnson, Robert. *Hard Time: Understanding and Reforming the Prison.* Belmont, CA: Wadsworth, 2002.

Johnston, Norman. "Evolving Function: Early Use of Imprisonment as Punishment." *The Prison Journal* 89, no. 1 (2009): 10–34.

Kerley, Kent R., Marisa C. Allison, & Rachelle D. Graham. "Investigating the Impact of Religiosity on Emotional and Behavioral Coping in Prison." *Journal of Criminal Justice* 29, no. 2 (2006): 69–93.

Kerley, Kent R., Heith Copes, Richard Tewksbury, & Dean A. Dabney. "Examining the Relationship between Religiosity and Self-Control as Predictors of Prison Deviance." *International Journal of Offender Therapy and Comparative Criminology* 55, no. 8 (2011): 1251–1271.

Kerley, Kent R., Todd L. Matthews, & Troy C. Blanchard. "Religiosity, Religious Participation, and Negative Prison Behaviors." *Journal for the Scientific Study of Religion* 44, no.4 (2005): 443–457.

Koenig, Harold G. "Religion and Older Men in Prison." *International Journal of Geriatric Psychiatry* 10 (1995): 219–230.

Kornhauser, Ruth R. *Social Sources of Delinquency: An Appraisal of Analytic Models.* Chicago: University of Chicago Press, 1978.

Larson, David B., & Byron R. Johnson. *Religion: The Forgotten Factor in Cutting Youth Crime and Saving At-Risk Urban Youth.* New York: Manhattan Institute, 1998.

LaVigne, Nancy G., Diana Brazzell, & Kevonne Small. *Evaluation of Florida's Faith-and Character-Based Institutions.* Washington, DC: Urban Institute Justice Policy Center, 2007.

MacKenzie, Doris Layton, Lynnie I. Goodstein, & David C. Blouin. "Personal Control and Prisoner Adjustment: An Empirical Test of a Proposed Model." *Journal of Research in Crime and Delinquency* 24 (1987): 49–68.

Maruna, Shadd, Louise Wilson, & Kathryn Curran. 2006. "Why God Is Often Found behind Bars: Prison Conversions and the Crisis of Self-Narrative." *Research in Human Development* 3, no. 2–3 (2006): 161–184.

Meade, Benjamin. *Moral Communities and Jailhouse Religion: Religiosity and Prison Misconduct.* El Paso, TX: LFB Scholarly, 2014.

Meade, Benjamin. "Examining the Factors That Predict Religiosity among Prison Inmates." Paper presented at the annual meeting of the American Society of Criminology, Washington, DC, November 2015.

Meade, Benjamin, & Benjamin Steiner. "The Effects of Exposure to Violence on Inmate Maladjustment." *Criminal Justice and Behavior* 40, no. 11 (2013): 1228–1249.

Middleton, Russell, & Snell Putney. "Religion, Normative Standards, and Behavior." *Sociometry* 25, no. 2 (1962): 141–152.

O'Connor, Thomas P. "Introduction: Religion-Offenders-Rehabilitation: Questioning the Relationship." *Journal of Offender Rehabilitation* 35, no. 3–4 (2002): 1–9.

O'Connor, Thomas P., & Michael Perreyclear. "Prison Religion in Action and Its Influence on Offender Rehabilitation." *Journal of Offender Rehabilitation* 35, no. 3–4 (2002): 11–33.

Pass, Michael G. "Religious Orientation and Self-Reported Rule Violations in a Maximum Security Prison." *Journal of Offender Rehabilitation* 28, no. 3–4 (1999): 119–134.

Pisciotta, Alexander W. *Benevolent Repression: Social Control and the American Reformatory-Prison Movement.* New York: New York University Press, 1994.

Reisig, Michael D., Scott E. Wolfe, & Travis C. Pratt. "Low Self-Control and the Religiosity-Crime Relationship." *Criminal Justice and Behavior* 39, no. 9 (2012): 1172–1191.

Rothman, David. *Conscience and Convenience: The Asylum and its Alternatives in Progressive America.* Boston: Little Brown, 1980.

Rothman, David J. "Perfecting the Prison: United States, 1789–1865." In Norval Morris & David J. Rothman (Eds.), *The Oxford History of the Prison: The Practice of Punishment in Western Society* (pp. 11–129). New York: Oxford University Press, 1995.

Sampson, Robert J., & John H. Laub. *Crime in the Making.* Cambridge, MA: Harvard University Press, 1993.

Schroeder, Ryan D., & John F. Frana. "Spirituality and Religion, Emotional Coping, and Criminal Desistance: A Qualitative Study of Men Undergoing Change." *Sociological Spectrum: Mid-South Sociological Association* 29, no. 6 (2009): 718–741.

Skotnicki, Andrew. *Religion and the Development of the American Penal System.* Lanham, MD: University Press of America, 2000.

Stark, Rodney. "Religion as Context: Hellfire and Delinquency One More Time." *Sociology of Religion* 57, no. 2 (1996): 163–173.

Steiner, Benjamin, H. Daniel Butler, & Jared M. Ellison. "Causes and Correlates of Prison Inmate Misconduct: A Systematic Review of the Evidence." *Journal of Criminal Justice* 42, no. 6 (2014): 462–470.

Steiner, Benjamin, & John Wooldredge. "Inmate versus Environmental Effects on Prison Rule Violation." *Criminal Justice and Behavior* 35, no. 4 (2008): 438–456.

Steiner, Benjamin, & John Wooldredge. "Implications of Different Outcome Measures for an Understanding of Inmate Misconduct." *Crime & Delinquency* 59, no. 8 (2013): 1234–1262.

Steiner, Benjamin, & John Wooldredge. "Comparing Self-Report to Official Measures of Inmate Misconduct." *Justice Quarterly* 31, no. 6 (2014): 1074–1101.

Sturgis, Paul W. "Faith behind Bars: An Explicit Test of the Moral Community Hypothesis in the Correctional Environment." *Journal of Offender Rehabilitation* 49, no. 5 (2010): 342–362.

Sundt, Jody L., & Francis T. Cullen. "The Role of the Contemporary Prison Chaplain." *The Prison Journal* 78, no. 3 (1998): 271–298.

Sundt, Jody L., Harry R. Dammer, & Francis T. Cullen. "The Role of the Prison Chaplain in Rehabilitation." *Journal of Offender Rehabilitation* 35, no. 3–4 (2002): 59–86.

Sykes, Gresham. *The Society of Captives.* Princeton, NJ: Princeton University Press, 1958.

Thomas, Jim, & Barbara H. Zaitzow. "Conning or Conversion? The Role of Religion in Prison Coping." *The Prison Journal* 86, no. 2 (2006): 242–259.

Ulmer, Jeffrey T., Scott A. Desmond, Sung Joon Jang, & Byron R. Johnson. "Religious Involvement and the Dynamics of Marijuana Use: Initiation, Persistence, and Desistence." *Deviant Behavior* 33 (2012): 448–468.

Van Voorhis, Patricia. "Measuring Prison Disciplinary Problems: A Multiple Indicators Approach to Understanding Prison Adjustment." *Justice Quarterly* 11, no. 4 (1994): 679–709.

Wooldredge, John, Timothy Griffin, & Travis Pratt. "Considering Hierarchical Models for Research on Inmate Behavior: Predicting Misconduct with Multilevel Data." *Justice Quarterly* 18, no. 1 (2001): 203–231.

Wright, Kevin N. "Developing the Prison Environment Inventory." *Journal of Research in Crime and Delinquency* 22, no. 3 (1985): 257–277.

Wright, Kevin N. "Prison Environment and Behavioral Outcomes." *Journal of Offender Rehabilitation* 20 (1993): 93–113.

Young, Mark C., John Gartner, Thomas O'Connor, David Larson, & Kevin Wright. "Long-Term Recidivism among Federal Inmates Trained as Volunteer Prison Ministers." *Journal of Offender Rehabilitation* 22, no. 1–2 (1995): 97–118.

CHAPTER SEVEN

The Effects of Religion on the Prisonization of Incarcerated Juveniles in Faith-Based Facilities

Lonn Lanza-Kaduce, Jodi Lane, and Kristen Benedini

Researchers have known for some time that religion (measured in various ways) bears a small but consistently negative relationship to delinquency and crime. For example, in 2001 Baier and Wright conducted a meta-analysis of 60 studies and reported an average effect size of r=−.12 (with a median of −.11). Given this common finding, religion is sometimes cited as being a "protective factor" that offsets the risks of developing antisocial attitudes and engaging in problem behaviors. Indeed, casting religion in this instrumental way is now common. A recent Google search (conducted January 28, 2016) of "religion as a protective factor" yielded pages of postings claiming that religion was protective, among other things, for mental health problems, drug use, suicide, early onset of alcohol and drug use, resilience, unhealthy behavior, delinquency and crime, and crime severity.

The consistency of the relationship between religion and delinquent or criminal behavior may be one of the reasons for the expansion of faith-based correctional programs, especially during the George W. Bush presidency. Those faith-based programs can be consistent with mainstream criminological theory. For example, Akers, Lane, and Lanza-Kaduce (2008) offer bonding, social learning, and restorative justice foundations for expecting faith-based programs to facilitate an inverse relationship. Religion should inhibit crime to the extent that religion (1) is a bond to conventional beliefs and behaviors, (2) offers conforming definitions and provides law-abiding associations with others who present positive models and reinforce conforming behaviors, and (3) endorses beliefs and interactions within communities that facilitate reintegrative shaming and that encourage transgressors to show remorse and others to forgive. These theoretical underpinnings show that religion can operate both by countering that which is antisocial and by fostering that which is prosocial. Note, however, that these theories raise the prospect that protective advantages may be due to processes like conventional bonds and associations rather than religion per se (see Duwe et al. 2015).

Despite the consistent relationship and the effort to put religion to good use in faith-based programming, much remains unknown about the nexus between religion, and both attitudes and behaviors. The purpose of this chapter is to explore one of the possible linkages using data from a faith-based program instituted in boys' and girls' juvenile residential correctional facilities in Florida. The instigation for digging deeper is twofold. First, the final report evaluating the Florida faith-based program (Lane, Lanza-Kaduce, Akers, & Cook 2009, 2010) contains a seeming disconnect: both religious attitudes and religious behaviors dramatically increased for the program participants during incarceration from that reported prior to commitment, but surprising numbers of those same youth reported isolation and alienation. Too many residents had adjusted poorly to their incarceration; they reported negative attitudes and feelings about it, some of which suggested prisonization, which is an antisocial reaction to incarceration. Those negative consequences harkened the words of John Stratton, an old professor of one of the authors, who insisted that rehabilitation or treatment gains cannot be realized until prisonization is overcome. His warning provided the second source of motivation for this investigation. Perhaps prisonization offsets the protective benefits of religion.

The research question for this chapter is quite simple: What is the relationship of religion to prisonization? If religion is indeed a protective factor against the antisocial that also promotes prosocial orientations, then more religion should inhibit prisonization. Religion has been measured in different ways (e.g., attitudes such as how important religion is or how religious someone is, affiliation with specific religious groups like Catholics or Buddhists, beliefs such as fundamentalism or atheism, and behavior such as participation in religious services or activities), and not all measures may relate to prosocial or antisocial orientations or behaviors in the same way. The research for this chapter will focus on both attitudinal and behavioral measurements of religion.

The chapter is organized into three sections. The first section is a literature review summarizing what is known about (1) prisonization and its relationship to norms and behaviors that are imported into incarceration and those used to adjust or adapt to confinement, and (2) the relationship of religion to prosocial and antisocial attitudes and behaviors relevant to corrections. The second section will describe the research methodology from the Florida evaluation that collected data measuring religion (both that imported into incarceration and that used during incarceration), prisonization, and various control variables (e.g., sex, race, age, prior record, fear of victimization outside before incarceration and inside during incarceration, and a sense of injustice about events leading up to residential placement). The final section will present the research results and a discussion of their implications.

Literature Review

Prisonization: Importation into and Adjustment to Incarceration

The dependent variable in this research problem is prisonization. The examination of prisonization is important for several reasons. First, research links prisonization to behavioral outcomes inside, which may also create issues for prison population management. Second, prisonization is an indicator of antisocial adjustment during incarceration, and other measures of poor adjustment are related to higher recidivism postrelease (e.g., see Hill 1985; Wolfgang 1960–1961). Third, prisonization may be an impediment to treatment in those facilities that do offer treatment.

Since the 1940s, scholars have recognized that correctional facilities constitute a unique setting with its own set of norms that influences those confined to it (Clemmer 1958; Garabedian 1963; Sykes 1958). Clemmer's (1977, 175–76) classic definition is a good starting point: "we may use the term *prisonization* to indicate the taking on in greater or lesser degree of the folkways, mores, customs, and general culture of the penitentiary." Even though he recognizes that the length of time one is incarcerated matters, he argues that "every man who enters the penitentiary undergoes prisonization to some extent," and he refers to a "swallowing-up process" at entry (1977, 176). Clemmer clearly anticipates, for example, that many inmates learn how to break rules (e.g., gambling) and to distrust and hate the prison staff (1977, 177). He goes on to list some "universal factors of prisonization" that include accepting an inferior role, developing new habits about eating, dressing, working, sleeping, and adopting new language (1977, 177). He also clearly asserts that the features of "prisonization which concern us most are the influences which breed or deepen criminality and anitsociality . . ." (1977, 177). In other words, from the time of its scholarly recognition, prisonization has been seen as a risk factor.

Historically, two theoretical accounts have been given for understanding the inmate social systems in correctional facilities (Leger & Stratton 1977). One focuses on the adaptation inmates have to make to the pains of imprisonment (for an early statement, see Sykes & Messinger 1960). Indeed, Clemmer's universal prisonization factors focus on those functional adaptations. The second, however, emphasizes the way in which the social system is affected by inputs from the outside, features that are imported into confinement. Clemmer was not unaware of that reality either. He discusses how criminals returning to the prison bring with them different lessons for taking on the social system of the prison (1977, 176). Thomas (1970) was one of the first scholars to note the compatibility of and utility of using both functional adaptation and importation explanations (see also Akers, Hayner, & Gruninger 1974). Both prison-specific influences and extra-prison influences have been found to have consequences in confinement (Gillespie 2002; Thomas 1977). Negative consequences of higher levels of prisonization are numerous and might include harmful behaviors such as self-mutilation, suicide, and resistance to facility rules (Gillespie 2002; Matthews 1999).

Although Clemmer (1977) discusses prisonization in the context of the long stays at a male penitentiary, the reaction to incarceration has been documented in other settings. Even in short-term jail admissions, the "swallowing-up process" requires some kind of adjustment. For present purposes, what is important is that the phenomena is found in both boys' and girls' juvenile facilities.

Two studies are illustrative. The first is Giallombardo's (1974) classic study of the *Social World of Imprisoned Girls* in which she recounts how adolescent girls adjust to confinement, including the way familial structures and kin ties are imported into the facility from the outside and adjusted inside to cope with the deprivations there. Giallombardo argues that this emphasis on family and kinship reflects the fact that, for girls, the most serious deprivations of incarceration are the separation from family and friends that accompanies their loss of freedom. Giallombardo also documents, much like Clemmer (1977) discusses, the ways in which the informal social system at the facility deals with a series of issues inside like protection, work, and food. To use Clemmer's words, there is clearly a "taking on in greater or lesser degree of the folkways, mores, customs, and general culture" of the correctional facility.

The second study is of boys in a facility outside of Chicago. Lanza-Kaduce and Radosevich (1987) examine the reactions of delinquents to their dealings with police, court processing, and incarceration and link them to substance use while incarcerated. The study borrows from Matza's (1964, 61) argument that "law contains the seeds of its own neutralization" to the extent that a subculture of youth withdraw legitimacy because the application of law contributes to a shared sense of injustice. According to Lanza-Kaduce and Radosevich (at 132) the features of that sense of injustice primarily address procedural justice shortcomings during police and court processing (i.e., "justice is seen as synonymous with fairness"). The study uses a sense of injustice scale derived from measures of Matza's features of fairness: cognizance, consistency, competence, commensurability, and comparison. That scale predicts self-reported substance use among the institutionalized males (both inside and while on weekend furloughs). Lanza-Kaduce and Radosevich also factor analyze 23 attitude items that had been used to measure prisonization and reactions to incarceration. They use oblique rotation because they expect dimensions of prisonization to be interrelated. Five factors emerged: isolation (e.g., be careful about who you're friendly with here), alienation (e.g., have no influence on how treated here), commitment (have more freedom than you think here), antiguard sentiments (e.g., guards push us around), and counselor sentiment (counselors do jobs well). The prisonization dimensions do discriminate substance use (across a range of substances) but not as well as the sense of injustice scale. They report isolation as the prisonization dimension that was most often related; a greater sense of isolation was associated with more use of marijuana, stimulants, and depressants.

The Role of Religion

Religion as generally protective against crime and delinquency. This chapter's research is premised on the assumption that religion contributes to prosocial orientations and behaviors and is protective against antisocial ones. Research has consistently indicated a small to moderate significant inverse relationship between religion and crime (Baier & Wright 2001; Johnson et al. 2000). A number of meta-analyses have confirmed that religiosity is linked to decreased offending behavior for both adolescents and adults. Using two measures of religious involvement (church attendance and perceived importance of religion to an individual in his or her life) and three outcome measures (alcohol use, illicit drug use, and nondrug delinquency) in a meta-analysis of 62 studies, Kelly and coauthors (2014) find religious involvement is inversely associated with problematic behavior in all six of the bivariate relationships examined. These effect sizes range from small (-0.16 for the importance of religion attitudinal measure/alcohol use relationship) to moderate (−0.22 for the church attendance/drug use relationship).

In a meta-analysis of 270 studies on the link between religiosity and delinquent/criminal behavior that used samples of both adolescents and adults, Johnson and Jang (2010) find that about 90 percent of the studies (244 of 270) report an inverse relationship between religiosity (measures of religiosity include religious attendance, study of scripture, religious commitment, religious belief, subjective religiosity or religious experience) and some kind of criminal behavior measure. Researchers find mixed results or no significant association in about 9 percent of the studies (24 of 270). The findings of these systemic reviews are consistent with others that have been completed on the protective effect of religion on criminal activity (Baier & Wright 2001; Johnson et al. 2000; Johnson, Thompkins, & Webb 2002). It is also noteworthy that stronger relationships between religiosity and criminal behavior appear to be found in studies that are more methodologically sound (Akers et al. 2008).

Results appear to vary, however, according to how religion is measured (Johnson 2008). For example, Evans and coauthors (1995) find that engagement or participation in religious activity inhibits adult criminal behavior but that the religious beliefs and religious values of those participants are not related to offending.

A recent study involving juveniles confounds the potentially important distinction between different measures of religion. Using data from a nationally representative sample of adolescents, Salas-Wright and coauthors (2012) conduct latent class modeling to assess the relationship between religion and teen drug use, violent behavior, and delinquency. A behavioral measure (attendance at religious services) and an attitudinal one (personal religious belief) are combined to categorize sample participants into different classes. Compared with the religiously disengaged class of adolescents, religiously devoted youth who regularly attend are significantly less likely to engage in fighting behavior. The religiously devoted participants are also less likely to engage in theft than religiously disengaged teens. There are, however, no significant differences between religiously private individuals and religiously disengaged individuals in fighting and theft behavior (Salas-Wright et al. 2012).

Other research by Salas-Wright and associates (Salas-Wright, Vaughn, & Maynard 2014) indicates that the effect of religion on criminal behavior is consistent across developmental stages (from adolescence to adulthood) for both males and females. Using a large nationally representative sample of both adolescents and adults, Salas-Wright and coauthors (2014) find that both religious service attendance and private religious beliefs are significantly and negatively related to theft and drug-selling behavior throughout adolescence and adulthood.

The religion/crime relationship may also vary according to the criminal outcome being measured. For example, one study reports that religious attendance affected the use of some substances but not others among a sample of adolescents and adults (Hill & Pollock 2015). Caution may be in order when making general statements on the protective effects of religion if study results vary by different offending behaviors.

Religion as protective in correctional populations. Early prison institutions in the United States included faith-based programming as part of a larger philosophy to rehabilitate offenders (Johnson 2008). In recent years, with consistent evidence that religion is associated with decreased criminal behavior, scholars have studied the impact of faith-based programs in institutional settings more systematically. In 2001, George W. Bush signed an executive order establishing the White House Office on Faith-Based and Community Initiatives, which helped overcome barriers faith-based programs and religious organizations were facing while applying for grant money to assist current and former prisoners (Johnson 2008).

Lane (2009) posits that the underlying philosophy of faith-based programs may matter. Faith-based programs can range from those sponsored by religious organizations that do not have a specific spiritual component to "faith-saturated" programs that emphasize faith and aim to effect a spiritual change in the program participant (DiIulio 2004). In a unique example of a faith-saturated program, the Texas state prison system implemented the Bible College Program. Program participants enrolled in a four-year course to become ministers and earned a bachelor's degree in biblical studies at the end of the program. Duwe and coauthors (2015) report that Bible College program participation is negatively associated with disciplinary infractions, lowering it by 65 percent for minor misconduct and 80 percent for major misconduct. Though these findings are promising, Bible College is a unique intensive program that is atypical of other faith-based prison programs.

Several studies have evaluated faith-based programs in the community. Two studies have measured the impact of faith-based programming among substance-abusing juveniles in noncorrectional settings. Both DiIulio (2004) and Lee et al. (2014) report that program participation might be associated with abstinence and decreased risk of relapse. However, there was a high dropout rate of program participants in one of these studies (DiIulio 2004), so its findings should be interpreted with caution.

Two other studies focus on the InnerChange Freedom Initiative (IFI), a faith-based prisoner reentry program. Duwe and King (2012) find that Minnesota inmates participating in the program were less likely than matched controls to be rearrested, reconvicted, and reincarcerated about three years postrelease. On the other hand, Johnson and Larson (2003) report no significant differences in recidivism between participants in a Texas InnerChange Freedom Initiative and controls 18 and 24 months postrelease (although the program had a high rate of noncompleters).

Other studies report mixed results or no relationship when assessing the effect of religion on institutional and/or postrelease behavior among adult males. Johnson and coauthors (1997) find that inmates in the Prison Fellowship (PF) Program in four New York State prisons did not significantly differ from members of a comparison group in terms of prison disciplinary infractions and arrests one year postrelease. However, a subgroup of the Prison Fellowship participants most active in Bible study (a behavioral measure of religion) are reported as being less likely than other program participants to be arrested one year postrelease. Using a sample of Federal Bureau of Prisons inmates participating in the Life Connections Program, a support program taught by spiritual guides, Camp and coauthors (2008) find that program participants are less likely than control group participants to engage in serious forms of prison misconduct. This relationship is not significant when considering less serious forms of misconduct and both types of misconduct (less serious and more serious) simultaneously, however (Camp et al. 2008).

Two studies from Florida correctional facilities report no relationship between religion and recidivism: one using a sample of incarcerated adults and one using a sample of incarcerated juveniles. Florida's Faith- and Character-Based Institutions in Lawtey and Hillsborough reportedly have had little impact on recidivism for adult participants after 12 months. However, there were few releases of program participants from prison during that time (LaVigne, Brazzell, & Small 2007). Lane and coauthors (2009, 2010) report that participation in Florida's Faith and Community-Based Delinquency Treatment Initiative (FCBDTI) implemented in juvenile facilities was not associated with law violations during commitment or during a short postrelease follow-up period (Lane et al. 2009, 2010). Indeed, it is the lack of outcome effect in the FCBDTI despite increases in measures of religion (participation and personal religious attitudes) during program exposure that prompts this investigation of the relationship of religion to the intermediate outcome of prisonization. Perhaps prisonization overrides religion's usual protective effect.

Results of other studies suggest that faith-based programming may reduce institutional problem behavior. For example, Clear and Sumter (2002) and O'Connor and Perreyclear (2002) report that involvement in religious programs and higher levels of religious commitment while in prison are associated with fewer disciplinary infractions among male inmates in state prisons. In a rare study involving female prisoners, Levitt and Booker-Loper (2009) find that women who participated in religious programs and perceived receiving high support from these programs while in state prison perpetrated fewer aggressive acts and committed fewer serious institutional infractions than did those in two comparison groups: those who did not attend religious activities as well as those who attended but perceived receiving less support.

Findings on the impact of faith-based programming have been mixed, and studies assessing these programs face a number of methodological and design issues. These issues include lack of random assignment, no comparison groups, and self-selection bias (Mears et al. 2006). Another problem may be the inconsistency across studies in how religion is measured. The operationalization of religion may also affect results when assessing the effects of faith-based programs on prisoner behavior (Dodson et al. 2011; Johnson et al. 2002). There may be an important distinction between behavioral measures (like attendance or participation in religious activities) and attitudinal measures (like the self-reported importance of religion or the extent to which respondents identify as being religious). Yet another problem with the evaluations of faith-based programs reflects the lack of articulating the programs' theoretical premises. Too often they do not clarify the mechanisms through which the program is thought to impact participant behavior, something that hinders the development of effective programs (Camp et al. 2008).

One study suggests the complexity in what may be happening and illustrates the importance of attending to how religion is measured and the importance of articulating theoretical processes. Even if only the behavior of religion is studied, different ways to measure it can yield different results when additional theoretical processes are taken into account. In a small sample of recently paroled male inmates, Kerley and coauthors (2010) report that greater participation in religious services *is* related to less institutional deviant behavior but that engagement in private prayer while in prison and watching religious broadcasts on television in prison *are not* related to deviant behavior when *self-control* is taken into account. Incorporating theoretically derived controls may provide a more nuanced understanding of the impact of religion.

Importation of religion and religious adaptation in faith-based correctional programs. Prisonization has been rarely addressed in research into the effects of faith-based programs. Because prisonization is thought to be a result of both imported factors and adjustment to the deprivations of incarceration, there may be differential effects of imported religious features (whether the individual participated in religious activities or held religious beliefs before prison) from adaptive religious behaviors and beliefs while in prison. Indeed, religion inside may be a newfound or rediscovered adjustment to life's problems generally or more specifically to prison life, even if merely a ruse (see, e.g., Clear & Cole 1994, 361–62). Researchers often fail to distinguish between preincarceration and incarceration religious beliefs and behavior.

Johnson and Larson (2003) present results from a study to address the personal experiences of religion among program participants that was conducted with targeted focus groups of 125 adult male participants in the InnerChange Freedom Initiative in Texas. They report that in 54 percent of 125 interviews, participants indicated a newfound faith or rediscovery of faith while in the program. This suggests that religious beliefs are often not imported into prison, and that the effect of religious programming is a factor in adjustment to prison. Recall, however, that their findings show no significant differences in recidivism between the faith-based participants and controls 18 and 24 months postrelease. Lane et al. (2009, 2010) also report major increases in both attitudes about religion and participation in religious services among juveniles who were exposed to faith-based programs in Florida residential facilities. Again, however, they find little evidence of postrelease gains in behavior.

The Research Problem Restated

One study, unrelated to faith-based programming, keys on the basic research question concerning the general link between religion and prisonization.

Gillespie (2002), using a sample of over 1,000 inmates in three state prisons, reports that religious participation in prison is negatively associated with prisonization (i.e., more participation in religious activities relates to less prisonization). Note, however, that Gillespie's religion measure taps only the behavior dimension during incarceration, and she does not deal with importation of religion into prison.

The current effort seeks to expand the inquiry in several ways. First, it examines both attitudinal and behavioral measures of religion (the importance of religion and attendance at religious services, respectively). Second, it looks at those measures for the time frame before confinement (religion that would be imported) and during confinement (religion that would be adaptive to incarceration). Third, it focuses on both male and female juveniles in faith-based programs during confinement. The effort involving both male and female juveniles should shed light on what kind of religious measure or measures relate to prisonization and how the time frame of those measures affect the relationship, if at all. The analysis will incorporate control variables, some of which are theoretically derived: sex, age, race, prior arrests, a sense of injustice about events leading up to confinement, and fear of victimization (both before and during incarceration). We hope to gain a more nuanced understanding of the extent to which religion may be protective by using prisonization, both because prisonization is an important outcome in its own right for understanding life during confinement but also because it is a probable intermediate outcome linked to behaviors both during incarceration (e.g., disciplinary reports) and after release (e.g., recidivism).

Methodology

Context

The data for this study are from the larger evaluation of the Florida Faith and Community-Based Delinquency Treatment Initiative or FCBDTI (Lane et al. 2009, 2010). This project was funded from 2004 to 2008. The Federal Office of Juvenile Justice and Delinquency Prevention (OJJDP) provided the Florida Department of Juvenile Justice (DJJ) with $3.5 million to implement the program, which included an evaluation component administered by two of the authors. The program itself provided faith-based personnel (e.g., chaplains), volunteer mentors, religious activities brought in from the outside, and secular evidence-based services (Thinking for a Change, Character Education, Strengthening Families Program, and Motivational Interviewing) to juveniles in three medium and two high-risk residential facilities across the state. Two of the facilities (one medium and one high risk) were for girls. Participants were volunteers in that at a commitment hearing they had to agree to participate in the faith-based program to be considered for the initiative.

The FCBDTI program used an open-forum approach (Lanza-Kaduce & Lane 2007), allowing youths to practice their chosen faiths with the support of program staff and volunteers, especially mentors. Standardized training was provided for program staff and volunteers. The intervention was designed to be uniform across sites and mixed cognitive behavioral programming (e.g., Thinking for Change) with religious components. The religious features included chaplains on site to deal with residents both individually and through group activities like devotions/prayer groups. The chaplain would also coordinate with religious groups in the community so that they could provide activities for residents. In addition, the chaplains would help arrange one-on-one mentoring from community volunteers. Because of the open forum approach, the chaplain would help match residents with religious mentors unless the youth requested a secular community volunteer. The goal was to match youths with mentors of their preferred faith, as long as it was a state-recognized religion. In truth, the majority of staff working on the faith based programming considered themselves "called" to the faith-based program, resulting in a milieu of faith more generally. That is, program staff more generally often participated in faith-based activities and discussions.

General findings from the evaluation project showed little effect of the program on recidivism or recidivism severity but did show that the program had some impact on incident reports inside the facilities and that religion became more salient for youths after they entered this program. These findings led us to the current analysis.

Sample and Data Collection

As part of the larger evaluation project, researchers conducted an interview with youths while they were inside the facilities. The interview instrument was 35 pages long, contained 313 questions, and lasted approximately 45 minutes to an hour. Interviews occurred between October 15, 2005 and November 30, 2006. The interview sample included 150 juveniles committed to any of the five participating FCBDTI sites. This number is smaller than the 262 youths who were referred to the FCBDTI from April 1, 2005 to June 30, 2006 for a variety of reasons. Eight youths refused an interview, some were released (n=37) or transferred to another facility (n=5) before researchers were able to interview them, and for the remaining (n=62) we were unable to obtain proper documentation of initial consent (from both a parent/guardian and the youth) to participate in the research phase of the initiative, which was required by the university institutional review board.

Measures

Dependent Variable

Our dependent variable is *prisonization*, a measure that has import for understanding the adaptation to confinement as well as an important intermediate outcome thought to be linked to future behavior, including subsequent delinquency or crime. The measure is constructed from 10 interview questions using a Likert response format running from 1=strongly disagree to 4=strongly agree. We added each respondent's answers and divided by 10. Four of the items use reverse coding (R) to prevent response sets. The items, which have been used in other research (e.g., Lanza-Kaduce & Radosevich 1987), are:

1. We are treated as individuals here. (R)
2. I feel like a caged animal here.
3. You need to be careful about who you're friendly with here.
4. To tell staff your problems is a sign of weakness.
5. The best way to get along here is to keep your mouth shut.
6. Residents have no influence on how they are treated here.
7. Residents are allowed to make decisions here. (R)
8. We have more freedom here than you might think. (R)
9. The rules here make good sense most of the time. (R)
10. You need to look out for yourself here; no one else will.

A reliability analysis shows that the items scale (Cronbach's alpha=.729). The mean is 2.61; the median falls between 2.5 and 2.6; and the standard deviation of the scale is 0.38 for the 129 cases included multivariate analyses. The actual scale scores range from 1.8 through 3.8.

Independent Variables

Our primary independent variables of interest focus on religion, before and while in the program. Because religion has different measurement dimensions, we use both attitudinal and behavioral approaches. The following interview items asked about respondents' attitudes toward religion: (1) Before you came to the facility, how important was religion in your life and (2) since you've been in the facility, how important is religion to your life? The responses ranged from 1=not at all important through 4=very important. Because of the important theoretical distinction between importation into confinement and adaptation to confinement, no effort was made to try to combine these attitudinal measures. *Religion's importance before* confinement has a mean of 2.29 and a standard deviation of 0.98; *religion's importance during* confinement has a mean of 3.03 and a standard deviation of 0.96. Interestingly, as we noted earlier, the mean score on the importance of religion increased during participation in the faith-based program. Note that we also examined a parallel attitudinal measure of religion that asked respondents to indicate how religious they considered themselves to be both before and during confinement, using a five-point scale ranging from not religious at all to very religious. Analyses using the religiosity attitude yielded results very similar to those obtained from analyses of the importance of religion and, therefore, are not included in this chapter.

The behavioral dimension of religion asked about participation in religious activities. It is tapped by questions regarding how often respondents attend religious services. One interview question focused on attendance in the year before confinement; another question zeroed in on attendance during confinement. The six response alternatives run from never (coded 0) through daily (coded 5). *Religious participation before* confinement among the 129 respondents in the analyses has a mean of 1.43 with a standard deviation of 1.31. *Religious participation during* confinement has a mean of 3.07 and a standard deviation of 1.27. Note the higher mean during confinement in the faith-based program.

Control Variables

Prior arrests. The interview asked youths about their involvement in a checklist of 17 different kinds of criminal activity during the year before they were committed to the facility. The stem of the question read:

> This is a list of activities that you may have been involved in during the year before you were committed to this facility. Remember that what you say is confidential. Please just think about these questions, and tell me whether you were involved in each activity during the year before you came to this facility.

Youths first indicated how many times they did each activity in the year prior to commitment; they then reported how many times they were arrested for the respective crime categories during that year. Because everyone in the sample was committed to a residential facility, all of them have records. For that reason, we focus on the arrests in the year prior to commitment to see if frequency of official trouble is related to prisonization. We computed a variable by adding all the frequencies for arrest in the year prior to commitment for the 17 items on the delinquency checklist. Nine youths reported they were confined in the year prior, so they were assigned to one prior arrest—they had to have at least one arrest at some point and one prior was the modal arrest category in the sample. The raw summed values for the 17 crime categories range from 0 to 132 and are badly skewed. Therefore, for the analysis they have been collapsed to four ordinal categories of *prior arrest*: 0=no priors before the arrest that led to confinement; 1=one prior arrest before the one leading to confinement; 2=two or three prior arrests; 3=four or more prior arrests. The mean is 1.69 and the standard deviation is 0.94.

The delinquency checklist included the following behaviors: (1) damaged or set fire to property; (2) broke into a house, building, or car in order to take something; (3) robbed or held up a place of business; (4) robbed a person; (5) tried to or beat somebody up or threatened someone with a weapon; (6) stole or boosted something; (7) stole a car, truck, or motorcycle; (8) used check or credit card illegally; (9) obtained prescriptions illegally; (10) ran cons or scams; (11) dealt or delivered drugs; (12) provided sex for money; (13) committed or attempted homicide; (14) committed or attempted sex by force; (15) been in gang or posse fights; (16) possessed marijuana or hashish; and (17) possessed hard drugs such as cocaine, crack, heroin, PCP, and LSD.

Fear of victimization. Because fear of crime victimization may hinder one's ability to be prosocial, we include two measures of fear as controls. One deals with fear on the outside prior to commitment to control for emotional states that may be imported into confinement. The other captures fear during confinement. Part of the swallowing up process that awaits everyone who enters confinement presents grounds for fear, even if just fear of the unknown for less experienced entrants. Of course, the conditions of confinement also can breed fear. The prospect of various kinds of violence during incarceration is real; as Pollock (2004, 102) concludes, "prison never has been, and probably never can be, free from fear."

Fear of victimization before confinement is derived from a summated scale that has been constructed from reports of fear of 13 different types of victimization on the outside. These included (1) having your property damaged by gang graffiti or tagging; (2) having someone break into your home while you were away; (3) having a gang member commit a home invasion robbery against you; (4) being raped or sexually assaulted by a stranger; (5) being a victim of a drive-by or random gang-related shooting; (6) being physically attacked or assaulted by a gang member; (7) being harassed by gang members; (8) being a victim of a carjacking; (9) being shot while you were walking down the street; (10) being robbed; (11) being beat up by somebody or being threatened with a weapon; (12) having your car, truck, or motorcycle stolen; and (13) being murdered. Two interview items dealing with victimization by police are not included because of the conceptual overlap with perceived injustice at the hands of police that is covered in the sense of injustice measurement and is discussed below. We asked respondents how "personally afraid" they were of each kind of victimization in their "community before" being committed; the responses for each of the 13 items could range from 1 not afraid to 4 very afraid. We divided the sums by 13. The Cronbach's alpha is high (.947), but the summated scale frequencies are highly skewed across over 30 different values. Therefore, the scale scores for fear of victimization before confinement are collapsed into five ordinal categories for the analyses: 1 = 1 (not afraid on any item); 1.08–1.46 = 2 (a little fear on one or several items); 1.54–1.92 = 3 (some fear on some items); 2.15–2.92 = 4 (fear on many items); 3.00–4.00 = 5 (high fear on multiple items). After collapsing, the mean is 2.37 with a standard deviation of 1.24.

Fear of victimization during confinement is also derived from a summated scale of responses to eight types of victimization on the inside. These are (1) having property stolen or damaged by another resident, (2) being harassed by another resident, (3) being physically attacked or assaulted by another resident, (4) being raped or sexually assaulted by another resident, (5) being murdered by another resident, (6) being harassed by staff, (7) being physically attacked or assaulted by staff, and (8) being raped or sexually assaulted by staff. For this measure, we asked respondents how "personally afraid" they were of the eight types of victimization while they lived in the facility, and the responses again run from 1 = not afraid to 4 = very afraid. The summed scores show reliability (Cronbach's alpha = .893) but the distribution is highly skewed. For use in the analyses, the scores are collapsed into three ordinal categories: 1 = no fear on any item, 2 = a little fear on a few items, and 3 = some fear on some items. After collapsing the categories, the mean is 1.67 with a standard deviation of 0.75.

Sense of injustice. Since the Lanza-Kaduce and Radosevich (1987) article, the research on injustice has been dominated by a focus on procedural injustice, led by the work of Tom Tyler (see, e.g., Tyler 1990; Tyler & Huo 2002). That line of research has not utilized Matza but has drawn distinctions among different dimensions of justice, differentiating procedural issues from substantive and distributive ones. Rather than pit one type of justice against others, the approach taken in this study is to broaden the measure so we incorporate different kinds of injustice.

The interview schedule included measures of procedural justice, substantive justice, and distributive justice from which we constructed a composite sense of injustice measure. The focus of the questions was on the events that led up to the respondents' commitments. For procedural justice, we use two interview questions: "Overall, how fairly were you treated by the police," and "Overall, how fairly were you treated by the judge?" Question responses range from 1 = very fairly to 4 = very unfairly). For substantive justice, we asked respondents to indicate their agreement (1 = strongly disagree to 4 = strongly agree) with the statement, "It should be against the law to do what I did." For distributive justice, we asked respondents their level of agreement (1 = strongly disagree to 4=strongly agree) with "I deserved to be sent here for what I did." The composite is a count of responses across the four items that indicate a sense of injustice. For the procedural justice questions, we count responses of "unfairly" and "very unfairly"; for the substantive and distributive justice items, we count "strongly disagree" and "disagree." The resulting count has scores that can range from zero through four. Its mean is 1.28 and its standard deviation is 1.22.

Personal characteristics. We control for the respondents' race, sex, and age at the time of the interview. For race, we use a dummy variable (*white*), so that Whites are coded 1 and all others are coded 0. Forty-six of the respondents are White. For *sex*, males are coded 1 and females 0. One hundred eight respondents are males. We also include the youth's *age* (in years) on the day researchers conducted the interview. The average age is just under 16 years old.

Plan of Analysis

We present the descriptive statistics for the measures used in the multivariate analyses in the discussion of their measurement. The multivariate strategy is to regress the dependent variable (the *prisonization* scale) on the respective indicators of religion and the controls using the SPSS ordinary least squares regression function. Although the prisonization scale is ordinal, it should have enough ordinal categories (see Kim 1975; Labovitz 1970) and is sufficiently normally distributed to support the regression analysis. The independent and control variables are entered simultaneously. There is no evidence of multicollinearity. The analyses employ listwise deletion of missing values, which results in 129 cases. With this relatively small number of cases (especially given the small number of females), the decision rule for statistical significance is the 0.10 probability level.

The prisonization analyses are pursued in two series of regressions. One series examines the attitudinal measures of religion (*religious importance before* and *religious importance during* confinement), and the other series deals with the behavioral dimension (*religious participation before* and *religious participation during* confinement). For each series, we ran three separate models. The first model focuses on the effect of religion before incarceration, controlling for sex, age, race, prior arrests, fear of victimization before commitment on the outside, fear of victimization during confinement, and a sense of injustice. The second model regresses prisonization on religion during confinement and on the list of controls. The third includes both the before and during measures of religion with the controls. The pattern of results is highly similar across all three runs in the respective series, so only the results for the third analysis including both the before and during religion measures are presented.

Results and Discussion

Results

To investigate the relationship between religion and prisonization, two series of multiple regression analyses are performed using different measures of religion. One focuses on an attitudinal measure: the importance of religion (both before commitment and during confinement). The other examines a behavioral measure: participation in religious activities (before and during).

The first results to be presented are those for regressing prisonization on the importance of religion. The model regresses prisonization on the importance of religion before incarceration and the importance of religion during confinement, controlling for sex, age, race, prior arrests, fear of victimization before commitment on the outside, fear of victimization during confinement, and a sense of injustice regarding events leading to confinement. The independent and control variables are entered simultaneously using listwise deletion of cases with missing values.

Table 7.1 shows the regression results for that model. We present the unstandardized coefficients, standard errors, standardized beta coefficients, significance or probability level, and zero-order correlations in the table columns. There is no evidence of multicollinearity; the strongest intercorrelation among independent variables was .532 between fear of victimization before and during confinement.

Table 7.1   **Prisonization Regressed on the Importance of Religion before and during Confinement with Controls (n = 129)**

	B	SE	β	p-value	r
Religion imported before	.011	.039	.028	.779	.074
Religion imported during	−.050	.036	−.124	.173	−.082
Age	.006	.026	.020	.814	−.015
Sex	−.263	.095	−.245	.007	−.231
White	−.058	.072	−.073	.421	−.150
Prior arrests	.047	.033	.115	.164	.105
Fear of victimization before	.037	.031	.119	.242	.193
Fear of victimization during	.090	.052	.177	.086	.276
Sense of injustice	.092	.027	.292	.001	.225
(Constant)	2.44	.496		.000	

R = .481; R^2 = .231; Adj. R^2 = .173

The importance of religion (either before or during confinement) is unrelated to prisonization. There is no evidence that a religious attitude is protective against the antisocial orientation that prisonization represents. Some of the controls, however, do predict prisonization. According to the standardized beta coefficients, the count of items indicating a sense of injustice is most strongly related to prisonization (β=.292; p=.001). Those indicating more injustice regarding their processing are more prisonized. Similarly, sex is moderately related (β=−.245; p=.007); the girls are more prisonized than the males in these faith-based facilities. Greater fear of being victimized while inside weakly relates to higher prisonization (β=.177; p=.080).

Table 7.2 presents the regression results for participating in religious services (both before and during commitment). We also include the control variables (sex, age, race, prior arrests, fear of victimization before commitment on the outside, fear of victimization during confinement, and a sense of injustice regarding police and court processing) in the regression. We present the unstandardized coefficients, standard errors, standardized beta coefficients, significance or probability level, and zero-order correlations in the table columns. Again, there is no evidence of multicollinearity.

The important difference in using a behavioral measure of religion is that one of the participation measures is somewhat protective. More regular participation in religious activities during confinement relates to less prisonization (β=.189, p=.028). Participation before commitment has no such salutary effect (β=.054, p=.544). Two control variables again predict prisonization in this model. The count of items indicating a sense of injustice is again most

Table 7.2 **Prisonization Regressed on Participating in Religious Services before and during Confinement with Controls (n=129)**

	B	SE	β	p-value	r
Religious participation before	.016	.026	.054	.544	.095
Religious participation during	−.057	.026	−.189	.028	−.109
Age	.004	.025	.014	.866	−.015
Sex	−.266	.092	−.257	.005	−.231
White	−.050	.067	−.062	.458	−.150
Prior arrests	.060	.033	.147	.075	.105
Fear of victimization before	.052	.031	.170	.096	.193
Fear of victimization during	.078	.052	.153	.137	.276
Sense of injustice	.091	.026	.290	.001	.225
(Constant)	2.462	.470		.000	

R=.500; R^2=.250; Adj. R^2=.193

strongly related to prisonization (β=.290; p=.001). Those indicating more injustice regarding their processing are more prisonized. Sex is once again moderately related (β=−.257; p=.005); the girls are more prisonized than the males. In the model that examines the behavioral measures of religion, fear of victimization before (rather than during) confinement is significantly, albeit weakly, related to prisonization (β=.170, p=.096). From the zero-order correlations, it appears that fear of victimization during confinement is related to prisonization (r=.276). That zero-order relationship does not hold up in the multivariate analysis, probably because fear during confinement is related to other variables that predict prisonization: fear before confinement (r=.532), sex (r=−.304), and religious participation before confinement (r=.253).

The findings can be summarized quite succinctly. The primary research question is whether religion is protective against the antisocial orientation that is prisonization. Importantly, the research finds that an attitudinal measure of religion is not protective regardless of whether it refers to religion before or during confinement. The importance of religion does not relate to prisonization. (Recall that a second attitudinal measure, identifying as being religious, also does not relate to prisonization.) One of the behavioral measures, however, does appear to be protective. More frequent participation in religious activities during confinement predicts lower prisonization.

Before moving to a discussion of the role of religion, we would be remiss not to note another pattern of findings. A sense of injustice, sex, and some measure of fear of victimization relate to prisonization. Indeed, these variables should be raised from their secondary role as controls because they may be as important as religion for understanding prosocial and antisocial orientations and what facilitates or blunts treatment. Given that prospect, the control findings also warrant further discussion.

Discussion

Religious participation, but not religious attitude, is inversely related to prisonization in this sample of faith-based program participants. This difference in the impact between religious behavior and religious attitudes on other attitudes and behaviors has been reported before (see Evans et al. 1995). The refinement this analysis adds is that it is religious participation during incarceration, rather than that which was experienced beforehand, that matters.

Theoretically, the import of religion's behavioral dimension fits well with the argument of Akers et al. (2008) that both social bonding and social learning help account for how religion can be protective. The convergence of participation in religious activities on the inside with bonding theory is most clearly seen in the theory's emphasis on conventional involvements (Hirschi 1969). Going to religious activities should bond confined residents to the program and help protect them from prisonization and its isolation, alienation, lack of commitment to the program, and hostile attitudes toward staff and counselors.

Religion's behavioral dimension also fits well with the behavioral origins of social learning theory. By participating in religious activities, the confined youth are exposed to conforming definitions in the context of law-abiding associations with others who present positive models and reinforce conforming behaviors. One behavioral consequence should be less prisonization, itself a kind of definition of the situation that Akers (1985) would characterize as a kind of subvocalized behavior. As behavior, it, too, is expected to be learned in a process of differential association that involves exposure to definitions, modeling, and operant conditioning.

The importance of the behavioral measure of religion in this research adds to the literature but does not resolve the issue of how to measure religion. Here, behavior (participation) is contrasted only with an overarching religious attitude (the importance of religion to the respondent). A more comprehensive effort should explore specific beliefs (e.g., in hell, original sin, life after death, reincarnation) or distinctive belief systems (e.g., fundamentalism, atheism).

This research highlights how prosocial programming confronts complications that may need to be taken into account during planning, implementation, and evaluation. The complications are both structural and processual. The finding that girls are more prisonized than boys is provocative, especially since research on girls' facilities is rarer. The finding harkens back to Giallombardo's (1974) argument that girls experience the loss of ties to family and friends as serious deprivations. That loss may be more pronounced for them than it is for boys. Structurally, the sex difference in this research is consistent with the argument that girls seem to be in a different place from boys and experience incarceration differently. Prisonization may need to be addressed especially for girls before treatment gains will be optimized. This prospect begs the question of whether other structural arrangements may condition how incarceration is experienced and how programming is affected. Scholars have increasingly recognized that girls and boys involved in the juvenile justice system have unique risks and needs that are best addressed through gender-responsive programming (Bloom, Owen, & Covington 2005). Future research should focus on how sex differences in juvenile facilities play out.

The important role of a sense of injustice in these findings also holds implications for the design, implementation, and evaluation of prosocial programs. A greater sense of injustice predicts more prisonization. One of the differences in this research is in the way sense of injustice is measured. Lanza-Kaduce and Radosevich's (1987) prior research, which derived measures from Matza (1964), and the research emanating from Tyler (e.g., 1990) rely heavily on procedural justice. They generally report that injustice perceptions make compliance less likely. The current research adds substantive and distributive or outcome justice to the procedural dimension to measure the sense of injustice. This broader measure is the variable that most strongly relates to the antisocial orientation that is prisonization.

Inasmuch as the focus of the sense of injustice in this study is on the events that led up to the confinement, that perception seemingly would have been imported into the facility and its effect on prisonization is over and above that of religious participation. We do not know how much perceived injustice may blunt the protective features of religion, but research may need to shift to that possibility insofar as the effect size of religion is not as large as religious leaders would hope. Perhaps there are a number of experiences and attitudes that would mediate, moderate, or suppress how much religion is protective.

One of the complications, however, may be causal ordering. Irwin (1980) argues that incarceration can cause a reinterpretation of the events that led to confinement, and he explicitly includes perceptions of justice at all phases of the system. If so, there may be a causal order issue that cannot be addressed with these cross-sectional data. Perhaps the incarceration itself leads to a reinterpretation of the preconfinement events so that the sense of injustice is an extension of prisonization as much as an antecedent to it. Given evidence that perceived injustice affects subsequent compliance, the prospect that incarceration experiences (including programming) could act back either to mitigate or aggravate the sense of injustice complicates the design and implementation of programming and suggests an important focus for evaluation of program effectiveness. At the very least, the sense of injustice warrants more research and needs to be linked to behaviors and orientations before, during, and postconfinement.

Our finding regarding fear of victimization also illustrates a potential challenge for the design, implementation, and evaluation of prosocial programming. In this sample, fear that is imported plays a role in the analysis featuring religious attitudes, while fear that stems from the incarceration itself affects prisonization in the religious participation analysis. The findings raise the prospect that fear may be a risk factor and/or a block to protective factors. They suggest that residential treatment programs need to incorporate the prospect of fear in their design, implementation, and evaluation.

Given the small sample and the fact that all the respondents were involved in a faith-based initiative in their juvenile facilities, the findings from this research must be viewed with some caution. Certainly, replication would be in order. The reasons for losing cases in this sample (failure to get consent to be researched, transfer to another facility, and refusal to be interviewed despite initial consent) all suggest that our data come from more rather than less cooperative residents. Those who are more isolated and resistant (features of prisonization) are less likely to be included. In addition, the faith-based programming probably made more religious activities available more often and encouraged attendance at them than would occur in other facilities.

Without the faith emphasis inside, prisonization may have been worse and the religious participation less. Still, these findings are not out of line with the extant research. There is much to be learned yet about how and when religion may serve protective functions and how concomitants of our justice system like the sense of injustice and prisonization may come into play.

Finally, this research is based on the premise that prisonization is reflective of antisocial orientations and an intermediate outcome linked to larger consequences. Two questions arise: (1) Is prisonization like other antisocial orientations and thus an important outcome to study in its own right? and (2) Is prisonization a risk factor that relates consistently to other outcomes and behaviors, including disciplinary problems, reintegration upon release, and recidivism? Additional research is needed to address these questions.

Bibliography

Akers, Ronald L. *Deviant Behavior: A Social Learning Approach* (3rd ed.). Belmont, CA: Wadsworth, 1985.

Akers, Ronald L., Norman Hayner, & Werner Gruninger. "Homosexual and Drug Behavior in Prison: A Test of the Functional and Importation Models of the Inmate System." *Social Problems* 21 (1974): 410–422.

Akers, Ronald L., Jodi Lane, & Lonn Lanza-Kaduce. "Faith-Based Mentoring and Restorative Justice: Overlapping Theoretical, Empirical, and Philosophical Background." In Holly Ventura Miller (Ed.), *Restorative Justice: From Theory to Practice (Sociology of Crime, Law and Deviance, Volume 11)* (pp. 136–166). Bingley, UK: Emerald, 2008.

Baier, Colin J., & Bradley R. E. Wright. "If you Love Me, Keep My Commandments: A Meta-Analysis of the Effect of Religion on Crime." *Journal of Research in Crime and Delinquency* 38 (2001): 3–21.

Bloom, Barbara, Barbara Owen, & Stephanie Covington. *Strategies for Women Offenders: A Summary of Research, Practice, and Guiding Principles for Women Offenders.* Washington, DC: National Institute of Corrections Bulletin, U.S. Department of Justice, 2005. Available at http://static.nicic.gov/Library/020418.pdf

Camp, Scott D., Dawn M. Daggett, Okyun Kwon, & Jody Klein-Saffran. "The Effect of Faith Program Participation on Prison Misconduct: The Life Connections Program." *Journal of Criminal Justice* 36 (2008): 389–395.

Clear, Todd R., & George F. Cole. *American Corrections* (3rd ed.). Belmont, CA: Wadsworth, 1994.

Clear, Todd R., & Melvina T. Sumter. "Prisoners, Prison, and Religion: Religion and Adjustment to Prison." *Journal of Offender Rehabilitation* 35 (2002): 127–166.

Clemmer, Donald. *The Prison Community* (Re-issued ed.). New York: Holt, Rinehart and Winston, 1958.

Clemmer, Donald. "The Process of Prisonization." In Robert G. Leger & John R. Stratton (Eds.), *The Sociology of Corrections: A Book of Readings* (pp. 175–180). New York: Wiley, 1977.

DiIulio, John J. "Getting Faith-Based Programs Right." *Public Interest* 155 (2004): 75–88.

Dodson, Kimberly D., Leann N. Cabage, & Paul M. Klenowski. "An Evidence-Based Assessment of Faith-Based Programs: Do Faith-Based Programs "Work" to Reduce Recidivism?" *Journal of Offender Rehabilitation* 50 (2011): 367–383.

Duwe, Grant, Michael Hallett, Joshua Hays, Sung Joon Jang, & Byron R. Johnson. "Bible College Participation and Prison Misconduct: A Preliminary Analysis." *Journal of Offender Rehabilitation* 54 (2015): 371–390.

Duwe, Grant, & Michelle King. "Can Faith-Based Correctional Programs Work? An Outcome Evaluation of the InnerChange Freedom Initiative in Minnesota." *International Journal of Offender Therapy and Comparative Criminology* 57 (2012): 813–841.

Evans, T. David, Francis T. Cullen, R. Gregory Dunaway, & Velmer S. Burton, Jr. "Religion and Crime Reexamined: The Impact of Religion, Secular Controls and Social Ecology on Adult Criminality." *Criminology* 33 (1995): 195–224.

Garabedian, Peter G. "Social Roles and Processes of Socialization in the Prison Community." *Social Problems* 11 (1963): 139–152.

Giallombardo, Rose. *The Social World of Imprisoned Girls*. New York: Wiley, 1974.

Gillespie, Wayne. *Prisonization: Individual and Institutional Factors Affecting Inmate Conduct*. New York: LFB Scholarly, 2002.

Hill, Gillian. "Predicting Recidivism Using Institutional Measures." In David P. Farrington & Roger Tarling (Eds.), *Prediction in Criminology* (pp. 96–118). Albany: State University of New York, 1985.

Hill, Milton C., & Wendi Pollock. "Was Hirschi Right? A National-Level Longitudinal Examination of Religion as a Social Bond." *Deviant Behavior* 36 (2015): 783–806.

Hirschi, Travis. *Causes of Delinquency*. Berkeley: University of California Press, 1969.

Irwin, John. *Prisons in Turmoil*. Boston: Little, Brown, 1980.

Johnson, Byron R. "The Faith Factor and Prison Reentry." *Interdisciplinary Journal of Research on Religion* 4 (2008): 1–21.

Johnson, Byron R., Spencer De Li, David B. Larson, & Michael McCullough. "Religion and Delinquency: A Systematic Review of the Literature." *Journal of Contemporary Criminal Justice* 16 (2000): 32–52.

Johnson, Byron R., & Sung Joon Jang. "Crime and Religion: Assessing the Role of the Faith Factor." In Richard Rosenfeld, Kenna Quinet, & Crystal A. Garcia (Eds.), *Contemporary Issues in Criminological Theory and Research: The Role of Social Institutions* (pp. 117–149). Belmont, CA: Wadsworth, 2010.

Johnson, Byron R., & David B. Larson. *The InnerChange Freedom Initiative: A Preliminary Evaluation of a Faith-Based Program*. Philadelphia: Center for Research on Religion and Urban Civil Society, 2003.

Johnson, Byron R., David B. Larson, & Timothy C. Pitts. "Religious Programs, Institutional Adjustment, and Recidivism among Former Inmates in Prison Fellowship Programs." *Justice Quarterly* 14 (1997): 45–166.

Johnson, Byron R., Ralph B. Tompkins, & Derek Webb. *Objective Hope: Assessing the Effectiveness of Faith-Based Organizations: A Review of the Literature.* Philadelphia: Center for Research on Religion and Urban Civil Society, University of Pennsylvania, 2002.

Kelly, P. Elizabeth, Joshua R. Polanin, Sung Joon Jang, & Byron R. Johnson. "Religion, Delinquency, and Drug Use: A Meta-Analysis." *Criminal Justice Review* 40 (2014): 505–523.

Kerley, Kent R., Heith Copes, Richard Tewksbury, & Dean A. Dabney. "Examining the Relationship between Religiosity and Self-control as Predictors of Prison Deviance." *International Journal of Offender Therapy and Comparative Criminology* 55 (2010): 1251–1271.

Kim, Jae-On. "Multivariate Analysis of Ordinal Variables." *American Journal of Sociology* 81 (1975): 261–298.

Labovitz, Sanford. "The Assignment of Numbers to Rank Order Categories." *American Sociological Review* 36 (1970): 515–524.

Lane, Jodi. "Faith-Based Programming for Offenders." *Victims and Offenders* 4 (2009): 327–333.

Lane, Jodi, Lonn Lanza-Kaduce, Ronald L. Akers, & Carrie Cook (September 2009). *Final Report of the Florida Faith and Community-Based Delinquency Treatment Initiative (FCBDTI) Evaluation.* Submitted to the Office of Juvenile Justice and Delinquency Prevention and the Florida Department of Juvenile Justice (revised February 2010).

Lanza-Kaduce, Lonn, & Jodi Lane. "Initiating Faith-Based Juvenile Corrections—Exercising without Establishing Religion." In Marilyn D. McShane & Franklin P. Williams III (Eds.), *Youth Violence and Delinquency: Monsters and Myths* (pp. 131–148). Westport, CT: Praeger, 2007.

Lanza-Kaduce, Lonn, & Marcia Radosevich. "Negative Reactions to Processing and Substance Use among Young Incarcerated Males." *Deviant Behavior* 8 (1987): 131–148.

LaVigne, Nancy G., Diana Brazzell, & Kevonne Small. *Evaluation of Florida's Faith- and Character-Based Institutions: Final Report.* Washington, DC: Urban Institute, 2007.

Lee, Matthew T., Paige S. Veta, Byron R. Johnson, & Maria E. Pagano. "Daily Spiritual Experiences and Adolescent Treatment Response." *Alcoholism Treatment Quarterly* 32 (2014): 271–298.

Leger, Robert G., & John R. Stratton. *The Sociology of Corrections: A Book of Readings.* New York: Wiley, 1977.

Levitt, Lacey, & Ann Booker-Loper. "The Influence of Religious Participation on the Adjustment in Female Inmates." *American Journal of Orthopsychiatry* 79 (2009): 1–7.

Matthews, Roger. *Doing Time: An Introduction to the Sociology of Imprisonment.* New York: St. Martin's Press, 1999.

Matza, David. *Delinquency and Drift.* New York: Wiley, 1964.

Mears, Daniel P., Caterina G. Roman., Ashley Wolff, & Janeen Buck. "Faith-Based Efforts to Improve Prisoner Reentry: Assessing the Logic and Evidence." *Journal of Criminal Justice* 34 (2006): 351–367.

O'Connor, Thomas P., & Michael Perreyclear. "Prison Religion in Action and Its Influence on Offender Rehabilitation." *Journal of Offender Rehabilitation* 35 (2002): 11–33.

Pollock, Jocelyn M. *Prisons and Prison Life*. Los Angeles: Roxbury, 2004.

Salas-Wright, Christopher P., Michael G. Vaughn, David R. Hodge, & Brian E. Perron. "Religiosity Profiles of American Youth in Relation to Substance Use, Violence, and Delinquency." *Journal of Youth and Adolescence* 41 (2012): 1560–1575.

Salas-Wright, Christopher P., Michael G. Vaughn, & Brandy R. Maynard. "Buffering Effects of Religiosity on Crime: Testing the Invariance Hypothesis across Gender and Developmental Period." *Criminal Justice and Behavior* 41 (2014): 673–691.

Sykes, Gresham M. *The Society of Captives*. Princeton, NJ: Princeton University Press, 1958.

Sykes, Gresham M., & Sheldon L. Messinger. "The Inmate Social System." In Richard Cloward (Ed.), *Theoretical Studies in the Social Organization of the Prison* (pp. 5–20). New York: Social Science Research Council, 1960.

Thomas, Charles W. "Toward a More Inclusive Model of the Inmate Contra-Culture." *Criminology* 8 (1970): 251–262.

Thomas, Charles W. "Theoretical Perspectives on Prisonization: A Comparison of the Importation and Deprivation Models." *Journal of Criminal Law and Criminology* 68 (1977): 135–145.

Tyler, Tom R. *Why People Obey the Law*. New Haven, CT: Yale University Press, 1990.

Tyler, Tom R., & Yuen Huo. *Trust in the Law: Encouraging Public Cooperation with the Police and the Courts*. New York: Russell Sage, 2002.

Wolfgang, Marvin E. "Quantitative Analysis of Adjustments to the Prison Community." *Journal of Criminal Law and Criminology* 51 (1960–1961): 607–618.

CHAPTER EIGHT

Religion Postprison: Roles Faith Played in Colson Scholars' Convict-to-Collegian Transition

Judith A. Leary

The United States incarcerates its citizens at rates unparalleled by other international justice systems, even in comparison to the most undeveloped and underdeveloped countries. Due to the "tough on crime" era that reigned for over three decades, the nation's prison population grew by more than 350 percent from 1980 to 2010, despite the fact that overall crime had declined and that the general population had grown by only 33 percent during these years (Schmitt, Warner, & Gupta 2010). Across the nation, prisoners mass-exodus these often-overcrowded facilities, daily returning to a society lacking meaningful reentry supports relevant to their significant obstacles (Petersilia 2003). Unfortunately, researchers, social scientists, and policy makers have so consistently overlooked the powerful potential of religious faith to serve as a meaningful support for both prison survival and successful prisoner reentry, that scant research evidence has existed on faith-based programs until recent decades (Delgado 2012; Eisenberg & Trusty 2002; Johnson 2002, 2011; Johnson & Larson 2003; Johnson, Larson, & Pitts 1997; Mears 2007; Zimmer 2005).

This historic gap in the research is partially attributed to a lack of study participants. Even on campuses where postrelease offenders form a sizable group, there are no universally accepted means to identify them, and they are often quite reticent to identify themselves due to a number of factors, including social stigma (i.e., "invisible stripes"), institutionalization, societal labeling, and the postrelease collateral consequences they face—all of which may also affect their willingness to attend events or access services created for them (Copenhaver, Edwards-Willey, & Byers 2007; Goffman 1968; Haney 2003; LeBel 2012; Pager, Western, & Bonikowski 2009; Paternoster & Iovanni 1989; Stoll & Bushway 2008). Doubtless these factors and other access-related challenges have contributed to the paucity of certain themes in the correctional literature, not the least of which have been the role of religious faith in the prison environment and the role of religious faith in the lives of offenders postrelease.

This qualitative study supplements the extant research by considering the postrelease role that religious faith played in the higher education transitions of a particular group of ex-offenders known as the Colson Scholars. Ex-offender scholarship programs, such as the need-based Charles W. "Chuck" Colson Scholarship program at Wheaton College, are exceedingly rare and are generally situated on faith-based campuses (Holding et al. 2010), but are essential to our understanding of ex-offenders' abilities to cope with transition associated with freedom following periods of incarceration. In order to establish sufficient context for this research, an introduction to postrelease realities of ex-offenders is provided. Following this introductory material, the liabilities the Colson Scholars identified are presented, and finally, the significant mitigating role that religious faith played as an asset, a coping mechanism, a rationale for disclosure, and a developmental outcome is explored. Implications for research and practice are offered subsequent to the findings.

Literature Review

Since 95 out of every 100 prisoners eventually reenter U.S. society, in-prison demographics closely mirror profiles of released offenders reentering local communities (Petersilia 2003). Persons of color, especially young African Americans from low socioeconomic backgrounds, are heavily overrepresented throughout correctional institutions, and a growing body of literature investigates the possible social, psychological, and political causes and ramifications of these racial disparities in the American criminal justice system (Alexander 2012; Tonry 2010). Joan Petersilia (2003, 21) illustrated the profile of the average U.S. prisoner as follows:

Today's inmate is likely to have been in custody several times before, has a lengthy history of alcohol and drug abuse, is more likely to be involved in gang activities and drug dealing, has probably experienced significant periods of unemployment and homelessness, and may have a physical or mental disability. Most of them have young children, with whom they hope to reunite after release, although in most cases, their children will have infrequently visited them during their incarceration. A significant number of inmates will have spent weeks, if not months, in solitary confinement or supermax prisons, devoid of human contact and prison program participation.

Indeed, inmates reentering society today will have served more time, be less educated, and be less marketable than those who have been released in previous cohorts (Pager 2007; Petersilia 2003). Ex-offenders seeking to enter educational programs in order to access employment are generally first-generation, underrepresented, low-income students who suffer from serious complications due to their high rates of illiteracy, learning disabilities, and mental/emotional/behavioral disorders, making them particularly high risk for attrition (Brazzell et al. 2009; Crayton & Neusteter 2008; Erisman & Contardo 2005; Falk & Blaylock 2010; Gorgol & Sponsler 2011; Harlow 2003; Leone, Wilson, & Krezmien 2008; Levin 2007; Petersilia 2003; Tewksbury, Erickson, & Taylor 2000). Although "little data are available on the involvement of formerly incarcerated individuals in educational programs in the community" (Brazzell et al. 2009, 12), even less is known about how faith might influence the transition into higher education for those who attempt it.

Religious Faith Characteristics

The religious faith observances of correctional populations have the potential to shed light on how this factor might influence in-prison experiences and postrelease behaviors. Federal chaplains surveyed by the United States Commission on Civil Rights (2008, 13) reported that just over two-thirds of the inmates in their spiritual care profess some sort of Christian faith (compared to 78 percent of the general population) while alternatively identification with "[non-Christian] faiths [is] higher among inmates than in the U.S. adult population." State chaplains reported similar adherence rates while expounding on the extrareligious challenges prisoners face postrelease (Boddie & Funk 2012). Seventy-five percent considered in-prison and postrelease religious programming "absolutely critical" to inmates' rehabilitation success, while nearly that same number also cited job resources, housing help, and quality job training as equally important, even naming substance abuse treatment and mental health treatment as *the two most critical factors* for successful prisoner reentry (Boddie & Funk 2012). In fact, a growing body of research suggests that well-rounded faith-based programs addressing these intersecting factors may be uniquely situated to provide a range of reentry supports to ex-offenders and may be more outcome-effective and cost-effective than similarly situated secular programs (Holding et al. 2010; Johnson 2011; O'Connor & Perreyclear 2002; Zimmer 2005).

Religious Faith and Criminality

According to Byron Johnson (2011, xi), "Faith-motivated individuals, faith-based organizations, and the transformative power of faith itself are proven keys in reducing crime and improving the effectiveness of our criminal justice system." Indeed, research suggests that in-prison religious activities are effective in helping change-motivated and solution-seeking prisoners understand their criminal culpability, replace antisocial tendencies with prosocial behaviors, adjust to abrupt and prolonged losses of freedom, and experience hope in spite of their circumstances (Camp et al. 2006; Clear & Sumter 2002; Kerley, Matthews, & Blanchard 2005; Zimmer 2005). Offenders involved in such in-prison faith-based programming have likewise spoken of spiritual transformation "consistent with [themes, behaviors and attitudes] thought to be essential in order to achieve rehabilitation" (Johnson 2011, 131). Research consistently shows that prisoners' increased involvement in religious activity while incarcerated has been associated with fewer in-prison infractions and disciplinary confinements (Clear & Sumter 2002; Kerley, Matthews, & Blanchard 2005; O'Connor & Perreyclear 2002).

Extant research also reveals longitudinal effects that suggest the benefits of religious involvement extend beyond prison walls and continue to play a critical role in offenders' desistance from criminal activity postrelease as measured by recidivism rate, or the rate at which former inmates are rearrested, reconvicted, or reincarcerated, generally within a three-year period (Eisenberg & Trusty 2002; Johnson & Larson 2003; Johnson, Larson, & Pitts 1997). Johnson (2011) reviewed 273 studies published between 1944 and 2010 relating religiosity variables to crime and delinquency variables, finding that 90 percent of the studies revealed an inverse relationship between the two. This result led him to conclude that a "faith-based program combining education, work, life skills training, mentoring, and aftercare . . . [can] influence in a paradigm-shifting way the prisoner reentry process . . . with the expectation that this approach will substantially enhance achieving the secular and correctional goal of rehabilitation" (116, 121).

Methodology

The purpose of this research was to fill critical gaps in the correctional education literature by investigating ex-offenders' experiences in higher education. A transition can be defined as "any event or nonevent that results in changed relationships, routines, assumptions, and roles" (Anderson, Goodman, &

Schlossberg 2011, 39). Nancy Schlossberg's (1984) transition theory provided a fitting interpretive framework through which to understand and classify participants' experiences with its structural emphases on *self, situation, supports,* and *strategies,* which aided the crafting of interview questions and the organizing of the participants' responses around the five key themes of investigation. These included (1) assets and liabilities, (2) coping mechanisms, (3) factors influencing disclosure of ex-offender status, (4) educational outcomes, and (5) ways in which Wheaton College provided or could have provided support.

Phenomenological Qualitative Inquiry and the Postpositivist Paradigm

Although phenomenological qualitative research was the most appropriate fit to answer the research questions centering on participants' perceptions of their lived experiences as Colson Scholars (Creswell 2012), my philosophical paradigm and its assumptions are more subjective and lead me to identify myself as a postpositivist researcher. The three quintessential postpositivist research tenets include (1) axiologically, a researcher's values inevitably influence the research questions and outcomes; that (2) epistemologically, a researcher's theory, hypotheses, or framework (i.e., a priori theory) inevitably influences the research; and that (3) ontologically, our understandings of reality are constructed and fragment apprehensions of a singular overarching reality or truth (Guba & Lincoln 1994; Merleau-Ponty 1962; Tashakkori & Teddlie 1998; Teddlie & Tashakkori 2011). Postpositivist assumptions and Merleau-Ponty (1962) phenomenological methods (i.e., with emphases on perceptions, bodily interaction with the world, and subjectivity) share similar perspectives and are entirely congruent (Clark 1998; Racher & Robinson 2003).

As a postpositivist, I understand that my identity, assumptions, and values regarding religious faith and criminality in my roles as a Christian and a criminal justice practitioner relate to my research. Although this means that my findings are incapable of being unbiased, I consistently attempted to own and identify those biases through processes of positionality and reflexivity. Surely I came to this project with basic beliefs as to the importance of faith in reentry and the role it plays in ex-offenders' lives, but I also knew that if I were to influence my participants' responses with my own ideas, the research would be unsound and unethical.

Subsequently, I closely and actively listened to my participants and their interpretations of reality in order to grasp their perspectives—while practicing epoché and bracketing my own perceptions—and do justice to their experiences (Jones, Torres, & Arminio 2013). Jones et al. (2013) explained epoché as the reflection and identification of one's preconceived notions relevant to the research and defined bracketing as the willful attempt to withhold judgment or appraisal of the research inquiry in focus by setting aside, or suspending those presumptions from affecting the research process. There are substantive disagreements to the extent researchers can truly practice epoché and bracketing, leaving Jones et al. (2013) to suggest that researchers might rather expose their preconceptions with as full of a disclosure as possible so that readers understand where the interests of the researcher may have interacted with the research process.

Research Setting and Context

Although the Colson Scholarship at Wheaton College is unique in its provision for education, life formation, and leadership training of ex-felons, it also fully covers tuition, room, and board for those who meet the application criteria and are selected by the scholarship committee (Institute for Prison Ministries 2016b). To qualify, an applicant must (1) be a Christian, (2) be an American citizen, (3) have a felony record, (4) be out of prison and established in a local church for at least one year, and (5) submit standardized test scores and transcripts (Institute for Prison Ministries 2016a). The application process also includes the submission of a completed application; a three-to-four paragraph essay including the individual's statement of faith, statement of goals, and statement of incarceration; incarceration and parole information releases and permission waivers; and three recommendations. Ineligible for the program are felony arsonists, felony sexual offenders, habitual violent offenders and felony offenders under psychiatric care or taking antipsychotic medication (Institute for Prison Ministries 2016a). Funded Scholars many enroll in any of Wheaton College's 40 major programs.

Wheaton College, in Wheaton, Illinois, is a selective private residential interdenominational college founded in 1860 (Benne 2001; Wheaton College 2016a). The college's mission is that it "serves Jesus Christ and advances His Kingdom through excellence in liberal arts and graduate programs that educate the whole person to build the church and benefit society worldwide" (Wheaton College 2016b, para. 2). As of 2016, Wheaton enrolls approximately 2,400 undergraduates and 480 graduate students who attend from all 50 U.S. states, 45 distinct countries, and over 55 church denominations. Twenty percent of Wheaton's collegians identify as American ethnic minority students. Wheaton is a top-ranked college by such prestigious entities as *The Fiske Guide to Colleges, Kiplinger, The Princeton Review, U.S. News and World Report, The Insider's Guide to the Colleges, Colleges That Change Lives, Forbes,* and *The Ultimate Guide to America's Best Colleges.* According to Wheaton College, only 20 percent of its full-time students in the 2014–2015 academic year were Pell Grant recipients. The Colson Scholarship certainly removes a significant financial barrier to college for students who receive it; based on a four-year tuition scale at the current rate, Colson Scholars' total financial award is estimated to be over a $165,000 value (Wheaton College 2016a).

Participant Recruitment and Selection

The sampling strategy for this study was criterion sampling (Creswell 2012), and the criterion was having completed a bachelor's degree at Wheaton College as a recipient of the Colson Scholarship. The early choice to delimit potential participants by this criterion allowed me to remove certificate-level-only students, masters-level-only students, noncompleting and current students from participation, narrowing the potential participant pool to 17 individuals to invite. No women were in the group of 17, meaning that no women would be represented in the final participants; while unfortunate, this should be considered more of a reality of incarcerated populations proportionally, built-in limitations on recruitment to women, and suspicions that women have differing primary priorities upon release than education.

Wheaton's liaison had contact information for 16 of the 17 men remaining and sent them an e-mail including my recruitment letter and informed consent form explaining the purpose of the study, the value of participants' responses, what they could expect, their rights and responsibilities, the risks involved, and a confidentiality pledge, all in accordance with approved research ethics protocols. Contacting potential participants through the institutional liaison protected their confidentiality, as the liaison did not know which Colson Scholars chose to participate and I never had information for those who did not participate. Participants also chose pseudonyms to protect their confidentiality; however, when certain demographic details appeared to have great potential for revealing participants' identities despite the pseudonym, those details were reported in aggregate form. Over the course of three weeks, potential participants received two invitation e-mails and one regular postal letter. Recruitment remained open three weeks, and within another month, six Scholars had chosen to participate in the three-hour interviews—an acceptable representation for phenomenological research given Morse's (1994) urging that no fewer than six participants be utilized and Creswell's (1998) range recommendation falling between 5 and 25.

Aggregate Participant Data

Despite the fact that only six individuals were interviewed, participants represented a surprisingly diverse demographic cross-section. As to race, three identified as Black, two White, and one Latino. One had graduated from high school, while the other five passed general education development tests (GEDs) while incarcerated. All entered Wheaton as full-time students averaging 34 years of age, and their attendance at Wheaton spans the four decades of the scholarship's existence. All participants entered Wheaton with transfer credits; as a result, the average stay at Wheaton was only three years.

The Colson Scholar participants' majors spanned Biblical and Theological Studies, Communication, Sociology, Christian Education, Clinical Psychology, and Evangelism. All participants lived on campus while at Wheaton; two entered with families, three were unmarried students, and one was married and subsequently divorced while at Wheaton. Currently, five of the interviewees are still in their first marriages, while the one who was divorced at Wheaton has since remarried.

These six Scholar participants are either fathers or stepfathers to 17 children; 3 of these are young children, 6 are teenagers, and 8 are adults. None of their adult children have attended Wheaton. All participants reported working while earning their degrees, averaging 24 hours weekly. Currently, none of the participants receives governmental assistance, and all are employed: two in prison ministry, two as owner-operators (one blue-collar, one white-collar), one in higher education, and one in independent contractor work as a local delivery driver. Only one participant recidivated after his Wheaton experience.

Data Collection and Analysis

Participants chose interview locations near their homes, and I began the face-to-face interviews by reviewing the parameters, risks, and benefits of the informed consent form. I followed the interview protocol that had undergone faculty scrutiny and multiple revisions until it contained questions I believed were well-crafted to foster rich feedback and facilitate answering the research questions. The semistructured interview format not only enhanced my understanding of participants' experiences, but also allowed for misconceptions to be clarified as they occurred and provided space for the acceptance and support of disclosures (Moustakas 1994). All interviews were completed during summer 2014.

I returned attention to the practice of epoché and bracketing as I reviewed the interview transcriptions and throughout the content data analysis and synthesis processes, including the phenomenological reduction, imaginative variation, and textural description phases (Jones, Torres, & Arminio 2013; Merleau-Ponty 1962; Moustakas 1994; Racher & Robinson 2003; van Manen 1990). I immersed myself in the data and manually themed, coded, and categorized the six interview transcripts (Creswell 2012), identifying deductive codes related to Schlossberg's (1984) transition theory and inductive codes not identified with the theory.

Once these themes were gathered and identified, I engaged the participants in a "member-checking" discussion to ascertain whether or not I had genuinely captured their experiences (van Manen 1990). Five of the six participants gave me the "phenomenological nod" that they saw their own experiences in the heart of the findings as captured (Munhall 1994), although one participant failed to respond to two e-mail attempts to contact him. The other five participants' consistent approval of the themes is just one measure of quality supporting the trustworthiness of my findings.

Measures of Quality and Trustworthiness

The quality of this research is undergirded by my graduate-level study of qualitative research philosophy and methods, my prisoner reentry research work leading a data collection team conducting interviews across 15 Ohio correctional facilities, and the in-depth risk classification interviews I have conducted with several hundred inmates over my 13-year correctional career. I also enhanced the quality of my findings by paying rigorous attention to detail throughout the study, and by applying the four parallel criteria of trustworthiness: credibility, transferability, dependability, and confirmability (Lincoln & Guba 1985). In this study, credibility was enhanced by peer debriefing, intercoder reliability checking, member checking, and researcher reflexivity through informal journaling (Creswell 2012; Guba & Lincoln 1989). Transferability was addressed by providing thick descriptions of the research setting and context and thoroughly describing the Colson Scholarship (Creswell 2012; Guba & Lincoln 1989). Dependability was increased by documenting the decisions I made in a researcher journal throughout the process, providing thick description while acknowledging my own researcher biases, using strong quotes, employing deductive and inductive coding, and conducting external audits to support the findings (Creswell 2012; Guba & Lincoln 1989; Saldana 2009). Finally, confirmability was improved by performing audits that ensured that the data and findings originated from the research interviews, documenting my biases and experiences in my journal, noting the logic behind the conclusions I reached, increasing immersion in the relevant data, providing a high level of attention to subjectivity and reflexivity, and member checking the findings to discern whether I adequately interpreted and represented what the participants offered as events and experiences significant to their higher education transitions (Creswell 2012; Guba & Lincoln 1989; Morrow 2005).

Potential Limitations and Ethical Considerations

Despite this level of care, several potential limitations may have negatively affected the quality of the study, including a lack of sufficient prolonged engagement, the potential for researcher bias, and the potential for a power and privilege dynamic (Creswell 2012). Prolonged engagement over repeated visits with participants (who were dispersed as far as Florida, Massachusetts, and Illinois) was impractical due to the project's time constraints and my commitment to interview the participants in person, although multiple interviews may have enhanced the findings. Also, I hold many biases from my experiences as a Christian and as a criminal justice practitioner; and, although I took great pains throughout the research process to bracket these preconceptions and keep them from projecting themselves onto the participants' responses and my representation of their experiences, it is possible that these biases had some mitigating effect on the research. To abate this possibility, I extensively utilized peer checks and expert reviews of the themes, codes, categories, and findings to ensure that I was not omitting or overvaluing certain responses because of personal bias. Finally, a subtle power-privilege differential may have been present, especially among participants who may have had negative experiences within the criminal justice system, although I did not share my correctional experience until after the end of the interview, if at all. There's also the possibility that invitees who received the scholarship but recidivated may have been too ashamed to participate, or that invitees who may have had bad experiences at Wheaton may have refused to participate due to misinterpreting the study as a pro-Wheaton marketing attempt (since the invitation came from the Wheaton gatekeeper), although I have no evidence that either of these affected the quality of the findings.

Findings

The prominent and essential role the participants reported their religious faith playing throughout their transitional process provided insight into its meaning for them as individuals and how powerful such a variable might be for the reentry of the greater ex-offender population. The research revealed that faith was significant to the participants' higher education transition in four distinct ways: as an asset offsetting a host of perceived liabilities, as a coping mechanism helping participants persist despite these perceived liabilities, as a reason for the disclosure of participants' criminal past, and finally as a developmental outcome of the higher education transition. The findings begin with a longitudinal look at participants' stories—and more specifically the dysfunction and abuse of their upbringings—to provide historic context to their perceived liabilities.

Histories Marked by Dysfunction and Abuse

Although not every participant experienced abuse in his home, four of the six shared harrowing stories of verbal, emotional, physical, or sexual abuse, or a combination. Often these tales of abuse were exacerbated by caregivers' substance abuse, and continued to affect participants deeply even into adulthood. Alpha described himself as growing up in a "pretty dysfunctional family."

> My parents divorced when I was ten. . . . [Mom was] a single mother with seven children. . . . My father had an alcohol problem. . . . That's the kind of environment that we grew up in. . . . An example, my father—after my mother had left him, when he found out where he thought we lived—he [drove] by and shot out the windows of the house next door. So, that level of dysfunction. . . . [even] going to the bars on the weekends with them.

Alpha elaborated that this lifestyle left the children to fend for themselves, bouncing from house to house and boarding with whatever relative or friend would accept them.

Nate experienced a similar level of familial dysfunction exacerbated by bouts of physical abuse:

> I was taking Ritalin when I was five years old. . . . My whole family . . . [told me] I was a retard. So, I grew up and that's what I thought of myself. . . . I ran away. . . . I had no reason to come home. . . . My stepdad just wanted to beat me all the time. . . . Your whole life you're told that you're never going to be anything. . . . My dad just . . . just feared for me more than anything, that somehow the problems I was having as a child, would really affect me as an adult, as they did. But he was hoping that somehow through discipline he could help me. . . . I just think that for him the discipline became fear and just got out of hand.

Nate described how this mistreatment left him seeking the love and acceptance absent from his childhood, leading him into the drug subculture, prison, and ultimately causing him to struggle upon his arrival at Wheaton: "I simply didn't have any framework in my emotional life or in my experiences for being a friend, or for making friends [and] for letting people in, because all my life I had been running from people."

John gave a similarly heartbreaking account of emotional neglect and abandonment and the effect this lack of parental guidance and love had on his young life. He described a father who left shortly after he was born and a mother who gave him away to a grandmother when he was young. After several more adults in his life deserted him, John concluded that it was actually his mother's initial abandonment that left him searching for purpose:

> I had the question, "Why did I even exist?" Like when I was twelve . . . I was in a foster home, and I [went] for a visit with my mom, and I knew she didn't want me. . . . I'm twelve years old thinking, "God . . . why did you create me to live here, suffer, die, and go to hell?" That was my basic worldview. It was an ultimate question. . . . I didn't feel worthy of existence. . . . My mother had never said she loved me—well, she told me once when I was thirteen, when somebody told her to tell me. And she hadn't said it [again] until I was thirty-two. So from thirteen to thirty-two, no love.

These emotionally dysfunctional upbringings often resulted in substance abuse and other destructive behaviors; criminal arrest was perhaps inevitable, and at least four of the six participants identified themselves as drug offenders. The connection between these upbringings and substance abuse was clearest in the case of Shawn, who specifically referenced episodes of childhood sexual abuse and felt that these abuses resulted in posttraumatic stress disorder, leading him to self-medicate with drugs and alcohol, and eventually incarceration. The trajectory of most Colson Scholar participants seemed to include dysfunctional upbringings in abusive environments and/or abuses of controlled substances, providing context for the other liabilities they identified.

Compounding Liabilities

Schlossberg (1984) categorized the personal and demographic characteristics and psychological resources most likely to influence the healthy sense of self and well-being of individuals in transition as "assets" and "liabilities." The liabilities participants mentioned having influenced their higher education transitional process included aforementioned histories of dysfunction and abuse, underdeveloped educational skills, a campus environment they felt exacerbated these liabilities, factors related to age and family, financial instability and indebtedness, and relationship-building difficulties. Participants' lack of academic skills, underestimation of Wheaton's rigor, and overestimation of their adaptability revealed their limited educational exposure—especially during classroom discussion where their feelings of inadequacy and difference seriously hindered their engagement and performance. Several factors that accompanied Scholars' increased ages also intensified scholastic challenges and family tensions, such as deaths in the family (and time redirected to funerals, grieving, and estate settling), greater sleep deprivation, lower energy levels, and increased pressure to achieve multiple marriage and family goals simultaneously—meaning academic learning paralleled learning how to be a husband, a father, an employee, and even relearning what it meant to be free.

Despite also identifying marital and family relationships as an asset, participants felt that these relationships were liabilities in that they placed valid claims on the Scholar's discretionary time and energy, leaving married participants to feel guilty for their study time, and single participants to observe that their married peers may have "missed out" on Wheaton student life and community. Incoming financial instability or indebtedness exacerbated this dynamic as time spent gaining and maintaining employment to support one's family could have been invested in the pursuit of academic success or family and campus relationship building. Psychological distance between participants and student peers created by gaps in age, personal histories, emotional capacity, life stages, academic preparation, financial resources, and common interests presented significant barriers to relationship building. According to Nate, these liabilities necessitated overcoming emotional dysfunction and disavowing past manipulative motives in order to experience healing and develop quality relationships. All Colson Scholar participants reported some combination of these concurrent liabilities weighing heavily on their transitions. Although many factors helped these participants to persist—secular and sacred—none seemed to play as significant and consistent a role as religious faith.

The Role of Faith in Colson Scholars' Higher Education Transitions

Against this backdrop of compounding liabilities, the Colson Scholar participants described faith playing multiple significant roles in their higher education transition. The interviews revealed that various aspects of religious faith played four distinct roles of influence for these Scholars, including (1) as a liability-offsetting asset, (2) as a coping mechanism, (3) as a reason for disclosure, and (4) as a developmental outcome.

Faith as a Liability-Offsetting Asset

Participants' liabilities could have been insurmountable if not offset by the intact strengths that aided them in familiarizing themselves with the new norms and expectations of college life (i.e., their assets). Although they mentioned several of these assets—including family and community support, wisdom and maturation that came with age, greater preparation for college-level coursework than their institutionalized peers, and dedication to their goal of earning their college degree—no asset was as predominantly mentioned as their faith. Participants consistently described how their active faith led them to attempt college, sustained them throughout their stay, and prepared them for life after graduation. Nate described his conversion as the very impetus for his application:

> I was about as through with living as a person can possibly be . . . in a holding facility . . . all by myself . . . no sound other than my own heartbeat . . . . It's when God called my name; and told me He loved me, wanted to heal me, wanted to change my heart and give me a new life, and all I had to do was surrender. . . . To finally realize that, that God loved me and had a purpose for my life, was just amazing. . . . In that moment it changed everything about my life . . . 180 degrees. . . . I would have never [gone to college] except because of my faith [and] never gotten through it except because of my faith. I mean, it's my faith in God that there is something far greater than us at work in life, and God has a plan and a purpose. And the beauty of our salvation in the gospel is that God is inviting us to join Him in the work that He's in the world doing, and that we can participate in that. He actually calls us into it, wants us to join in the labor. . . . It's from that perspective that I went to school.

John also reported faith as the primary catalyst for his choice to study theology at Wheaton:

> It was taking too long to develop a thorough knowledge of what I believe as a Christian and why and how to articulate it. . . . Having a theology background would enable me to be a better thinker, a better explainer of my faith. . . . That was probably the key influence. . . . Once I got hold of what it meant to be a Christian, to live in Christ, I got a taste of that, then I grew hungrier and hungrier and hungrier. . . . I was able to interact with people from different worldviews and religious perspectives, and I was able to lead certain people to Christ. . . . That was a very exciting period in my life spiritually speaking, and so that was like a chief motivator, like a catalyst to propel me. . . . So going to Wheaton was kind of a Mecca . . . for me in terms of my spiritual development and education . . . it was like a journey, spiritually speaking. . . . So when . . . I applied to Wheaton . . . that was the main thing that strengthened us for the process, because we were going to be leaving our comfort zone, leaving our network, our support groups, and going to an unfamiliar place. At the same time, looking at the next level where God was taking us, that was a spiritual high.

Jonah concurred that his faith foundation, and the opportunity to grow that faith, gave him strength and was central to his decision to come to Wheaton:

> I think faith had a big part for me. I was not necessarily even thinking about going back to college and so going to a Christian college was a big motivating factor. If this had been a scholarship to, I don't know, Duke, I probably would have said no. And I know that sounds somewhat foolish, but . . . this being a Christian institution led me to believe that I would be able to in some way wrestle with my faith even more. . . . I felt that Wheaton College with the reputation it had of being a great institution of faith and learning . . . would be an awesome opportunity to continue to just learn more about God. So my faith played a big part in me even coming here. . . . [The scholarship] is kind of like you won a lottery, you know? I wasn't really even playing a number. And so for me that was one of those God things.

Alpha described his faith as his relationship with Jesus Christ that existed long before his arrival at Wheaton and gave him a foundation of strength from which to persevere:

> [Faith] prepared me for endurance, and gave perspective, a lens from which to just encounter life. . . . The dynamics of my family life never take away the personal responsibility for personal action, but when you look at people's behavior in a vacuum, obviously external influences can control that socioeconomic environment that they're nurtured in and it tends to have an

impact. . . . If you were to look at my extended family, you'll see that dysfunction generation after generation and what makes the difference—fortunately in my case—it was being introduced to the gospel through some family members and other people that God placed in my life that produced that light of hope for change. . . . a relationship with the Lord Jesus Christ—and that change which was there pre-Wheaton.

Participants repeatedly cited their faith as an asset that would offset their varied liabilities, and the significance and centrality they attributed to their faith cannot be overstated. Faith not only helped lead them to Wheaton, but also helped them persevere once at the college—revealing that their faith was not only a liability-offsetting asset but also a vital coping mechanism.

Spiritual Resources and Religious Service as Coping Mechanisms

Individuals cope with stressors by employing psychological resources and other coping mechanisms that act as basic strategies from which their relationships to transitions can be effectively managed (Anderson, Goodman, & Schlossberg 2011; Schlossberg 1984). Learning the coping strategies this group of underrepresented students employed to counter the stressors they faced may provide previously unknown insights into the coping of the general ex-offender population.

Rigorous academic demand at Wheaton drove the participants to develop coping resources that included seeking out tutors and professors and growing in self-sufficiency and self-efficacy. Additionally, participants named the spiritual resources of prayer, the guidance of the Holy Spirit, and the grace of God as distinct factors encouraging their progress through higher education. Throughout academic challenges, employment responsibilities, and familial health issues, their faith and spirituality kept them stable. For example, Nate asserted that he found spiritual help in his quiet times with God: "If I didn't stay on my face praying all the time . . . I would have never made it through there. . . . I know that it was in the quietness of those times and in my devotions that I had every day that God used them to keep me on task and to keep me inspired and encouraged."

The Scholars interviewed also emphasized seeing religious service as the primary reason for their higher education pursuits and as a significant contributor to their ability to persevere. Participants described the pursuit of education as an opportunity to please God, represent Christ well, represent ex-offenders well, and set a good example for their children or for future Colson Scholars. John elaborated that

several times I felt like withdrawing, but what motivated me to stay was the scholarship is a tremendous gift and I didn't want to squander [it]. I thought about people coming behind me, you know? If I don't finish, if I don't do a good job, they may shut the program down or somebody else that could have benefitted wouldn't because of my waste. . . . So I want to represent Christ and the Colson Scholarship in a way that seeks to glorify God. . . . Some people don't appreciate what they're given, they just squander it and blow it. And as convicts, you'd expect that. You'd expect somebody to get discouraged and give up. So I had a lot riding on me.

Adaptability became an essential characteristic these pioneering Colson Scholars embraced for the greater good. After sharing horror stories of roommate problems, Jonah cited serving others as a reason and means to cope:

It humbled me. . . . I had to kind of temper myself and not complain. . . . I just endured a lot so that the scholarship could live. . . . I felt like the cause was bigger than me. . . . For my family I needed to do it, for me, and for God as well, [and for] ex-offenders everywhere. . . . I also wanted to really just do good even for a kid coming out of the ghetto. . . . All those things were motivating factors for me.

The other Scholars interviewed were also cognizant of how their successes and failures might affect ex-offenders who would later attempt the program. Kenneth saw himself as a trailblazer whose motivation of equipping himself for Christian service caused him to press on:

I saw myself as a pioneer, an ex-convict coming to the campus of Wheaton College which is supposed to be the Harvard of Christian schools, you know? . . . You don't get an education for yourself; you get it to serve others. . . . So quitting was never an option. . . . I dedicated myself to study because I knew I couldn't fail, and I had to think about the guys coming behind me. . . . As Christians we have to be equipped to serve others, so higher education was a vehicle through which I would become much better equipped.

The employment of spiritual resources and the goal of self-development for Christian service were coping mechanisms participants identified that counteracted their stressors and motivated them to persist despite their challenging liabilities. Not only did the faith factor serve as a liability-offsetting asset and a coping mechanism, but it also gave participants a reason to share their stories of triumph against all odds.

Spiritual Transformation as a Reason for Disclosure

Among the rationales participants gave for disclosing their criminal pasts were sharing their spiritual transformations, representing their peers behind bars, offering hope to others, and embracing their self-redefinitions. The primary purpose for disclosing was spiritual motivation, as participants described their stories as merely a part they played in God's grand narrative. Participants seemed to welcome invitations to speak of their pasts, seeing others' natural curiosity as an opportunity to speak freely of their spiritual conversions. Kenneth described this dynamic as follows:

> As long as we use [our stories] for the advancement of the gospel, why not disclose? So I was very open [and] vocal about where I came from. I knew I was representing Christ. . . . I had no problem whatsoever if people knew who I used to be, and they had to find out who I am now—in Christ! It's a big difference. . . . Romans 1:16 [says], "Don't be ashamed of the gospel for it is the power of God, for anybody, for everyone who believes." So I took that to heart!

Similarly, Shawn said such invitations gave him "an opportunity to talk about how Jesus had transformed my life from this scumbag who spent most of his time . . . smoking coke and drinking and partying all day and all night, to what and who I am now." As the interviews progressed, it became evident that faith served not only as an asset, coping mechanism, and reason for disclosure; it also helped answer life's "big" questions—a concept integrally tied to worldview development.

Faith and Worldview Development as Outcomes

Schlitz, Vieten, and Miller (2010) described a worldview as a complex and coherent conceptual framework that develops over time, and includes beliefs, assumptions, attitudes, values, and ideas that influence how individuals comprehend and interpret reality. James Olthuis (1985) suggested that there are universal ultimate questions and answers regarding our identity and purpose, the existence and source of deity and the true path to happiness, that constitute our worldview frameworks and give our lives context, direction, and meaning. He held that these worldviews were often based more on faith than deliberate rational thought and that they morphed "as faith deepens, as insight into reality grows, and as individuals and cultures themselves move on to new stages in their development" (9).

Participants consistently reported entering Wheaton with an underdeveloped understanding of a faith-centric worldview and that the biblical and theological perspective they gained at the college bolstered their faith, significantly shaping their worldviews. Alpha submitted that

> going to Wheaton . . . helps you grasp and wrestle with those questions: Who am I? Where did I come from? Who is God, and what role does that

play in my life? What am I supposed to do with this life? It helped answer some of those questions, and equipped you to be able to think and understand the world that you live in and how it works. . . . [to] answer the theological questions of who we are and what God is requiring of us.

Jonah agreed that "my faith . . . the college has just enlarged that in such a way that I'm not even sure I can measure it."

Wheaton provided participants with access to the tools, time, and environment for growth in theological awareness, religious faith, and critical thought in order to formulate their worldviews while answering life's deep and abiding "big questions" (Parks 2000). John elaborated:

[Wheaton professors] talked about spiritual formation quite a bit. . . . It wasn't just about the learning [but] the overall picture. The term they used is "faith and learning." . . . That was in the forefront of our minds. And we did devotions in class, and professors prayed for the students. . . . It gave me a sense of purpose and it kind of completes something that was missing there for a long time and answers a question for me . . . [from] when I was 12, "Why am I even here?" And that's one of the major worldview questions people ask. . . . Wheaton has helped to shape me in that way.

Nate added that through exposure to the type of critical theological thinking that Wheaton offered, students grew more comfortable applying theology to life in order to answer these ultimate questions through biblically informed worldviews:

The spiritual formation that I received as a result of my education at Wheaton is—priceless. The very way that I think about life was really formed through my being exposed to critical . . . deep and passionate theological thinking. . . . Researching and reading the ancient authors and the early church fathers, and really seeing how the work of theology was done over a long period of time, and being able to know that you can stake your life on it, that has changed me. As opposed to before I went to Wheaton . . . I was really full of passion and zeal, but no knowledge. . . . I just couldn't believe that, after everything I had done and all the people I had hurt, that God was really at work in my life to provide opportunities for me to grow as a person and to learn, and to educate my heart and my mind. . . . So to be given the chance to really grow and be exposed, and to have my faith sharpened, and really be able to perceive deep things, and scriptural truths, and theological truths, is just a phenomenal opportunity. . . . Receiving a higher education is a rare and incredible privilege . . . [and even rarer is] the kind of education that's available at Wheaton College.

Alpha described the importance of this faith development to life after Wheaton as follows: "You transition to the real world and you take all that stuff you had there and apply it. . . . That [faith] is still able to maintain you and keep you on course." Nate also explained how his Wheaton experience continues to have a pervasive effect on his faith development: "Everything . . . challenged my faith, informed my faith, convicted my faith, and stretched my faith. . . . It affects every way I think in my life today because of the information . . . and the challenges and the knowledge [to which] I was exposed." Indeed, the faith development that a Wheaton education encouraged remained long after the graduation ceremonies concluded. Jonah even felt this faith development drove him to minister to others post-Wheaton:

> I have an understanding of [God] because someone else helped me get it, so . . . I think I'll die trying to help other people get a better understanding of . . . ultimate truth. . . . Maybe I will go out one day and minister to a homeless guy and he'll remove himself from the streets, and become a disciple and then go disciple. . . . It's far-fetched, but it's like, when people have purpose, I just think their response is different, and you need educated people to actually give it to them—the blind can't lead the blind.

Implications for Research and Practice

Understanding the role of faith in participants' higher education transitions not only fills a critical gap in the extant research, but also has implications for future research and practice. For future research, two inquiries birthed from this research seem most salient: (1) How might faith development theoretical models look differently for ex-offender students? and (2) How does the Christian-identification scholarship requirement affect promotion and recruitment? In addition to these suggestions, implications for practice pertaining to recidivism and potential scholarship replication are offered.

Implication for Research

Extant models of student development theory (e.g., Fowler's 1981 stages of faith development) may not adequately reveal how ex-offenders' religious faith develops following periods of incarceration. On one hand, the effects of institutionalization and the embrace of the prison code (Goffman 1961; Haney 2003; Johnson 2011) may stunt potential Colson Scholars' faith development while incarcerated so that they are not in age-typical stages upon release from prison. On the other, the variety and regularity of faith-based offerings and time available to attend them inside prison combined with the high level of introspection and religious motivation generally descriptive of this particular population, may actually result in potential Scholars having a more robust faith development than their peers upon release (Maruna, Wilson, & Curran 2006).

Second, the Colson Scholarship currently exists on a Christian liberal arts college campus with Christian identification as a qualification; although not unusual, the stipulations placed on private donor-endowed scholarships at niche-serving institutions doubtless have recruitment ramifications. Federal chaplains report that nearly one-third of the inmate populations under their spiritual care profess no religious faith or some religious faith other than a form of Christianity (United States Commission on Civil Rights 2008), which categorically excludes them from scholarship consideration; more research is needed to ascertain what secular and alternative faith options might exist for these individuals. Future research could also identify how the scholarship opportunity is shared with potential candidates and how effectively the program is able to draw qualified applicants for admission. Since 77 percent of state chaplains report high incidence of "religious [identification] switching" (Boddie & Funk 2012), the possibility of feigned short-term conversions for the purpose of scholarship eligibility also exists.

Implication for Practice

The first implication for practice pertains to recidivism. The five Scholars interviewed who did not recidivate consistently cited personal dispositions and spiritual resources as the determining factors, while the Scholar who did recidivate (technically giving this participant pool a 17 percent recidivism rate) suggested that an embittered Colson Scholar dropout influenced him toward criminal activity. That faith may have played a role in the five postrelease success stories is certainly not inconsistent with the extant literature; however, caution should be exercised against making broad statements regarding faith's impact on recidivism based on this study as it provides little direct information regarding the specific connection between the two variables, nor was it methodologically designed to do so (Gehring 2000). It would also be inappropriate to utilize this particular study as proof positive that higher education in a faith-based setting results in lowered recidivism for several specific reasons: (1) participants self-selected into this study (potentially introducing self-selection bias), (2) recidivism for noninterviewed Colson Scholars may vary, (3) individual characteristics known to affect recidivism were not controlled, (4) sample size was small, (5) participants attended the program across various decades and had diverse interactions, (6) participants had extremely variant criminal records, (7) no direct questions related to factors influencing recidivism were in the interview protocol, and (8) there are similar secular programs to which the Colson Scholarship can be compared.

A second implication for practice pertains to participants' interest in scholarship replication. For now, the question remains whether or not campuses of other faith identities or even secular campuses would provide similar spiritual supports and theological content to what the Colson Scholar participants reported as essential to their faith and worldview development at Wheaton. Most Scholars interviewed believed expansion to other institutional types was possible, although they felt successful replication would require the host institution to develop Wheaton's pervasive emphases of genuine empathy, community belonging, redemptive belief, spiritual formation, social justice, high-level faculty involvement, and supportive infrastructure, which they believed ensured the scholarship's success over time. A few felt that the program might be less successful at secular institutions, although two participants disagreed, believing that secular campuses would provide Scholars with more diverse faculty, more diverse student bodies, and greater access to higher education for those who qualified but were not academically competitive enough for Wheaton. Participants cited reasons for expansion, including (1) limited educational opportunities for ex-offenders, (2) belief in the possibility of change, (3) an opportunity for those who have been blessed to give back to others less fortunate, (4) an opportunity to effect change for a worthy population, and (5) enabling future Scholars to attempt higher education while remaining geographically close to already established healthy reentry networks. One participant warned against short-circuiting proper risk management practices for the purpose of rapid duplication.

Time will tell whether the benefits replication could bring will outweigh the risks. Whether certain institutional types are best-suited to support the complex role and development of religious faith in the lives of ex-offender scholarship recipients also remains to be discovered and documented. Meanwhile, the Colson Scholarship at Wheaton College provides situation and context to the influential role religious faith can play in former convicts' reentry transition to noncriminal lifestyles in community through college participation.

Bibliography

Alexander, Michelle. *The New Jim Crow: Mass Incarceration in the Age of Colorblindness.* New York: New Press, 2012.

Anderson, Mary, Jane Goodman, & Nancy K. Schlossberg. *Counseling Adults in Transition: Linking Schlossberg's Theory with Practice in a Diverse World* (4th ed.). New York: Springer, 2011.

Benne, Robert. *Quality with Soul: How Six Premier Colleges and Universities Keep Faith with their Religious Traditions.* Grand Rapids, MI: Eerdmans, 2001.

Boddie, Stephanie C., & Cary Funk. "Religion in Prisons: A 50-State Survey of Prison Chaplains." Technical Report. Pew Forum on Religion & Public Life, 2012. http://www.pewforum.org/2012/03/22/prison-chaplains-exec

Brazzell, Diana, Anna Crayton, Debbie A. Mukamal, Amy L. Solomon, & Nicole Lindahl. "From the Classroom to the Community: Exploring the Role of Education during Incarceration and Reentry." Paper presented at the John Jay Reentry Roundtable on Education, New York, March 31, 2009. http://www.urban.org/publications/411963.html

Camp, Scott D., Jody Klein-Saffran, Okyun Karl Kwon, Dawn M. Daggett, & Victoria Joseph. "An Exploration into Participation in a Faith-Based Prison Program." *Criminology & Public Policy* 5, no. 3 (2006): 529–570.

Clark, Alexander M. "The Qualitative-Quantitative Debate: Moving from Positivism and Confrontation to Post-Positivism and Reconciliation." *Journal of Advanced Nursing* 27, no. 6 (1998): 1242–1249.

Clear, Todd R., & Melvina T. Sumter. "Prisoners, Prison, and Religion: Religion and Adjustment to Prison." *Journal of Offender Rehabilitation* 35, no. 3–4 (2002): 125–156.

Copenhaver, Anna, Tina L. Edwards-Willey, & Bryan D. Byers. "Journeys in Social Stigma: The Lives of Formerly Incarcerated Felons in Higher Education." *Journal of Correctional Education* 58, no. 3 (2007): 268–283.

Crayton, Anna, & Suzanne Rebecca Neusteter. "The Current State of Correctional Education." Paper presented at the John Jay Reentry Roundtable on Education, New York, March 31, 2008. http://www.urban.org/projects/reentry-roundtable/roundtable10.cfm

Creswell, John W. *Qualitative Inquiry and Research Design: Choosing among Five Traditions.* Thousand Oaks, CA: Sage, 1998.

Creswell, John W. *Qualitative Inquiry and Research Design: Choosing among Five Approaches* (3rd ed.). Thousand Oaks, CA: Sage, 2012.

Delgado, Melvin. *Prisoner Reentry at Work: Adding Business to the Mix.* Boulder, CO: Lynne Rienner, 2012.

Eisenberg, Michael, & Brittani Trusty. "Overview of the InnerChange Freedom Initiative: The Faith-Based Prison Program within the Texas Department of Criminal Justice." Technical Report. Texas Criminal Justice Policy Council, 2002. http://www.lbb.state.tx.us/Public_Safety_Criminal_Justice/Reports/IFI.pdf

Erisman, Wendy, & Jeanne B. Contardo. "Learning to Reduce Recidivism: A 50-State Analysis of Postsecondary Correctional Education Policy." Technical Report. The Institute for Higher Education Policy, 2005. http://www.ihep.org/sites/default/files/uploads/docs/pubs/learningreducerecidivism.pdf

Falk, Charles F., & Bruce K. Blaylock. "Strategically Planning Campuses for the 'Newer Students' in Higher Education." *Academy of Educational Leadership Journal* 14, no. 3 (2010): 15–38.

Fowler, James W. *Stages of Faith: The Psychology of Human Development and the Quest for Meaning.* San Francisco: Harper & Row, 1981.

Gehring, Tom. "Recidivism as a Measure of Correctional Education Program Success." *Journal of Correctional Education* 51, no. 2 (2000): 197–205.

Goffman, Erving. *Asylums: Essays on the Social Situation of Mental Patients and Other Inmates.* Garden City, NY: Anchor Books, 1961.

Goffman, Erving. *Stigma: Notes on the Management of Spoiled Identity.* Englewood Cliffs, NJ: Prentice Hall, 1968.

Gorgol, Laura E., & Brian A. Sponsler. "Unlocking Potential: Results of a National Survey of Postsecondary Education in State Prisons." Technical Report. Institute for Higher Education Policy, 2011. http://www.ihep.org/sites/default /files/uploads/docs/pubs/unlocking_potential-psce_final_report_may _2011.pdf

Guba, Egon G., & Yvonna S. Lincoln. *Fourth Generation Evaluation.* Newbury Park, CA: Sage, 1989.

Guba, Egon G., & Yvonna S. Lincoln. "Competing Paradigms in Qualitative Research." In Norman K. Denzin & Yvonna S. Lincoln (Eds.), *Handbook of Qualitative Research (pp. 105–117).* Thousand Oaks, CA: Sage, 1994.

Haney, Craig. "The Psychological Impact of Incarceration: Implications for Post-Prison Adjustment." In Jeremy Travis & Michelle Waul (Eds.), *Prisoners Once Removed: The Impact of Incarceration and Reentry on Children, Families, and Communities (pp. 33–66).* Washington, DC: Urban Institute Press, 2003.

Harlow, Caroline Wolf. *Education and Correctional Populations.* Bureau of Justice Statistics. NCJ 195670. Washington, DC, 2003.

Holding, Cory, Trace Dace, Simon Schocken, & Rebecca Ginsburg (Eds.). "Prison Higher Education Programs: An Incomplete Assessment." The Education Justice Project, University of Illinois at Urbana-Champaign. Unpublished manuscript, 2010.

Institute for Prison Ministries 2016a. "Applying for a Colson Scholarship." Accessed February 20. Billy Graham Center for Evangelism at Wheaton College. http://www.wheaton.edu/BGCE/Training-Ministries/Prisons-Corrections /IPM/Colson-Scholarship/Apply

Institute for Prison Ministries 2016b. "The Charles W. Colson Scholarship." Accessed February 20. Billy Graham Center for Evangelism at Wheaton College. http://www.wheaton.edu/BGCE/Training-Ministries/Prisons-Corr ections/IPM/Colson-Scholarship

Johnson, Byron R. "Assessing the Impact of Religious Programs and Prison Industry on Recidivism: An Exploratory Study." *Texas Journal of Corrections* 28 (2002): 7–11.

Johnson, Byron R. *More God, Less Crime: Why Faith Matters and How It Could Matter More.* West Conshohocken, PA: Templeton Press, 2011.

Johnson, Byron R., & David B. Larson. *The InnerChange Freedom Initiative: A Preliminary Evaluation of a Faith-Based Prison Program.* Philadelphia: University of Pennsylvania Center for Research on Religion and Urban Civil Society, 2003.

Johnson, Byron R., David B. Larson, & Timothy C. Pitts. "Religious Programs, Institutional Adjustment, and Recidivism among Former Inmates in Prison Fellowship Programs." *Justice Quarterly* 14, no. 1 (1997): 145–166.

Jones, Susan R., Vasti Torres, & Jan Arminio. *Negotiating the Complexities of Qualitative Research in Higher Education: Fundamental Elements and Issues* (2nd ed.). New York: Routledge, 2013.

Kerley, Kent R., Todd L. Matthews, & Troy C. Blanchard. "Religiosity, Religious Participation, and Negative Prison Behaviors." *Journal for the Scientific Study of Religion* 44, no. 4 (2005): 443–457.

LeBel, Thomas P. "Invisible Stripes? Formerly Incarcerated Persons' Perceptions of Stigma." *Deviant Behavior* 33, no. 2 (2012): 89–107.

Leone, Peter E., Michael Wilson, & Michael P. Krezmien. "Understanding and Responding to the Education Needs of Special Populations in Adult Corrections." Paper presented at the John Jay Reentry Roundtable on Education, New York, March 31, 2008. http://www.urban.org/projects/reentry-roundtable/roundtable10.cfm

Levin, John S. *Nontraditional Students and Community Colleges: The Conflict of Justice and Neoliberalism.* New York: Palgrave MacMillan, 2007.

Lincoln, Yvonna S., & Egon G. Guba. *Naturalistic Inquiry.* Beverly Hills, CA: Sage, 1985.

Maruna, Shadd, Louise Wilson, & Kathryn Curran. "Why God Is Often Found behind Bars: Prison Conversion and the Crisis of Self-Narrative." *Research in Human Development* 3, no. 2–3 (2006): 161–184.

Mears, Daniel P. "Faith-Based Reentry Programs: Cause for Concern or Showing Promise?" *Corrections Today Magazine* 69, no. 2 (2007): 30–33.

Merleau-Ponty, Maurice. *Phenomenology of Perception.* Translated by Colin Smith. London: Routledge & Kegan Paul, 1962. First published 1945.

Morrow, Susan L. "Quality and Trustworthiness in Qualitative Research in Counseling Psychology." *Journal of Counseling Psychology* 52, no. 2 (2005): 250–260.

Morse, Janice M. "Designing Funded Qualitative Research." In Norman K. Denzin & Yvonna S. Lincoln (Eds.), *Handbook of Qualitative Research* (pp. 220–235). Thousand Oaks, CA: Sage, 1994.

Moustakas, Clark (Ed.). *Phenomenological Research Methods.* Thousand Oaks, CA: Sage, 1994.

Munhall, Patricia. *Revisioning Phenomenology: Nursing and Health Science Research.* New York: National League for Nursing Press, 1994.

O'Connor, Thomas P., & Michael Perreyclear. "Prison Religion in Action and Its Influence on Offender Rehabilitation." *Journal of Offender Rehabilitation* 35, no. 3–4 (2002): 11–33.

Olthuis, James H. "On Worldviews." *Christian Scholar's Review* 14, no. 2 (1985): 1–12. http://understandingworldreligions.com/books_pdf_worldviews/Olthuis_On_Worldviews.pdf

Pager, Devah. *Marked: Race, Crime, and Finding Work in an Era of Mass Incarceration.* Chicago: University of Chicago Press, 2007.

Pager, Devah, Bruce Western, & Bart Bonikowski. "Discrimination in a Low-Wage Labor Market: A Field Experiment." *American Sociological Review* 74, no. 5 (2009): 777–779.

Parks, Sharon Daloz. *Big Questions, Worthy Dreams: Mentoring Young Adults in Their Search for Meaning, Purpose, and Faith.* San Francisco: Jossey-Bass, 2000.

Paternoster, Raymond, & Leeann Iovanni. "The Labeling Perspective and Delinquency: An Elaboration of the Theory and an Assessment of the Evidence." *Justice Quarterly* 6, no. 3 (1989): 359–394.

Petersilia, Joan. *When Prisoners Come Home: Parole and Prisoner Reentry.* Oxford, NY: Oxford University Press, 2003.

Racher, Frances E., & Steven Robinson. "Are Phenomenology and Postpositivism Strange Bedfellows?" *Western Journal of Nursing Research* 25, no. 5 (2003): 464–481.

Saldana, Johnny. *The Coding Manual for Qualitative Researchers.* Thousand Oaks, CA: Sage, 2009.

Schlitz, Marilyn Mandala, Cassandra Vieten, & Elizabeth M. Miller. "Worldview Transformation and the Development of Social Consciousness." *Journal of Consciousness Studies* 17, no. 7–8 (2010): 18–36.

Schlossberg, Nancy K. *Counseling Adults in Transition: Linking Practice with Theory.* New York: Springer, 1984.

Schmitt, John, Kris Warner, & Sarika Gupta. "*The High Budgetary Cost of Incarceration.*" Technical Report. Center for Economic and Policy Research. Washington, DC, 2010. http://www.cepr.net/documents/publications/incarceration-2010-06.pdf

Stoll, Michael A, & Shawn D. Bushway. "The Effect of Criminal Background Checks on the Hiring of Ex-Offenders." *Criminology and Public Policy* 7, no. 3 (2008): 371–404.

Tashakkori, Abbas, & Charles Teddlie. *Mixed Methodology: Combining Qualitative and Quantitative Approaches,* Vol. 46. Applied Social Research Methods Series. Thousand Oaks, CA: Sage, 1998.

Teddlie, Charles, & Abbas Tashakkori. "Mixed Methods Research: Contemporary Issues in an Emerging Field." In Norman K. Denzin & Yvonna S. Lincoln (Eds.), *The SAGE Handbook of Qualitative Research* (4th ed., pp. 285–299). Los Angeles: Sage, 2011.

Tewksbury, Richard, David John Erickson, & Jon Marc Taylor. "Opportunities Lost: The Consequences of Eliminating Pell Grant Eligibility for Correctional Education Students." *Journal of Offender Rehabilitation* 31, no. 1–2 (2000): 43–56.

Tonry, Michael. "The Social, Psychological, and Political Causes of Racial Disparities in the American Criminal Justice System." *Crime and Justice* 39, no. 1 (2010): 273–312.

United States Commission on Civil Rights. *Enforcing Religious Freedom in Prison.* Washington, DC, 2008. http://www.usccr.gov/pubs/STAT2008ERFIP.pdf

van Manen, Max. *Researching Lived Experience: Human Science for an Action Sensitive Pedagogy.* New York: State University of New York Press, 1990.

Wheaton College 2016a. "College Profile." Accessed February 22, 2016. http://www.wheaton.edu/About-Wheaton/Profile

Wheaton College 2016b. "Mission." Accessed February 23, 2016. http://www .wheaton.edu/About-Wheaton/Mission

Zimmer, Bolko. "Effect of Faith-Based Programs in Reducing Recidivism and Substance Abuse of Ex-Offenders." *Journal of Community Corrections* 14, no. 1 (2005): 7–19.

CHAPTER NINE

Prison, Religion and Conversion: The Prisoner's Narrative Experience

Malcolm L. Rigsby

A problematic issue of our time is increasing desistance among chronic offenders and reducing the recidivism rate. Religion is one of several treatment programs that prisons may integrate with other outcome-based initiatives, thereby enhancing potential for individuals desiring a transformative change to realize their goal. It is often said in prison that religion is left at the front gate. Perhaps in part, this is a reason why a great deal of literature has focused on religion as a tool for institutional security rather than the potential for pro-social identity shifts that accompany the religious conversion experience. Many researchers who study religion and identity transformation in prison conclude that as a society, we neglect the study of religion as part of an overall rehabilitative prison treatment program (Camp et al. 2006; Camp et al. 2008; O'Connor 2004b; O'Connor & Bogue 2010; O'Connor & Duncan 2008). Unfortunately, concerns over radicalization and terrorism in the United States after terrorist attacks in September 2001 have placed religion in prison under a social and political microscope. However, this concern over radicalization has served a positive outcome in enhancing the potential for objective and well-designed research exploring the transformative experiences of prison converts.

In fall 2011, I initiated a pilot study with the goal of generating viable knowledge about conversion in prison. The goals of the study were to use inmate narratives to assist the participants, criminal justice practitioners, religious leaders, and social science professionals in how religious conversion is a nuanced process by which subtle distinctions interact, leading to a systematic transformation in identity where individuals, helpers, and the strain of structural environment affect the need for solutions in self (Barringer 1998; Butler 1978; Cilluffo et al. 2007; Fox 2005; Hamm 2007, 2009).

Qualitative methodology enabled me to explore conversion as a process in prison and develop a grounded theory in regard to transformative identity in prison (Marshall & Rossman 2006; Patton 2002; Snow 2003). Participants included chaplains, 11 men and 4 women, as well as 22 male prisoners. Of these, 11 were converts to Islam and 11 were converts to Christianity. Interviews included basic demographic questions but consisted primarily of open-ended questions designed to elicit deep narrative accounts and stories about the individual's life (Becker 1998; Denzin 1989; Denzin & Lincoln 1994; Guba 1981; Krefting 1991; Marshall & Rossman 2006; Patton 2002; Strauss & Corbin 1998). The sample was drawn from a state prison system in the United States.

Assumptions and Research Questions

Prisons tend to create a micropopulation where a combination of strain sources such as stigma, labels, victimization, or loss associate with outcomes such as fear, anger, and hate. Within this system exists a desire for knowledge about self and belonging within the community. Religion as a structural component of understanding the unknown provides one means of satisfying a need for knowledge (Hannaford 2015).

Several research questions were generated, but the primary one is: what are the personal and social reasons given by the participants for conversion and how does the process unfold? Additional related questions emerged as the study progressed and narratives were analyzed. For instance, what is the role of community identity? Participants expressed their goal to transform pro-socially, expressing the need for responsibility and accountability, and this not only to themselves but also to others. Perhaps the most critical component of change is the "helper." All but one prisoner spent a great deal of time discussing the role of a helper in their success in their transformative journey.

Of the 22 participants, each of which was assigned an anonymous name from the Greek alphabet, all but one specifically asked me to refer to him not as an "inmate" but as a "prisoner." Therefore, my use of "prisoner" is one of honor because the participants asked me to identify them in their own terms. Typical of the majority, it was Zeta that said, "I'm no inmate, that sound too clean, I'm a prisoner. That's my identity. That's the way the world sees me and I must recognize that and correct it so when I get out I can deal with people calling me ex-con." Although the word "prisoner" has a negative connotation and is a societal label stigmatizing people, I honor the participants in assisting to give them a voice (Becker 1963; Goffman 1959, 1961, 1963).

The Need for Prisoner Life Stories

A Neglected Population

Maruna et al. (2006) indicated the need for research using narrative in finding deep meaning of the process of prisoner religious conversion. Through this process, the prisoner receives a forum and a venue to express the social identity that emerges during and after conversion. Maruna and colleagues call on the academic community to help prisoners explore their new sense of social community and identities, thus helping them actively participate in rehabilitative identity construction.

The relevant literature discloses a social and a political need underscoring the need to understand religious conversion in prison. Socially, it is imperative we learn more about how religion provides a means for the prisoner to adjust to, manage, and cope with prisonization through the transformation of self and community. All people seek means by which to perceive order in the world. Such a perspective or philosophy of life is called a worldview (Kluckhohn 1962: 409 [1944]; Lofland & Skonovd 1981; Lofland & Stark 1965). Some scholars believe that religion serves as an anchoring and sustaining resource that identifies and locates us in the world (Kimball 2002; Nagel 1994; Sadri 2006, 2007; Yinger 1970). Other scholars focus on nationalism as the major source of identity (Acuff 2008; Anderson 1983; Baldwin 1993; Connor 1972; Gilpin 1975; Morgenthau 1952; Spykman 1942; Waltz 1979). Scholarly analysis of the complex concept of identity has become increasingly important to contemporary life (Abdelal et al. 2006). Research shows that when people feel disenfranchised, lost, or strained in their lives, they seek alternative identities (Anderson 1983; Connor 1972; Horowitz 2000, 90–6). When identity associated with nationalism is strained, individuals may seek alternatives. Those experiencing strain are likely to turn to a religion, or to change their religion as a means of seeking new beliefs and bonding relationships that provide alternative directions for identity (Downton 1980, 392–93; Kox et al. 1991, 227–40; Gardner 2004, 50; Goddard 2006; Heirich 1977, 664; Nagel 1994). Differing tendencies of identity conceptualized in terms of antisocial or prosocial values, beliefs, and behavior may develop with the transforming identity (Armstrong 2000, 2009; Cavanaugh 2006; Cinoğlu 2010; Cleveland & Bunton 2009; Cox 1984, 2009; Geertz 1958, 1966; Kimball

2002; Lofland & Stark 1965; Yinger 1970). When people give up one worldview for another, they experience the process of conversion.

Equally important is the role of religion in bringing about change in self-identity that may remain steadfast after release and thereby reduce the likelihood of recidivism. Religion as a social institution provides beliefs and practices, and creates a body of associations with others of similar beliefs and practices. Such activities, learning experiences, and support mechanisms provide individuals with prosocial bonds and controls over egoism (Durkheim [1915] (1965), [1915] (2001); Hirschi 1969; Sadri 2006, 2007). The academic call substantiates the use of religion as one of multiple treatment programs for prosocial change in the individual. Researchers from several disciplines studying religion, crime, and treatment programs for the incarcerated are calling for better understanding of the role of religion in prison treatment and reentry programs (Maruna et al. 2006; Norcross & Wampold 2010; O'Connor 2004a, 2004b; O'Connor & Bogue 2010; O'Connor & Duncan 2008; Pew 2012; Worthington et al. 2010). The American Psychological Association (APA) recently conducted a meta-analysis of studies on the impact of including religion and spirituality in a person's treatment, and concluded that doing so was "demonstratively effective" (Norcross & Wampold 2010; Worthington, Hook, Davis, & McDaniel 2010). According to the APA, it is now an "evidence-based practice" for psychologists to include religion or spirituality, whatever that may be, in their patients' treatment, because doing so makes their treatment more effective.

The political rationale calls for studies examining how religion may be used to create antisocial transformation such as terrorist ideology. Such an endeavor must be carefully embarked on with due deference to the U.S. Constitution's protection of religious freedom. Fear of terrorism has led to heightened scrutiny of the role of Islam as a tool for active and widespread recruitment to terrorism (King 2011; Lieberman 2006a, 2006b; Neumann 2010; Pistole 2003). Although a legitimate concern, our constitution requires that "safety to the public" be balanced against "infringement of religion" (Green 2011; Richardson 2011; U.S. Commission on Civil Rights 2008). The general position here is if there are distinctions between Islam and Christianity and social behavior, only facts not claims must be considered and weighed carefully before regulating free practice of religion.

Some studies make the claim that terrorist ideologies may use religion as a gathering point within prisons (Cilluffo 2007; Cilluffo et al. 2007; Fighel 2007; Hamm 2007, 2009; Sadri 2009). Two studies are particularly relevant to radicalization and religion in prisoner populations. Mark Hamm's study recruited prisoner participants and interviewed them seeking their understandings of how the conversion to a religion may affect whether they become more prosocial or antisocial, or whether they may be receptive to terrorist recruitment (Hamm 2007, 2009). In late 2011, the Pew Research Center Forum on Religion and Public Life conducted a 50-state survey of prison chaplains (Pew 2012). Although this study provides significant insight into religion in prison, it still fails to include the prisoners as participants. Moreover, it fails to provide the deep meaning required to generate a testable theory on conversion and transforming identities. Since Hamm fails to compare Christian and Islamic converts in prison, and Pew fails to incorporate prisoner narratives, this research responds to the gap in the literature (Rigsby 2012, 2014).

Gaining access to speak directly with prisoners about their lives and experiences is not easy to accomplish. The nature of prison itself creates a danger to the residents and workers. Emphasizing this point is the recent Pew Forum on Religion and Public Life study, which states:

> The U.S. Bureau of Justice Statistics routinely reports on several characteristics of the U.S. prison population, such as age, gender and racial/ethnic composition, but it does not usually report on the religious affiliation of inmates, and independent surveys of inmates rarely are permitted. Thus, the Pew Forum survey offers a rare window into the religious lives of inmates through the lens of prison chaplains. (Pew 2012)

Then in footnote 9 to the above quote, Pew indicates the following:

> Prisoners are rarely allowed to participate in research studies of any kind, partly because of prior abuses of their involuntary availability for such studies. To be permitted, studies usually must demonstrate a clear cost-benefit calculation in the prisoners' favor, such as the benefit from receiving a particular medical treatment. The possible 'psychic rewards' to inmates of being able to express their opinions and describe their experiences on a survey questionnaire, or the value of the information to the public, generally are not considered by correctional authorities to justify a survey of inmates. (Pew 2012)

In the United States, today there are almost 1,100 state and federal prisons of which most have at least one chaplain, and many have volunteer chaplains. Of the approximately 1,450 state prison chaplains, 730 participated in the Pew survey. Among several findings, the Pew study noted that people of faith have hope that the introduction of religion to the penitentiary environment will inspire prosocial transformation. Although this study provides significant insight into religion in prison, it still fails to include the prisoner himself as a participant. Studies offering prisoners a voice in explaining their search for identity and life management through religion are limited and largely neglected (Camp et al. 2006; Cilluffo 2007; Cilluffo et al. 2006; Cilluffo et al. 2007; Emerson 2009; Fighel 2007; Hamm 2007, 2009; Levin 2003; O'Connor & Duncan 2008).

Selected Conversion Theory

Entry to prison is like a funnel, channeling a disenfranchised and strained population into a tiny environment. In this process, those suffering frustration and anger are funneled into a recruiting process (Cilluffo et al. 2006, 2007; Gerwehr & Daly 2006, 77; Hamm 2007, 2009; Lofland & Stark 1965, 863). Recruitment is believed to be a multistage process in which individuals suffering strain are potential converts to a religion (Hamm 2007). This population seeks belonging, community identity, and knowledge about how to manage their lives in the prison environment as they face the reality of navigating the "system" (Maruna et al. 2006).

In prison, many prisoners turn to religion in order to seek a new worldview to foster a sense of belonging, identity, and management of life issues (Cilluffo et al. 2006, 2007; Fighel 2007; Goffman 1961, 1963; Maruna et al. 2006; Neumann 2010; O'Connor 2004a, 2004b; O'Connor & Duncan 2008). Others may turn to religion as a means of transformation of self. Religious dogma has been used to create and strengthen a social bond in the form of community identity that justifies, mobilizes, and enforces common beliefs and values (Sadri 2006, 2007). Lofland and Stark (1965) have proposed a value-added model of conversion to a deviant perspective, in which the individual:

1. Experiences enduring, acutely felt tensions,
2. Within a religious problem-solving perspective,
3. Which leads the individual to define oneself as a religious seeker,
4. Encounter the Divine Precepts (DP) at a turning point in one's life,
5. Wherein an affective bond is formed (or preexists) with one or more converts,
6. Where extra-cult attachments are absent or neutralized,
7. And, where, if to become a deployable agent, the individual is exposed to intensive interaction.

This model of conversion provides a construct of identity, where the convert experiences strain, seeks Divine solutions, encounters the Divine, forms bonds, and a community emerges (Lofland 1977; Lofland & Skonovd 1981; Lofland & Stark 1965).

Desire for a worldview to explain direction in life may lead them to be susceptible to developing different tendencies of transformation and community identity. When humans give up one worldview for another worldview they experience conversion, which refers to a "turning around" or changing course of life that involves the adoption of and internalization of a new religious belief from that previously held. The convert may therefore exhibit both a subjective inner change as well as an outward behavioral change. For those who convert, the phenomenon is often accompanied by change in values, beliefs, and normative behavior. Lofland and Stark's original model of conversion may, with modification, be extended and refined so that it applies particularly well in the prison setting.

Using an integrative approach by referring to labeling and stigma theories and drawing on principles of value-added theory, social bond theory, and the theory of neutralization, Lofland and Stark's theory of conversion may be refined and advanced to assist in understanding the prison experience of conversion and predicting tendencies in transforming identity for prisoners that seek to change. In establishing a basis for this approach, five foundational threads have been connected: religion as a means of individual identity, religion as a source of community identity, religion as a source of worldview community identity, the role of religious dogma, and the level of commitment to structure in religion that justifies beliefs, values, and norms. We have examined the public fear that religion is being used to assist in recruitment of terrorists, and this has led to widespread speculation that has been alleged prejudicial. Nevertheless, we have noted that religion has been tied to outcome-based treatment programs that may assist prisoners in transforming their lives and desisting from crime. Hence, to predict these potential outcomes in sociality it is critical to understand the conversion experiences and transformative process of individuals in prison. The findings yield a baseline for more research.

Overview of Themes

In this study, conversion was understood as a change of religion or a change of religious orientation within a religion, entailing "a turning around" in the direction of life. Converts give up one worldview for another (Downton 1980; Gardner 2004; Goddard 2006; Heirich 1977; Kox et al. 1991; Nagel 1994). Central to "a turning" is the concept of commitment or recommitment to group membership interaction. I made the assumption that conversion and recommitment are inseparable to devotion and membership solidarity and are measurable by increased interaction with the community of the faith and members of the group. This interactive process affects the disengaging of an old identity and engaging of a new one. The primary research question was designed to seek understanding of both social and personal reasons for prisoner conversion. Personal and social reasons became contextual themes. Personal reasons were discussed in relation to the concept of desire to understand self and to change life relationships. Social reasons were related to the concept of helpers. Helpers were described as media and people, of which people were the most referenced type of helper. Media referred to were religious texts, music, and video including films, the Qur'an, and the Bible. People referred to were primarily other prisoners, followed by family, friends, and associates from the free world, volunteers, and chaplains. In reference to reasons for conversion, chaplains were least cited by prisoners. These findings were supported by the study conducted by Hamm (2007). Early in the analysis of the chaplain interviews and prisoner narratives, it became apparent that these two contextual themes were emerging from the concepts of understanding self and understanding self in relation to others.

Personal Reasons for Conversion

Personal reasons for conversion were defined as autonomous and an internal desire to change one's own self-identity for some reason based on individual needs, desires, or feelings. Desired outcomes from seeking religion were expressed in the context of seeking material and emotional returns. Desire to change was expressed in terms of relationship with the Divine and in terms of expectations that would be realized once change began to take place. Desire to change was expressed by some participants in spiritual context and others in religious context. In most narratives both personal and social reasons were closely intertwined. In such cases a judgment call was made as to the predominant factor in the individual's turning point in conversion. The participant I called Psi stated, "Christ came to me at that point at a really inconvenient time in my life because all the anger and everything I had at that point had led me to joining a group of skinheads. Now through this relationship I'm learning through Christ I can no longer live by their ideals."

Some participants reported that not all who say they convert are "real." In other words, some individuals turn out of desire to change themselves while others seek to use religion as a means to hide or work the environment of prison for their own advantage. Interestingly Hamm (2007) noted that while chaplains he interviewed stated that prisoners often use religion as a tool to manipulate the system, none of his interviews with prisoners uncovered any evidence of this practice. Likewise, in this study, none of the prisoner participants themselves admitted their own manipulation of the system. However, the narratives often indicated that some prisoners come initially to chapel programs and may seek out multiple religions to gain privileges that may create status among the general prison population. Items of religious clothing and symbols, dietary needs, and participation in religious assemblies serve as typical examples. Most of the narratives portrayed the personal need to understand self and change in relation to society. Several needs, desires, and feelings were expressed in terms of bottoming out and escape, need for value in terms of respect, curiosity, anger, turning points, and need for structure in terms of accountability and responsibility. These terms and concepts were voiced repeatedly in response to need for identity and arose in relation to conversion. One prisoner described what it was like to be in need of "one more chance" to understand himself and "get it right before it was too late" and how he finally saw the real him:

> One day Allah smacked me in the head and He says have you had enough yet? Look in the mirror. I looked in the mirror and seen this gray headed guy, full beard. Wow, who is that? That wasn't the image I seen of myself. Who is that? I kept looking and I'd go back once in a while and I'd look again. I seen that little twinkle in my eye and I recognized who that was. I caught a glimpse and I liked the glimpse I caught of me. There you are, you have been hiding all this time now it is time to be yourself and give up yourself [Sigma].

Several participants expressed the feeling of bottoming out, need for escape, and the need for value in self as reasons for turning to religion, faith, or spirituality. When asked about a turning point in his life and decision to convert Omega said:

> I had just came out of suicide watch and I was sitting and crying and I said God I know I can't run my life. It keeps on being proven I can't run my life. I give up on trying to do this so I am going to try to do it your way. . . . isolation gave me that shift and I think I was able to focus on me, know me, develop a relationship with me, become more mindful and things of that sort.

Feelings of being "bottomed out" were also described in the following ways: "I had to get out of the cell. I bottomed out. I was just, I felt so beat up and done. Almost like a dog when you beat it down to that point where you try to pet it, it just ducks its head" [Xi], and "I was at the point of being broken and had nowhere else to look. . . . Everybody that loved me up to that point had hurt me. Having everything stripped that you valued. Nowhere else to look, you were so far down you have no choice but to look up. It was just a point where I needed help . . . point of total brokenness . . . Spirituality can say the existence of an "other" real us. Inadequacy." [Psi], and "I pretty much tried everything else and none of this is working for me. . . . After the first week it just snapped, my life got better instantly. If it works why fix it? I have never had that happen with the Catholics or the Christians. I've went to mass before and I've sat in church and sang hymns and none of that worked for me. . . . what I need to change and how to change it and why I was doing the things I was doing. . . . I was just tired of living everyday life half awake, half asleep like a zombie" [Upsilon].

Escape and finding value in self may reflect the individual's desire to change the self and turn away from old ways. However, others may not want to change themselves but only seek to resist or escape their surroundings or become less visible. As discussed by Goffman (1961, 1963), total institutions seek to reduce the members to a common denominator before attempting resocialization. Prisoners may seek change or conversely present themselves as changing. Some narratives noted that reasons for turning to religion were based on a need to resist or escape the institution or groups, rather than flee from an old identity of self:

> It happened in 2007 when they came and got me in the middle of the night and they chained me up and they put me in the black box in the back of a van and drove me from Ft. Madison, Iowa to Wilsonville, Oregon which was 3 days on the road chained up with just nature outside of the window of a moving van. In isolation is where spirituality came back outside of religion. The spirituality is why I couldn't be broken but the religion is how I justify the fight to myself. Spirituality doesn't want anything, spirituality doesn't have an agenda. I didn't understand the power of spirituality at the time so I interpreted it as religion and I submerged myself into different denominations of Islam mainly the Nation of Islam and the Moorish Science Temple of America, Christianity because that was my roots, some Buddhism [Pi].

Besides curiosity, anger was a reason also expressed by several participants. One individual described his turning point this way:

> I was curious so I had attended the Wickens for a while about a year and a half and didn't immerse myself in it but I was searching because I was mad at God. There is a difference between following a religion and having a relationship with your creator. It wasn't until I came here and heard that message taught that I realized that that is the void that I needed filled in my life was that relationship. . . . relationship and peace of mind. . . . Coming in here took you away from some of that freedom that allowed you to do some things you were wanting to do. . . . . you have to fall all the way to the ground before you realize that what you are doing in your life is the wrong thing. That is when you recognize the reality versus the world's way. Understanding relationship with something else with acceptance and responsibility. Woke up! When I realized that my faith in Jesus Christ as my lord and savior wasn't a religion it was a relationship [Iota].

Although most of the narratives expressed emotional factors in the turning point or decision to convert, there were examples of physical events that may have affected personal well-being.

> One day I fell all the way, missed every rung on the ladder and I went splat, face first, facing the concrete, fell through it in fact, ended up in DSU here

from there to IMU [*intensive management unit*] in April of 1993 alone, no one else around me 24/7 365 days a year, I did a year. I ended up in that. I decided then that I gotta do something. If I don't change and mean it this is what I got to look forward to the rest of my entire life. It got to a point for me that I was tired of that. I walked away from it. I ended up on my knees, I prayed earnestly for the first time in my life I was genuine. I asked Christ to come into my heart and forgive me and have mercy on me. . . . I am searching for who I am [Delta].

A typical response to questions about the reason for and the point of conversion often included a discussion about seeking one's identity as included in Delta's response above. Another often-mentioned need in the context of this theme was the need for individual worth. Typically, value as a person related to value with other people. Several narratives established that the interest in a particular religion arose in part from the need for structure, accountability, and responsibility in relating with other people. The following response reflects how one individual described his watching members of a particular group and determined there was some structure and responsibility within the group:

Brothers I observed in prison had a peace about them and had structure in life. They just asked me if there was anything I needed, they are there for me. It just made me think and I was watching each one of them and I've known them for a while and I know how they are and they are real peaceful. I just started noticing that more and more and I thought that is what I need. . . . I just felt like everybody had left me. . . . I woke up in the hospital about a day later in the hospital after surgery. The doctor told me it was a miracle I am even alive. He said he doesn't even know, can't explain why and that made me think why am I still alive? Now I know it is obviously God didn't want me to go. There was a movie that I saw Les Miserables . . . [Omicron].

Omicron goes on to explain how the priest's gift of the valuable silver created a duty and responsibility that Jean Valjean must then "live up to." This duty serves to reconstruct and transform him into a new and accountable person.

Accountability and responsibility seem to relate to turning in identity and becoming a new person in transformation. Learning the answer to "who am I?" was often cited in transformation: "I had to really learn who I was. Either you want to be free or you don't want to be free. Ultimately it always goes back to whether a person is really wanting to change." [Nu]

I felt an overwhelming need for compassion. I sat in the cell and watch one of my cellies overdose on drugs and couldn't do anything to help him because the guys on the tier are having drugs and they don't want anybody up there and we made this pact before we did it. Don't call the cops. I sat there and watched my friend die. That is how callous and uncaring I had become. I had no idea of myself or anything else. Being able to get in touch with myself and ask myself questions and look at myself in the mirror and wonder why, not wonder why I'm here [Rho].

Most of the participants discussed this ongoing and never-ending process referred to as transformation. To transform, one individual indicated you must first know where you are. Accountability and structure also seemed to be expressed in terms of having something to follow: "I wanted to start finding something to follow, at least take me away from all the drugs and all the stealing." [Mu] "Putting structure into your life, a discipline, a structure. Prison was a big influence." [Kappa] "[A] Power said to me, okay we tried your way, now this is what is going to happen. Took all those worldly things away from you. You don't have the vices that you had out there on the streets. So this is what we are going to do, we are going to get back into the word. I'm going to groom you. . . . Felt like this [*prison*] was a grooming field." [Epsilon]

One participant who had always considered himself religious concluded that when he began to teach in chapel, he realized that he had not truly understood his religion. He stated that in order to become responsible one must continue to learn. He expresses that those who help others convert to a religion have a responsibility:

While I'm teaching them I say you know what I want to learn more because while I am teaching them I was learning some new stuff too. I don't know my faith. So I said I need to know that. I have time to do it. So if I don't do it, it is on me because honestly out there I didn't know that there is so much that I should learn so now I realize I don't know a lot. That is the reason that I started to pay attention . . . That touched me a lot and made me go back and see what am I doing . . . There are brothers I still see them as brothers, they study with us for 2 years, 3 years when I was here in their last 2, 3 years. They never took their Shihada but every Friday they came they listened to Kusbah and they pray with us which they pray with us but they never took their Shihada. I never judge them I never got upset with them because if they say I still need to believe 100%. If I don't then I'm a hypocrite. Hypocrites are the lowest of the low as a human being in Islam. They will go to lowest hell because that is why they know it that is why they said I want to make sure that I want to be a Muslim. That is why they study with us [Lambda].

Social Reasons for Conversion

Social reasons for conversion were defined as nonautonomous externally driven associations that create or assist the desire in another for change in identity. A common narrative theme was the need and desire to change self in order for relationships with others to improve. Participant Eta put it this way, "I need to work on me before I am able to present myself back to them or be asking them for anything or wanting anything from them." Desire, participant Rho indicated, relates to, "When they realize that [*desire for self-change*] and they know that there is somebody there that can help or there is a program in place that can help, that is where you need to be." This desire for change in self is critically watched in prison. Most of the interviews discussed "being real" and that the general population, including prison personnel and prisoners including gangs, continually "watched" those who professed to have changed their lives through religion. Being real enabled the men to walk the line in prison. Those who were considered real by gang members were allowed to leave the gang without the shedding of blood or loss of life. Failure to be considered "real" made the effort to leave a gang detrimental to life. This quality of being real and the way in which relationships are not only entered into, but also departed from in context of being real is explained as follows:

> Once I started making that transition, they recognized it and saw that I was pulling away but there was a point to where they also recognized when I was there. When I was there, I was there. When I'm not there, I'm not there. Some guys still tow the rope they want to be okay I'm religious on this aspect but yet at the same time I'm still going to be wrapped in on this aspect. For me there was no rope to be towed and I made sure they recognized that from the gang. My life is this way and this is where I'm going so there wasn't if they approached me with the greeting what is going on blood, there wasn't no what's going on blood in return [Alpha].

Being real also equated to the way a convert approached his new relationship with the Divine:

> Me and Allah just weren't on the same page. It took me a little bit of time to understand me and it hit me like, you tried to make a deal, you tried to be slick, you tried to be sneaky, manipulative. You tried to make a deal. That was your foundation of you doing, following his rules and commitments. That didn't work. Now it is more of well I learned that I have to do this, I have to make a new commitment [Tau].

There was also the need to make the desire for accountability relate to something other than to self; it extended to the rest of society, family, and victims: "What I've done is a waste. I cut a man's life short from his family and cut my life short from the family at the same time. Victims on both sides of the fence. That is when you really see what is happening. It is an eye opener." [Rho]

Desire for acknowledgment also seemed to accompany the need for social relationships. Many narratives related the feeling of loss in the midst of many and that this loneliness leads to seeking attention, using other people for gain, half-hearted efforts at leading a productive life, and lack of self-esteem. The following participant statements give the general theme of need for social inter-action and relationships that lead to turning points: "It is a weird feeling being around hundreds of people all the time and feeling alone." [Psi] "Here in prison you have people who are trying to make up stories, make up lies, make up anything sometimes that is just to entertain themselves, other times it is to get other people to do actions, manipulate." [Chi]

> It was like being boxed in; my friends were more or less bought. They weren't real because real friends will be there when the going gets tough. I finally realized that with all my other past relationships I know now why the relationships at home, the relationship with my first wife, my second wife, all my friends I grew up with, I know why those relationships fell apart. God wasn't part of it. There was nothing there. That is why I have the relationships I have today I have is because God is a part of those rela-tionships. It has nothing to do with a religion. It is about a relationship [Delta].

"I need to belong to people in order for me to feel better about myself." [Tau]

This last statement by Tau may shed light on a reflexive relationship that self-identity may have to community identity. Desire to change and turning points in religion were often described in the context of "helpers." Helpers assist the individual in deciding to make a commitment to change one's life and take on a "duty" to obtain knowledge and seek understanding of the Divine, self, and others. Helpers were described in the social context of human relation-ships with chaplains, other prisoners, friends and family not in prison, as well as noted public figures. Several cited the importance of literature in helping them come to understand the need for change and religious affiliation.

As in this study, Hamm (2007) concluded that chaplains were not often reported by prisoners as a reason for conversion. However, in the Pew study (2012) chaplains overwhelmingly self-reported their need to be religious counselors and leaders of worship. In light of this, it may be the high ratio of prisoners to chaplains that helps to explain why the prison narratives indi-cate that chaplain-assisted conversion is seldom reported. Nonetheless, some interviewees noted that a relationship with a particular chaplain was instru-mental in helping them learn about and come to seek religious community: "I did contact Chaplain [omitted] and he was able to supply me with a bible and I went to several religious services and have had meetings with the chap-lain to discuss my particular case. So therefore, he has been very, very supportive. The chaplain and I was able to share things with him that he encouraged." [Chi]

According to chaplains, 74 percent reported that conversion or proselytizing attempts among prisoners are either very common (31 percent) or somewhat common (43 percent) (Pew 2012). All narratives in my study indicated either direct or indirect proselytizing efforts by those other than chaplains. They had either been approached by another, or had heard of others being recruited by someone other than chaplains, usually other prisoners. Several narratives illustrate these social reasons for conversion: "Other inmates, a few people here who invited, come on down to the church. We actually would sit on the bunk and crack the Bible and do a little impromptu Bible study just one on one together. That helped me maintain or get back to sanity is the best way to describe it and then go from there." [Chi] "My dad he is in here too, he introduced me to a couple of people and said you might want to listen to what they have to say." [Upsilon]

> It was a buddy of mine, elder, he was fighting this case for like 10 years and he was in hole for 10 years and that is almost unheard of. He ended up winning and going back to county. When he was down in county he wrote us he got converted, I took my Shihada. There was an individual within our community that really supported me in my walk and helped me learn things and understand things [*and speaking of his duty to proselytize*] if I bring you in to our mosque I'm not to pressure you to become a Muslim. My job is to bring you in, treat you how I'd want you to treat me. Hopefully try to answer any of your questions or point you in the right direction. I'm not supposed to apply any pressure so therefore you can make your own decision and your own commitment. [Tau]

"When you come to prison and you are around people [*Muslims*] like that, 'we want to tell you something.' What they laid on me blew my mind because nobody ever talked to me like that where I would listen and I was in a place where I could listen and learn. So I sat down and I listened." [Sigma]

Other helpers came from associations, family, friends, and even public figures that filtered in from the world. A pattern that emerged was related to being responsible for self and to others and being accountable to others for actions. Sometimes these social helpers pushed, restored faith in humanity, supported, set an example to strive for, and sometimes created remorse, as the following quotes illustrate:

> Those I loved back home pushed me to seek to change. [Zeta]

> They would help the family out in other ways without me even knowing about it, a box of groceries would land on the doorstep. They were out of state and when their wives would come in on the weekend they would send their wives over to my wife's business, who is a nail tech and they would

get their nails done. They would pay for that but they would leave an envelope with a tip. There was a lot more than a tip in there. I started seeing the beginnings of what real relationships were, how they worked, in a strange environment, odd as it would be. I start paying attention to that. [Delta]

Kenneth Copeland. I love him, and Gloria Copeland they have been a big blessing in my life. [Phi]

I had always seen Muslims all over the country, on street corners selling Muhammad speeches and stuff like that . . . juice and bean pies. They were good too. Then they had their little restaurants and the people were very respectful and when you talked to the brother they had knowledge. They could quote things to you. You look at them and they were clean, they dressed in Muslim with bow ties and they were clean. They were very respectful towards everybody. [Sigma]

[*I was in here*] almost 30 years in here for killing a man I woke up one day and my mom had said to me on the phone about she says I think you want to be there; because you aren't doing anything to get out. I had heard other people say that to me to that too. It was something my mom told me—I'm tired of coming down there. I'm tired of having to come into that prison. You need to get out of there. I don't want you in there. That was kind of a catalyst to be able to snap my head back and think man you need to do something. [Rho]

Synthesizing the Findings

In analysis of the personal and social accounts of conversion, the most cited social reasons for conversion that emerged were used in context of an independent "desire" arising from the strained environment of prison. Desire related to how the decision to seek out identity first arose and grew. Regarding the decision to seek out identity, the desire was a personal choice that often accompanied a discussion of both inner desires to understand self and a willingness to learn and change one's life. This type of desire was coded as a personal reason for conversion. Simultaneously a desire was discussed in terms of external associations, with other prisoners, or continuing relationships with family and friends in the "free world." These external sources of desire were coded as social reasons. Desire to convert was described as related to the element of "time." In prison, there is an abundance of time to enable what had been neglected before incarceration. Time led to "reflection" on self, the meaning of life, and other matters including family and victims. Those expressing greater group experience with the religion couched their conversions in terms of group practices and symbols. These group experiences reinforced their initial decision to gain knowledge and understand themselves through religion. Those who reported more spirit-filled experiences, in initially deciding to seek out their identity, spoke less of group experiences, practices, and symbols of religion. Sometimes social reasons preceded personal reasons, other times they were discussed simultaneously, and yet in others, personal reasons came first.

A Strained Turning Point

A critical stage was a "turning point" in developing new community identity and bonds, and recognizing the duty to make "commitment" a part of daily life. It was interesting that desire for understanding of self that was discussed in relation to time and strain of prison was distinguished from the type of desire regarding commitment. Although time aided reflection, the desire to reflect was presented in the context of "bottoming out," "anger," "seeking to avoid authority," or trying to "make the best of it." The desire for commitment was spoken of in relation to the concept of portraying one's self as "real." Being real in prison is an important quality that both gains and reinforces one's placement in community and relates to respect, prestige, and esteem.

A Desire to Know and Change

In addition to the desire to learn about one's identity, there was a desire to change. Change emerged from motivations to seek out material, spiritual, and/or social rewards and/or gains. Some tried to satisfy material rewards in an instrumental fashion while others sought out expressive rewards.

Accompanying the desire to change was a thirst for "gaining knowledge." Perhaps time allows prisoners a respite in which to gain knowledge, and that knowledge enhances desire. I asked participants throughout the interviews to rank desire and knowledge in their own ultimate decision to convert. Most stated that desire must come first, but often bottoming out was close in time. Many had sought out alternatives for change. Some participants noted seeking out prison cultures such as gang membership or academic knowledge, science or social-personal management counseling to obtain understanding of self before turning to religion. These findings are similar to Hamm (2007), where many of the participants reported searching out many religions, reading books on psychology, religion, sociology, political science, and attending many types of both secular and sectarian counseling and mentoring programs.

The Importance of Helpers

In discussing their quest for knowledge, participants referenced the importance of "helpers," who seemingly served vital roles in transforming

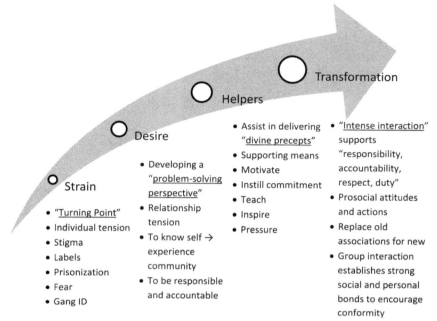

Figure 9.1   Pathways to Transformation

identities. Chaplains as helpers were almost entirely left out of the discussion. This finding is consistent with Hamm, where he cites the massive administrative duties of chaplains and the highly disproportionate ratio of chaplains to prisoners (2007). Some helped by pressuring the member to continue to seek knowledge, and others helped by providing instruments and pathways to knowledge. As knowledge developed, helpers assisted the individual in entering the next stage involving "understanding," "respect," "accountability," "responsibility," and "self-esteem." These were coded both regarding "self-identity" and "community identity." For example, respect was something desired that could lead to better self-esteem, and then accountability and responsibility. Conversely, as the individual's understanding of value, accountability, and responsibility advances, the community returns respect, calls for, and reinforces the need for mutual accountability. This process instills greater responsibility in the individual both in terms of self and toward other members of the group and society. This process was often cited in the context of coming to "love and respect yourself before being able to love and respect others."

Figure 9.1 reflects the pathway to transformation discussed by the participants. In deciding to make a religious commitment and seek personal transformation, it is interesting that the participant narrative life accounts reveal a pathway to transforming one's self in terms of individuality and in community belonging. Social context arising in strain linked to their desire for self-understanding and a simultaneous need for community belonging and social commitment to others. Notwithstanding strain and desire the transformative process required a third ingredient. Helpers assisted the desiring individual, equipping them with the knowledge as well as the requisite duty, responsibility, and commitment to self and others in order to successfully begin their journey of change through religion. Some noted strain was a critical ingredient in their road to change. Others noted that a sincere helper who enabled them to take an active part in change was a precursor to desire to change. Sometimes these elements almost converged in a moment of strain. However, in most life accounts the transformative journey through religion clearly began with strain and progressed to a turning point and the realization of the desire to change one's being. This spurred individuals to seek a dedicated teacher and helper who taught them duty, love, responsibility, and respect through a journey of intense interaction with self and others. In the nuanced paths to transformation in prison, it appears the role of the helper is the most critical ingredient in assisting the individual to convert and transform.

Conclusion

Narrative life accounts provide better firsthand analysis of strategies that prisoners employ not only to cope with prisonization but also to better understand themselves, their community, and their overall placement in society. For those seeking to change, religion offers a means for transformation in identity and belonging. Deeper understanding of the nuances in this multipath process is required. Common features of the life stories reflect a need to cope with the past as well as current identity and relationships with others in society. For those seeking religion as a means for prosocial transformation, this appears to be of great importance in helping people to take an active role in desisting from criminality and thereby reducing the likelihood of recidivism. Within this process we cannot ignore the importance of the helper's role. This research is of value to prison administrators, chaplains, psychologists, and counselors in better equipping them to understand how faith-based programs can be viable and productive correctional treatment programs. These programs may assist prison administrators and by contributing to a safer environment and by helping offenders to transform. By allowing felons active self-help roles, we promote their receptivity to develop a socially responsible self. These findings support the need for interdisciplinary approaches that holistically integrate one's religion as part of an overall treatment program by incorporating theological, psychological, and sociological programs.

Bibliography

Abdelal, Rawi, Yoshiko M. Herrera, Alastair Lain Johnston, & Rose McDermott. "Identity as a Variable." *Perspectives on Politics* 4, no. 4 (2006): 695–711.

Acuff, Jonathan. "One Nation under God: Nationalism, Religion, and Collective Violence." Conference Paper, International Studies Association, 49th Annual Meeting, San Francisco, CA, March 2008 (http://search.ebscohost.com /login.aspx?direct=true&db=aph&AN=42974703&site=ehost-live).

Anderson, Benedict. *Imagined Communities: Reflections on the Origin and Spread of Nationalism.* New York: Verso, 1983, Revised 2006.

Armstrong, Karen. *The Battle for God.* New York: Knopf, 2000.

Armstrong, Karen. *The Case for God.* New York: Knopf, 2009.

Baldwin, David A. "Neoliberalism, Neorealism and World Politics." In David A. Baldwin (Ed.), *Neorealism and Neoliberalism: The Contemporary Debate.* New York: Columbia University Press, 1993 (http://books.google.com/books?id =J-5086iinx0C&pg=PA3&dq=baldwin+neoliberalism+1993&cd=1#v =onepage&q=baldwin%20neoliberalism%201993&f=false).

Barringer, T. A. "Adult Transformations inside a Midwest Correctional Facility: Black Muslim Narratives of their Islamic Conversion." Unpublished doctoral dissertation. DeKalb: Northern Illinois University, 1998, AAT 9918698.

Becker, H. *Outsiders: Studies in the Sociology of Deviance.* New York: Free Press, 1963.

Becker, H. *Tricks of the Trade: How to Think about Your Research While You're Doing It.* Chicago: University of Chicago Press, 1998.

Butler, K. "Muslims Are No Longer an Unknown Quantity." *Corrections* 4 (1978): 55–63.

Camp, S., D. Daggett, O. Kwon, & J. Klein-Saffran. "The Effect of Faith Program Participation of Prison Misconduct: The Life Connections Program." *Journal of Criminal Justice* 36 (2008): 389–395 (http://www.crim.umd.edu/faculty /userfiles/113/Campetal2008.pdf).

Camp, S., J. Klein-Saffran, O. Kwan, D. Daggett, & V. Joseph. "An Exploration into Participation in a Faith-Based Program." *Criminology and Public Policy* 5, no. 3 (2006): 529–550.

Cavanaugh, William. "Does Religion Cause Violence." Presented at the University of Western Australia, Perth, Australia, May 29, 2006.

Cilluffo, Frank, Jan Lane, Sharon Cardash, Josh Magarik, Andrew Whitehead, Gregory Saathoff, Jeffrey Raynor, Arnold Bogis & Gina Lohr. "Out of the Shadows: Getting Ahead of Prisoner Radicalization," in A Special Report by The George Washington University Homeland Security Policy Institute, Washington, DC, and The University of Virginia Critical Incident Analysis Group, Charlottesville, VA, 2006 (http://www.healthsystem.virginia .edu/internet/ciag/publications/out_of_the_shadows.pdf).

Cilluffo, F. J. "Prison Radicalization: Are Terrorist Cells Forming in U.S. Cell Blocks?" In Hearing before the Committee on Homeland Security and Governmental Affairs, United States Senate No. 109–954, One Hundred

Ninth Congress, Second Session, September 19, 2006. Washington, DC: U.S. Government Printing Office, 2007 (http://www.healthsystem.virginia.edu/internet/ciag/publications/senate_hearing_on_prison_radicalization_2006.pdf).

Cilluffo, F. J., S. L. Cardash, & A. J. Whitehead. "Radicalization: Behind Bars and Beyond Borders." *The Brown Journal of World Affairs* XIII, no. 2 (2007): 113–122.

Cinoğlu, Huseyin. "Sociological Understanding of the Relationship between Terrorism and Religion." *International Journal of Human Sciences* 7, no. 2 (2010): 200–209 (https://j-humansciences.com/ojs/index.php/IJHS/article/view/1081/578).

Cleveland, William L., & Martin Bunton. *A History of the Modern Middle East* (4th ed.). Boulder, CO: Westview Press, 2009.

Connor, Walker. "Nation-Building or Nation-Destroying?" *World Politics* 24, no. 3 (1972): 319–355.

Cox, Harvey. *Religion in the Secular City*. New York: Simon and Schuster, 1984.

Cox, Harvey. *The Future of Faith*. New York: Harper Collins, 2009.

Denzin, N. *Interpretive Interactionism*. London: Sage, 1989.

Denzin, N., & Y. Lincoln. *Handbook of Qualitative Research*. Thousand Oaks, CA: Sage, 1994.

Downton, James V., Jr. "An Evolutionary Theory of Spiritual Conversion and Commitment: The Case of Divine Light Mission." *Journal for the Scientific Study of Religion* 19, no. 4 (1980): 381–396 (http://www.jstor.org/stable/1386132).

Durkheim, Emile. *The Elementary Forms of the Religious Life*. Translated by Joseph Ward Swain. New York: Free Press. Originally published in London: George Allen and Unwin, [1915] 1965.

Durkheim, Emile. *Emile Durkheim: The Religious Forms of the Religious Life*. Translated by Carol Cosman. Oxford, NY: Oxford University Press. Originally published in London: George Allen and Unwin, [1915] 2001.

Emerson, Steven. "Radicals in Our Prisons: How to Stop the Muslim Extremists Recruiting Inmates to Terrorism," *The New York Post*, May 23, 2009. NewYorPost.com, 2009 (http://www.nypost.com/p/news/opinion/oped columnists/item_mm7BW6pcTbzbjhri6DmuHM/2).

Fighel, J. "The 'Radicalization Process' in Prisons." Paper presented at NATO workshop, Eilat, December 25, 2007, Online Article Series, International Institute for Counter-Terrorism, 2007 (http://www.ict.org.il/Portals/0/Articles/Radicalization%20in%20Prisons.pdf).

Fox, U. "Captive Converts: What Makes Islam So Attractive to Prisoners?" *The Times Online, The London Times*, London, August 11, 2005 (http://www.timesonline.co.uk/tol/comment/article554614.ece).

Gardner, Howard. *Changing Minds: The Art and Science of Changing Our Own and Other People's Minds*. Cambridge, MA: Harvard Business School, 2004.

Geertz, Clifford. "Ethos, Worldview and the Analysis of Sacred Symbols." *The Antioch Review* Winter (1958): 421–437.

Geertz, Clifford. "Religion as a Cultural System." In Michael Banton (Ed.), *Anthropological Approaches to the Study of Religion* (pp. 1–46). London: Tavistock, 1966.

Gerwehr, S., & S. Daly. "Al-Qaida: Terrorist Selection and Recruitment." In *McGraw-Hill Homeland Security Handbook*. Boston: Rand, 2006 (http://www .rand.org/pubs/reprints/RP1214).

Gilpin, Robert. *U.S. Power and the Multinational Corporation: The Political Economy of Foreign Direct Investment*. New York: Basic Books, 1975.

Goddard, Stacie E. "Uncommon Ground: Indivisible Territory and the Politics of Legitimacy." *International Organization* 60 (2006): 35–68.

Goffman, E. *The Presentation of Self in Every Day Life*. New York: Anchor Books, 1959.

Goffman, E. *Asylums: Essays on the Social Situation of Mental Patients and Other Inmates*. New York: Doubleday, 1961.

Goffman, E. *Stigma: Notes on the Management of Spoiled Identity*. New York: Simon and Schuster, 1963.

Green, A. U.S. Representative Texas 9th District. Committee on Homeland Security. Chairman, *Hearing on the Threat of Muslim-American Radicalization in US Prisons*, June 15, 2011 (http://www.gpo.gov/fdsys/pkg/CHRG-112hh rg72541/pdf/CHRG-112hhrg72541.pdf).

Guba, E. "Criteria for Assessing the Trustworthiness of Naturalistic Inquiries." *Educational Resources Information Center Annual Review Paper* 29 (1981): 75–91.

Hamm, M. "Terrorist Recruitment in American Correctional Institutions: An Exploratory Study of Non-Traditional Faith Groups," 2007. NCJRS Document 220957 (http://nij.ncjrs.gov/publications/Pub_Search.asp?category =99&searchtype=basic&location=top&PSID=27).

Hamm, M. S. "Prison Islam in the Age of Sacred Terror." *The British Journal of Criminology* 49 (2009): 667–685.

Hannaford, Alex. An interview with Malcolm L. Rigsby in "Letters from Death Row: Faith Behind Bars." *The Texas Observer,* June 12, 2015 (https://www .texasobserver.org/death-row-inmates-religion).

Heirich, Max. "Change of Heart: A Test of Some Widely Held Theories about Religious Conversion." *The American Journal of Sociology* 83, no. 3 (1977): 653–680 (http://www.jstor.org/stable/2778148).

Hirschi, Travis. *Causes of Delinquency*. Berkeley, CA: University of California Press, 1969.

Horowitz, Donald. *Ethnic Groups in Conflict*. Berkeley, CA: University of California Press, 2000.

Kimball, Charles. *When Religion Becomes Evil: Five Warning Signs*. San Francisco: HarperCollins, 2002.

King, P. U.S. Representative New York 2nd District. Committee on Homeland Security. Chairman, *Hearing on the Threat of Muslim-American Radicalization in US Prisons*, June 15, 2011 (http://www.gpo.gov/fdsys/pkg/CHRG -112hhrg72541/pdf/CHRG-112hhrg72541.pdf).

Kluckhohn, Clyde. *Navaho Witchcraft*. Boston:Beacon Press, [1944] 1962.

Kox, Willem, Wim Meeus, & Harm't Hart. "Religious Conversion of Adolescents: Testing the Lofland and Stark Model of Religious Conversion." *Sociological Analysis* 52, no. 3 (1991): 227–240 (http://www.jstor.org/stable /3711357).

Krefting, Laura. "Rigor in Qualitative Research: The Assessment of Trustworthiness." *The American Journal of Occupational Therapy* 45 (1991): 214–222.

Levin, Brian. "Radical Religion in Prison: How are Prison Officials to Balance Security Interests and the Right to Racial Supremacists to Pursue Religion? The Jury's Still Out." Intelligence Report, Issue Number 111. *Southern Poverty Law Center*, 2003 (http://www.splcenter.org/get-informed/intelligence -report/browse-all-issues/2003/fall/radical-religion-in-prison).

Lieberman, J. "Senate Homeland Security Committee Meeting Examines Terrorist Recruitment in U.S. Prisons." Paper presented at the Senate Committee on Homeland Security and Governmental Affairs, Washington, DC, 2006a (http://hsgac.senate.gov/public/index.cfm?FuseAction=Press.Majority News&ContentRecord_id=2a9666a3-9ca1-4bc4-a895-d009d0801f14& Region_id=&Issue_id=).

Lieberman, J. "Lieberman Hails Report on Threat of Homegrown Terror in Prisons." Paper presented at the Senate Committee on Homeland Security and Governmental Affairs, Washington, DC, 2006b (http://hsgac.senate.gov /public/index.cfm?FuseAction=Press.MajorityNews&ContentRecord_id =34d8a9fe-8b65-45ba-b3ff-016b75e553b8&Region_id=&Issue_id=).

Lofland J., & R. Stark. "Becoming a World-Saver: A Theory of Religious Conversion." *American Sociological Review* 30 (1965): 862–874.

Lofland, John. *Doomsday Cult: A Study of Conversion, Proselytization, and Maintenance of Faith.* New York: Irvington, 1977.

Lofland, John, & Norman Skonovd. "Conversion Motifs." *Journal for the Scientific Study of Religion* (December 1981): 7–85.

Marshall, C., & Rossman, G. B. *Designing Qualitative Research* (4th ed.). Thousand Oaks, CA: Sage, 2006.

Maruna, S., L. Wilson, & K. Curran. "Why God Is Often Found behind Bars: Prison Conversions and the Crisis of Self-Narrative." *Research in Human Development* 3, no. 2–3 (2006): 161–184.

Morgenthau, Hans J. "Another 'Great Debate': The National Interest of the United States." *American Political Science Review* LXVI (December 1952): 961.

Nagel, Joane. "Constructing Ethnicity: Creating and Recreating Ethnic Identity and Culture." *Social Problems* 41, no.1 (1994):152–176.

Neumann, Peter R. *Prisons and Terrorism: Radicalisation and De-radicalisation in 15 Countries.* International Centre for the Study of Radicalisation and Political Violence (ICSR). King's College, London, 2010 (http://icsr.info /publications/papers/1277699166PrisonsandTerrorismRadicalisationan dDeradicalisationin15Countries.pdf).

Norcross, J., & B. Wampold. "What Works for Whom: Tailoring Psychotherapy to the Person." *Journal of Clinical Psychology* 67 (2010): 127–132.

O'Connor, T. P. "What Works, Religion as a Correctional Intervention: Part I." *Journal of Community Corrections* 13, no. 4 (2004a): 11–27.

O'Connor, T. P. "What Works, Religion as a Correctional Intervention: Part II." *Journal of Community Corrections* 14, no. 1 (2004b): 11–27.

O'Connor, T. P., & B. Bogue. "Collaborating with the Community, Trained Volunteers and Faith Traditions: Building Social Capital and Making Meaning to Support Desistance. In F. McNeill, P. Rayner, & C. Trotter (Eds.), *Offender Supervision: New Directions in Theory, Research and Practice* (pp. 301–322). New York: Willan, 2010.

O'Connor, T. P., & J. B. Duncan. "Religion and Prison Programming: The Role, Impact, and Future Direction of Faith in Correctional Systems." Offender Programs Report. *Civil Research Institute* 11, no. 6 (2008): 81–96.

Patton, M. Q. *Qualitative Research & Evaluation Methods* (3rd ed.). Thousand Oaks, CA: Sage, 2002.

Pew. "Religion in Prisons: A 50-State Survey of Prison Chaplains." The Pew Research Center, The PEW Forum on Religion & Public Life, released March 22, 2012. Washington, DC, 2012 (http://www.pewforum.org/2012 /03/22/prison-chaplains-exec).

Pistole, J. S. "Terrorist Recruitment in Prisons and the Recent Arrests Related to Guantanamo Bay Detainees." Federal Bureau of Investigations. Congressional Testimony of John S. Pistole, Assistant Director, Counterterrorism Division, FBI before the Senate Judiciary Committee, Subcommittee on Terrorism, Technology, and Homeland Security, October 14, 2003 (http:// www.fbi.gov/congress/congress03/pistole101403.htm).

Richardson, L. U.S. Representative California 37th District. Committee on Homeland Security. Chairman, *Hearing on the Threat of Muslim-American Radicalization in US Prisons*, June 15, 2011 (http://www.gpo.gov/fdsys/pkg /CHRG-112hhrg72541/pdf/CHRG-112hhrg72541.pdf).

Rigsby, M. L. *Religious Conversion in Prison and Its Directions: Community Identity, Religious Dogma, and Exclusivist or Inclusivist Religiosity in American Prisons.* Texas Woman's University, Denton, TX. Ann Arbor, MI: ProQuest, 2012.

Rigsby, M. L. "Religious Conversion in Prison: Prosocial v. Antisocial Identities." *International Journal of Education and Social Science* 1, no. 4 (2014): 61–77 (http://www.ijessnet.com/wp-content/uploads/2014/11/7.pdf).

Sadri, M. "From Irony to Inclusion: Early Models of Interfaith Dialogue." *Interreligious Insight* 4, no. 1 (January 2006): 8–18.

Sadri, M. "Suicidal Homicide: A Durkheimian Approach." In S. Ozeren, I. Dincer, D. Gunes, & M. Al-Badayneh (Eds.), *Understanding Terrorism: Analysis of Sociological and Psychological Aspects.* NATO Science for Peace and Security Series, E: Human and Societal Dynamics, Vol. 22, 2007.

Sadri, M. "Terrorism: Notes on a Communitarian Approach. In S. Ekici, A. Ekici, D. A. McEntire, R. H. Ward, & S. S. Arlikatti (Eds.), *Building Terrorism Resistant Communities.* Washington, DC: IOS Press, 2009.

Snow, D. "Thoughts on Alternative Pathways to Theoretical Development: Theory Generation, Extension, and Refinement." Paper presented at the Workshop on Scientific Foundations of Qualitative Research, the Sociology

Program of the National Science Foundation, Arlington, VA, July 11–12, 2003. Retrieved May 29, 2012 (http://web.ku.edu).

Spykman, Nicholas J. *America's Strategy in World Politics*. New York: Harcourt Brace, 1942.

Strauss, A., & J. Corbin. *Basics of Qualitative Research: Techniques and Procedures for Developing Grounded Theory* (2nd ed.). Thousand Oaks, CA: Sage, 1998.

U.S. Commission on Civil Rights. *Enforcing Religious Freedom in Prison*. Washington, DC: U.S. Government Printing Office, 2008 (http://www.usccr.gov /pubs/121008_EnforcingReligiousFreedomInPrison_StatutoryReport .pdf).

Waltz, Kenneth. *Theory of International Politics. Reading*, MA: Addison-Wesley, 1979.

Worthington, E., J. Hook, D. Davis, & M. McDaniel. "Religion and Spirituality." *Journal of Clinical Psychology* 67 (2010): 204–214.

Yinger, J. Milton. *The Scientific Study of Religion*. New York: McMillan, 1970.

CHAPTER TEN

Reading Scripture in Exile: Favorite Scriptures among Maximum-Security Inmates Participating in Prison Seminary Programs

Joshua Hays

Reading and study of the Bible is central to many faith-based programs within correctional settings. These programs are among the most prevalent and cost-effective methods for inmate rehabilitation and range from informal Bible studies and worship services led by volunteers in local jails, to fully accredited bachelor's degree programs available to maximum-security inmates in several states. The centrality of the biblical text unites these otherwise disparate programs along a continuum of varying frequency, intensity, and staffing requirements.

Scholars have acknowledged the prominence of Bible reading and study among inmates, but which passages prove meaningful to inmates has received scant attention. Furthermore, some prior research has suggested that inmates almost universally interpret Scripture with a simplistic literalism that highly personalizes the text. Under this assumption, the reader takes each passage in its most surface sense and then makes immediate application to the personal experience of incarceration. Interviews with 85 maximum-security inmates enrolled in Bible college degree programs tell a different story. These men readily identify particular verses that have proven meaningful to them, often without prompting. They often interpret these texts in nuanced ways that defy the caricature of crass literalism and only then apply these interpretations to their personal experiences.

Literature Review

References to Bible reading or study within criminological literature often emerge as indicators of religiosity, a notoriously difficult concept to define sociologically (see Benda & Corwyn 2001). Attention given to a sacred text such as the Bible offers one method of operationalizing this elusive description to supplement other measures such as religious service attendance or self-report of religious belief. Johnson (1987), for instance, constructed an index of inmates' self-reported religiosity from five variables, including inmates' response to the question, "Do you believe in the Bible?" The resulting self-report index in turn combined with chaplains' perceptions of inmates' religiosity and church attendance to form a more complete composite measure of religiosity. Although helpful toward operationalizing religious faith and practice, this approach tends to reduce engagement with the Bible into binary terms. Inmates provide a yes or no response to inquiries about their use of the Bible, but these answers cannot illuminate the depth, frequency, or subject of inmates' reading.

Subsequent research of faith-based programs sponsored by Prison Fellowship, a nonprofit Christian ministry to prisoners, found that high participation (defined as 10 or more sessions per year) in Bible studies corresponded with significantly lower rearrest rates over a one-year follow-up period (Johnson, Larson, & Pitts 1997). This effect diminished over time but remained significant up to three years after release (Johnson 2004). These studies suggest a dosage effect whereby highly involved participants benefit postrelease from Bible study while lower-frequency participants do not. This finding moves beyond the binary understanding of inmate Bible reading but still does not speak to which passages prove meaningful to inmate readers.

A federal judge ruled another Prison Fellowship program, the InnerChange Freedom Initiative (IFI), unconstitutional as offered in an Iowa prison, but IFI continues to operate in Texas and Minnesota (see Sullivan 2009). Odle (2007) critiques IFI for its "all pervasive use of Biblical text to underscore and explain nearly all aspects of the InnerChange program," taking particular issue with the citation of Matthew 18:25–35 within the program's "Accountability Covenant" (289). This citation of a specific text from the Gospel of Matthew begins to shed light on the passages deemed relevant by the *providers* of faith-based services, in this case Prison Fellowship, but the question remains whether inmates connect with and value these same passages. IFI participants signed and affirmed the Accountability Covenant as a condition of their participation in the program, but the verses mentioned therein are not necessarily the ones most meaningful to them.

Seemingly the only study to identify specific passages referenced by inmates is, unsurprisingly, a qualitative one. Kerley and Copes (2009) examine strategies attested by inmates to maintain their fresh identity following religious conversion, and Bible study figures prominently in this process. The authors organize these strategies under the headings "connecting with positive others in formal and informal settings, sharing their stories with those in need, and reflecting on their daily choices" (Kerley & Copes 2009, 228). Scripture study emerges in the narratives about the first two of these three methods. Religious inmates assemble together for "group scripture study," citing as their justification "this scriptural precept: 'Let us not give up meeting together, as some are in the habit of doing, but let us encourage one another—and all the more as you see the Day approaching' (Hebrews 10:25)" (235). With regard to sharing their stories, inmates "frequently reference the scriptural concept of the 'Great Commission' [Matthew 28:19–20] as a chief reason for sharing" (237). They also describe this practice using agricultural metaphors drawn from the Gospels: "In particular, many inmates made direct reference to this scripture: Again Jesus said, "Simon son of John, do you truly love me?" He answered, "Yes, Lord, you know that I love you." Jesus said, 'Take care of my sheep' (John 21:16)" (237–38).

By their personal appropriation of this agricultural metaphor spoken to the apostle Simon, these inmates do indeed display the tendency toward personalization often assumed within the literature, but they do so in a more sophisticated way than the stereotype of superficial literalism suggests. Clear and colleagues (2000) contend that inmates "often take a literal interpretation of the teachings of their faith" and "seem to experience religion as a basic truth that is presented without complexity or nuance in the holy teaching." Through such surface readings, "the rhetoric of religious fervor can take on the quality of intolerance" (58). Although Clear and colleagues are right to warn of the dangers of superficial literalism leading to intolerance, they present no evidence of this literalism among inmates. They name no specific passages or interpretations to support their claim. No doubt Clear and colleagues could readily identify numerous examples, just as ministers and Bible teachers among the broader public provide similar examples, but the point is that these examples of oversimplification and reductionism are not unanimous or necessarily even representative in correctional settings or the free world.

Clear and colleagues continue to argue that inmates gravitate toward sacred texts, whether the Bible, the Qur'an, or another corpus, because these texts "constitute complete explanations of the rights and duties of a human life" that inmates can employ as a pattern to fashion a new, more prosocial way of life (60). These "total systems" offer "a packaged alternative to previous ways of living" comparable to 12-step programs like Narcotics Anonymous and others (61). Here they echo the earlier research of Switzer (1984), who contends, "Some men become interested in the Bible during the early stages of confinement for the same reasons that other men read self-help oriented literature, and for the same reasons most men lose interest" (18). On the authority of a single chaplain, Switzer posits that 5–6 percent of inmates sustain interest in the Bible throughout their incarceration, doing so to maintain connections with the outside world whether through actual contact with religious volunteers or through the psychological connection established by participating in an activity shared with free society. One inmate attests personally to this connection with volunteers who "send us some Bible scriptures and stuff like that, where we can keep ourselves going on with the Lord" (Kerley & Copes 2009, 233).

Given the prominence of the Bible within faith-based rehabilitation programs and the proliferation of these programs in recent years, lack of attention to passages most meaningful to inmates seems a curious omission. Criminologists have utilized the sheer act of Bible reading as a variable to operationalize religiosity more broadly, and studies have documented the positive impact of sufficiently frequent Bible reading on recidivism rates. Meanwhile, critics have identified the Bible passages explicitly underlying some faith-based programs such as IFI. The complementary Bible preferences of the inmates receiving these services, however, have yet to receive documentation beyond rather sweeping generalization. Some researchers have dismissed inmate interpretation of Scripture as simplistically literal and utilitarian, a coping mechanism to script a new identity or to maintain social ties to the outside world. The exceptions to this trend in the literature, such as Kerley and Copes (2009), are few indeed. The conspicuous omission of inmate perspectives on the texts central to their religious lives diminishes their voice with regard to the programs aimed at their rehabilitation and dismisses the authenticity of their spiritual beliefs and practices, which often are both vibrant and creative.

Methodology

This chapter aims to fill this void in the literature using both survey data and personal interviews. The Baylor Survey of Life in Prison (BSLP), conducted by the Institute for Studies of Religion at Baylor University, surveyed the entire population (n=2,249) of Main Prison at the Louisiana State Penitentiary in Angola, Louisiana (more popularly known as Angola). This facility is the largest maximum-security prison in the United States, housing over 6,200 inmates. Its Main Prison complex is the largest unit at Angola, which also includes four other "camps" in addition to its medical treatment and hospice center. Main Prison houses the Angola extension center of the New Orleans Baptist Theological Seminary (NOBTS), which offers a fully accredited bachelor of arts degree in Christian ministry to academically and disciplinarily eligible inmates at no cost to the students or to taxpayers. Main Prison also houses 17 inmate-led religious congregations meeting in three chapel facilities and in other educational spaces. NOBTS inmate graduates have established most of these congregations, but several of them predate the establishment of the NOBTS extension at Angola in 1995. Administered in the spring of 2015, the BSLP asked inmates about a range of topics including attitudes toward prison administration, spiritual beliefs and practices, emotional self-perception, prison programming options, religious identity, worship participation, exposure to the Bible College, criminal history, educational background, and other demographic information (see Hallett et al. 2016).

This data provide context for over 100 interviews conducted with Angola inmates between September 2013 and May 2015. From these interviews, the responses of 30 inmates who identified particular Bible passages of special significance are discussed. These 30 men include 26 NOBTS graduates, three students currently enrolled at the time of the interview, and one nonparticipant who pastors an inmate congregation predating the seminary.

Qualitative data includes 55 in-depth interviews with inmates at the Darrington Unit of the Texas Department of Criminal Justice (TDCJ). The Darrington Unit offers an accredited bachelor of science degree in biblical studies provided by the Southwestern Baptist Theological Seminary (SWBTS). Implemented in 2011, this seminary program draws inspiration from the NOBTS program at Angola, but Darrington notably lacks inmate-led congregations. Inmates are allowed to participate in worship leadership (e.g., preaching, teaching, and music) under the authority of the chaplain, but TDCJ policy currently forbids the establishment of fully autonomous prison congregations (see Duwe et al. 2015). Interviews at Darrington took place between November 2013 and April 2014, and all participants were seminary students at the time of the interview.

Interviews were conducted privately at both facilities using an IRB-approved protocol with provision for additional follow-up questions. The responses relevant to this chapter came in reply to the question "Do you have a favorite Scripture or Bible verse?" Those inmates who identified a particular passage often quoted it and were eager to explain more about its personal significance to them. These qualitative findings in the inmates' own words offer significant insight into the role of sacred texts in faith-based rehabilitation programs and about inmates' self-understanding of their own spiritual identities.

Survey Findings

Survey responses to the BSLP establish the prevalence, frequency, and distribution of personal Bible reading among inmates at Angola. Researchers

Table 10.1 Frequency of Privately Reading a Sacred Text (e.g., Bible, Qur'an, Torah)

Frequency of reading	Protestant, %	Catholic, %	Total Christian, %	Islam, %	BC grads, %	Population, %
Daily	42.9	28.2	38.5	40.5	55.7	34.3
At least several times a week	63.3	42.5	57.1	58.4	77.9	51.4
At least weekly	74.9	57.8	69.8	67.9	87	64.3
At least 2–3 times a month	82	67.3	77.7	75.0	92.1	71.5
At least monthly	85.9	76.8	83.2	84.5	94.4	76.7

asked, "Outside of attending religious services, about how often do you currently spend private time reading the Bible, Qur'an, Torah, or other sacred book?" Cross-tabulating responses with inmates' current religious identification reveals that Protestant Christians read a sacred text more often than any other religious group, with nearly 43 percent reporting daily reading and three-quarters reading at least weekly (see Table 10.1). Catholics read sacred texts less often than Protestants, Muslims, or the population as a whole. Still, the total population of Christians including Protestants and Catholics read the Bible with greater frequency than the population at large. Frequency of this combined Christian Bible reading tracks remarkably closely with Muslims' reading of the Qur'an.

Unsurprisingly, Bible College graduates report reading with greater frequency than any other group. Over half of graduates read daily (55.7 percent), three-quarters several times a week (77.9 percent), and 87 percent at least weekly. Membership and attendance within Angola's congregations also fosters private Bible reading. Among attending congregation members, 46.7 percent read Scripture daily. Another 21.4 percent read several times per week, and 13.8 percent read about weekly. In sum, 81.9 percent of active congregants read a sacred text *at least* weekly, which is more frequent than any self-identified denominational grouping and nearly as often as Bible College graduates. This level of reading engagement comparable to the college graduates is all the more remarkable given that 65 percent of Angola inmates have less than a high school education. Educational staff members estimate that 30 percent of the prison population is functionally illiterate. (Per LSP Demographics Report provided by prison staff, as of July 8, 2013, 65.33 percent of inmates claim 11 years or fewer of education; 28.14 percent claim 8 years or fewer.)

Interview Findings

Interview responses move beyond who is reading a sacred text and how often, and include information about which texts have the most lasting significance for readers. Given the focus on Bible college students and graduates, all texts cited were from the Christian Bible. Interviewees identified 30 passages from the Old Testament and 66 from the New Testament as their favorites or as passages of special significance (several of the 85 interviewees named multiple passages). Within the Old Testament, the Psalms were most popular, being named 8 times. New Testament citations focused on the epistles traditionally attributed to the Apostle Paul (38 times), followed by the Gospels (18), and the other epistles (9). Of particular interest are the individual verses recurring in multiple interviews. The most popular of these verses was Romans 8:28 (named 8 times): "We know that all things work together for good for those who love God, who are called according to his purpose." (All Scripture citations come from the New Revised Standard Version.)

In 7 different instances the interviewees named some portion of Philippians 4:11–13:

> Not that I am referring to being in need; for I have learned to be content with whatever I have. I know what it is to have little, and I know what it is to have plenty. In any and all circumstances I have learned the secret of being well-fed and of going hungry, of having plenty and of being in need. I can do all things through him who strengthens me.

Finally, Jeremiah 29, containing the prophet Jeremiah's letter of encouragement and instruction to the Jewish people living in exile in Babylon, and the words of Jesus in John 3:16 tied for third with 6 mentions each. Table 10.2 provides a further listing of all passages named more than once.

Several interviewees declined to name a specific passage as their favorite, often for theological reasons. One man refused to choose a favorite on the grounds of his love for the entire Bible. Elaborating on his choice, he reported that he has no favorite Scripture in the same way that he has no favorite child. Similarly, others were hesitant to commit to a single verse or passage in a lasting way but then identified Scriptures especially relevant to their immediate circumstance. One inmate at Angola recounted declining an offer to change his housing assignment and requesting instead to remain in the West Yard, which is widely regarded as the most difficult environment of Main Prison.

Table 10.2 Scriptures Named Most Frequently by Inmates

Scripture reference	Frequency
Romans 8:28	8
Philippians 4	7
Jeremiah 29	6
John 3:16	6
Galatians 2:20	5
Job 23:10	3
Philippians 3	3
2 Timothy 2:15	3
Proverbs 3:5–6	2
Matthew 6:33	2
Romans 5	2

Note: In some instances references to overlapping verses have been consolidated into a reference to an entire chapter (e.g., Phil 4:11–13; Phil 4:13; Phil 4:13–17 → Philippians 4).

He did so to continue leading a Bible study there for inmates returning to dorms after leaving the disciplinary cell blocks. He chose to remain because he recognized that "the harvest is white" (John 4:35). Another inmate asked, "How can David be 'a man after God's own heart' if he was a murderer, a liar, and an adulterer?" alluding to 1 Samuel 13:14 and its personal significance to his own situation. His answer: "Forgiveness." Finally, two inmates independently referenced Acts 5:38–39 when questioned about the future prospects for the seminary at Angola. They replied with reference to deliberations of the Jewish ruling council during the trial of Peter and the other apostles when the Jewish leader Gamaliel cautioned, "[If] this plan or this undertaking is of human origin, it will fail; but if it is of God, you will not be able to overthrow them—in that case you may even be found fighting against God!" The Bible college graduates perceive the seminary in a similar vein. At some stage it may complete its divine mission and close shop, but until then no administrative obstacle will prove insurmountable.

Through close reading of the verses chosen as most significant by inmate Bible college graduates, four key themes emerge. First, prisoners demonstrate a clear affinity for passages that connect directly with their present experience of incarceration. Second, while inmates frequently choose favorites popular in the free world, they interpret these Scriptures with sensitivity to both the literary context of the Bible and their own lived context of imprisonment that belies the caricature of superficial proof-texting. Third, through this interpretive process, inmates identify personally with a wide range of characters from throughout the biblical narratives. Fourth, through both contextual interpretation and personal identification, inmates reshape their own self-understandings by engaging with the text.

Connections with the Experience of Incarceration

First, prisoners gravitate toward passages that connect with their experience of captivity. This point of connection may come either through a text's provenance or its subject matter. Among the New Testament documents, prisoners favor the letters attributed to the Apostle Paul, and among this corpus the most often cited texts come from the "Prison Epistles," letters traditionally believed to be written by the apostle during his multiple experiences of incarceration by the Roman Empire. As mentioned above, inmates, like many other Christians, draw encouragement from Paul's description of finding strength through contentment in Philippians 4:11–13. What is taken for granted by many religious adherents in the free world, but vitally important to prisoners, is the context surrounding this exhortation. Paul writes his Philippian correspondents, "I rejoice in the Lord greatly that now at last you have revived your concern for me; indeed, you were concerned for me, but had no opportunity to show it. . . . In any case, it was kind of you to share my distress" (Phil 4:10, 14). Surrounding his words regarding contentment, Paul thanks the Philippian church for sharing his distress, namely, his deprivation via imprisonment. His entire letter was occasioned by the generosity of outside believers contributing to his material needs and thereby supplying what his state captors did not. Meanwhile, inmates today find that Paul's words regarding contentment help to decrease their anxiety. According to one interviewee, they "allow me to focus less on my own situation and things out of control; instead, I take them to God" in prayer.

Another favorite among the Prison Epistles is 2 Timothy, traditionally regarded as Paul's last known letter prior to his execution in Rome. One inmate named 2 Timothy 1:7 as his favorite: "God did not give us a spirit of cowardice, but rather a spirit of power and of love and of self-discipline." This preference for power over cowardice is normal within a conventional inmate culture that privileges bravado and intimidation, but the verse subverts and redefines these normal notions of power with the qualifications of love and self-discipline, traits far too absent from most prison environments. Again, the immediate context speaks to the author's experience of imprisonment: "Do not be ashamed, then, of the testimony about our Lord or of me his prisoner, but join with me in suffering for the gospel, relying on the power of God" (2 Tim 1:8). Contemporary inmates connect with Paul's concern that loved ones might grow ashamed. The apostle also speaks to the decline in relationships typically occurring because of incarceration. He writes, "Recalling your tears, I long to see you so that I may be filled with joy" (2 Tim 1:4). Late in his letter he pleads for a visit (4:9), mourns those who have abandoned him (4:10–11, 16), and requests basic items to bring comfort to his austere experience (4:13). All of these needs ring true to those who share Paul's experience of incarceration.

In the midst of this loneliness and deprivation, however, Paul continues to exhort his protégé Timothy, "Do your best to present yourself to God as one approved by him, a worker who has no need to be ashamed, rightly explaining the word of truth" (2 Tim 2:15). Many interviewees selected this verse as their watchword, thus recognizing its significance to the men. In fact, the seminary at Darrington incorporated this Scripture into a mural in its main corridor.

Although the Old Testament seldom addresses prison in the same way as Paul's letters, enforced captivity looms large through the Jewish experience of exile. Much of the prophetic literature addresses an audience in captivity. The books of Jeremiah and Ezekiel and many of the psalms are particularly representative of this context. Perhaps unsurprisingly, then, this material is among the most popular from the Old Testament with contemporary prisoners. Jeremiah 29 is one of the most beloved passages with inmates. Like the Philippians 4 passage, Jeremiah 29 is equally popular with believers outside of prison, but our interviewees demonstrated a particular interpretive sensitivity to the passage's exilic origin. This contextual sensitivity introduces the second major theme of inmates' biblical reading and interpretation.

Interpretive Sensitivity to Literal Context and Lived Experience

Inmates often favor passages equally popular among other Christian believers, but they frequently interpret them with attention to both literary context and their personal experience as prisoners. This distinct interpretation and application of common favorites discredits the caricature that prisoners always read Scripture in a flat, superficial manner. Jeremiah 29 offers one of the best examples. At the heart of this passage is the promise of verse 11: "For surely I know the plans I have for you, says the LORD, plans for your welfare and not for harm, to give you a future with hope." In the free world this promise for hope and prosperity proves especially popular during commencement season, adorning greeting cards and all manner of gifts for graduates. Inmates, however, are quick to point out (along with many other interpreters) that this assurance comes from a particular historical setting reflected in its literary context: it is a promise to exiles. Jeremiah addresses a community in captivity due to both their own failures and the injustice of their civil leaders. As one inmate put it, "God does not forget about his people. Even during chastisement, he loves you." As he understands it, the plans for welfare and future hope described here are not promises for physical freedom or material prosperity but for the sustained presence of God. As the following verses continue, "Then when you call upon me and come and pray to me, I will hear you. When you search for me, you will find me; if you seek me with all your heart . . ." (Jer 29:12–13).

Another inmate applies this same passage in a very specifically personal way, but he does so with the same sensitivity to its historical context and original audience. He points out that Israel faced 70 years in exile (Jer 29:10). Recognizing this original significance of the text, he then bridges it to his own personal experience. He is currently serving consecutive sentences of 40 and 30 years, giving him the same duration of "exile" as ancient Israel. With this personal touchstone, he finds in Jeremiah 29 a pattern for his life while incarcerated. He adopts as his own directive the instruction of verse 7 to "seek the welfare of the city where I have sent you into exile, and pray to the LORD on its behalf, for in its welfare you will find your welfare." He recognizes the prison as his "city" and senses a responsibility to seek its good through both action and prayer. It is not the city he would choose to inhabit any more than Israel chose Babylon, but it is the city where he resides nonetheless, and so he seeks its welfare for its sake and his own.

A third inmate from a different prison elaborated even further on his responsibilities in light of Jeremiah 29. He explained the passage's context of captivity and offered an allegorical interpretation applying the specific instructions of verses 5–6 to his situation: "Build houses and live in them; plant gardens and eat what they produce. Take wives and have sons and daughters; take wives for your sons, and give your daughters in marriage, that they may bear sons and daughters; multiply there, and do not decrease." In a contemporary context without the possibility of building or marriage and little opportunity for gardening, this prisoner takes "build houses" as an instruction to "build yourself," cultivating a newly faithful and prosocial identity. Rather than planting gardens, he plants "seeds of the gospel" among his fellow prisoners (connecting Jeremiah 29 with agricultural metaphors for preaching used by both Jesus [Mark 4:1–8 and pars.] and Paul [1 Cor 3:5–7]). Finally, he applies the command to multiply to the growth of believers in the church rather than to biological reproduction. Like the previous interviewee, he also notes the responsibility to pray on behalf of his community, including his captors. Based on a prophetic message to ancient Israel, this contemporary inmate feels a sacred responsibility to intercede for the correctional officers and wardens of his prison.

Personal Identification with the Narratives of Biblical Characters

The third theme to emerge from the interviews is inmates' identification with a wide range of biblical characters. These comparisons usually emerged unsolicited during interviews, often in response to questions about a favorite passage. Characters named included both men and women from both testaments and ranged from figures as prominent as David and Paul to those as obscure as Mephibosheth (see 2 Samuel 9). Many of the parallels are relatively straightforward. One man compared his experience of incarceration to that of Jonah "living in the whale." Another draws solace from the story of doubting Thomas' restoration to faith during his own periods of doubt. Yet another finds encouragement in David's forgiveness and restoration following his spiral into successive moral failures. Many of the men identify with the apostle Paul as a fellow prisoner as described above.

Other identifications, however, are much more nuanced but equally valid. One prisoner compared his experience to the life of the apostle Peter in a somewhat unexpected way. As the father of a 12-year-old daughter whose mother is also incarcerated, this inmate identifies with Peter's need to "trust God to provide for his family while following Christ in ministry imperfectly." Like many prisoners, this man is concerned for the safety and well-being of his child and pained by his forced separation from her, but in Scripture he has found a model of trust in God to care for family members that he cannot serve personally.

Perhaps the most unusual identification was with the Old Testament character Mephibosheth, grandson of Israel's first king Saul. The story of Mephibosheth is found in 2 Samuel 9. Here Saul's successor King David seeks someone from his predecessor's lineage "to whom [he] may show kindness for [Saul's son] Jonathan's sake" (2 Sam 9:1). A servant tells David of Mephiboseth, "a son of Jonathan . . . crippled in his feet" (9:3). David summons this man, who likely expects to be executed as a potential rival claimant to the throne; instead, David honors the man and invites him to dine at the royal table for the rest of his life. One Louisiana inmate identified with Mephibosheth, citing his own experience of "brokenness through abuse and neglect" as an analogue to Mephibosheth's chronic injury. Like Mephibosheth, this man expected the worst when brought before judicial authorities, but instead he now understands himself as "invited to a place at the king's table" through his Christian faith.

This same man identified with aspects of the life narratives of many biblical characters. He compared himself with the Samaritan woman in John 4 broken by her own guilt at Jesus's words but then told of living, spiritual water. He also likened himself to the man born blind but healed by Jesus, saying, "There is no greater way for God's glory to be revealed than through a situation you did not create." The explanations of these contrasting identifications point toward the tension in many inmates' self-understandings. They recognize and sometimes freely acknowledge their guilt with its accompanying regret and brokenness (like the Samaritan woman) but also see themselves as victims of situations beyond their control (like the man born blind). This tension captures the ambiguities inherent within the criminal justice system amid the interplay between personal agency on the one hand and structural disadvantage on the other. Finally, like the man healed from a legion of demons by Christ, he sees himself as someone who was formerly violent, sought out by Jesus for a specific purpose, and told to return to those who formerly knew him best where his transformation would make the greatest impact.

Identity Transformation

This transformed self-understanding and attendant sense of mission is the final theme to emerge from the interviews, and is a product of both contextual interpretations of Scripture and personal identification with its complex characters. Maruna and colleagues (2006) explain how incarceration creates for prisoners a "crisis of self-narrative." One response to that crisis is the experience of religious conversion and the accompanying creation of a "conversion narrative." The authors argue that these narratives accomplish "shame management" in five ways:

1. Creates a new social identity to replace the label of prisoner or criminal.
2. Imbues the experience of imprisonment with purpose and meaning.

3. Empowers the largely powerless prisoner by turning him into an agent of God.

4. Provides the prisoner with a language and framework for forgiveness.

5. Allows a sense of control over an unknown future. (Maruna et al. 2006)

Favorite Scriptures identified by inmates correlate well with Maruna's five functions. Galatians 2:20, named by five different inmates, speaks to the "new social identity": "[It] is no longer I who live, but it is Christ who lives in me. And the life I now live in the flesh I live by faith in the Son of God, who loved me and gave himself for me." Ezekiel 36:26 serves a similar purpose with its emphasis on "a new heart" and "a new spirit." As described already, this new identity provides purpose and meaning as prisoners perceive themselves as witnesses to their families, prison communities, and communities of origin. Within these newfound roles, prisoners serve as agents of God who "strive first for the kingdom of God and his righteousness" (Matt 6:33).

Maruna and colleagues place "a language and framework for forgiveness" fourth on their list, but perhaps it should come first given the logical progression and prominence among inmates' most frequently cited Scriptures. The experience of forgiveness logically precedes creation of a new identity, from which purpose, meaning, and empowerment follow. Galatians 2:20 therefore holds relevance here also. Other popular passages also foreground forgiveness, along with divine love, most notably in John 3:16 and Romans 5:8:

> For God so loved the world that he gave his only Son, so that everyone who believes in him may not perish but may have eternal life.
> But God proves his love for us in that while we still were sinners Christ died for us.

Finally, conversion narratives built on frequent and thoughtful meditation on the Bible grant prisoners a sense of control within chaotic environments. Proverbs 3:5–6 captures this assurance well: "Trust in the LORD with all your heart, and do not rely on your own insight. In all your ways acknowledge him, and he will make straight your paths." For men facing highly tenuous futures and accustomed to reliance on their own insight, often with disastrous consequences, the promise of straight paths provides hope and stability.

Conclusions and Recommendations

This mixed-methods study of long-term inmates participating in prison seminary programs in Texas and Louisiana offers new insight into the Scripture reading habits and preferences of prisoners. Survey data from Angola prison in Louisiana show that both Christian and Muslim inmates privately read a sacred text significantly more often than the general population. Among Christian inmates, Protestants read the Bible more frequently than Catholics. Unsurprisingly, seminary graduates read Scripture more frequently than any other group, but actively participating congregation members without comparable education also read more often than self-identified Muslims, Christians, or even the more frequently reading Protestant subset.

This heightened reading by congregational participants who have not attended the Bible College indicates a desire for biblical literacy among religious general population inmates. The primary barrier to this *biblical* literacy, however, is the lack of *basic* literacy among inmates. According to the U.S. Department of Education, 16 percent of adult prison inmates test below basic prose literacy, and only 3 percent tested as fully proficient. Survey findings also indicate racial disparity as White inmates test higher than Black inmates, while both groups outperform Hispanic inmates. Fifteen percent of Black inmates tested below basic literacy with only 1 percent proficient, and 35 percent of Hispanic inmates fell below basic with 2 percent proficiency (Amodeo, Jin, & Kling 2009; Greenberg et al. 2007). The specific circumstance at Angola is even more desperate with as much as 30 percent of the population functionally illiterate.

Such prevalent illiteracy coupled with prisoners' desire to read Scripture for themselves suggests that religious volunteers and ministries ought to consider basic literacy education as both a powerful spiritual *and* social intervention in inmates' lives. Offering literacy instruction will enable prisoners to read sacred texts and other religious materials but also to further their formal education, participate in a fuller array of rehabilitative programs, and improve prospects for employment upon release. Such literacy programs would likely face much less constitutional scrutiny than other types of religious programs. Christians already have precedent for this type of literacy promotion as a form of outreach through the work of both international missionaries and domestic evangelists (Barros 1995; Christoph 2009; Harries 2001).

Meanwhile, qualitative interviews in both Texas and Louisiana dispel the misconception that inmates who are able to read the Bible privately do so in exclusively simplistic ways. Although some no doubt apply the texts in highly personalized ways without consideration of context, others demonstrate rich and sometimes novel interpretive practices. Incarcerated readers gravitate toward passages that connect to their personal experience of imprisonment and then interpret those passages with sensitivity to both the literary context of the verses and their own context of imprisonment. They also identify particular biblical characters whose narratives resonate with their own experience in some way. Sometimes these practices yield highly personalized and even idiosyncratic applications, but often they serve to reorient the readers' lives and provide a new sense of purpose and responsibility to their neighbors, both fellow inmates and correctional officers. Biblical interpretation offers a foundation for construction of their own "conversion narratives" highlighting the themes enumerated by Maruna and colleagues.

This work has focused on Christian readings of the Bible as a result of the religious self-identification of the great majority of seminary students interviewed. Although survey data allowed limited comparisons with the reading habits of Muslims, ethnographic work should follow to explore their reading of the Qur'an and other sacred literature. Comparable work with inmates of other faith traditions would also strengthen understanding of prisoners' religious practices. Future research may also explore more detailed comparisons with Christian inmates who have not attended a seminary program or other formal religious education. Again, survey results allowed comparison of reading frequency at Angola but not an in-depth exploration of the specific reading habits and interpretive practices of these men. Finally, future work could explore the reading of sacred texts by religiously nonaffiliated inmates. With little previous attention given to the specific content of inmates' sacred reading, much exploration remains to be done.

Bibliography

Amodeo, A., Jin, Y., Kling, J., & United States. Employment and Training Administration. *Preparing for life beyond prison walls: The literacy of incarcerated adults near release.* Washington, DC: U.S. Dept. of Labor, Employment and Training Administration, 2009.

Barros, M. C. The missionary presence in literacy campaigns in the indigenous languages of Latin America (1939–1952). *International Journal of Educational Development* 15 (1995): 277–287.

Benda, B. B., & Corwyn, R. F. Are the effects of religion on crime mediated, moderated, and misrepresented by inappropriate measures? *Journal of Social Science Research* 27 (2001): 57–86.

Christoph, J. N. Each one teach one: The legacy of evangelism in adult literacy education. *Written Communication* 26 (2009): 77–110.

Clear, T. R., Hardyman, P. L., Stout, B., Lucken, K., & Dammer, H. R. The value of religion in prison: An inmate perspective. *Journal of Contemporary Criminal Justice* 16 (2000): 53–74.

Duwe, G., Hallett, M., Hays, J., Jang, S. J., & Johnson, B. R. Bible college participation and prison misconduct: A preliminary analysis. *Journal of Offender Rehabilitation* 54, no.5 (2015): 371–390.

Greenberg, E., Dunleavy, E., Kutner, M. A., & National Center for Education Statistics. *Literacy behind bars: Results from the 2003 national assessment of adult literacy prison survey.* Washington, DC: National Center for Education Statistics, Institute of Education Sciences, U.S. Dept. of Education, 2007.

Hallett, M., Hays, J., Johnson, B., Jang, S. J., & Duwe, G. *The Angola prison seminary: Effects of faith-based ministry on identity transformation, desistance, and rehabilitation*. Oxford, UK: Routledge, 2016.

Harries, P. Missionaries, Marxists and magic: Power and the politics of literacy in south-east Africa. *Journal of South African Studies* 27 (2001): 405–427.

Johnson, B. R. Religiosity and institutional deviance: The impact of religious variables upon inmate adjustment. *Criminal Justice Review* 12 (1987): 21–30.

Johnson, B. R. Religious programs and recidivism among former inmates in Prison Fellowship programs: A long-term follow-up study. *Justice Quarterly* 21 (2004): 329–354.

Johnson, B. R., Larson, D. B., & Pitts, T. C. Religious programs, institutional adjustment, and recidivism among former inmates in Prison Fellowship programs. *Justice Quarterly* 14 (1997): 145–166.

Kerley, K. R., & Copes, H. "Keepin' my mind right": Identity maintenance and religious social support in the prison context. *International Journal of Offender Therapy and Comparative Criminology* 53 (2009): 228–244.

Maruna, S., Wilson, L., & Curran, K. Why God is often found behind bars: Prison conversions and the crisis of self-narrative. *Research in Human Development* 3 (2006): 161–184.

Odle, N. Privilege through prayer: Examining Bible-based prison rehabilitation programs under the Establishment Clause. *Texas Journal on Civil Liberties & Civil Rights* 12 (2007): 277–311.

Sullivan, W. F. *Prison religion: Faith-based reform and the Constitution*. Princeton, NJ: Princeton University Press, 2009.

Switzer, D. Literature in prison. *Journal of Correctional Education* 35 (1984): 18–19.

Appendix: List of All Passages Cited by Interviewees

Deut 15:16	Ps 142
Jos 1:8	Prov 3:5–6
Job 1:21	Eccl 7:8
Job 13:15	Isa 6:8
Job 23:10	Jer 17:7–8
Job 38:1–4	Jer 29
Ps 19:14	Jer 29:7
Ps 27:13	Jer 29:11
Ps 51	Ezek 36:26
Ps 91	Hos 4:6
Ps 103:10	Hab 2:2
Ps 119:49–50	Matt 5–7
Ps 119:128	Matt 6:33

Luke 1–3

Luke 6:22–38

John 1:12

John 3:16

John 14:1–3

John 14:6

John 15:7

John 17:9

Rom 5:1–8

Rom 5:8

Rom 8:28

Rom 12:1

1 Cor 10:13

1 Cor 13

2 Cor 5:17

Gal 2:20

Eph 4:1–6

Eph 6:19–20

Phil 2:4

Phil 2:13

Phil 3:10–12

Phil 3:13

Phil 3:13–14

Phil 4:11

Phil 4:11–12

Phil 4:13

Phil 4:13–17

Phil 4:19

2 Tim 1:7

2 Tim 2:15

Titus 1:16

Heb 4:16

Heb 6:10

Heb 13:3

Jas 1:22

Jas 5:16

1 Pet 5:6–8

2 Pet 1:16

2 Pet 3:9

1 John 4:4

Rev 3:20

CHAPTER ELEVEN

Backgrounds and Motivations of Prison Chaplains

Andrew S. Denney

Prison chaplains are one of the oldest, yet least studied, positions within American corrections. As of 2012, there were 1,600 chaplains employed at approximately 1,100 state and federal prisons in the United States (Pew Research Center 2012). Moreover, the passage of the Religious Land Use and Institutionalized Persons Act (RLUIPA) in 2000 that further buttressed inmate rights to identify with and perform religious rites has served as a catalyst for a number of high-profile lawsuits (see U.S. Department of Justice 2010). As such, it is crucial to understand the backgrounds and motivations of prison chaplains, as is the purpose of this study, to assist with recruitment and retention efforts in order to ensure that inmate religious rights are upheld and further safeguard the department of corrections at the state and federal levels against future lawsuits.

Literature Review

Historically, prison chaplains have served as a mainstay inside American corrections. However, the monumental increase in correctional budgets—at the state and federal levels—over the past approximate 30 years has led to many states looking for ways to save money. For example, state and federal correctional budgets went from $20 billion in 1982 to $74 billion in 2007 (U.S. Department of Justice 2009). Consequently, prison chaplains have felt the effects of budget shortfalls with states like South Carolina cutting 24 of its 47 chaplains in 2001 after a $33.6 million budget shortfall (St. Gerard 2003). Despite these budget cuts, the passage of RLUIPA in 2000 has underscored the importance of chaplains in the correctional setting and perhaps even provided further justification for the continued existence of this storied role within corrections that serves as an "agent for change" (Glaser 1964).

Brief History of Prison Chaplains

Prison chaplains have served as a constant presence inside American corrections, dating back to the waning years of the 1700s (Skotnicki 2000). The strong belief of religious groups at this time, primarily from the influence of the Quakers, firmly attached religion as a perceived necessary requirement to reform individuals and turn them away from a life of crime. The term *penitentiary* is even rooted in the religious practice of doing *penitence*, or repenting from one's sins (Thibaut 1982). Therefore, this belief of the necessity for religious instruction was essential for the moral reform of an offender, thus becoming firmly entrenched as the primary goal of American corrections for the first approximate 100 years of its existence.

Because of this purported need and requirement of religion and faith for the moral reform of inmates inside American prisons, Catholic and Protestant chaplains were employed by prisons and entrusted with overseeing the moral reform of inmates. The job duties assigned to chaplains during this time ranged from leading religious services to overseeing the reentry aspect of inmates as they transitioned back into society (Skotnicki 2000). Some scholars have even argued that chaplains held the same level of power as wardens within prisons during the 1800s (Skotnicki 2000). Though this strong influence of chaplains within the institutional setting was undeniable during this time, the importance of religion began dissipating in the early 1900s with a gradual emphasis towards positivism.

Throughout the 20th century, the emphasis of religion and the moral reform of inmates substantially declined as the medical model of corrections took hold. As such, the role and direct religious responsibilities of chaplains also suffered. This emphasis of positivism saw teachers, psychiatrists, and others fulfilling the roles that chaplains once occupied (Skotnicki 2000). With this strong historical presence inside American corrections and the shift away from religious reform of an inmate as being a central goal of corrections, this led some scholars to question the role that modern chaplains serve inside American prisons.

Current Role of Prison Chaplains

As a consequence of the shifting role in American corrections throughout the 20th century and an increasing amount of volunteers fulfilling the duties once charged to chaplains, scholars began examining the role that modern chaplains were performing in prisons as research on the modern roles of prison chaplains prior to the 1990s had been sparse (see Sundt & Cullen 1998, 2007; Sundt, Dammer, & Cullen 2002). Sundt and Cullen (1998) found that modern prison chaplains spend the overwhelming majority of their time performing administrative roles. Specifically, most chaplains report that their time is spent overseeing volunteers from the surrounding community that come in to work with inmates and coordinating institutional faith-based programming (Sundt & Cullen 1998). This finding was confirmed in a relatively recent 50-state survey that examined the roles of modern prison chaplains by the Pew Research Center (2012), finding that 93 percent *administer* or *organize religious programs.*

Sundt and Cullen (1998) also found that chaplains view counseling inmates as a primary task. This finding too was later confirmed by the Pew Research Center (2012) with 57 percent of chaplains reporting that counseling sessions, in addition to leading religious worship and individual instruction, are among the most important perceived aspects of their job. This role is crucial since religion has been identified in prior research as assisting with an inmate's transition into the prison setting (see Clear, Stout, Dammer, Kelly, Hardyman, & Shapiro 1992; Johnson 1987; Johnson, Larson, & Pitts 1997; Pass 1999). However, the evolution of the prison chaplain role has also led to the emergence of new role issues.

Role Issues

Role issues associated with key positions within prisons, such as stress attached to the role of correctional officers, have been the subject of widespread research over the past approximate 30 years (see Cullen, Link, Wolfe, & Frank 1985; Finn 1998; Tewksbury, Higgins, & Denney 2012). With this focus on correctional officer stress, some scholars began examining both the sources and presence of stress among prison chaplains in their modern position. While examining the potential sources of stress, Hicks (2012) identified that a substantial portion of this stress is derived from conflict between chaplains (noncustodial role) and correctional officers (custodial role). Additionally, stress has been attributed to the shifting role of chaplains from ministerial duties to more administrative tasks (Sundt & Cullen 2007). Consequently, the potential for role ambiguity and stress remains as the chaplaincy position seemingly continues to shift toward a more administrative role, perhaps even leading to burnout where a chaplain leaves the institutional role entirely.

One may assume that those who occupy a position within corrections and experience stress in the workplace may lead to eventual burnout, as has been the case in research examining correctional officer stress (Cullen et al. 1985; Finn 1998; Tewksbury et al. 2012). Overall, however, research suggests that prison chaplains are generally satisfied with their position within prisons (see

Pew Research Center 2012; Sundt & Cullen 2007). For example, Sundt and Cullen (2007) found that most chaplains in their sample reported being *very* or *somewhat* satisfied with their occupation at 99 percent. A more recent examination of prison chaplain job satisfaction by the Pew Research Center (2012) found too that most chaplains were satisfied with their jobs, albeit at a lower percentage (64 percent were *very satisfied* and 30 percent were *somewhat satisfied*) than what was found by Sundt and Cullen (2007). Although research suggests that most chaplains are satisfied with their positions, research has also suggested that a significant minority (30 percent) of chaplains report feeling *a lot of* pressure with their roles (Sundt & Cullen 2007). With the apparent trend of the chaplain role shifting toward a more stress-laden administrative role, understanding the backgrounds and motivations of prison chaplains are imperative to study as they may serve as crucial recruitment and retention tools for the department of corrections in the near future as burnout among prison chaplains may increase.

Backgrounds and Motivations of Prison Chaplains and Faith-Based Prison Volunteers

To date, few studies have examined the backgrounds and motivations of prison chaplains, especially in a qualitative sense. Most prior research pertaining to prison chaplains has only focused on information regarding the attitudes and beliefs of various criminal justice system components, policies, and/or practices. Such components include the role of punishment, belief toward rehabilitation, job satisfaction attitudes, and perceived work dangers (see Beckford 1999; Hicks 2008, 2012; Sundt & Cullen 1998, 2007; Sundt et al. 2002). However, few identified studies have focused on the backgrounds and motivations of both employed prison chaplains and lay ministers in the correctional setting (see Kerley, Bartkowski, Matthews, & Emond 2010; Kerley, Matthews, & Shoemaker 2009), or volunteers with prison ministries (see Kort-Butler & Malone 2015; Tewksbury & Collins 2005; Tewksbury & Dabney 2004).

One of the first studies to examine this issue by Kerley and colleagues (2009) focused on interviews with 30 prison chaplains employed by the Mississippi Department of Corrections and lay ministers that volunteered their services for the prison. In particular, Kerley et al. (2009) focused on the four general themes of (1) their approach to prisons/prison ministry, (2) the role of faith on changing inmate behaviors and attitudes, (3) goals of ministerial work, and (4) the role of the chaplains and lay ministers in the creation of social networks for inmates upon their release. Kerley et al. (2009) found that the vast majority of the prison chaplains and lay ministers attended church early on in their life, mostly converting to Christianity between the ages of 5 and 15, and had continued this trend of heavy church involvement well into adulthood. Moreover, many held positions within their local congregations, such as pastor, music ministers, and business managers while employed as a chaplain or in addition to their volunteer role. Lastly, they found that respondents reported their position within the prison—as an employee and a volunteer—as a "calling" that was part of a larger purpose from God whereby they often received enjoyment from interacting with inmates of different faiths from their own.

Kerley et al. (2010) examined the religious values that may serve as motivation for both prison chaplains and lay ministers that volunteered for prison ministries in Mississippi in addition to the inherent tension between traditional conservative Protestant punitive values and inmate programming. Kerley at al. (2010) built on what was found in Kerley and colleagues (2009) that respondents believed their work was a "divine calling" in that they were doing what God had planned for their life. Additionally, they noted that they became involved in prison ministry from connections they had formed at some point in their life, including but not limited to, having a relative or friend incarcerated, their own incarceration, and having worked inside a prison prior to their ministerial work. Respondents also discussed developing continued compassion across their interactions with inmates that ultimately served as a way to navigate their future interactions with inmates through a sense of comfort with inmates and the prison environment as a whole.

Kort-Butler and Malone (2015) echoed the theme found in the two prior works of prison-ministry volunteers having a divine calling to their work. This is a theme that has also been found in prior work examining prison ministry volunteers (Tewksbury & Collins 2005; Tewksbury & Dabney 2004) and even faith-based halfway house volunteers (Denney & Tewksbury 2013). For example, Tewksbury and Dabney (2004) found that 50 percent of prison volunteers in their sample reported being "called" by God to share their faith with inmates. Kort-Butler and Malone (2015), similar to Kerley et al. (2010), also found that prison ministry volunteers often sympathized with inmates because of feeling a connection with inmates based on poor choices that they too had made while also experiencing transformation in their own personal lives from inmate interactions. This transformative effect has too been found in prior studies examining similar populations (see Denney & Tewksbury 2013; Kerley et al. 2010).

Although prior studies have loosely examined the backgrounds and motivations of prison chaplains, no such identified studies have done so directly. The importance of this topic is crucial as RLUIPA and the increased focus on prison chaplaincy as an administrative role in recent years perhaps has changed the overall nature of who seeks out and stays employed as a prison chaplain. Therefore, the expansion of research directly into the backgrounds and motivations of prison chaplains employed by the department of corrections is crucial for understanding who is attracted to this position, why, and what qualities of the position potentially can be emphasized by the department of corrections to recruit and retain key personnel.

The Present Study

Despite many changes in the overall job duties and social position of prison chaplains throughout the United States, prison chaplains still maintain an important position and fulfill an essential role for the department of corrections at both the state and federal levels. Not only do prison chaplains perform necessary functions inside the prison to assist inmates and staff with personal issues (see Clear, Hardyman, Stout, Lucken, & Dammer 2000), but they also help safeguard their respective agency against lawsuits for the alleged/actual violation of protected inmate religious rights with the passage of RLUIPA in 2000. The goal of the present study is twofold: first, to understand the detailed backgrounds of individuals that have chosen prison chaplaincy as an occupation, including key demographic information, personal upbringing, and overall life experience; and second, to understand what motivated these individuals to join the occupation initially, and what may serve as a motivation to continue their work. Findings from this study will assist state and federal department of corrections with recruitment and retention efforts for one of the oldest positions inside U.S. prisons.

Methods

The current study involves one-on-one interviews of prison chaplains employed with a state-level department of corrections in a midwestern state in the United States. The midwestern state department of corrections does not support or endorse any findings in the present study. All participants were prison chaplains employed at the time of the interview for their respective department of corrections. Approval was made through the department of corrections and the institutional review board of the author's former university.

Once approval was received, the author was provided a list of all chaplains currently employed by the department of corrections. Potential respondents were e-mailed by their supervisor an invitation to participate. If interested in participating, chaplains were then instructed to contact the author to schedule an interview date and time. In total, 21 of the 34 total chaplains (61.8 percent) agreed to participate; however, two eventually declined due to scheduling conflicts. The final participation total was 19, yielding a 55.9 percent participation percentage. Responses collected reflect the personal and professional backgrounds of prison chaplains in addition to their motivations for initially beginning and continuing their work as a prison chaplain. Data collection took place in the late winter and early spring of 2015.

Participants

Participants in the present study were prison chaplains that were employed through the state's department of corrections or contracted out to one of the state's private prisons. Those contracted to a private prison (n=3: 15.8 percent) still fell under the purveyance of the state department of corrections' chaplain office on all matters pertaining to the chaplaincy position. However, their job duties and freedom to create new programs varied slightly from those at state-run institutions.

A total of 19 participants were interviewed in the present study, including both males (n=13; 68.4 percent) and females (n=6; 31.6 percent) (see Table 11.1). Participants were either the sole chaplain of their facility, or one of a possible two or three chaplains employed at an individual institution. Ages of participants ranged from 42 to 65 years of age with a mean of 53.1, a mode of 61, and a median of 51.

There were only two races/ethnicities represented among the participants, Caucasian and African American. Fully 17 of the participants identified themselves as Caucasian with two identifying themselves as African American. The majority (n=12) of participants were married. However, a significant minority self-reported as being either single (n=5) or divorced (n=2).

All participants reported having a minimum of a bachelor's degree. However, the minimum degree needed for this position according to the respective department of corrections' policy is a masters in divinity (MDiv). The majority of participants had the minimum educational qualification of either a MDiv (n=11), a combination of a MDiv and another graduate degree (e.g., MBA or MS) (n=2), or a doctorate in divinity (n=1). Four of the participants had only obtained a bachelor's degree. There were a total of 12 Christian denominations represented (see Table 11.1).

Total time in their current chaplaincy position ranged from seven months to 18 years. However, only two chaplains reported having more than 7 years of experience at 17 and 18 years, respectively. The average time in one's current position was 6.3 years. Pseudonyms have been assigned to participant names to protect their identity.

Data Collection

Data for the present study were collected through a combination of face-to-face and telephone interviews with chaplains employed by the department of corrections previously identified. Each interview lasted between 60 and 90 minutes. Interviews were conducted in a private setting, typically within the chaplain's office, a coffee shop, or a restaurant. A semistructured interview guide was used to guide the discussion around central themes.

Table 11.1　Descriptive Statistics

Measure	%	M
Demographics		
Sex		
Male	68.4	
Female	31.6	
Race		
Caucasian	89.5	
African American	10.5	
Age		53.1
Marital status		
Single	26.3	
Married	63.2	
Divorced	10.5	
Education		
Bachelor's	21.1	
Master's	5.3	
Master's in Divinity	57.9	
Combination	10.5	
Doctorate in Divinity	5.3	
Denomination		
African Methodist Episcopalian	10.5	
Assemblies of God	21.1	
Baptist	5.3	
Baptist Fundamentalist	5.3	
Church of Christ Christians	5.3	
Lutheran	10.5	
Methodist	5.3	
Missouri Lutheran Synod	5.3	
Nondenominational	5.3	
Pentecostal	21.1	
Protestant	15.8	
Quaker	10.5	

The specific themes in the interview guide included the following: personal upbringing, family life, employment history, any interaction(s) with offenders throughout their lifetime, prior ministerial experience, personal motivations for holding the chaplaincy position, and personal rewards derived from their occupation. All interviews were audio-recorded and transcribed in full. Once key themes emerged, each transcript was reread numerous times to ensure the accuracy and completeness of all identified themes. Generally, a minimum of approximately 25 interviews is considered to be needed for theoretical saturation to occur (Charmaz 2006; Morse 1994). However, Guest, Bunce, and Johnson (2006) found that themes can appear at as few as six interviews, and theoretical saturation can even occur at 12 total interviews. Results reflect the primary themes of the data.

Results

With the goals of the present study being to understand key backgrounds and motivations of prison chaplains, the focus of the present study went beyond prior research foci on job duties. Three separate themes emerged pertaining to the backgrounds of prison chaplains, and four individual themes for chaplain motivations. For backgrounds of prison chaplains, these three themes were a (1) blue-collar background, (2) strong religious upbringing, and (3) instability in ministerial work. For motivations of prison chaplains, these four themes were (1) the chaplaincy position offering stability, (2) being "called" to the chaplaincy, (3) the ability to effect positive change on inmates, and (4) being exposed to different religions and faiths. Findings suggest that most chaplains seek the position out of a desire for stability in their personal and professional life after a lifetime of moving and instability in prior ministerial work.

Findings overwhelmingly demonstrate that chaplains do not actively seek to become a prison chaplain, but that they fall into the chaplain role after instability in their ministerial careers. Participants discussed being raised in mostly blue-collar households with a central focus on the importance of religion. This strong religious atmosphere within their household led most on a path to seek a career in ministry. However, most prison chaplains experienced extreme difficulty finding a consistent position in ministry in pay, hours, and location. Most chaplains sought the position because of its offerings for benefits (e.g., consistent pay, health insurance) not attributed in prior ministerial work and were largely not "called," contrary to what prior research suggests (see Hicks 2008; Kerley et al. 2009, 2010). Moreover, the shift in the modern-day chaplain role to a primarily administrative position—what has largely been considered a potential catalyst for chaplain burnout (see Sundt & Cullen 2007)—has now seemingly led to attracting an entirely new employee base. Therefore, this shift in motivation for prison chaplains from being "called" to the position being seen as more of a stable occupation may further push the chaplaincy position into the administrative role that it has seemingly become.

Backgrounds

Blue-Collar Background

Many chaplains reported growing up in a blue-collar background. Specifically, eight discussed in detail their blue-collar upbringing (e.g., father was automobile mechanic, school custodian, military member). This information is important because it becomes apparent that this background assisted chaplains both with being able to relate to inmates and being used to the consistent moving that is often associated with their later ministerial profession. Melissa, a chaplain for six years, discussed her upbringing when she said that, ". . . I grew up in a very normal [family], my dad worked in a factory, grew up in a big family, so there were a lot of rules and structure, which now, I really absolutely understand and uphold."

Pamela, an African American female chaplain employed for two years, discussed her upbringing with a single mother in an inner-city area in how her personal background assisted her with forming connections with inmates as part of her chaplain duties:

> . . . [I] grew up in a lot of neighborhoods that the guys grew up in, you know I try not to tell them that as much, so a lot of neighborhoods, a lot of schools they went to, because a lot of the guys are from [name of the city] . . . so about 40% of our population is from there. . . .

Pamela goes on to say how this background assists her in understanding the inmate population that she works with:

> Coming from some of the same background as some of the guys, the single parent piece, low income piece, having to navigate some of those things and you know, throw in African American in a facility [that] really has 40% African Americans, so you know understanding all those . . . that was actually a good thing.

Molly discussed how her father was in the military and how she moved numerous times as a child saying that, "Dad was in the military, so we did move around a bit. And, so [I] lived in California, Colorado, Spain, which is where I got the Spanish. A couple other places that I don't remember, I was too young." The consistent moving and acclimation to a new community also simultaneously reinforced the second main theme of a strong religious upbringing, largely because of the relatively stable social outlet that it provided regardless of where the individual was now living.

Strong Religious Upbringing

The religion and the tradition that an individual is raised in can have drastic impacts on one's life that shapes various aspects of their long-term personal and professional life (Bridges & Moore 2002). This largely seemed to be the case for this sample in seeking a career in ministerial work as 12 total participants reported being raised in a strong religious household. This is similar to findings by Kerley and colleagues (2009) that most chaplains and prison ministry volunteers were heavily involved in church, both as a child and adult. One respondent, Ben, reflected on his strong religious and almost sheltered upbringing with his father being a pastor:

> Yeah, I was really fortunate as I was raised with a loving family. My dad, my dad, he went to be a pastor when I was six or seven years old, and so I was raised as a pastor's kid. So, everything that I pretty much did in my life was centered around church or sports. That was really all I knew. You know, my parents were really conservative . . . I never went to a movie theatre until I was a freshman in college.

Several other chaplains also mentioned their fathers being pastors at their local church and how that behavior became ingrained in them at an early age. Eric shared this experience of being a Lutheran pastor as a tradition within his own family stating that:

> I was a pastor's kid, so it was pretty much, it was a part of my life from the get-go. And my father was a Lutheran pastor, my grandfather before him was a Lutheran pastor, all of his brothers were Lutheran pastors. So, there were five brothers in the family, all of them were ordained into the Lutheran ministry.

Other chaplains brought up that although their father was not a pastor of a local church, they still were highly active in many regards due to their parent's heavy involvement. Levi, a chaplain for 18 years, stated that:

> Well, I was raised, very strongly raised, in the church . . . we always attended, it doesn't matter what size the church was, we always attended whatever was the closest Assemblies of God church to our house . . . I picked that up from him [his father], as I was growing up, a strong involvement in local church and then just following that background. I have always had a strong relationship with the Lord.

Leon, a 65-year-old chaplain, echoed this experience when he stated, "We were always active in the church and stuff . . . from about the time that I was 10 years old, we went to church Sunday morning, Sunday night, Wednesday night, if the door was open, we were there." Roland, a Lutheran chaplain, provides further support for this theme by stating that, "I was never like new. My parents always brought me to church, went to church, so I am not new to the faith, so that has always been an important component. . . ." Another chaplain, Ken, even mentioned his life-changing experience, as an unknowing part of the "Jesus movement" as a teenager in Southern California in the 1960s and 1970s when he said that:

So I grew up in Southern California . . . I didn't even realize it . . . I actually grew up in the middle of what was called the 'Jesus movement' in Southern California . . . we would go there on Friday nights for concerts with people who eventually, obviously, became big recording artists . . . So . . . during the course of my growing up years, a lot of people mentored me, I grew up in a large church . . . I spent a lot of time in church just out of habit and stuff, that's what [my] family did.

Although the overwhelming majority of chaplains directly mentioned a strong religious upbringing (n = 12), a small minority of chaplains reported that they did not grow up in a Christian or religious household altogether. Specifically, three of the chaplains reported not growing up in a particularly strong religious household with two-third's of these chaplains stating that they grew up in a verbally and physically abusive household, often rife with substance abuse. Percy, a chaplain for three years and a former inmate himself, discussed his inconsistency in various religious traditions and faith as a teenager and young adult when he stated that:

I was off the wall practicing, I was just searching for fulfillment, truth, religion, you know I dabbled in witchcraft, dabbled in Satanism, dabbled in magic, tattooed my body up, getting high and drunk in prison. . . .

Percy further discussed how his lack of a strong religious upbringing led him to the streets, eventually influencing him to make a series of decisions that brought him to the prison as an inmate. This ultimately would become the same prison he would serve as a chaplain. Percy went on to state that his unique path and offender background, unlike most other chaplains, helped him form a connection with inmates that has helped in his chaplaincy role.

Despite the small minority of chaplains that did not grow up in a particularly religious household, the overwhelming majority of chaplains did share this experience. Moreover, most chaplains sought to continue their passion through attending Bible College. It is through their experience in Bible

College that many of them were set on a path to the ministerial world. This is where many began their eventual track toward prison chaplaincy, albeit unknowingly.

Instability in Ministerial Work

One of the most prevalent themes that emerged from the data was instability in their ministerial careers. *Instability* here refers to consistently changing jobs and moving throughout the country in order to find employment in the ministerial field. It is this instability that typically led to most eventually seeking the chaplaincy role due to the stability offered by its pay, hours, and location. Not one of the 19 chaplains that made up the sample of the present study originally set out to become a prison chaplain; however, the chaplain occupation was an opportunity sought out or offered to many after years in the ministerial workforce.

Linda, a 64-year-old chaplain, discussed how she reluctantly came into the prison chaplaincy, which at the time of the interview she had held this position for just over five years, saying, "I am 64 years old, so I came to this kicking and screaming . . . God had to work really hard to get me where I am. . . ." Leon, a 65-year-old chaplain only employed for three years, echoed this experience stating that:

> I am a relatively new prison Chaplain . . . I've been in ministry for like, 40 years . . . and like twenty years as a full time pastor, then I went part time for the other 20 or so years. During that time, I drove a truck and preached part time. And now I have heart issues, so I needed to find something else because I couldn't drive anymore, so I started over here as a substance abuse counselor and then a Chaplain position opened up, I applied, and got hired.

Percy mentioned that one of his favorite books is a fictional work that centers on a chaplain that, "wasn't making it in the pastoral world and became a chaplain. . . ." Thus, this suggests that instability in ministerial careers of prison chaplains is perhaps well known among the chaplain community. Ken, a 51-year-old chaplain, further supported this theme of "accidently" becoming a prison chaplain after years of experience in other ministries, but was drawn to the chaplaincy by the stability that the position offered, saying:

> Well kinda by accident truthfully . . . I have been a pastor for 16 years at four different churches and so, the last church that I left, my wife and I . . . we decided we didn't want to move, our kids were you know junior high and high school, late grade school. We have four boys, so we decided we

weren't going to move, so I actually left the church in April, my contract was up at the end of June.

Ben, a 46-year-old chaplain employed for seven years, shared a similar experience to Ken stating that:

> Well . . . I was a pastor for 16 years at three different churches, and really, the truth be told, I got to the point with my family where I didn't want to move and so I realized at some point that while being a pastor, I was going to have to move and I just didn't want to move them when they were kids and such. So, I knew it was time to try and find something else where I didn't have to move. . . .

The former statement further demonstrates how many chaplains grew tired of the consistent moving that was often a part of their occupation. As such, they sought out a position within their field that offered stability that was not afforded by other potential positions, primarily as pastors of small congregations.

Jenna, a 58-year-old female chaplain, discussed the financial hardships often associated with pastoral experience prior to seeking the position of a chaplain when she discussed the small sums of money she would make preaching in addition to having to become a substitute teacher for a local school system:

> Well, it was Sunday, it wasn't hourly. Flat rate per time I preached. They gave me $150 each time. And that would be for the whole day, including visiting those in the nursing home, and so I got $150 for doing that. And then, that same pastor, who was a very good friend of mine . . . he owned a double-wide trailer, and so he gave us a break on the rent as part of my work . . . I said [referring to unstable ministerial work] "thank you, but no thank you. . . ."

When discussing how she specifically became a prison chaplain, Jenna went on to state that:

> Well that wasn't on my plate of things to do. I did not set out to become a prison chaplain . . . I had been the co-pastor at a little church and an associate pastor at another one and was doing substitute teaching, so I had three little jobs. But nothing that would support my children. And so when he [her ex-husband] left us with very little notice . . . my [unemployment] caseworker said, "Have you ever thought of being a prison chaplain?" . . . [laughs], no way, that had never crossed my mind.

Martin, a Pentecostal chaplain for 17 years, further echoed this instability within prior ministerial work and all of the occasions he had to move:

> . . . the ministry I was doing up in Canada was with [name of ministry] in [name of city] . . . I was a program director there. And then before that, I worked about 6 months as an associate pastor at a small church in [name of city], Pennsylvania. But it was a disaster. It was the dumbest decision I ever made in my life . . . prior to that I was working for [name of organization] in the Dominican Republic as a boy's counselor . . . so I was there for about two years, I think. And before that I was in Miami going through missionary school . . . and prior to that, I went to Kenya. I was in Kenya for a year as an internship when I was in graduate school . . . I started out in Western North Dakota . . . and I served three congregations there at a time and then I went to another parish that was two churches at a time. Then, back to three churches at a time, then back to two churches at a time. And then, I moved to [name of state], I finally got single churches. The first one, that closed down, and the second one, that went a different direction.

This statement by Martin shares and underscores many of the same sentiments by other chaplains of the extreme instabilities associated with many ministerial positions in regards to pay and location. Understanding the instability issues attached to the ministerial roles experienced by many prison chaplains simultaneously accentuates the primary motivation that draws and keeps chaplains in their positions. It is through this instability that concurrently makes the chaplain role attractive, thus serving as the first primary motivation for holding the chaplaincy occupation.

Motivations

Stability

Because of the instability in most chaplain's ministerial careers, the stability offered by the department of corrections in pay, time, and location emerged as the primary motivation for most chaplains in the sample. Moreover, many chaplains mentioned the stability associated with the administrative duties of their position, serving as a secondary motivation for many. A total of 10 participants mentioned the stability in pay/time/location and/or administrative work as a key motivation to initially seek and remain in their position.

Sean, a 47-year-old chaplain who is a former correctional officer, discussed how he only returned to the prison system as a chaplain because he had completed his bachelor's degree in Bible college after he was diagnosed with cancer and the position offered needed benefits (e.g., pay and health care) saying:

I was officially ordained back in 2009 and took a ministry position near [name of city]. And they don't have enough money to pay, so I went back to the prison system, I had a bout of cancer . . . so I went back to that small amount, and I'm only in my 40s, so I had to, economic, I had to go back for income. And that was why I initially went back to the prison. And for benefits and stuff.

Leon also reflected on the benefits of this job after having heart issues in comparison to his prior positions as a part-time minister and truck driver when he stated:

Now, I only work 37.5 hours a week. I've never ever had a job like that in my life. I love this, 7:00 am to 3:30 pm, you know it's still daylight when I leave, now that part I really like . . . I mean, I am what, 16 miles from my house, home every night, sleep in my own bed . . . No, my word, no. There is just not too much to whine about.

Roland also spoke about the benefits of the job saying, "Right, well, actually, the benefits were not so bad, at least in my [opinion], probably better, but the consistency and that kind of thing. . . ."

Percy builds on this theme when he discussed how the consistency and stability of the chaplaincy position allowed him to follow other passions when he said:

. . . I love the field, I love the opportunities, that it gives me on a day-to-day basis. And, I like to do the same [thing] every day . . . I am actually building, I came on as an associate pastor at [name of ministry] . . . so I got my family, we started going to the day church . . . I ended up ministering the morning service and then I come two Sundays, well two Sundays I am at the morning service and two Sundays I am at the facility, my job here is flexible. I am in the facility 40 hours a week, sometimes 50–60 hours, 40 hours on a normal work week. That normally frees up my Sunday to go to Church with my family because I have volunteers that come in.

In addition to the stable hours, pay, and location that this occupation provides, several chaplains also discussed the administrative duties of the position as a key benefit, offering both a sense of comfort and stability. This is in contrast to prior research that has suggested administrative work of this role serving as a potential key source of burnout (see Sundt & Cullen 2007). One example of this where Pamela discussed how instead of paperwork and other administrative responsibilities serving as a detriment to her position, it actually was one of the most beneficial aspects of the occupation when she said,

"I don't mind the paperwork, I don't mind, I love that aspect of the job. I also liked that . . . you can really make the job your own. . . ." Here, the chaplain enjoys both the administrative aspect of the position, in addition to having the flexibility to do other initiatives in which they may be interested.

Furthering this theme, Ben stated that:

> . . . I am so simple minded; I like just the steadiness of it. Although every day is different, there is still a steadiness of it. I, I take security in that structure, I like that. And so, for the most part, though I may not know what I face when I come in, I know generally what I face when I come in and I, unlike being a pastor, for example, you know, being a pastor can just, it can just, go and do so much in so many different directions, there is some fun to that, but you also feel like the job is never done and you never go home and really for the most part, that is all I have ever done in my life, is pastoring. So here, when I leave, I leave, and I am done. I like that, compared to what I have had before . . . so I do like that, I do like the structure, I do like the repetition that there is, for me, a simple minded person, I find that very secure within my life.

Molly, a 48-year-old chaplain for only a year and a half, shared this sentiment for her attraction to the administrative process of the position when she said:

> . . . you know, honestly, I don't mind the administrative part. I like process. I'm task oriented by nature and so when I think of how I'm managing my job, I like to say, "how can I do this better, how can I do it faster, more efficiently?" So, I like both pieces of it honestly. I like the administrative part and I like the ministry part.

This same benefit was shared by Eric, a chaplain for nearly eight years, when he said, "What I like about it is . . . it gives me an opportunity to put some of my best gifts into practice. I've always thought of myself as kind of an administrator. And what I do, doing a lot of bureaucracy."

Even though many were both directly and indirectly attracted to the chaplaincy position through the stability—in benefits and administration—this did not serve as the only form of motivation for individuals initially seeking or even maintaining their chaplaincy position. Similar to prior research (Hicks 2008; Kerley et al. 2009, 2010), often chaplains discussed that their reason for occupying the chaplaincy position was part of a divine plan from God or a "calling." However, the frequency and overall role of being "called" to this specific occupation differed greatly when compared to what has been found in prior literature.

"Called" to the Chaplaincy

Having a "calling" or being "called" to one's occupation has been identified in prior literature as a key motivation, if not a necessary requirement, for prison chaplains and prison ministry volunteers (Hicks 2008; Kerley et al. 2009, 2010; Kort-Butler & Malone 2015; Tewksbury & Collins 2005; Tewksbury & Dabney 2004). Under half of the current sample (n=8) specifically referenced being "called" to the prison ministry. Moreover, the same number (n=8) of chaplains did not reference being "called" in any capacity to their current occupation. A small minority of chaplains (n=3) stated that they were "called" to ministry, generally, but not to prison chaplaincy, specifically.

Molly recalled her divine intervention that she had with God that led her on the path to become a prison chaplain saying that:

> . . . this might sound a little kooky, okay, but bear with me. I had a dream one evening that I was serving in a prison and I was inside the prison with other ministries, and God began to speak to me through one of the other ministers. God was saying, "come by, come by." So, normally, I don't pay attention to my dreams because, you know, dreams can just be way out there, but because in this particular dream, God was speaking, it caught my attention and so when I woke up from the dream, I said a prayer to the Lord and said, "Lord, if you're directing me to prison ministry, I need confirmation." And confirmation came that very next day.

Other chaplains, like Doris, a 50-year-old chaplain, did not share as vivid of an experience as Molly when she continued this theme, simply stating, "I felt it was a calling. . . ." Nathan, a 50-year-old chaplain who became a prison chaplain after his exposure to the role in a CPE (clinical pastoral education) requirement as part of his MDiv, also discussed his "calling" to the chaplaincy position when he stated:

> Well, I felt called to prison ministry and chaplaincy. I guess, because they are two different things. So, I made arrangements with the then director of religious services for [name of the agency] and met with him, and he thought it would be a good match to set me up here . . . it was a little struggle getting me on the interview list because I technically wasn't qualified at the time.

Nathan demonstrates that despite his not meeting the minimum qualifications to be hired, initially, his eventual job offer further underscored the "calling" of his position and that it was part of God's divine plan for his life. Nathan also considered the importance of being "called" to this profession when he statesn:

Make sure that you're called for it because it will eat you alive if you're not . . . It never stops and typically, especially for [name of state], we have a high ratio of offenders to chaplains. We have about 1800 offenders here for two chaplains. That gives us about 900 guys a piece and it's just really demanding. You combine that with all the administrative functions that we have to do and there's not, typically not enough time in the day to do every-thing that you need to do. If it's not something you really are called for, you love, it's just going to grind you up.

This example by Nathan demonstrates that feeling as if one is "called" for this position perhaps helps with issues related to burnout because it is a part of a divine purpose.

Percy further supports this notion of being "called" to the chaplaincy role and how it is a perceived part of a divine plan when he said, ". . . the whole time I was doing volunteer work . . . I actually got qualified for my interview for the department of corrections . . . [I] was like wow, this is what I was designed, this is why I was created, I felt this was my calling." Percy contin-ues this discussion reflecting on his experience as a former inmate and his interactions with chaplains throughout the years stating that, "I know many chaplains that are way better at Chaplaincy that are doing the work that I do that have never been to jail, but they have not been called." Therefore, Percy highlights this issue of some individuals perhaps occupying this role that are truly not meant for it, but only because they can perform the administrative functions now ascribed to the role. This is a subtheme supported by Jenna when she says, ". . . be sure God called you to do it. Because not everybody can be a prison chaplain. Just because you're a pulpit preacher doesn't mean you can be a prison chaplain. It's an entirely different scenario."

Melissa also supported this theme of sensing that becoming a prison chap-lain was part of a divine plan from God, even giving up part of a pension with a prior job to pursue this "calling":

I actually walked away from a job where I was close to retirement and I felt like this is where the Lord wanted me . . . I love this . . . That I know I am where God sent me to be, that is first and foremost. There is a peace know-ing you are in the will of God. I can't get everything done that I want to get done in a day's time, but I assure you, when I finally close my eyes at night, I can sleep in peace . . . the peace of knowing I am in the will of God makes all the rest of it okay.

Sean summarizes his feelings on why being "called" to this position is key and how it is a different "calling" entirely than that of a minister, stating that:

. . . it's a calling. It has to be [that] they feel truly called to minister to the inmates, not to, you know, and to the staff, because they feel God is actually placing them there and called to that. Because it's not the type of role that I could see a minister, someone God's called into the ministry and say, "okay, I think I'll pick being a Chaplain because there's a lot going on inside those systems." It's a city, it's a world of its own . . . If they don't feel called to it then, don't do it for the money, well certainly don't do it for the money . . . but, by all means, don't do it just because it's the only job they can find . . . you're going to end up doing more damage than you are good unless you feel God's calling [you] into it.

Some chaplains (n = 3) mentioned that although they were "called" to the ministry, they did not reference being "called" to prison chaplaincy, specifically. One example is where Levi, the longest tenured chaplain in the sample at 18 years that failed to promote to a Marine chaplain, stated that:

But I got a call into the ministry . . . went into the Bible college, which then went into seminary because for the military chaplaincy, they require a Masters in Divinity . . . was an associate pastor at several small churches . . . and then, I failed to promote, was put off of active duty because of that, and this prison here opened up, and I've been here, in May, it will be 19 years now. . . .

Roland continues this theme of being "called" to ministry, in general, and having his Lutheran church assign him where he is needed. For example, Roland states that, "So, it is a sense of call and in our structure you discern that through a bishop and so, and the bishop is the one who does the endorsing of a candidate or a person . . . we discerned together and then this position opened up. . . ." Regardless of whether chaplains felt they were "called" to their current position, were "called" through structure, or in the position for a steady job, another theme that emerged was that most felt they could affect positive change in inmate lives.

Effect Positive Change

The third theme for chaplain motivation to emerge was to effect positive change. This is a similar theme to that found in Kerley et al. (2009) of prison chaplains and prison ministry volunteers "planting seeds" and "harvesting." The overwhelming majority (n = 15) of the sample reported effecting positive change in the lives of inmates as being a primary motivation. Levi succinctly stated, "Working with the guys, seeing lives transformed," then he proceeded to provide an example of a specific former inmate who has turned away from a life of crime and is active in his own church because of Levi's influence.

Franklin, a 60-year-old chaplain employed for six years, emphasized his enjoyment to effect positive change in inmates' lives when he said:

> I like talking with the gentlemen, even when it means that someone in their family is sick or dying or dead, that's a pretty high-level contact and it's a good opportunity to reach out to them to let them know that, even if it doesn't seem like it very often. There are people here who care about them, praying for them . . . I appreciate digging out the materials to help people study and to grow as a person and as a Christian. . . .

Ben continues this theme reflecting on hearing the positive change in inmates after they have left the facility and those that benefit from his teaching while inside the prison when he said:

> We get calls periodically from inmates who have gotten out and they are doing well, and they say thank you for all that you did, those are gratifying. For me, personally, I really enjoy teaching . . . so, when I get a chance to do that and then I hear guys appreciate that and respond and react . . . that is just so rewarding for me.

Steven, a 42-year-old chaplain employed for three years, supported the notion discussed by Ben and others regarding the benefits from teaching when he said:

> I teach a systemic theology and I teach some pretty in-depth doctrinal things. And man, to watch how it transforms them it's just awesome. Light bulbs come on, you see people, like here I see girls who have been on medication their entire life, and they take it upon themselves to get off of it just because they become that much more stable in what they've learned. . . .

He then continues to discuss how he's personally heard some of his inmates recite catechism to their kids on the phone and the gratification that he receives from that.

Percy continues this theme of effecting personal change in others after reflecting on his poor experiences with a former chaplain when he was an inmate and discussing the change chaplains can effect by both their words and actions:

> What don't I like about my job? I like coming in . . . you speak to a lot of people and you don't know what seeds you planted, you know some of us plant, some of us water, but God gives the increase. But you don't know, you got people watching you, might not have ever talked to you, might not

have ever come to Chapel, but they are watching you . . . So, I think that is one of the biggest rewards, that we won't know until we get to the Kingdom to see whose lives you really impacted. . . .

Jenna further underscores this common thread shared by the vast majority of chaplains when she said:

. . . my favorite part of the job, spiritually speaking, is showing the boys that God loves them. That just because they've messed up, that doesn't mean God loves them any less. But some of them don't even know . . . And so, I love teaching them about how much God loves them and how to use their faith to make daily decisions and things like that.

A final example that summarizes the sentiment shared by most chaplains is when Gregg, a 45-year-old chaplain employed for seven years, stated:

. . . I like being able to meet guys where they are, help them where they're at in their journey and hopefully somehow . . . what I do helps them to see Christ in me and then maybe somehow, someway they might come to that decision in their own life, that's great. If by chance they decide to keep their own belief system and stay where they're at, whatever that may be, and yet somehow, someway, make some positive changes in their lives, then that makes me feel good. . . .

The last statement by Gregg summarizes the common sentiment shared by most chaplains that they want to have a positive impact on inmate lives in some capacity. It is clear that both through chaplains' limited teaching opportunities with inmates and in their daily interaction with inmates that most enjoy seeing their positive impact on inmates' lives. This statement also introduces the final motivational theme that emerged, the exposure to others' religious and faith practices.

Exposure to Different Faiths

The final and least prevalent subtheme of motivation that emerged from the data was being exposed to and learning other religions and faiths that differ from the chaplain's personal faith. This subtheme is similar to Kerley and colleagues' (2009) finding of prison chaplains and prison ministry volunteers' enjoyment of "meeting people where they are." A total of six participants discussed exposure to other religions and faiths as a primary benefit and motivation of their occupation. Moreover, many discussed having a relatively open approach toward religion and salvation.

Nathan discussed his interest with being exposed to different faiths when he said, "The vast variety of religions, or the variety of ways that you're expressing religion, I find it interesting. Because, I'm a student of religion. I'm an ordained Christian, but I'm a student of religion." Linda, a 64-year-old chaplain that has been employed for a little over five years, explained her position toward religion saying, "I kind of believe there are different ways to God, and that the purpose of religion is to come to a closer walk with God, as we know God. I'm a little off, so. . . . ." Linda then stated how many inmates approach her assuming that she is only open to Christianity and strict interpretations of the Holy Bible with inmates coming in with, "such a huge chip on their shoulder. You know the rock of Gibraltar. . . . They want to pick a fight about religion, well you've come to the wrong place honey." She then continued with an analogy to explain her personal position and to convey religion to interested inmates about the many shared components between different faiths:

> . . . there's always the cow analogy. The cow is milk, human beings take that milk and they make whole milk, they make skim milk, they make chocolate milk, they make ice cream, they make butter, they make sour cream, all of those things came from the same source. All of those things are what human beings have done to religion.

This statement by Linda highlights the open way in which a significant minority (n=6) of chaplains view religion. Roland echoed this sentiment toward being open to different religions when he stated:

> I have always been this economical type of animal, so I really like the setting because I am able to look and get dialogue, whatever you want to call it, from the other faiths, that is just the way I am set up, I am pretty open . . . because all of them have basic tenants that are similar. . . .

One chaplain, Ben, stated that his seven years as a prison chaplain has changed his perception and overall approach toward church. Moreover, he even suggests that he perhaps is struggling with his own faith due to his position as a chaplain when he stated:

> I think working in prison changes your whole perception of Church, and I am still wrapping my mind around that . . . I believe in the Church, I always have . . . I think it is crucial . . . But, as I am in here, and I see these people, and I see what is going on, I feel like that Church is missing the boat tremendously, but trying to figure out my niche now is difficult. So, that has been a struggle the last few years.

Discussion and Conclusion

This study has examined the backgrounds and motivations of prison chaplains for how they originally sought and remained in their occupation. Findings overwhelmingly suggest that modern chaplains did not actively seek to fulfill this role within prison; however, this position is only sought after years of inconsistent work within the ministerial field. Moreover, chaplains stay in their positions because they are now in a stable occupation in pay, time, and location in addition to a myriad of personal benefits derived from their direct role as a chaplain.

The first primary finding of this study is that many chaplains (n=8) discussed being raised in a primarily blue-collar household. Through discussing their stories, the importance of the blue-collar background became apparent for two reasons. First, many chaplains felt that they could put themselves "in the shoes" of inmates in which they were ministering. Second, chaplains were used to moving from city to city or state to state for their parent's, generally their father's, occupation. This is key because it places these individuals being used to moving at a young age, consistently being uprooted. Unknowingly, most chaplains reported a similar pattern once they began their ministerial careers. Thus, instability in the home life due to the largely blue-collar work of many chaplains' parents became ingrained within many chaplains at a young age. As such, the stability offered by the chaplaincy role with pay, hours, and work location would eventually appear as an attractive option later in life.

Chaplains also overwhelmingly (n=12) reported a strong religious upbringing. This should come as no surprise since a strong religious upbringing has been found to have a significant influence on one's religiosity well into adulthood (Bridges & Moore 2002). This finding also builds on Kerley et al. (2009) when they found that prison chaplains and prison ministry volunteers mostly were involved with a local church as children and typically converted to Christianity between early childhood and late adolescence.

This theme of a strong religious upbringing is crucial for two primary reasons. First, it seems to have instilled in chaplains a sense of normalcy regarding their attendance and participation within a local church. Second, many stated that their strong upbringing in the church set them with a desire or "calling" to attend Bible College in an effort to pursue a career in ministry. Thus, it appears that their strong religious upbringing serves as the catalyst that places them on the path to eventual ministerial work, ultimately leading to the occupation of a prison chaplain.

The final background theme and first motivational theme to appear is the instability in ministerial work and the stability offered by the chaplain role, respectively. Ten participants in the sample specifically mentioned the stability in pay, time, and/or location as serving as a primary attraction of the prison chaplain position. The instability that is attached to many ministerial roles among those in the sample appears imperative to the overall attractiveness of the chaplaincy roles to these individuals for several important reasons. First, it demonstrates the inconsistent nature of ministerial work. Second, the detriment of the instability attached to many ministerial roles indirectly serves as the primary motivation for those who fulfill the chaplain role. Therefore, it is possible that many modern prison chaplains experience burnout in their ministerial careers and subsequently turn to a career as a prison chaplain simply for the stability that the position offers in most department of corrections. Thus, it is the ministerial field that has led to burnout, and the chaplaincy position appears as an attractive alternative where they can still use their training and experience with more stability in pay, time, and location. It could also be that the evolution of the modern prison chaplain role to a primarily administrative position has altered the overall composition of those that are attracted to the position in the first place. Future research needs to examine whether this is an artifact of the hiring practices of the department of corrections in which the sample for the current study was derived, or if this is a common theme of modern prison chaplains across the United States.

The fifth major finding of the present study is that only eight of the chaplains reported being directly "called" to prison chaplaincy. This is in stark contrast to prior research on both prison chaplains and prison ministry volunteers that found most chaplains and those that work with inmates in a religious sense (e.g., lay ministers, volunteers) are "called" (see Hicks 2008; Kerley et al. 2009, 2010; Kort-Butler & Malone 2015; Tewksbury & Collins 2005; Tewksbury & Dabney 2004). It is possible that this finding is a product of the shifting role of the chaplain position from primarily a ministerial role to an administrative one (Pew Research Center 2012; Sundt & Cullen 2002). It is also possible that individuals simply seek the role of prison chaplain after experiencing burnout in their ministerial careers, thus seeking stability in both their personal and professional lives. Furthermore, it may be that instituting minimum educational requirements has dissuaded some individuals from pursuing their "calling" simply because they may not meet the educational requirements that are deemed necessary by the respective department of corrections for the position. Future research needs to explore the specific role that primarily administrative responsibilities or even minimum requirements (e.g., education), if any, have had on the "calling" of one to the chaplain role as the installation of minimum requirements may inadvertently restrict those who truly desire to fulfill this position.

The overwhelming majority of chaplains reported effecting positive change as a primary benefit and motivation of their role. This finding mirrored that of Kerley et al. (2009) regarding chaplains and lay ministers positively viewing their work as "planting seeds" and "harvesting." This also supports the

Pew Research Center's (2012) finding where chaplains view the counseling of inmates as one of their more important tasks.

It is possible that what job responsibilities chaplains view as the most important aspects of their occupation are influenced by what they receive the most personal gratification from, both directly and indirectly. It is also possible that prison chaplains view this aspect of their job as rewarding because seeing change is more apparent when working with offenders than when compared to traditional congregants within a church, as was found in Denney and Tewksbury's (2013) work on faith-based halfway house volunteers. That is, offender populations are more vulnerable where they are more likely to reveal personal struggles that likely carry a stigma (e.g., drug addiction, issues that are sexual in nature, the commission of various crimes) when perhaps traditional congregants would not be as privy to share such information due to potential social ramifications. With this, any positive effect that the chaplain is having on the life of an inmate may be more easily visible. Thus, prison chaplains may feel like they are having a true impact with their ministerial work with this particular population as opposed to the populations largely dealt with in their mostly negative experiences in ministerial work outside of the prison setting. Future research needs to explore the relationship between prior experiences with congregants and the intrinsic benefits of working with offenders to fully ascertain the nuances that may exist within this motivation.

The fourth and final motivation that emerged from the chaplaincy position is that a substantial minority (n=6) of chaplains were motivated by learning about other religions and faiths. It is possible that this a consequence of the passage of RLUIPA. That is, the passage and enforcement of RLUIPA has possibly driven out chaplains that are more fundamentalist in their personal views regarding religion and faith. It could also be that the chaplaincy position is now attracting those with a genuine interest in studying other religions and faiths. Moreover, it could be that continued exposure to numerous inmates from a variety of backgrounds and religious traditions has the tendency to change a chaplain's personal religious views over time. Future research should compare the religious ideologies of chaplains at the onset of their careers and track their religious ideologies as their careers progress.

Findings in the present study have three important policy implications. The first implication is that state departments of correction should actively recruit those that have both (1) prior experience in the ministry field and (2) those that have a "calling" to prison chaplaincy. This will ensure that those hired both have the experience necessary in ministry and a true desire to work with the inmate population.

The second policy implication is that a hiring agency should actively advertise the stability offered by the position in terms of pay, hours, and location. Emphasizing these benefits may serve one of two functions. One, it may attract highly qualified individuals in the ministerial field that may have not considered the prison chaplaincy position otherwise. Two, it may persuade those that are considering the change to prison chaplaincy, but are still unsure of its benefits to apply.

The third policy implication is that the department of corrections should allow chaplains the opportunity to teach and practice true aspects of ministry, opposed to strictly administrative tasks. Such a practice may ensure that chaplains actively witness any positive change they are imparting on inmate lives in which they receive gratification from, as is clear in the findings from this and other studies (see Kerley et al. 2009; Pew Research Center 2012). Therefore, the intrinsic reward gained by many from this approach may serve as motivation to stay in their current position for the foreseeable future, thus assisting with the turnover and retention of qualified and experienced chaplains.

Even though the present study provided useful information that can be used by policy makers in efforts to recruit and retain prison chaplains, this was not achieved without limitations. First, this sample included only chaplains from one state in the United States. Therefore, these findings are not necessarily generalizable to the wider prison chaplain population. Future research needs to explore themes that emerged in the current study to verify if these are common themes present throughout all modern chaplains, or if findings are only a reflection of the state's hiring practices.

The second limitation of this study is that the sample consisted of those that volunteered to participate through the initial invitation of their direct supervisor. As such, this process could have biased the sample to include those that wanted to appear favorable in the eyes of their primary supervisor by participating in the study. Future research should attempt to confirm the themes that emerged in the present study with a national survey that provides further anonymity to any participants.

A third limitation is that all interviews were conducted and all transcriptions were coded by the author. Thus, findings that emerged could have been influenced by the author's general worldview. Future research should use multiple interviewers and coders to help protect against any potential biases.

Despite the above limitations, themes found in this study, both reaffirming those found in prior research and additional themes, provides a solid framework for future studies on the backgrounds and motivations of prison chaplains. With the approximate 1.6 million inmates currently incarcerated at both the state and federal-level prisons in the United States (Kaeble, Glaze, Tsoutis, & Minton 2016), under RLUIPA, these individuals are guaranteed the right to practice their religion and/or faith as long as it is officially recognized by their respective department of corrections. In order to uphold this right and to safeguard state and federal department of corrections from lawsuits, the chaplaincy position is perhaps as important as ever. Unless future research continues to examine the backgrounds and motivations of this vital and understudied position in prisons, efforts to attract and retain the best candidates for these positions may jeopardize inmate rights while simultaneously increasing the liability of the department of corrections for inmate lawsuits.

Bibliography

Beckford, James A. "Rational Choice Theory and Prison Chaplaincy: The Chaplain's Dilemma." *The British Journal of Sociology* 50 (1999): 671–685.

Bridges, Lisa J., & Kristen A. Moore. *Religion and Spirituality in Childhood and Adolescence.* Bethesda, MD: Child Trends, 2002.

Charmaz, Kathy. *Constructing Grounded Theory: A Practice Guide through Qualitative Analysis.* Thousand Oaks, CA: Sage, 2006.

Clear, Todd R., Hardyman, Patricia L., Stout, Bruce, Lucken, Karol, & Harry R. Dammer. "The Value of Religion in Prison: An Inmate Perspective." *Journal of Contemporary Criminal Justice* 16 (2000): 53–74.

Clear, Todd R., Stout, B. D., Dammer, Harry R., Kelly, L., Hardyman, P. L., & Carol Shapiro. "Does Involvement in Religion Help Prisoners Adjust to Prison?" *NCCD Focus,* November 1992, 1–7.

Cullen, Francis T., Link, Bruce G., Wolfe, Nancy T., & James Frank. "The Social Dimensions of Correctional Officer Stress." *Justice Quarterly* 2 (1985): 505–533.

Denney, Andrew S., & Richard Tewksbury. "Motivations and the Need for Fulfillment of Faith-Based Halfway House Volunteers." *Justice Policy Journal* 10 (2013): 1–24.

Finn, Peter. "Correctional Officer Stress a Cause for Concern and Additional Help." *Federal Probation* 62 (1998): 65–74.

Glaser, Barney. *The Effectiveness of a Prison and Parole System.* New York: Bobbs-Merrill, 1964.

Guest, Greg, Bunce, Arwen, & Laura Johnson. "How Many Interviews Are Enough? An Experiment with Data Saturation and Variability." *Field Methods* 18 (2006): 59–82.

Hicks, Allison M. "Role Fusion: The Occupational Socialization of Prison Chaplains." *Symbolic Interaction* 31 (2008): 400–421.

Hicks, Allison M. "Learning to Watch Out: Prison Chaplains as Risk Managers." *Journal of Contemporary Ethnography* 41 (2012): 636–667.

Johnson, Byron R. "Religiosity and Institutional Deviance: The Impact of Religious Variables upon Inmate Adjustment." *Criminal Justice Review* 12 (1987): 21–30.

Johnson, Byron R., Larson, David B., & Timothy C. Pitts. "Religious Programming, Institutional Adjustment, and Recidivism among Former Inmates in Prison Fellowship Programs: A Research Note." *Justice Quarterly* 14 (1997): 145–166.

Kaeble, Danielle, Glaze, Lauren, Tsoutis, Anastasios, & Todd Minton. *Correctional Populations in the United States.* Washington, DC: Bureau of Justice Statics, 2016. Accessed February 27, 2016. http://www.bjs.gov/content/pub/pdf/cpus14.pdf

Kerley, Kent R., Bartkowski, John P., Matthews, Todd L., & Tracy L. Emond. "From the Sanctuary to the Slammer: Exploring the Narratives of Evangelical Prison Ministry Workers." *Sociological Perspective* 30 (2010): 504–525.

Kerley, Kent R., Matthews, Todd L., & Jessica Shoemaker. "A Simple Plan, a Simple Faith: Chaplains and Lay Ministers in Mississippi Prisons." *Review of Religious Research* 51 (2009): 87–103.

Kort-Butler, Lisa A., & Sarah E. Malone. "Citizen Volunteers in Prison: Bringing the Outside In, Taking the Inside Out." *Journal of Crime and Justice* 38 (2015): 508–521.

Morse, Janice M. "Designing Funded Qualitative Research." In Normal K. Denzin & Yvonna S. Lincoln (Eds.), *Handbook of Qualitative Research* (2nd ed.). Thousand Oaks, CA: Sage, 1994.

Pass, Michael G. "Religious Orientation and Self-Reported Rule Violations in a Maximum Security Prison." *Journal of Offender Rehabilitation* 28 (1999): 119–134.

Pew Research Center, the Pew Forum on Religion and Public Life. "Religion in Prisons: A 50-State Survey of Prison Chaplains." 2012. Accessed September 23, 2014. http://www.pewforum.org/2012/03/22/prison-chaplains-exec

Skotnicki, Andrew. *Religion and the Development of the American Penal System.* Lanham, MD: University Press of America, 2000.

St. Gerard, Vanessa. "Tight Budgets Affect Prison Chaplain Jobs." *Corrections Today,* July 1, 2003, 65.

Sundt, Jody L., & Francis T. Cullen. "The Role of the Contemporary Prison Chaplain." *The Prison Journal* 78 (1998): 271–298.

Sundt, Jody L., & Francis T. Cullen. "Doing God's Work behind Bars: Chaplains' Reactions to Employment in Prison." *Journal of Offender Rehabilitation* 45 (2007): 131–157.

Sundt, Jody L., Dammer, Harry R., & Francis T. Cullen. "The Role of the Prison Chaplain in Rehabilitation." *Journal of Offender Rehabilitation* 35 (2002): 59–86.

Tewksbury, Richard, & Sue Carter Collins. "Prison Chapel Volunteers." *Federal Probation* 69 (2005): 26–30.

Tewksbury, Richard, & Dean Dabney. "Prison Volunteers: Profiles, Motivations, Satisfaction." *Journal of Offender Rehabilitation* 40 (2004): 173–183.

Tewksbury, Richard, Higgins, George E., & Andrew S. Denney. "Measuring Work Stress among Correctional Staff: A Rasch Measurement Approach." *Journal of Applied Measurement* 13 (2012): 394–402.

Thibaut, Jacqueline. "'To Pave the Way to Penitence': Prisoners and Discipline at the Eastern State Penitentiary, 1829–1835." *The Pennsylvania Magazine of History and Biography* 106, no. 2 (1982): 187–222.

U.S. Department of Justice, Bureau of Justice Statistics. "Correctional Populations." 2009. Accessed September 23, 2014. http://www.bjs.gov/content/glance /tables/corr2tab.cfm

U.S. Department of Justice. "Report on the Tenth Anniversary of the Religious Land Use and Institutionalized Persons Act." 2010. Accessed February 21, 2016. https://www.justice.gov/sites/default/files/crt/legacy/2010/12/15 /rluipa_report_092210.pdf

Restrictions on Inmate Freedom of Religious Practice: A National and International Perspective

Jason Jolicoeur and Erin Grant

Freedom of religious thought and practice is widely viewed as one of several substantive individual rights that collectively serve to differentiate American culture and society from others that exist around the globe. Indeed, in the minds of many, the individual rights and protections that are accorded to American citizens by foundational documents like the Constitution and the Bill of Rights are viewed as being exceptional, sacrosanct, and all encompassing. Sentiment of this nature invariably contributes to the many myths that have come to characterize the nature of contemporary American society. Although certainly important and at least theoretically inimitable, the substantive and procedural protections that are enjoyed by American citizens are far from universal or unalterable when viewed through a lens of applied practice. Rather, these constitutional and procedural protections might better be examined through a contextual lens as fluid and mutable concepts if they are to be more precisely understood and appreciated. Context and characteristic both contribute to the creation of an environment that is more or less conducive to the full exercise of recognized individual rights and collective freedoms in contemporary American society. This is true of virtually all of the cherished freedoms that Americans profess to hold dear. For instance, the Supreme Court has noted that free speech protections are not absolute and that the government can regulate them to varying degrees when speech is found to be obscene, slanderous, or meant to incite fights or violence against others (Ruane 2014).

Freedom of religion is another notable civil liberty in American society that in practice has not been held to be complete or absolute. Instead, reasonable restrictions on the freedom of religious practice are noted in relevant legislation and have been allowed by the courts. To illustrate, the Supreme Court has ruled that reasonable restrictions on the free practice of religion are permissible, at least in instances when the alternative would allow for open violations of existing criminal statutes (*Employment Division v. Smith* 1990). Decisions of this nature underscore the reality that limitations can be placed on the religious freedoms extended to all Americans. However, these restrictions are more pronounced for some groups within American society than for others. More specifically, some inordinate prohibitions on the free exercise of religion have been established for inmates in America's correctional institutions. Prohibitions of this nature tend to stand in stark contrast to the religious freedoms indeed in the Bill of Rights. As a result, an unusual and sometimes contentious dialogue has developed concerning the intersection of mass incarceration and the freedom of religious practice in American society. Moving forward, American society likely will continue to struggle with trying to live up to idealized expectations regarding religious freedom within a societal context that is characterized by the imprisonment of a larger percentage of its population than virtually any other in the history of human civilization. Further, this dilemma is not a uniquely American one as many countries around the globe struggle with balancing the competing interests of religious freedom and public safety concerns.

International Provisions Safeguarding Freedom of Religious Practice

Ensuring the freedom to practice religion freely can be difficult even in the very best of circumstances. Even in homogeneous societies where widespread agreement characterizes religious affiliation, problems can arise. Subtle denominational differences and understated variations in practice can contribute to tension between religious groups and competition among them. In practice, this competition can contribute to social and legal efforts to limit and control the spiritual behaviors of religious groups that are seen as different or unusual. Perhaps then, it is not unexpected that ensuring the right to the free practice of religion becomes eminently more complicated from a global perspective when competing religions, typically with vastly differing principles and practices, must be considered. This is especially true in areas with racially and ethnically diverse populations where adherents to different religions are expected to undertake a collective existence. In even the best of situations unintentional actions or institutionalized factors can contribute to disparities in the ability to practice religion freely. In more extreme instances, religiously linked hostilities can become a flashpoint for some of the very worst examples of human behavior. Indeed, some of history's most blatant instances of mass criminal atrocities have been driven, at least in some part, by ideological differences that can be linked to the religious beliefs of the indigenous populations involved.

Armed human conflict repeatedly has been the context in which human atrocities readily occur. The human costs associated with these atrocities have contributed to international efforts to establish standards of behavior meant to control the most heinous abuses. Much of this international humanitarian legislation has the overarching intention of protecting soldiers and civilians alike during times of war. Although legislation of this nature was not specifically designed to ensure the protection of the freedom of religious practice for protected populations, it has often done so in an indirect or collateral manner. This is because specific provisions included within larger international humanitarian legislation often address issues that are at least tangentially related to the freedom of religious thought and practice. Perhaps most importantly, for purposes of the current discussion, much of the existing international humanitarian legislation, including provisions related to the freedom of religious practice, was created specifically to protect the large prisoner populations that are commonly taken during the course of armed human conflict. Initially, many of the humanitarian standards governing the treatment of prisoners of war were informally agreed on by the relevant combatants (Morrow 2002). Over time, many of these informal standards became more widely accepted and eventually were increasingly likely to be codified in some formalized manner.

Some of the first legislation of this type originated from what is commonly known as the Geneva Convention. In spite of common misconceptions, the Geneva Convention was not a singular event. Rather, it refers to a series of gatherings or conventions that occurred during the course of the 19th and 20th centuries. One goal of these meetings was to collectively establish minimum standards regarding the treatment of those injured, taken prisoner, or interned during the course of armed human conflict (Crawford 2010). Over time, the specific standards that were developed during each individual gathering, referred to as conventions or protocols, were codified as a body of international law. Collectively, they have become the contemporary international standards that govern the treatment of civilians, soldiers, and those taken prisoner during times of war. The first mention of religion in the conventions refers to generalized protections that prohibit the adverse treatment of protected populations based on their religion, faith, or a variety of other factors (International Committee of the Red Cross 1983). A more direct reference to the freedom of religious practice concerns civilian prisoners and notes that they must be granted the same rights as soldiers and that they must be allowed to practice their own religion under the guidance of religious leaders of their own faith (International Committee of the Red Cross 1983).

Other international legislation has been established to preserve religious freedom of practice for confined populations outside times of armed conflict. One of the best examples of legislation of this nature is the International Covenant on Civil and Political Rights (ICCPR). The ICCPR is international legislation that originated in the United Nations General Assembly and was ratified by the bulk of the world's countries by the latter half of the 20th century (Joseph & Castan 2013). The ICCPR has a broad and sweeping focus on a variety of different political, legal, self-preservation, and freedom of expression protections. However, religious freedom of thought and practice is also a significant focus of this legislation. The legislation specifically notes that all individuals, including prisoners, should have free conscience to pursue the religious beliefs of their choice and should be able to freely practice those beliefs with minimal state intrusion (Joseph & Castan 2013). Further, the legislation notes that individuals have a right to be protected from discrimination or adverse action based on their religious affiliation or the nature of their religious beliefs. In spite of the widespread acceptance of this legislation, there is evidence that in many countries, government officials and citizens alike are able to violate its provisions, including those related to religious freedom, with general impunity (Dziedzic 2013; Seibert-Fohr 2009). Incarcerated populations are at an especially high risk for violations of this nature, given their relatively low social status, lack of public visibility, and generally weak social power. This is an especially significant issue given that impunity from responsibility for human rights violations may contribute to more and more serious violations of these rights in the future (Seibert-Fohr 2009). Lack of compliance and the complications associated with the enforcement of international legislation may result in legislation that is adopted by individual countries taking on increased importance in relation to the provision of religious freedoms for incarcerated populations.

American Constitutional Provisions Related to the Freedom of Religious Practice

In the United States, founding constitutional documents like the Constitution and the Bill of Rights underscore the civil liberties and human rights that citizens enjoy. The vast majority of these freedoms apply, at least in some manner, to the many individuals subject to correctional supervision. In regard to the freedom of religious thought and practice, one specific clause from among these many constitutional provisions is of substantive importance. More specifically, the First Amendment of the Bill of Rights stands apart from other constitutional provisions given its direct recognition of the inherent religious freedoms and protections afforded to the public. This broad constitutional amendment also addresses a number of additional constitutional protections, such as freedom of speech, freedom of the press, and freedom of assembly. Although many of these protections were initially viewed as applicable only at the federal level, they were eventually made binding on individual states through the Fourteenth Amendment.

The First Amendment introduced two key principles that have helped shape the concept of religious freedom in American society for more than two centuries. Each of these principles has had an influence on how the courts interpret what religious freedom is and in what instances it can be restricted. In doing so, these two key principles have also had an influence on the efforts of public policy makers and correctional administrators as they relate to the ability of incarcerated populations to practice freely the tenets of their religious beliefs. The first of these two key principles or concepts is the Establishment Clause and the second is the Free Exercise Clause. Each of these concepts is important individually, but collectively they take on an even greater significance in regards to their ability to protect and enlarge, and in some instances restrict and constrain, religious freedoms.

The Establishment Clause holds that the government cannot establish an official state religion nor mandate public adherence to such a religion (Greenawalt 2006). Contrary to some public misconceptions, this clause does not provide an outright exclusion from state involvement in religion. Rather, the courts have interpreted this specific clause to mean that the state is prohibited from either the excessive promotion or the unnecessary obstruction of any particular religion or set of religious beliefs (*Lemon v. Kurtzman* 1971). The Establishment Clause itself does not address directly the legitimacy of any specific restrictions that the government can place on incarcerated individuals in correctional environments to practice freely their religious beliefs.

Instead, this clause specifically prohibits the government from establishing a particular religion to which correctional inmates must belong, or from the inordinate promotion of any particular set of religious beliefs. The specific justification and extent of limitations to the free exercise of religion are more directly addressed by the Free Exercise Clause and by case law decisions, which have established relevant contextualized legal precedent. The importance of the Establishment Clause for correctional populations lies in its assurance that the government cannot mandate religious adherence, or lack thereof, to any particular religion or set of religious tenets. In doing so, it expressly assures that inmates, within certain parameters, have a constitutional right to religious participation and practice in a faith of their choosing.

The Free Exercise Clause has exerted a more direct and measurable impact on the ability of both free and incarcerated Americans to practice freely the observable artifacts of their individual religious beliefs. The Free Exercise Clause has primarily served to protect religious freedoms rather than to provide a legislative apparatus for their restriction. This is because the Free Exercise Clause holds that individuals should be allowed to practice freely the religion of their choice in the manner they wish (Greenawalt 2006). However, these protections, while broad, are not universal nor are they absolute. The freedoms inherent in the Free Exercise Clause pertain only to religious practice and behavior so long as they do not run contrary to legitimate state interests, do not violate accepted standards of moral behavior, and do not pose an undue threat to public safety and well-being. Acceptable state-sanctioned restrictions reflecting these limitations can be seen in court edicts reviewing the applicability of the Free Exercise Clause that have allowed the military to draft individuals whose religious beliefs mandate pacifism (*Welsh v. United States* 1970), to restrict plural families in spite of religious precepts allowing them (*State of Utah v. Green* 2004), and upholding laws requiring the vaccination of children in instances when parental religious beliefs preclude them (*Prince v. Massachusetts* 1944).

Limitations of this nature are especially significant because they are likely to be encountered with a great deal of regularity within American correctional institutions. Few would argue legitimate goals of the correctional system include the smooth functioning of individual correctional institutions, the safety and protection of correctional staff and inmates, and the prevention of inmate escapes. Concerns of this nature contribute to the creation of a legitimate state interest in restricting inmate behaviors that are thought to threaten or undermine institutional efficacy or facilitate an environment conducive to violence or escape. It is the enhanced significance of factors such as these in the correctional environment that contributes to the development of greater restrictions on the free practice of religion within the confines of penal institutions.

Although significant in their own right, the constitutional protections related to the freedom of religious practice are only one of a number of factors that collectively define spiritual autonomy in American correctional institutions. These constitutional protections might best be viewed and understood as broad general rights, rather than specific ones. Although applicable to incarcerated populations, these constitutional protections were not specifically developed for them and therefore do not explicitly address specific aspects of their conditions of incarceration. These broad religious protections are more clearly delineated for correctional populations by national legislation, which provides a more focused and direct evaluation of the extent of religious freedoms in the correctional context and the nature and type of legitimate restrictions that can be placed on these freedoms for incarcerated populations.

National Legislation Intended to Protect Freedom of Religious Practice

Although a great deal of federal legislation refers to religious freedom in at least some manner, there are three particularly important pieces of legislation that have a disparate influence on the contemporary state of religious freedom of practice, or lack thereof, within the American correctional system. Each of these, while distinct and separate from the constitutional protections previously discussed, is also linked to this legislation to varying degrees. For instance, the Civil Rights of Institutionalized Persons Act (CRIPA), which was passed by Congress in 1980, offers constitutional protections to incarcerated individuals through the provisions of the Establishment and Free Exercise Clauses that were discussed previously. The intent of CRIPA is to protect vulnerable populations by prohibiting the deprivation of constitutional rights in a variety of high-risk communal living populations (U.S. Commission on Civil Rights 2008). The influence of CRIPA is not limited to correctional environments, but instead extends to a variety of shared public institutions, such as mental health facilities and nursing homes. In instances where a given institution is found to have engaged in a pattern of violating resident rights, the government has the ability to undertake litigation. Any undertaken litigation can focus on a variety of remedies, including ensuring institutional compliance, protecting the rights of residents, and allowing an avenue for the redress of grievances. It is CRIPA's connection to the First Amendment that provides the attorney general with the authority to investigate claims that religious freedom protections have been violated and the specific verbiage of the legislation itself that extends this authority to incarcerated populations.

The contentious nature of prisoner rights in contemporary American society is underscored to at least some degree by legislative reactions to the inmate use of CRIPA as an avenue for the redress of grievances. The Prison Litigation Reform Act (PLRA) was established in 1996 to address concerns that prison inmates were abusing their rights by filing frivolous lawsuits based on unsubstantiated claims. These lawsuits were thought to be attempts to "clog the system" and to demonstrate prisoners' disdain for the correctional environment. Interestingly, the PLRA has resulted in a substantive reduction in inmate claims concerning their conditions of confinement (Belbot 2004). As a result, the government is in essence legislatively restricting the use of one of the primary mechanisms by which prison inmates might have sought a means of exercising the rights granted to them through CRIPA legislation. Dichotomies of this nature only serve to graphically illustrate the controversial nature of prisoner rights in general and freedom of inmate religious practice in particular.

Research indicates that the public appears to have a dubious attitude toward inmates (Cullen, Fisher, & Applegate 2000). On the one hand the public appears to want inmates to be punished, but on the other they simultaneously want them to be rehabilitated and reformed. Perhaps then, it is not surprising that these same conflicting attitudes might be reflected in societal efforts to protect inmate rights while at the same time supporting legislation that restricts these rights. CRIPA sought to ensure that prison officials were cognizant that inmates do not fully and completely relinquish their freedom of religious practice rights upon incarceration. However, legislators have also recognized that restrictions on this freedom are inevitable given the nature of the prison environment.

The Religious Land Use and Institutionalized Persons Act (RLUIPA) of 2000 attempted to provide a legal test by which institutions might recognize when these inevitable restrictions are justifiable and will be able to pass legislative and legal scrutiny. The RLUIPA established a strong legal standard commonly referred to as strict scrutiny as the justifying basis of restrictions on religious freedom of inmates. This standard requires that any restrictions on freedom of religious practice in correctional environments must be justified by a compelling state concern and that these restrictions must be implemented with inmates in the least restrictive and intrusive manner possible (U.S. Commission on Civil Rights 2008). In essence, correctional institutions must critically evaluate both the original justification for any restrictions placed on inmate religious freedoms and the manner in which those restrictions are implemented if they are to be considered legitimate. Considerations of this nature are significant as they will ultimately prove to be important when established or evolving correctional policies and practices regarding religious freedom are evaluated in reference to an inmate allegation of a constitutional violation. Restrictions that pass this test are likely to become institutionalized, while those that do not will be revised or discarded altogether.

Finally, the Religious Freedom Restoration Act (RFRA) of 1993 acted as a predecessor to the RLUIPA by establishing the same type of strict scrutiny standard that was advocated in that act nearly a decade before its creation. The goal of the RFRA was to help ensure the preservation of religious freedom and autonomy of religious practice, albeit in a more general context than was the case with the legislation that we have examined, which specifically targeted correctional populations. In fact, if the religious rights of any particular group were a driving factor behind the creation of the RFRA, it was those of the Native American community, as it was feared that their spiritual beliefs were potentially being threatened by ongoing government actions (U.S. Commission on Civil Rights 2008). Although the RFRA is linked to the establishment of the strict scrutiny standard in relation to restrictions on religious freedom, it is not its only significance in regard to religious protections. Legal scrutiny of the RFRA resulted in a determination that its application to the states was not constitutionally permissible. This finding contributed to the creation of an additional level of legislation intended to protect religious freedoms at the state level.

State Legislation Intended to Protect Freedom of Religious Practice

In *City of Boerne v. Flores* (1997), it was determined that the manner in which the RFRA legislation was being implemented with the states amounted to a constitutional violation. However, this finding did not extend to the manner of application of this legislation within the federal system. As a result, the various provisions of the RFRA and its related religious freedom protections continue to have an impact at the federal level, but their significance and applicability to the states have waned. Many state legislators perceived that these developments created a potential vacuum in the legislative standards and the extent of religious freedom protections offered to individuals at the state level. Officials in many states responded by creating legislation similar to the RFRA in an attempt to fill the pressured void created by the Flores decision. Since the time of the Flores decision 21 states have undertaken the task of establishing state-specific legislation that largely mimics the RFRA (McCrea 2016). The intent of this legislation was similar to that associated with the original RFRA, but was necessarily more individualistic in nature given the process by which it was created. As a result, some minor variations in state-level RFRA legislation can be observed when comparing and contrasting those states that have enacted legislation of this nature (McCrea 2016). In essence these developments have created a two-tiered system of RFRA legislation for some inmates. For these inmates, relief for constitutional violations of free exercise protections can be sought in either federal or state courts depending on the context in which the reported violation occurs and the specific nature of the alleged behaviors.

Overview of Existing Legislation

The freedom of religious thought and practice is a fundamental constitutional right that is protected by a complicated web of legislation at the international, national, and state levels. Although much of this legislation provides general societal protections that indirectly extend to inmates, there is also a substantive body of legislation specifically targeted toward correctional populations. In some ways, legislation of this nature represents the very best ideals of humanity and human society. However, lofty ideas regarding the intrinsic nobility of the human spirit that must, by necessity, allow individuals to choose freely the spiritual path to which they aspire can come into conflict with the realities of daily life in contemporary society. This contrast is especially stark when applied to prison inmates and correctional environments. In this environment, the harsh realities of prison life and government interests can collide with the higher ideals that contributed to the passage of religious freedom legislation. In most societies, some level of balance has been sought between the competing ideals of full religious freedom for inmates and the application of reasonable restrictions to ensure the efficacy of correctional institutions. Those two competing goals have been aptly demonstrated by the legislation that has been examined in this chapter. The religious protections extended to prisoners by the Geneva Convention have been balanced by the recognition of compelling state penal interests, and the ability to seek legal redress of violations of religious rights through CRIPA has been offset by the limitations imposed by the PLRA.

In practice, all of the legislation that has been examined thus far is further contextualized and clarified by the legal precedents that are established via case law decisions. These decisions determine what the legislation examined thus far means in the day-to-day lives of American prisoners. For instance, the strict scrutiny test established by the RFRA and RLUIPA must be put into practice, and it is only through actual judicial scrutiny that the real meaning of this standard can be understood. In turn, the manner in which this standard is defined will influence the ultimate success or lack thereof that inmates experience when pursuing action to remedy restrictions that they feel are inhibiting their ability to practice freely their religious beliefs. The importance of judicial review does not undermine the significance of the legislation itself. Indeed, case law precedent and judicial review would be an impossibility if relevant legislation was not first created.

It may be best to understand legislation and judicial review as independent, yet related, concepts. Collectively they contribute to an evolving and fluid conceptualization of what inmate freedom or religious practice means and which types of restrictions on this practice are viewed as legitimate and acceptable. Given the significant influence that judicial interpretation has on inmate religious freedom, several key cases will now be examined. An overview of a limited number of key cases will serve to underscore the importance of judicial interpretation and to clarify the current state of inmate religious freedoms within the American correctional system.

General Case Law Provisions

For much of the penal history in the United States, prisoners were considered slaves of the state, and thus forfeited all rights. There were few state or federal statutes guiding prison standards or proscribing the manner of inmate treatment (Bernstein 1976). The few standards that did exist provided little in terms of guidance for prison officials and even less in terms of safeguards for prisoners. Early attempts to seek guidance or legal redress, especially related to prisoner's rights, were strictly limited or denied altogether as a result of the "hands-off doctrine" that characterized the legal orientation toward correctional administration during much of the 20th century. The purpose of the hands-off doctrine was to ensure a separation of powers and to prevent courts from not becoming actively involved in correctional governance (Bernstein

1976). In practice, this contributed to a very limited role for the courts in the general day-to-day operation of prison institutions. Courts were unable to supervise prison officials or to interfere with the rules and regulations that were created to govern correctional facilities. The hands-off doctrine was driven by the perception that members of the judiciary should defer to those with penological experience concerning the governance of correctional institutions since they lacked the requisite expertise in prison administration (Fox 1972). It was feared that, to do otherwise, would undermine the power of prison officials thus creating a "slippery slope" in which all aspects of prison life and policy would eventually be supervised by the judicial branch (Fox 1972).

With few exceptions, prison administrators were given absolute deference in regard to the creation of prison policies until the 1960s when the hands-off doctrine experienced a period of decline, culminating with a "hands-on approach" to correctional oversight (Oei 1988). The hands-on period was characterized by an increased willingness among members of the judiciary to involve the courts in the ongoing operations of the correctional system. Due to the ability of the judiciary to determine bail settings, as well as conditions of parole and pretrial release, it follows that the treatment of inmates and the conditions of their confinement would also be reviewable by the courts (Fox 1972). It was during this time that the Warren Court began examining the rights of accused individuals prior to conviction, which intuitively led to the examination of the rights of the incarcerated. At the same time, prisoner rehabilitation and treatment became important correctional goals adding greater emphasis to calls for a renewed evaluation of prisoners' rights (Solove 1996). One major issue the courts faced when embarking on these efforts was an absence of precedent to guide their collective actions when making decisions concerning the rights of prisoners. Although it seemed apparent to the courts that prison inmates did not possess the same rights as those enjoyed by free citizens, it also seemed clear that the rights not infringing on their status as prisoners or threatening a legitimate institutional concern remained (Oei 1988).

Johnson v. Avery (1969) was among the first cases permitting a more hands-on approach by the courts. Although this case did not provide direct guidance in terms of religious rights, it was one of the first cases in which the Court addressed prisoners' constitutional rights in a general sense. In Johnson, the defendant was disciplined for aiding a fellow prisoner in drafting a writ of habeas corpus. The Court ruled that, unless there were reasonable alternatives provided for those in need of assistance in the creation of such writs (e.g. illiterate or indigent prisoners), the state could not bar inmates from aiding one another. This concept of reasonable alternatives created a lasting legal precedent that would be found in other cases relating to the First Amendment rights of prisoners, including those directly affecting the religious rights of prisoners.

Since the transition to a "hands-on period" in judicial oversight, the Court has shown an increased willingness to intervene in the standards set by prison administrators regarding the First Amendment rights to practice religion. This is at least partially due to the historical relationship between religion and prisons in the United States (Bernstein 1976). Religious groups, most notably Quakers, founded the U.S. prison system based on aspirations that criminals might become law-abiding citizens through immersion in a prosocial correctional environment. Religion continued to be a correctional tool used throughout prison history to help inmates reclaim their religious identity and to rehabilitate themselves prior to release (Bernstein 1976).

Today, religious involvement is still thought to have a number of benefits for inmate populations. Involvement in prison religious activities permits inmates to learn prosocial behaviors through involvement with others in constructive and cooperative ways (Kerley, Matthews, & Blanchard 2005; Welty 1998), and many prisons coordinate with members of local faith congregations to offer religious programs for inmates (Kerley, Bartkowski, Matthews, & Emond 2010; Kerley, Matthews, & Shoemaker 2009). Reducing an inmate's ability to practice religion may lead to an increased risk of recidivism postrelease (Welty 1998). Given the importance of religious participation in regard to a variety of important inmate outcomes, it is logical that freedom of religious participation would be one of the factors reviewed by the courts.

A number of landmark cases have provided guidelines for decision making when it comes to the First Amendment rights of prison inmates. These cases include *Procunier v. Martinez* (1974), *Pell v. Procunier* (1974), and *Turner v. Safley* (1987). Each of these cases will now be briefly examined in an attempt to establish the framework that will influence the decisions made in the cases to follow. *Procunier v. Martinez* did not directly deal with the issue of inmate freedom of religious practice. However, it was still an important case because it helped to establish the legal test by which later cases concerning religious freedom would be determined. In siding with inmates regarding the censorship of their mail, the Court held that when limits are placed on First Amendment freedoms, institutions must demonstrate that those limits are reasonably necessary to further a legitimate penological government interest and that they are no greater than necessary to protect that interest. It was during these proceedings that the Court noted a lack of accepted standards for protecting prisoners' rights and for preventing the unnecessary involvement of prison administration. The test that the Court implemented is reflective of the strict scrutiny standard previously examined and focused on the reasonableness of the government interest and the intrusiveness of its implementation.

Shortly after Martinez, other cases testing the First Amendment standards established in Martinez began to emerge. In *Pell v. Procunier* (1974) a policy prohibiting face-to-face media interviews with certain inmates was upheld. The reasonableness standard was invoked in this case, forcing prison administration to demonstrate the reasonableness of the regulation in question and requiring prisoners to demonstrate otherwise. In Pell, the Court found that the government interest in question was reasonable because there were other means of communication between inmates and the media. Together, Martinez and Pell underscored not only the standard by which First Amendment claims would be judged by the courts, but also a demonstrated willingness on behalf of the judiciary to decide such cases based on that standard even if it meant entering judgments in the favor of inmates (Oei 1988).

A little over a decade later, *Turner v. Safley* (1987) examined the issue of intrusiveness in regards to how institutional restrictions on inmate life were implemented. The complainant in this case alleged that two prison regulations were unconstitutional. The first regulation forbade or severely restricted mail between inmates in different correctional institutions. The second regulation required the prison superintendent's permission for inmates to marry, which was often only provided when there were compelling circumstances, such as pregnancy or the birth of an illegitimate child. The Court upheld the first regulation while striking down the second. The Court held that both regulations infringed in some manner on prisoner rights, but that only one was offset by reasonable state interests. Citing institutional safety concerns, the Court argued that denying mail between inmates was reasonable. However, using the standards set forth in Martinez, the Court determined that the regulation on denying inmate marriage altogether was overly broad and was not implemented in the least restrictive manner possible. In Turner, the Court set out to formulate a clearer standard of review for the constitutional claims of prisoners, one which takes into account the needs of the facilities and the inmates (Oei 1988).

In Turner, the Court also established a minimal scrutiny test for instances in which inmates alleged that a constitutional right, including those involving the freedom of religious practice, was being infringed on (Solove 1996). The Court held that any prison regulation that restricts rights must balance that restriction with the legitimate penological objectives that the prison is attempting to advance. The examination must consider whether the regulations that burden the fundamental rights of prisoners are based on exaggerated institutional concerns (Oei 1988). In considerations of this nature, Turner required the evaluation of a number of factors. Not only must the restriction in question be reasonably related to a legitimate penological interest, such as security, rehabilitation, or the exhaustion of limited institutional resources, but also inmates must be provided with reasonable alternative means of exercising the restricted right, if possible. This factor is particularly important in cases considering the freedom to exercise religion, as will be seen later in the chapter.

Much of the existing literature on the constitutional rights of prisoners, especially involving First Amendment protections, has credited Martinez, Pell, and Turner with establishing the general legal guidelines by which courts will decide cases involving allegations of unlawful institutional restrictions. With these general standards established, the courts could move forward with the evaluation of the legality of more specific institutional policies and practices that limited inmates' freedom of religious thought and practice. These cases ultimately proved to have a more direct impact on the manner in which prisoners could practice their religious beliefs behind prison bars. Some of the first issues evaluated pertained to whether correctional institutions actively favored certain religions over others and in doing so were actively engaging in patterns of religious discrimination. The following section will discuss the cases that collectively established the precedent for determining whether a correctional institution has, in fact, been discriminatory in creation of prison regulations related to the free practice of religion.

Legal Prohibitions against Religious Discrimination

Incarceration inevitably requires at least some restriction on the otherwise unrestricted exercise of inmate rights. However, courts have repeatedly held that this does not mean that all inmate rights can be curtailed or that allowable restrictions are limitless, including those rights related to the free practice of religion (Solove 1996). Martinez, Pell, and Turner provided guidelines to determine how one's religious rights may be protected. This is an important standard given that difficulties faced by administrators (e.g., limited finances, outdated facilities, and increasing prison populations) can lead to religious intolerance within the prison context (Solove 1996). This intolerance may result in limits being placed on prisoner rights not only in situations when it is absolutely necessary and reasonable to do so, but also in situations when doing so might simply be the most convenient manner of preventing institutional issues and avoiding the possibility of potential dangers to staff, inmates, and society as a whole (Solove 1996).

Historically, the religious rights guaranteed to both prisoners and free citizens alike in American society have tended to center on Christian religious beliefs, most notably those associated with Catholic and Protestant faith traditions (Thomas & Zaitzow 2006). However, the 1960s evidenced greater diversity in the American religious landscape with an accompanying rise in the number of individuals belonging to less common faiths. The increasing number of Muslim inmates was an especially significant development in this regard as these inmates were willing to push for greater equality through the courts. As the courts began to process more cases from Muslim inmates seeking religious equality on par with that experienced by members of mainstream Christian denominations, the future of religious rights in prison began to take shape (Thomas & Zaitzow 2006). The willingness of the courts to entertain challenges from inmates belonging to less frequently practiced faiths initially was minimal (Solove 1996). Many of the later challenges alleging religious discrimination would be decided based on legal precedents established in the early cases involving Muslim inmates.

Prison administrators originally denied any sort of official Muslim faith. These refusals to recognize the religion were justified based on institutional assertions that they were necessary to ensure institutional security given the alleged political and racist nature of the Black Muslim movement in the American prison system (Bernstein 1976). Two of the first representative cases were *Fulwood v. Clemmer* (1962) and *Cooper v. Pate* (1964). In Fulwood, the Court evaluated whether Black Muslims adhered to beliefs that could be properly classified as a religion for legal purposes and whether these beliefs espoused violence and racial hatred. In its decision in this case, the Court officially recognized the Black Muslim movement as a legitimate institutional religion. Additionally, the Court concluded that there was insufficient evidence to conclude that adherents of the Black Muslim movement espoused racial hatred or advocated violence as part of their practices. As a result of this decision, Black Muslims were granted the same religious protections and privileges that had previously been extended to mainstream Christian denominations (Bernstein 1976). As evidence of this evolving judicial policy, the Supreme Court ruled in *Cooper v. Pate* (1964) that it was discriminatory for a correctional institution to place a Black Muslim inmate in a segregated housing unit simply because of his religious beliefs.

In a related case (*Cruz v. Beto* 1972), a Buddhist prisoner serving a sentence in a Texas Department of Corrections facility alleged that he was not permitted to use the chapel, correspond with religious advisers, or share religious materials with other inmates. The inmate argued that the restrictions amounted to a violation of First Amendment freedom of religion protections and filed a lawsuit against the Texas Department of Corrections seeking legal relief. The district court originally dismissed the case out of deference to prison officials. However, the Supreme Court reversed this decision in ruling that denying inmates a reasonable opportunity to pursue religious faith without fear of retribution, even when they possess unconventional religious beliefs, was indeed a violation of inmates' First Amendment rights (Thomas & Zaitzow 2006).

Collectively, these cases underscored the notion that prison officials could not discriminate against specific types of religions, so long as those religions were viewed as legitimate. In doing so, they established a precedent that favored the protection of the First Amendment rights of a much broader group of religious inmates than had previously been the case in the American correctional system. The ultimate operational implication of the decisions in these cases is that prison administrators are prohibited from discriminating against the practices of any particular religion. However, none of these cases provided a legal prohibition against prison administrators limiting the practice of all religions, so long as they are willing and able to do so equally and without preference (Fox 1972). For protections of this nature, one must look toward cases such as Turner, which require that certain specified conditions be met before inmate religious rights can be infringed upon. The following section will further the current discussion by providing an evaluation of selected cases that scrutinized institutional restrictions on specific types of religious practices.

Restrictions on Services, Sabbath, and Clergy

Given their restricted housing status, incarcerated individuals inevitably will have more limited access to religious services and to spiritual leaders. For instance, inmates are physically incapable of attending worship services during their work assignments, regular headcounts, and prison-wide lockdowns. Although some restrictions of this nature are to be expected, questions regarding the extent of legitimate constraints remain. Many cases have examined this issue to determine the extent to which access to services and clergy must be provided to inmates by prison administrators. Among the earliest cases related to the extent of religious access was *Gittlemacker v. Prasse* (1970). In this case, the Court examined whether prison administrators were required to provide a religious leader for each religion represented within the inmate population. The claim made by the inmate was ultimately dismissed by the Court based on the standard created in *Turner v. Safley* (1987). In deciding the case, the Court noted that the prison had not imposed unreasonable barriers on inmates of a variety of faiths regarding opportunities to practice their religious beliefs. Facilities for worship were provided on prison grounds and regulations allowed clergy members from a variety of faiths to visit the institution. The Court noted that the administration was not required to provide all faiths with faith-specific clergy members. According to the Court, doing so would be cost prohibitive given the large number of different religions that must coexist within prisons.

Twenty years later, in *Young v. Lane* (1990), inmates alleged that their First Amendment rights were violated due to the absence of a Jewish religious official and the inability to offer inmate-led religious services in the absence of a qualified clergy member. Prison administrators argued that this regulation was intended to prevent challenges to institutional security because inmate-led religious meetings could be used as a means of concealing criminal associations and allowing the transmission of information that could be used to undermine institutional goals and smooth correctional operations. In this case the court sided in part with inmates in determining that prison inmates should be provided with opportunities for peer-led religious services in the absence of qualified clergy members. In responding to the security concerns raised by prison administrators, the court noted that any and all peer-led religious services could take place under the supervision of correctional personnel to prevent threats to safety or potential violations of institutional policy (*Young v. Lane* 1990).

Religious holy days are another issue pertaining to religious practice. To people of faith, holy days are sacred periods that play a pivotal role in their faith. As such, these days must be honored in the manner prescribed by established religious tenets. Conflict can arise when institutions are faced with inmate populations that recognize different and potentially conflicting holy days. In *O'Lone v. Estate of Shabazz* (1987), a number of Muslim prisoners in New Jersey claimed that they were denied their religious rights through institutional polices that prohibited their attendance at Friday religious services. Using the factors that had been set out in Turner, the Court dismissed the inmate allegations that the prison policy had infringed on their religious rights. This decision was based on evidence that Muslims could exercise their religious freedoms in other manners, including daily prayers, conferencing with religious leaders, and eating specialized diets during Ramadan (*O'Lone v. Estate of Shabazz* 1987).

Restrictions on Religious Literature and Religious Artifacts

Literature and other religious paraphernalia play a significant role in the practice of all faiths. The desire for adherents to access literature and artifacts as a part of practicing their faith is understandable, but so are institutional efforts to limit this access in an attempt to reduce contraband and to limit violence. Cases related to limitations of this nature often hinge on the nature of the specific religious items that institutions have decided to restrict. For instance, should a particular religion mandate the use of decorative religious swords as part of its practice, correctional institutions could make a compelling argument they should have the right to restrict them. However, it is less clear whether institutional policies restricting access to spiritual literature because it is thought to advocate racial animosity are legitimate. Given the inherent differences between religious literature and religious artifacts, each of these items will be considered separately and cases representing the position that the courts have taken on each will be examined.

Inmate access to the Muslim periodical, *Muhammad Speaks,* has been addressed in multiple cases alleging the suppression of religious freedom. In *Rowland v. Sigler* (1971), the complaining inmate had a subscription to *Muhammad Speaks* purchased for him by a family member. An institutional policy restricted inmate periodicals to only those that were included on an officially sanctioned reading list. As a result, the inmate was denied access to the periodical. In evaluating the inmate's claim, the court ruled that the correctional institution had failed to demonstrate the existence of a compelling justification for the restriction. The court noted that without a demonstration by the state that the publication would create a security risk to the institution or that purchasing the publication would create a financial hardship for the institution, the materials would need to be released to the inmate. This was an interesting case given that the inmate in question was not a Muslim and only sought the publication out of personal interest, rather than religious conviction. In a related case, *Long v. Parker* (1972), the same publication was denied by correctional authorities, but this time to a Muslim inmate seeking it for religious purposes.

After examining the evidence in the case, the court ruled that when alleging unconstitutional restrictions of religious materials, inmates must demonstrate to the courts that the publication in question is religious literature essential to the practice of their faith. Further, inmates must prove that members of other religious groups are granted access to similar types of religious publications.

Finally, the court ruled that to justify restricting religious materials based on safety considerations, penal institution must prove that those materials present a "clear and present danger" to institutional safety (*Long v. Parker* 1972). General concerns that religious materials might cause an increase in hostilities or violence were viewed as insufficient to justify banning them from prison inmates altogether. Again, factors related to equality of treatment across religions, sincerity of inmate religious beliefs, and severity of threat to institutional safety were key factors in the determination of this case. These elements remain critically important in deciding cases of this nature today.

In addition to religious literature, religious artifacts are important elements for most faith traditions. As a result, the institutional suppression of these items has brought frequent court challenges from religious inmates. In many cases of this nature, courts have been charged with comparing institutional claims that religious artifacts posed safety and security concerns against inmate claims that doing so placed an unreasonable burden on their ability to freely practice their religious beliefs. *Mark v. Nix* (1993) is an example of a case in which this type of calculation was required. The inmate in this case had a rosary with a crucifix that was confiscated by prison officials who feared the crucifix could be used to unlock restraint devices. The inmate was given a replacement rosary without the crucifix attached, but felt that the compromise amounted to an unconstitutional restriction on his right to religious practice. The court ruled in the institution's favor holding that the institution had justified the legitimacy of the institutional safety concern and that it had offered a reasonable alternative to the inmate that allowed him to practice his religious beliefs.

Dietary Restrictions

Dietary restrictions are a common part of many religions and tend to reflect significant aspects of the faiths that require them. In many instances religious dietary guidelines are intended to either underscore important religious teachings or principles, or to ensure the devotion and commitment of adherents. Given their large numbers within the American prison population, Christian dietary restrictions are relatively easy for correctional officials to accommodate. However, the special dietary restrictions associated with less common religious groups pose a more substantive challenge for penal institutions. For this reason, many of the legal challenges involving the denial of special dietary requests have involved uncommon religions with fewer followers. When determining the extent to which correctional institutions must accommodate the dietary guidelines of less common faiths, the courts have held that inmates have a duty to demonstrate the sincerity of their religious beliefs as they relate to the dietary restrictions in question, and that their requests do not impose an excessive burden on the correctional institution that houses them.

The provision of kosher and Muslim meals has been the subject of an inordinate number of legal challenges related to the denial of faith-based dietary restriction cases. During the course of evaluating challenges of this nature, the courts have held that inmates with sincerely held religious beliefs are eligible for special meals consistent with their spiritual beliefs if it does not present an undue burden on the institution to provide them (*Kahane v. Carlson* 1975). This is true even if the inmate is a recent religious convert who is not viewed as an official member of the faith in question by religious officials (*Jackson v. Mann* 1999).

Inmates with insincere or fictitious religious beliefs are not eligible for the religious protections extended to inmates with sincerely held religious beliefs. However, the courts have also noted that while institutions can deny religious dietary requests for inmates with insincere religious beliefs, institutional assessments regarding the sincerity of religious beliefs cannot be made based on mere speculation or secondhand knowledge (*McElyea v. Babbitt* 1987). In instances when sincere religious beliefs mandate special dietary restrictions, correctional institutions are under no obligation to create a new menu when modifications of the existing menu will suffice (*Kahey v. Jones* 1988).

Restrictions on Physical Appearance

Many contemporary religions have established specific standards of dress and appearance to which followers are expected to adhere. In a correctional environment these standards can come into direct conflict with institutional regulations mandating minimal standards of physical appearance. As was the case with other restrictions we have examined, much of the litigation related to faith-based restrictions on physical appearance originated with inmates belonging to less conventional religions. This section will discuss three such cases, which have addressed the practices of wearing beards, maintaining long hair, and wearing religious clothing.

In *Moskowitz v. Wilkinson* (1977), the Court examined instances in which prisoners wear beards as part of their religious convictions. Despite being disciplined on multiple occasions, an Orthodox Jewish prisoner continually refused to remove his beard, which was a violation of prison regulations. After a survey of state prisons revealed that more institutions permitted beards than prohibited them, the Court held that the policy banning beards was likely not linked to legitimate institutional safety concerns and was therefore an unconstitutional religious restriction. In a related case, *Gallahan v. Hollyfield* (1982), a Native American inmate refused to cut his long hair for spiritual reasons. In that case, it was determined that the inmate's lack of compliance was driven by sincere religious convictions as part of a recognized religion. The court did not find the state's safety argument compelling, reasoning that prison officials could provide a less intrusive means of ensuring institutional security. The court reasoned that the inmate's hair could be searched for contraband whether it was long or short.

The courts have not always found in favor of inmates in cases involving religiously linked physical appearance restrictions. In fact, inmates have typically had difficulties in establishing claims of this nature (Boston & Manville 2010). In *Hines v. South Carolina Department of Corrections* (1998), inmates of different religious faiths collectively alleged that the Department of Corrections was infringing on their religious rights through a policy that mandated short hair and clean-shaven faces. The policy had been put in place due to institutional concerns regarding gang activity, prison security, and inmate discipline. Inmates who refused to comply were not forced to submit to the institutional regulation, but were reclassified to a higher security area. The court ruled in favor of the state finding their institutional safety argument compelling and noting that in this instance the policy was applied equally to inmates of all religious faiths, rather than being applied in a discriminatory manner to members of only certain faiths.

The legal complexity of issues such as these can also be seen in a pair of cases addressing similar issues, but reaching different findings. The wearing of headpieces is a common practice in both Jewish and Muslim faiths. However, this practice is also frequently a violation of institutional regulations for fear the headpieces will be used to denote gang affiliation or hide contraband. In *Young v. Lane* (1990), a Jewish prisoner challenged institutional restrictions prohibiting yarmulkes, a religious headpiece. In siding with the inmate the court held that the institutional policy was not shown to be adequately related to institutional security concerns. The court noted that institutional policies allowed inmates to wear baseball caps, which were just as likely to be used to indicate gang affiliation and more likely to be used to transport contraband. Two years later, in *Muhammad v. Lynaugh* (1992), the Court ruled in favor of a correctional institution concerning a very similar issue. In this case, Muslim inmates were restricted from wearing Kufi caps, a form of religious headpiece. The institutional justifications for the restrictions were similar to those proffered in the Lane case. The court upheld the Kufi restrictions in noting that the institutional restriction was only enforced when inmates were in public parts of the institution. Allowing inmates to wear religious headgear in their cells and in the chapel provided ample opportunities for the exercise of their religious freedoms, and were not offset by the otherwise reasonable restrictions imposed.

Conclusion

The free exercise of religion can be a contentious subject under even the best of circumstances. Religious adherence and doctrinal differences can drive conflict among those in society with mainstream religious beliefs, those with no religious affiliation, and those with nonmainstream religious beliefs. Conflicts of this nature are especially difficult in the context of how the state distributes its resources. It is a great challenge, then, for states to determine the veracity and appropriateness of religious rights among those in correctional facilities.

The principle of least eligibility holds that prisoners are among those in society least deserving of society's benefits and protections, including those protections associated with religious liberty. At the same time, the United States prides itself on the individual rights and liberties that it provides to even the least deserving of its citizens. These concerns are evident in legislation that has been passed in an attempt to provide legal protections for the religious rights of correctional populations. However, the challenges associated with the provision of these protections is demonstrated in court decisions prioritizing institutional safety and security. The issue of religious freedom, in correctional institutions and the general public, is a dynamic and evolving one that must balance a number of complex and competing factors in a challenging effort to find an elusive middle ground.

Bibliography

Belbot, Barbara. "Report on the Prison Litigation Reform Act: What have the courts decided so far?" *The Prison Journal* 84, no. 3 (2004): 290–316.

Bernstein, Andrea. "Free exercise of religion in prison: The right to observe dietary laws." *Fordham Law Review* 45, no. 1 (1976): 92–109.

Boston, John, & Daniel E. Manville. *Prisoner's self-help litigation manual (4th ed.).* New York: Oxford University Press, 2010.

Crawford, Emily. *The treatment of combatants and insurgents under the law of armed conflict.* New York: Oxford University Press, 2010.

Cullen, Francis T., Bonnie S. Fisher, & Brandon K. Applegate. "Public opinion about punishment and corrections." *Crime and Justice* 27, no. 1 (2000): 1–79.

Dziedzic, Peter. "Religion under fire: A report and policy paper on religious freedom in Tibet." *The Tibet Journal* 38, No. 3–4 (Autumn–Winter 2013), 87–113.

Fox, Barry M. "The First Amendment rights of prisoners." *Journal of Criminal Law and Criminology* 63, no. 2 (1972): 162–184.

Greenawalt, Kent. *Religion and the Constitution: Volume 1. Free exercise and fairness.* Princeton, NJ: Princeton University Press, 2006.

International Committee of the Red Cross. *Basic rules of the Geneva Conventions and their additional protocols.* Geneva: The Conventions, 1983.

Johnson, Barry M. "Prisoner's rights: Restrictions on religious practices." *University of Colorado Law Review* 42, no. 3 (1970): 387–402.

Joseph, Sarah, & Melissa Castan. *The International Covenant on Civil and Political Rights: Cases, materials, and commentary (3rd ed.).* New York: Oxford University Press, 2013.

Kerley, Kent R., John P. Bartkowski, Todd L. Matthews, & Tracy L. Emond. "From the sanctuary to the slammer: Exploring the narratives of evangelical prison ministry workers." *Sociological Spectrum* 30 (2010): 504–525.

Kerley, Kent R., Todd L. Matthews, & Troy C. Blanchard. "Religiosity, religious participation, and negative prison behaviors." *Journal for the Scientific Study of Religion* 44 (2005): 443–457.

Kerley, Kent R., Todd L. Matthews, & Jessica Shoemaker. "A simple plan, a simple faith: Chaplains and lay ministers in Mississippi prisons." *Review of Religious Research* 51 (2009): 87–103.

McCrea, Austin. "Religious policy adoption in the American states: Measuring and validating influence of the Christian Right." Electronic thesis or dissertation. Kent State University, 2016. https://etd.ohiolink.edu

Morrow, James D. "The laws of war, common conjectures, and legal systems in international politics." *The Journal of Legal Studies* 31, no. 1 (2002): 41–60.

Oei, Lorijean G. "The new standard of review for prisoner's rights: A Turner for the worse—Turner v. Safley." *Villanova Law Review* 33, no. 2 (1988): 393–436.

Ruane, Kathleen A. *Freedom of speech and the press: Exceptions to the First Amendment.* Washington, DC: Congressional Research Office, 2014.

Seibert-Fohr, Anja. *Prosecuting serious human rights violations.* New York: Oxford University Press, 2009.

Solove, Daniel J. "Faith profaned: The religious freedom restoration act and religion in the prisons." *Yale Law Journal* 106, no. 2 (1996): 459–491.

Thomas, Jim, & Barbara H. Zaitzow. "Conning or conversion? The role of religion in prison coping." *The Prison Journal* 86, no. 2 (2006): 242–259.

U.S. Commission on Civil Rights. *Enforcing religious freedom in prison.* Washington: United States Commission on Civil Rights, 2008.

Welty, Jeffrey. "Restrictions on prisoner's religious freedom as unconstitutional conditions of confinement: An Eighth Amendment argument." *Duke Law Journal* 48, no. 3 (1988): 601.

Court Cases

City of Boerne v. Flores. No. 95-2074 (1997).
Cooper v. Pate. 378 U.S. 546 (1964).
Cruz v. Beto. 405 U.S. 319 (1972).
Employment Division v. Smith. 494 U.S. 872 (1990).
Fullwood v. Clemmer. 206 F. Sup 370 (1962).
Gallahan v. Hollyfield. 670 F. 2d 1345 (1982).
Gittlemacker v. Prasse. 428 F. 2d 1255 (1970).
Hammans v. Saffle. 348 F. 3d 1250 (2003).
Hines v. South Carolina Department of Corrections. 148 F. 3d 353 (1998).
Jackson v. Mann. 196 F. 3d 316 (1999).
Johnson v. Avery. 393 U.S. 483 (1969).
Kahane v. Carlson. 527 F. 2d 492 (1975).
Kahey v. Jones. 836 F. 2d 948 (1988).
Lemon v. Kurtzman. 403 U.S. 602 (1971).
Long v. Parker. 455 F. 2d 466 (1972).
Mark v. Nix. 983 F. 2d 138 (1993).
McElyea v. Babbitt. 833 F. 2d 196 (1987).
Moskowitz v. Wilkinson. 432 F. Sup 947 (1977).
Muhammad v. Lynaugh. 966 F. 2d 901 (1992).
O'Lone v. Estate of Shabazz. 482 U.S. 342 (1987).
Pell v. Procunier. 417 U.S. 817 (1974).
Prince v. Massachusetts 321 U.S. 158 (1944).
Procunier v. Martinez. 416 U.S. 396 (1974).
Rowland v. Sigler. 327 F. Sup 821 (1971).
State of Utah v. Green. No. 20010788 (2004).
Turner v. Safley. 482 U.S. 78 (1987).
Welsh v. United States. 398 U.S. 333, 90 S. Ct. 1792, 26 L. Ed. 2d 308 (1970).
Young v. Lane. 733 F. Sup 1205 (1990).

PART 3

Religion in Prison outside the United States

Faith Provision, Institutional Power, and Meaning among Muslim Prisoners in Two English High-Security Prisons*

Ryan J. Williams and Alison Liebling

I: You said that twenty years ago there was a difference in the ways that Muslims identified themselves as Muslim . . . R: I think certainly there were fewer Muslim prisoners. The identity of Muslims wasn't that strong. So many Muslims didn't make a big fuss of attending Friday prayers, not attending Friday prayers. Prayers during workshop hours. Wearing of clothing. Islamic classes . . . There wasn't that much understanding of other faiths, per se, across the board, from the Prison Service . . . but slowly, slowly, over the years, prisoners started demanding Halal food, and wearing of [religious] clothing. Chaplaincy Headquarters got its act together. The structures changed. And people are more multi-faith,

*This work was supported by the Economic and Social Research Council (Ref. # ES/L003120/1). The writing of this chapter was supported by the Social Sciences and Humanities Research Council of Canada through a postdoctoral fellowship (Award Number 756-2014-0647) awarded to Ryan Williams.

inter-faith dimensions grew, and instilled it within the whole prison. And that's how identity amongst prisoners grew. (Sulieman, Chaplain)

"How do we take the power out of religion? Through the regime." (Leon, prison officer, fieldnotes)

Nearly two decades ago, Beckford and Gilliat (1998) identified the crucial problem for prisons in the face of increasing diversity and multiculturalism as one of recognizing equal rights for prisoners to practice their respective faiths. In this chapter, we argue that a new and more complex problem lies in understanding how institutional power flows through faith provision and impacts religious identity and meaning-making. Our starting point is to suggest that faith provision does not occur within a vacuum: it is deeply tied with the broader social and moral climates of particular prisons and interacts with the ways in which power and order are exercised in different prisons. Following Jacobs's classic prison sociological study of Stateville (1977), which describes very similar developments in the United States in the 1970s, we explore the relationship between religion, power, recognition, and identities of resistance. Religious provision and chaplaincy departments have become a site where different forms of institutional power are exercised. This bears upon the experiences of religious provision and shapes what religion comes to mean for prisoners, ranging from the assertion of identities of resistance to the exploration of avenues for personal growth where personal agency is exercised.

At the time of Beckford and Gilliat's work, religious affiliation on the whole was on the decline in the prisons of England and Wales, with small gains in the numbers of prisoners from minority faiths. Pastoral and religious care was narrow, evolving from a historical context where the Church of England had an exclusive hold over chaplaincy activities (1998, 25). Two decades have brought significant changes and increasing diversity within prisons. Diversity in the prisoner population has increased steeply with a significant rise in the numbers of Black and mixed-race prisoners and growth in the number and proportion of prisoners who self-identify as Muslim, a figure that has doubled in over a decade (Table 13.1).

Beckford and Gilliat's pioneering work described the "controversy" that surrounds diversity and faith provision in prison chaplaincies. But this controversy is situated today in a new context where the prison service manages new risks that intersect with religious identity, power, and extremism (Liebling & Arnold 2012; Liebling, Arnold, & Straub 2011; Silke 2014). This set of risks or concerns often intersect with the prison chaplaincies as spaces and the work of chaplains. Accommodating diversity, *and* drawing limits to its recognition in order to maintain a safe and efficient regime, is now a familiar struggle in the day-to-day operations of English high-security prisons.

This chapter explores the entanglements between faith recognition and provision, identity, and power in high-security prisons. As the pair of opening

Table 13.1   Prison Population by Religious Group (March 2016)

	Number	% of prison population	% pt. change on 2002	% general population, aged 15+
Christian	41,940	49.1	−9.0	61.3
Muslims	12,506	14.6	+6.9	4.0
Hindu	421	0.5	+0.1	1.5
Sikh	732	0.9	+0.2	0.7
Buddhist	1,558	1.8	+0.9	0.5
Jewish	406	0.5	+0.2	0.5
No religion	26,349	30.8	−0.6	24.1
Other	1,437	1.7	+1.1	0.5
Not recorded	92	0.1	+0.1	7.0
Total	85,441	100		

Source: Allen, Grahame, & Noel Dempsey. July 4, 2016. "Prison Population Statistics." London: House of Commons Library.

quotes highlights, the growth of a religious identity consciousness among prisoners and in the prison service has come to intersect in subtle ways with how institutions exercise power to maintain order and control. We argue in this chapter that these forms or means of order (Sparks & Bottoms 1995; Sparks, Bottoms, & Hay 1996) and the "moral climates" of prisons to which they are related (Liebling 2005) come to bear in subtle ways on the subjective experience of faith identity and contribute to a range of expressions of religious identity from resistance and protest to personal development.

The relationship between institutional forms of power and religious identities have largely evaded empirical description within the sociology of religion in prisons because "the perspective of inmates was . . . not thoroughly studied" (Becci 2015, 3), though Beckford and his colleagues provide a notable exception in their landmark study of Muslim prisoners in Britain and France (Beckford, Joy, & Khosrokhavar 2005). Moreover, attention to "power dynamics around religious diversity" is a relatively recent site of investigation (Becci 2015, 7). Our work is grounded in the empirical tradition of prison sociology (inter alia Clemmer [1940] 1958; Sykes [1958] 2003) and successive works that have sought to systematically compare prisons, their use of power, legitimacy and their "moral climates" (Liebling 2005; Sparks & Bottoms 1995; Sparks, Bottoms, & Hay 1996).

We draw on our recent study (with colleagues, Ruth Armstrong and Richard Bramwell. "Locating trust in a climate of fear: Religion, moral status, prisoner leadership, and risk in maximum security prisons." Ref. No. ES/L003120/1. The writing of this article was supported by the Social Sciences and Humanities Research Council of Canada through a postdoctoral fellowship [Award Number 756-2014-0647] awarded to Ryan Williams) of two high-security English prisons to explore how religious identity can take on different expressions and come to signify different meanings for prisoners in prisons with different moral climates and control styles. Before summarizing this study, we provide some background through detailing a study that set the tone for the current research.

Viewing Religion through a "Risk Lens": Whitemoor Prison 12 Years On

Liebling and Price studied staff-prisoner relationships in Whitemoor prison between 1998 and 1999 (Liebling & Price 1999, published in its second edition as *The Prisoner Officer*; with Shefer, 2010) and 12 years on in 2010–2011 (Liebling, Arnold, & Straub 2011). "Whitemoor 1" described a prison where relationships between staff and prisoners were generally good and where "relationships were the oil which smoothed the flow of a prison day in a way that implicitly meant more power (or a more effective utilization of power) for officers." Good relationships between staff and prisoners and "a good knowledge of prisoners led to increased power" among prison staff and a more ordered and controlled regime that was reasonably acceptable or legitimate in the eyes of prisoners (Liebling et al. 2010). There is a history in English prisons of maintaining order and control through enlisting the "willing cooperation" of prisoners (Bottoms & Sparks 1997, 50). "Legitimacy" refers to a state of affairs where order and control flow from good relationships between staff and prisoners, and through fairness of procedures, professional competence, and decent interpersonal treatment, or what the authors term interpersonal and procedural legitimacy (see further Sparks & Bottoms 2007).

Twelve years later, Whitemoor prison had changed. So too had the social context of imprisonment. A new prisoner population with a far higher proportion of Muslim, Black, and mixed-race prisoners meant that staff were less confident and sure-footed in building relationships and setting boundaries with prisoners. There were concerns by staff about being racist and uncertainties around what Islamic practices could be policed. Fears of radicalization were prevalent. This contributed to a "climate of fear" where religion was read through a "risk lens." There was a disruption of established hierarchies with more Black and minority ethnic and mixed-race prisoners, and more Muslim prisoners asserting their status on the wings. About half of the Muslims in Liebling et al.'s sample converted to Islam while in prison: "A mixture of coercion and the attractions of faith made turning to Islam appear as one solution to the problems of fear, lack of trust, and the existential crisis that prisoners faced" (Liebling & Arnold 2012, 414). Social relationships between prisoners were described as more "complex and less visible," and there were some real risks of serious violence.

There was an ambiguity in faith identity where it was difficult to disentangle sincerity from collective group identities used to coerce and dominate others. Faith was an avenue for self-exploration and development. Islamic identification provided a source of meaning and belonging, and a means to cope with the pains of imprisonment. But it was also part of a new power-base where Muslim prisoners came to exert power over other prisoners. The report of the research documented disconcerting evidence around Islam being used as a power base, raising difficult questions around the role of Islam in reshaping prisoner hierarchies, staff-prisoner relationships, and relationships and conflicts between prisoners. There were tensions between faith groups, with some reports that some Muslim prisoners sought to enforce Islamic norms on other prisoners, such as wearing underwear in the showers or not frying bacon in the kitchens. These challenges made empirical description of Islamic faith practices difficult.

There were new features of the contemporary prison experience. This included relatively young prisoners serving indeterminate sentences with 15–25 year tariffs. Coming to terms with such sentence lengths and uncertainty was difficult for prisoners. There were several prisoners convicted for terrorist-related offenses, serving their sentences within the main prison population, compounding new risks around radicalization and extremism in prisons.

There were also limited avenues for finding hope, recognition, and meaning in a political climate where there were concerns over "pampering long-term prisoners" leading to many creative activities in prisons being subject to a new "public acceptability test." This meant that some of the activities and sense-making outlets, relationships, and opportunities that had previously been available for prisoners facing long sentences were now unavailable. Liebling et al. (2011) described the chaplaincy in Whitemoor 12 years later as "depleted," with uncertainties over their "collective role, power and presence in the prison" (46). Liebling et al. (2011) also, however, identified the chapel as a source of hope, recognition, and humanity (39). The chaplaincy team were "deeply engaged in individual prisoner narratives and were able to offer guidance and support in ways that prisoners appreciated" (46). This contrasted with the work of psychologists who were described as being at the "opposite" end of a trust continuum (47). While psychologists were primarily involved in risk assessment (see Crewe 2009 for a discussion of the power of psychology departments), the "chaplaincy were trying to give people hope and meaning" (Liebling, Arnold, & Straub 2011, 47).

"Locating Trust in a Climate of Fear": Methods and Data

A four-member team (Alison Liebling, Ruth Armstrong, Ryan Williams, and Richard Bramwell) conducted a total of 10 months of fieldwork in two high-security English prisons, Full Sutton and Frankland, in 2012–2013. Fieldwork involved slow entry into each prison, taking time to observe and participate in the daily life of prisoners and staff in each prison. This involved attending staff meetings, prisoner adjudications, workshops and education sessions, cooking classes, chapel services, and observations and casual conversations on wing landings. As researchers we were afforded an unprecedented level of access and trust in both prisons. We were given keys that allowed us to navigate the prison unescorted, following the protocols of each prison and directions from staff on site.

We conducted interviews with 106 prisoners and 68 members of staff. The interviews often lasted several hours, and some were carried out over more than one sitting. The majority were digitally recorded, with permission, and fully transcribed. Interviews were usually conducted in private offices in education, workshops, or on the wings, with some interviews taking place in segregation units in closed conditions through acrylic glass. The interviews covered a range of topics including prisoners' backgrounds and experiences in prison. Appreciative methods framed questions that included what participants were "most proud of in their lives" (Liebling, Price, & Elliot 1999), and what brought them meaning, purpose, and hope. Interviewees were willing and deeply engaged in the interviews, often expressing appreciation for being able to talk openly about their experiences with us.

Ten of our interviewees were convicted for offenses against the Terrorism Act (TACT), and all of these except for one (who was reconsidering his relationship with Islam) identified as Muslim. Nearly half of the interview sample consisted of prisoners who self-identified as Muslim, with some of these having converted in prison. Twenty-nine percent of the sample were Christian, 8 percent were of "other" religious affiliations (including Sikh, Jewish, Rasta, pagan, and scientology), and 8 percent were not registered with a religious affiliation (Liebling et al. 2015).

We used imaginative ways of understanding each prison. One of the researchers organized a rap class in Full Sutton, and in Frankland we convened a dialogue group with prisoners in order to develop longer term relationships in order to come closer to understanding their experiences and the worlds they inhabited (see Liebling & Arnold 2015). We also collected a range of institutional data from each prison, including data on the volume of security information reporting (Liebling & Williams, in press) and practices for managing problematic prisoners ("no one to one contact" lists and "managing challenging behavior" procedures).

By the end of our fieldwork, we were a well known presence in both prisons. We felt part of the routine, entering the prison shortly after the influx of day staff and leaving the prison often 12 hours later after the shuffle of prisoners were locked behind their cell doors for the night, each wing's landing becoming eerily quiet. We became part of the banter that inevitably followed after a day shift as staff crowded together in small holding rooms while waiting for the series of automated doors to close before the next one could open on our way out. We knew the modus operandi of each prison, and observed differences between the wings.

Stateville: The "Authoritarian Regime" and Religious Provision

Jacobs's classic prison sociological study of an American prison in Illinois, Stateville, provides perhaps the earliest illustration of the relationship between institutional power in prisons and the forms of religious identity that emerge. It is also an early study of the recognition of prisoners' religious rights, though this is often overlooked among prison sociologists. Prison sociologists tend to refer to the study as an example of how resistant identities form under particular types of prison regimes and how in-prison dynamics are shaped by social change outside prison, and the forms of status and social structure that are brought into prison from the streets (see also Clemmer [1940] 1958). Here we offer a rereading of this classic work in view of the threefold intersection between prisoner rights and provisions, the type of prison regime and the way that order and control are exerted, and the religious identities that ensue.

Jacobs's study was part of the rich tradition of prison ethnographic research that recognized prisons as highly textured and dynamic places that are shaped and embedded within broader social currents. Jacobs situated the new challenges presented by Muslim prisoners within broader changes in the prisoner population, including increasing prisoner turnover, an erosion of a system of accommodation between staff and prisoners as "old cons" were granted parole, and a diversification of the prisoner population with a rise in the proportion of minorities. There was a "new racial consciousness" that "made cooperation between guards and inmates more problematic" (Jacobs 1977, 58). Outside prison, "the emergence of the civil rights movement on the streets" contributed to "politicizing the inmates at Stateville" (58). It reflected many of the social changes found in the English context over the past decade with increasing diversity of offenders and new religious and cultural differences that staff needed to negotiate as described in Liebling's studies summarized above.

Jacobs's work was situated within a unique social and political climate of the Nation of Islam, a movement that polarized relationships between adherents of the movement and the guards. The organization of Black Muslim prisoners around Black nationalism was significant on two accounts. First because

Muslim collectively "challenged the traditional relationship between keeper and kept" (58–59). Muslim prisoners defined the prison, for the first time, as a communal experience. Their activities of communal prayer, congregating on the recreation yards, and teaching and proselytizing were viewed as a problem for prison officials in the 1960s:

> For the Muslims, organizing was not simply a means to achieve certain advantages in the prisons. It was an end in itself. While Muslim leaders wrote frequently to the warden that their religion demanded their obedience to authority, their organizational activities and desire for communion necessarily brought them into conflict with the traditional system of authority. On the recreation yards, the Muslims clustered together in defiance of the prisons' rules. In most cases they dispersed when ordered to do so, but confrontations were not uncommon. In his reports to the warden the disciplinary captain described a pattern of defiance ranging from refusing orders to cursing, spitting at, and striking guards. (Jacobs 1977, 63)

Second, Muslim prisoners prepared the first list of demands, and these demands included requests for faith provision and recognition. Muslim prisoners "articulated their prison concerns in the vocabulary of political and social protest [c]laiming that they were being discriminated against on the basis of race and religion" (61). Six Muslim prisoners in segregation presented the prison authorities with the first written inmate demands in the history of the penitentiary in June 1964. From the present standpoint of hard-won equal rights for prisoners of different faiths to practice their religion in prison (Beckford & Gilliat 1998), most of the demands seem quite reasonable and are now part of the values of protecting civil liberties of prisoners practicing their faith and recognizing human rights. These demands included the use of the "Chapel for Islamic religious services once to two times a week"; to "purchase the Holy Quran and all other Islamic religious *periodicals*"; and to have "Kosher style" (halal) meals. Today, Muslim prisoners have access to each of these demands. Other demands were impossible for the prison to accommodate: "We demand the suppression, and 'Genocide' oppression of the Islamic religion be stopped forthwith, now, and forevermore"; and "we demand that Arabic books and African historical books be put on the High School curriculum" (Jacobs 1977, 61).

Jacobs observes the challenge for Stateville officials to concede to even the minimum and most reasonable of their demands:

> Permitting Muslims to possess a copy of the Quran did not on its face threaten prison security, but recognition of the Muslims as a bona fide religious group, entitled to all the deference and legitimacy of the traditional religions, was perceived as a grave threat to the moral order of the prison . . . (59).

Faith recognition served as a challenge to the authoritarian prison regime and dominant "moral order of the prison" that was uncompromising to prisoner rights. The "prison resisted every Muslim demand . . . what seemed to be at stake was the very survival of the authoritarian regime" (59). The tension was exacerbated by the "fervent hatred of the white race [that] escalated the traditional boundaries of conflict between guards and inmates and was an especially emotional issue for the white guard force drawn from southern Illinois's rigid caste systems" (59). The authoritarian regime operated with heavy-handed use of force by locking up their main leaders and curtailing their activities. In Jacobs's estimate, there were never more than 100 Muslim prisoners in an inmate population of more than 3,000 at any one time in Stateville, but Muslims were perceived as a serious problem.

The refusal to allow Muslims to have access to the Qur'an or a space to practice faith seems archaic by today's standards, but Stateville illustrates the interconnections between "heavy" forms of power employed by prison authorities operating through faith provision and forms of identities of resistance that emerged. In the following, we describe two English prisons, one operating a heavier form of power in relation to faith provision and the other operating a lighter form of power largely disconnected from faith provision, and we explore how identities of resistance and spaces for personal development emerged from these respective forms of order.

Two Prison Cultures

Our study was modeled on Sparks, Bottoms, and Hay's comparative study of legitimacy and order in two adult male English maximum security prisons in the 1980s. Their study examined how Albany and Long Lartin demonstrated very different ways of achieving order and operated their regimes through different ways of regulation. These forms of order had implications for the legitimacy of each prison. *Prisons and the Problem of Order* (Sparks, Bottoms, & Hay 1996) drew on ideas of legitimacy to compare the different means by which these two high-security prisons accomplished order. Albany placed a stronger emphasis on control and supervision and adapted a largely "situational" model of control. It seemed more punitive and harsher, or closer to what Crewe, Liebling, and Hulley later characterized as "heavier," with staff who were more "present" (Crewe, Liebling, & Hulley 2014). Long Lartin adopted a "softer" and more "social" form of control (a "negotiation model") and promoted closer relationships between prisoners and staff. Crewe, Liebling, and Hulley would describe this approach as "light-present" (2014). Crewe and colleagues observe that the lightness of a prison is not always favored, but that each model has its advantages and drawbacks. Although there was less friction between staff and prisoners in Long Lartin, relationships between prisoners were more complex and fractious, and led to higher levels of serious violence. The relaxed atmosphere enabled the development of a more complex informal economy, and a more structured and developed prisoner hierarchy. The heaviness of Albany was seen by prisoners as less legitimate than the regime of Long Lartin. The lightness of Long Lartin led to some reservations among more vulnerable prisoners in particular, including "poor regime organization, lack of boundaries and inadequate policing by staff."

In our study, the regime at Full Sutton was "heavy-present" (Crewe, Liebling, & Hulley 2014), with minor incursions being dealt with heavy-handedly. Security and other staff had an overbearing presence. Prisoners were subject to all forms of nondisciplinary actions (i.e., disciplinary action taken that is not subject to the adjudication process) such as being sent to segregation under rule 54 for good order and discipline, being subject to warnings that could lead to the removal of prisoners' Incentives and Earned Privileges (IEPs, which includes access to television and more visitations permitted per month), random and overly frequent checks of prisoners, their personal artefacts, and cells (e.g., "bolts and bars" checks, mandatory drugs tests, or volumetric controls, which means that prisoners have to pack up their possessions to fit them within a predefined volume allowance for X-ray purposes). Prisoners described these methods of control as "really heavy handed" (Saleem) and as "very strict" (Aamal). Dominic, a White in-prison convert to Islam, said that "they just go out of their way, like they are looking to press my buttons." Prisoners also could be removed from meaningful roles and positions such as being a wing cleaner or a "listener" without knowing the reasons why.

The general overuse of formal power and the distant staff prisoner relationships were punctuated by examples of officers who proved an exception, who were "good," "decent," and "human." Every prisoner could identify one or two officers they could trust, and whom they would go to if they needed something. Staff could work skillfully with prisoners, inquiring about concerns or behavior directly in order to better assess the situation and find the best means to help prisoners.

Conversely, prisoners frequently described Frankland prison as "friendly" and "relaxed," to the point of almost too relaxed on some wings. There was a lingering label that Frankland was a "racist prison" stemming from a historical incident, after which a prisoner who had attacked two members of staff was found not guilty because he had suffered psychological and racial mistreatment by staff. Staff were acutely aware of the dangers of being seen as "racist" after this verdict. Many of the Black, mixed-race, and Muslim prisoners whom we interviewed expressed a level of comfort while in Frankland compared to other dispersal prisons where Black, mixed-race and Muslim prisoners were treated with more suspicion and concern. They found that once they had arrived in Frankland, it did not conform to their expectations of Frankland as a "racist prison." Prisoners attributed this to "Geordie culture," which reflected a laid-back attitude and generally helpful demeanor of many staff. Abdul represents this lighter atmosphere in describing how officers perform routines of searching prisoners ("pat-downs") before moving to different parts of the prison:

> They [officers in Frankland] kind of have a laugh with you as they're searching you and on the way to go to Muslim prayers, you can have a bit of a joke with them and a laugh and a giggle, which makes the Muslims think and feel comfortable like oh, these guys are all right, you know, and it kind of breaks down that . . . you know, the friction.

The friendly and interpersonal atmosphere in Frankland came at some cost to bureaucratic and procedural legitimacy. Prisoners felt that their complaints were not adequately responded to, and in some instances, complaint and application forms for positions (e.g., work applications) were lost. Officers would often try to work out the problem with the prisoner without the forms, asking "tell me what's wrong and I'll see if I can sort it." This made complaints about particular officers, or complaints related to racism and discrimination, difficult. These different prison cultures, which we explore next, had significant implications for the work of chaplaincy departments and the forms of religious identity that were expressed.

Power in the Chaplaincy and Identities of Resistance: Full Sutton

Institutional power penetrated the chaplaincy department reflecting the "control style" and moral climate of Full Sutton. Institutional control was exercised in often indirect and subtle ways. It was overtly observed during our fieldwork when 15 officers stood outside noontime prayers as less than 30 prisoners conducted their ritual observances in a workshop. It seemed, and felt like, a display of force by staff.

The exercise of power was more subtly described by Leon (see epigraph), where the regime served as the means for taking "the power out of religion." The logic behind Leon's observation and strategy was that when religious practice is institutionalized and bureaucratized, prisoners are unable to exercise claims of disadvantage or discrimination through appealing to their rights because the rules and boundaries around what is and is not permissible are clearly drawn. This is a different method than the denial of religious provision and recognition described in Stateville, but nonetheless reflects a form of power that intersected with prisoners' rights. Staff could, for example, adjudicate prisoners for praying in a cell when there were more than three prisoners because the rules permitted a maximum of three in a cell at a time, and they could do so with confidence that they were not overstepping prisoners' rights. Power could be exercised by recognizing religious rights, but more accurately, by *drawing boundaries around religious* rights, and circumscribing prisoners' claims that certain practices or behaviors were "religious" and were therefore something that they were entitled to. Religious provision was granted, but it was never beyond the reach of institutional power.

Importantly, bureaucratizing Islamic practice in the interests of order and control shifted what Islam could mean for prisoners. It meant that religion became less of a personal choice and less of a communal act of participation done willfully through exercising agency, and instead reflected opposition and assertion: there was a clear dichotomy between compliance and noncompliance to institutional policies. The meaning and authenticity of the act was undermined as it became embedded within institutional power. Religious participation through the chaplaincy, as we explore below in relation to Friday prayers, became disingenuous and inauthentic. The institutional setting is not, of course, the sole determinant of how prisoners came to express their religious identity:

> I'm proud to be a Muslim, I'm proud to be something . . . something that's meaningful in my life, so . . . that's about it really . . . I ain't got no qualifications, I'm not proud of my A levels . . . [I] ain't got none of that shit, so . . . it's the only good thing that's come out of me. (Benjamin)

Against a background of little else to mark success or to bring meaning to his life, being a Muslim was of profound significance for Benjamin.

A second way that power came to flow through the chaplaincy was through practices related to the prevention and detection of radicalization. This practice was seen differently from the perspective of security staff and chaplains. Muslim chaplains had a vested interest in contributing to counterterrorism because it helped them to inform staff about Islam, in order that Muslim prisoners would not be stigmatized for ordinary religious practice. Chaplains provided care through increasing faith literacy among staff, responding to queries and attending security meetings. In so doing they were serving the interests of prisoners by mitigating misunderstandings and misconceptions about Islam. As chaplains frequently weighed in on evaluations of what is and is not risky in relation to faith practice, this cemented bonds between the chaplaincy and institutional power. It also placed chaplains in a precarious position that they were very careful to navigate. It heightened the possibility for what Liebling observed in her team's second Whitemoor study as an ambiguity over "whose side" a chaplain was on in prisoners' minds, and this contributed to prisoners asking whether they could trust the chaplaincy department (Liebling & Arnold 2012).

Two additional examples illustrate the way that the control style of Full Sutton impacted the activities of the chaplaincy department and shaped what Islamic faith and practice meant for prisoners.

The Politics of Religious Provision

Consider the following instructions to chaplains:

For many years there has been an inconsistency between high security prisons' facilities lists prompting complaints from prisoners and requests to make all the same . . . There are some items which are no longer permitted in the high security facilities list. Some of these items are currently perceived to be religious; however, they are not defined as such in PSI [Prison Service Instruction] 51/2011 Faith and Pastoral Care . . . These items will need to be destroyed, handed out on a visit or alternatively posted out, in which case the prison will pay for the postage to facilitate once an application has been received. These items are:

- Buddhism: Obsidian Stone
- Christianity: Posters
- Islam: Shamaag—Islamic headscarf; Lungi—clothing worn around the waist; Leather socks
- Judaism: Pendant
- Sikhism: Symbolic Pendant
- Sikhism: Symbolic Pendant; Prayer Beads

Prison Information Notice No. 043/2014 (April 22, 2014)

The local banning of the shamaag reflected an instance when institutional power and a heavy control style impeded into the activities of the chaplaincy through faith provision. Prisoners were notified of the ban through a Prison Service Instruction (a local document that notifies staff and prisoners of policy changes). Before the ban the shamaag was permitted as a religious artefact during Friday prayers, and it was common to see prisoners wearing the shamaag on the wing. The exact reasons for the ban were uncertain. Some prisoners claimed that it followed from a backlash against Muslim prisoners after a judge ruled that three Muslim prisoners who took a member of staff hostage were not guilty of holding the officer against his will (they were found guilty for assault). Others claimed it followed from the security concerns the item brought with it as it could be worn in a way that obscured a prisoner's face and prevented them from being identified on camera and by staff. The tension between providing for religious clothing and security was brought to light over the shamaag, and Full Sutton responded through an outright ban. (Other prisons developed clearer guidance on how the shamaag could be worn, thus permitting the religious item under the condition that it was worn in a way that did not obscure the face.) One officer remarked on these challenges, observing the everyday tensions in enforcing policies related to security when those policies intersected with religious provision:

They're talking about removing the shamaag, and . . . I think that's more of a fact down to a security issue, because it can cover a face up, things like that. But . . . some are saying it's not a religious item, some are saying it's a cultural item. Again, it creates two different areas. And when you're trying to tell a prisoner the reasons why you're doing something, and you've got two answers, it makes it very difficult. So when you go and approach somebody to say, "Please can we just have clarification," and you're not getting it, that's frustrating. (Sheryl, Wing Staff, Full Sutton)

The wholesale banning of the shamaag reflected a heavy-handed local policy. The directive contradicted article 8.2 of the PSI 51/2011 that states: "Prisoners must be allowed to wear dress, including headdress, that accords with the requirements of their registered faith" (13). Prison chaplains also advised against banning the shamaag.

The ban represented a means of exercising power through constraints on religious provision. Power punctuated faith provision, and this came to have significant consequences for how Muslims expressed their identity. One chaplain wore the shamaag the Friday after the ban as a passive sign of resistance against the ban, reclaiming the principle that religious artefacts should be under the purview of the chaplaincy. Any other Friday, such an act would have had little meaning beyond ordinary religious practice. But in the context of a regime that sought to curtail the identity of Muslims and limit religious rights and provisions, donning the shamaag came to be a highly symbolic act of defiance and an assertion of autonomy. This is reminiscent of events that took place in Jacobs's study and the resistance generated among Muslim prisoners where religious rights posed a "grave threat to the moral order of the prison."

The ban produced outrage among many prisoners, who saw the act as one of discrimination against Muslims. This outrage turned religious practice and clothing from objects of devotion and piety to political objects that were subject to institutional, and state, power. One prisoner exclaimed in frustration after Friday prayers that his "wing is the front line of Iraq" (fieldnotes). The battle lines had been drawn with the encroachment of institutional power into the chaplaincy. The ban of the religious headdress as a religious provision reflected a heavy control style.

The Sermon

In a chapter documenting the transformation of religious authority in Egypt, Charles Hirschkind carefully traces the links between religious authority, the exercise of state power, and practices of meaning-making and ethical self-cultivation. Hirschkind details how, following Egyptian independence in 1952, state control over institutions of religious authority accelerated, and the

Ministry of Religious Affairs came to bring mosques and religious specialists into alignment (Hirschkind 2006, 44). As Imams and sermons were integrated into the bureaucracies of the state under the national project of President Nasser, the sermon became "a device for working on and improving the raw human material that is to be the national citizenry" (49). The hand of the state extended into the daily life of Egyptians and against a backdrop of security concerns:

> . . . the utility of mosques has been redefined, to some extent, in panoptic terms, as structures for the localization, control, and supervision of bodies. In a dramatic shift, mosques have become sites where the state now listens to the audience for the incipient rumblings of contestation and militancy (50).

There were echoes of this infusion of state power into the sermon and the chaplaincy department after the murder of soldier Lee Rigby in Woolwich, London, in 2013. We were told by staff and prisoners that the sermon or *khutbah* delivered during Friday prayers that weekend was delivered by a sessional chaplain and that the sermon was "scripted by headquarters." The content of the sermon was "nationally supported," and it explicitly condemned the murder of Lee Rigby. The sermon was purportedly part of a government directive to respond appropriately to the Woolwich incident to the high-security prisons. Three Muslim prisoners walked out of prayers during the sermon, an event that attracted attention two days later when one of those prisoners, along with two others, took a member of staff hostage. The content of the sermon concerns us here because of how it represents the extension of institutional control into the chaplaincy space.

Kanye described to us that many prisoners were discontented with the sermon because they felt that it represented the prison service bringing politics into the chaplaincy. The sermon served to politicize the chaplaincy. The source of the controversy, therefore, did not lay in prisoners agreeing with any justification behind the murder. Similarly, the protest by some prisoners of not attending Friday prayers was related not to whether an Imam was "too moderate" (cf. Liebling, Arnold, & Straub 2011, 46). Instead, it reflected the way that power was used in the prison and the way that order was maintained. Resistance and protest were related to a transgressed boundary of what was perceived to be the legitimate role that the secular state should play in religion, and the boundaries within which the prison should operate in relation to religious provision. The sermon presented a point where this boundary was violated and the chapel, an otherwise neutral space for religious practice and pastoral care within the prison, came to be seen as a forum for the voice of the prison service, and by extension, an opportunity for the state to exercise its power. The scripted sermon served to reconfigure the space of the chaplaincy

from one of pastoral care to one of security and control, in a way that parallels Hirschkind's description of the state-sanctioned *khatib* or imam whose
sermons reflected a national project of identity and security.

This sermon contributed to a transformation in what religious practice and
attendance at Friday prayers could mean for prisoners. Assad described his
surprise at the way that power was exercised through Friday prayers around
the time of the hostage-taking:

> They got put in the Seg [segregation unit], just for not praying. And you
> just think, wow! It is a bit nuts. And even when the whole Friday thing
> stopped, people stopped going, governors were begging me to go to Friday
> service. I am like . . . who has heard of this? I've never seen a governor beg
> me to go to Friday service.

Seeing the chaplaincy area as a space of institutional power rather than as
a space for pastoral care, religious practice, and being in community, seeded
an arena where resistance became possible through the walking out of sermons or the refusal to attend Friday prayers. The absence of Muslim attendance
at Friday prayers was carefully monitored in the prison, and nonatten-
dance was seen as a marker of risk. Kanye expressed how Muslim prisoners
were singled out in these monitoring practices:

> **Kanye:** What happens is like when there was the last proper boycott
> where everyone refused to go [to Friday prayers], they took down every-
> one's name that didn't go . . . to get this person lifted or to get this person
> taken to the seg [segregation unit], and that caused an even bigger issue . . .
>
> **Interviewer:** And . . . if Christians don't want to go to Sunday service?
>
> **Kanye:** It's not an issue. This is something that's been brought up many
> times again . . . why is it that Muslims are different to Christians?

These examples draw attention to the way that Full Sutton turned the chaplaincy into a space for the supervision of bodies and the control of a narrative. Most often, the chaplaincy was a space for providing for religious faiths
in both prisons, but the way that power punctuated the chaplaincy in certain
times and in certain ways had significant consequences. It reflected a flow of
power that came to impact negatively on prisoners' views of legitimacy and
what Islam could mean for prisoners.

Within this transformed space new avenues opened up for prisoners to
express power against the institution. Refusing to attend Friday prayers
became a way for prisoners to exercise agency and to resist the institution.
It came to light during our interviews that many prisoners felt they could
practice their faith more authentically by not attending Friday prayers. The

reasons for this authenticity are more complex than we can detail here, and included the view that other Muslim prisoners in attendance were seen as being "there for the wrong reasons" (Darnell). But institutional power shaped what it meant for some Muslims to authentically practice their faith, and this involved avoiding Friday prayers. Staff described the increased attention paid to anyone seen to orchestrate or influence others to not attend Friday prayers:

> The spike in [security information] reporting after Lee Rigby's murder, and after the Imams had kind of challenged the fact openly in Friday prayers about, this isn't about Islam, and there was a bit of a reaction to the Imams saying this, because some of the prisoners didn't think it was their place to do it, to condemn the murder . . . Reporting spiked then, and some people were quite openly saying, "They're killing our brothers in foreign lands," and, "What do they expect?" and were kind of really vocalising a lot of stuff that you wouldn't normally expect to hear from prisoners. So there was a spike in reporting there about . . . and it was more about . . . it was more about support for extremist causes, or an anti-Western sentiment. Expressions of anti-Western sentiment. (staff member)

This expression of "anti-Western sentiment" can be understood within the broader context of the politicization of the sermon and the chaplaincy department through the "pursuit of security" (in Lucia Zedner's words 2000; cited in Liebling 2014). To be clear, the flow of institutional power in the chaplaincy was uneven, and this example did not fundamentally change the chaplaincy department and its role or the outlook of the chaplains. Our purpose, however, is to illustrate examples when the chaplaincy space was politicized by serving the interests of a national identity project. The monitoring for insipient risks of extremism among those in attendance or not in attendance draws attention to how efforts to anticipate and contain risk enabled prisoners to exercise resistance against the regime in the chaplaincy. Concurrently, it transformed the meaning of the chaplaincy for many Muslim prisoners, and rerouted religious authority and the location of religious practice from the chaplaincy to the wing.

Recognition and Personal Development in the Chaplaincy: Frankland

The chaplaincy department in Frankland by contrast was largely a space of obsolescence and only vague importance within the secular administration of the prison regime. Chaplaincy activities were distinct from other activities like prisoners' work or education because, as one chaplain described with some frustration, chaplaincy activities were not included as part of any formal criteria for risk reduction. This chaplain described the difficulty he had ensuring that prisoners were able to attend their two mandatory religious activities per week, as it created some difficulties for scheduling movements around the prison. Some prisoners were concerned that attending activities in the chaplaincy would count as an absence from their work or education that could count against them. The regime placed little value on the chaplaincy department as a source of "risk reduction" and was a mere requirement that the prison needed to fulfill satisfactorily.

Another chaplain described how prison management was only concerned with the chaplaincy to appease claims against the prison of being discriminatory or "racist" after the Thakrar incident, referred to above. Muslim prisoners were seen to be the main beneficiaries of this, with comments that the governor's budget for Muslim prisoners exceeded that of other faiths. There was an overcompensation to avoid Muslim prisoners' complaints, but chaplaincy provision was not otherwise seen as a site for achieving security in the way that it was in Full Sutton. From the perspective of prison management, it was an institutional requirement to provide for different faiths, and faith was recognized as somehow important to prisoners. Compared to the cynicism and scepticism around Muslim prisoners in Full Sutton (particularly converts to Islam), Frankland staff more often recognized some value to religion and the meaning it must have for prisoners: "I think religion is—it's probably important to them, because it helps them with their strength, and especially if they've been quite religious outside. It's just some have gone on an errant path, haven't they?" (staff, Frankland). This reflected part of the staff culture of Frankland prison. The prison's culture was more relaxed than at Full Sutton, and staff were less inclined to view religion through a "risk lens."

The Frankland chaplaincy team were not immune to institutional forces, but these operated in more subtle ways than at Full Sutton through timetabling that pushed the chaplaincy into the recesses of the day-to-day workings of the prison regime. Prisoners were reluctant to attend sessions in the chaplaincy that might interfere with their regular work and education, particularly where these fulfilled requirements within their sentence plans that enabled them to "progress" through their sentence and be eligible for decreases in their risk assessments. Frankland prison had two special units, the PIPE (Psychologically-Informed Planned Environment) and the Westgate Unit, which were psychologically informed rehabilitative environments for prisoners with complex needs, and these spaces heightened the relevance of psychologically driven activities as relevant to progress over activities within the chaplaincy department.

In contrast to Full Sutton, the comparative irrelevance of the chaplaincy department for the prison regime and for order and control had significant implications for what the chaplaincy department meant for prisoners. The chaplaincy served as a space for identity beyond the reach of institutional control. Innovative and creative endeavors by chaplains were permitted, and these allowed for a range of self-expression. For example, a prison band was organized, and it walked the tightrope of public acceptability, security, and creating space for personal expression. It was comprised of a motley crew, including a convicted terrorist offender, a Catholic, a Muslim, and a Protestant. One prisoner in the band suffered from severe depression. When seen on the wing he was lifeless and refused eye contact. During band practices and performances, he came alive, performing a solo to the cheer of the small crowd that communicated the depths of his experience. The loudness of the electric guitar, microphone, and drums was ear-piercing, his vocal cords strained under the release of raw emotion. It was impossible not to sense the heaviness and contradictions of the space and the performance. It felt emotionally dangerous, like boundaries were being pushed; it felt precarious, and that heightened its value and significance for all in attendance. That it was permitted, felt deeply respectful.

When a pair of boxer shorts was tossed at the lead singer, a gesture of humor to simulate female fandom with rock bands, officers were alert and on edge, but assessed the projectile as harmless as it draped off the singer's shoulder. The audience was small, about 20 prisoners, seated in three short rows, with staff on either side. A sense of anticipation grew on the wings in advance of concerts. There was positive energy, a sense of rupture in the mundane that was only equaled in religious festivals, particularly Friday prayers, in Full Sutton and during Ramadan. These activities were permitted but not without a struggle on behalf of chaplains seeking to continue with activities that presented some risks, and there was a sense that the band could be dismantled at any time if, for example, a piece of equipment or fastener went missing. Prisoners were careful to protect this opportunity from being lost in a way that paralleled the good behavior found in prison gyms, where prisoners risked losing gym privileges if they misbehaved. The research team were "performed for" on more than one occasion.

The chaplaincy provided a space for recognizing a broad array of religious and cultural backgrounds, beyond those "officially" recognized by the prison service. A Rastafarian group was convened by the Anglican chaplain, bringing together prisoners of African heritage to play drums, chat, drink tea, and eat biscuits—the pervasive fare in the chaplaincy. A Traveler group was also convened. They were watching a series on Traveler culture. A clip was playing of a brawl between two men who were fighting for leadership within the community. The chaplain explained this cultural aspect to the researchers and how these aspects of Traveler culture are not recognized. The group, he said, was popular among Travelers. Even though it seemed only an opportunity to meet with one's friends, it provided a space for the exploration of shared cultural heritage and identity. It allowed recognition of the diversity and inherent differences of human beings. A Christian bible study, with an evangelical tone, offered a time for praying for one another. Emotions were laid bare in ways that were not possible on the wings, even among those who had the most formidable reputations. A Quaker group had a Muslim prisoner in attendance who self-identified as a hybrid Muslim-Quaker. Another prisoner, Abdal, described a process of exploring the intersection of scientology and Islam:

> I'm a Scientologist. I . . . you know, it doesn't conflict with my religion, it's . . . I mean, my understanding of Scientology is about making you the best person you can be . . . Well, I've been looking at it over the last year, and I've not long become one, but I've been looking and reading the books and everything. It's basically about making you the best person that you can be. You know, it's not about religion in the sense of you must do this, you must do that. It's about any way you can do it is fine as long as it's successful. So you can be a Buddhist, a Christian and, you know, a Muslim, a Jew, whatever, there's no dogma to it.

Such explorations occurred within a space that was separate from the secular security regime. Friday prayers in Frankland contrasted with the above description in Full Sutton. During Friday prayers, officers sat behind partitions. Counterterrorism staff introduced themselves to offenders convicted of terrorist offenses, but these prisoners were otherwise free to practice their faith in the way they chose (some prayed at the front, others chatted at the back). The boundaries of power were transparent rather than hidden and did not directly penetrate chaplaincy activities. The moments and linkages that connected the chaplaincy to order and control in Full Sutton were less pronounced in Frankland, and this, we suggest, impacted how the chaplaincy department and its activities were experienced by prisoners. Prisoners attended the chaplaincy on their own accord, exercising agency to participate, and retaining ownership over their own personal development. It was, almost by accident, a space separate from the structures of domination that characterized the prison environment, and this had significant implications for the types of religious identity that prisoners described in Frankland and for what the chaplaincy department could achieve.

Conclusion

In this chapter we draw attention to the new context in which faith provision and chaplaincy activities operate. We compared two prison cultures and examined the different ways that power flows through, or around, activities within chaplaincies. Institutional power was seen to reconfigure what religious practice and identity came to mean for prisoners. Table 13.2 provides a summary of the observations made between two models of control, an "autonomous model" represented in Frankland where the activities of the chaplaincy department were mostly independent of means of order and control, and a

Table 13.2   Models of Order in the Chaplaincy and Religious Identity

	Autonomous model	Control model
Exercise of institutional power in the chaplaincy	Low	High
Personal agency in religious practice	High	Low
Chaplaincy and personal development	High	Low
Legitimacy of power	High	Low
Site of personal development	Chaplaincy	Wing
Characteristics of religious identities	Exploration, seeking, coping	Resistance, power

"control model" where heavy forms of order punctuated the activities of the chaplaincy.

In Full Sutton, diligent and "heavy" policing practices concerned with order, control, and the prevention of violent extremism (and associated projects of national citizenry) penetrated the chaplaincy department and impacted faith provision to create moments of tension. This polarized the objectives of providing for religious and spiritual care and performing the role of security to ensure order, control, and safety within prisons. These blurred lines presented a rupture in the delicate balance of trust within which prison chaplaincies operated. This rupture offset the fine balance between the responsibilities of pastoral care and faith provision for prisoners and the role of security, a tension that faith provision and chaplaincy departments will need to navigate for the foreseeable future.

In Frankland, the activities of the chaplaincy department were approached by the prison with indifference or with a vague acceptance of their importance for individual prisoners. The chaplaincy department was considered less essential to the security and operational infrastructure of the prison, and its activities were less impregnated with security-driven concerns. Although this contributed to a struggle among chaplains to have the importance of their work recognized within the broader prison regime, accommodations were made for a diversity of activities, including a prisoner band and Traveler group, and these activities served as meaningful sites for personal development and coping with the pains of imprisonment. Spaces were carved out that recognized cultural and religious diversity in imaginative ways, raising the issue of how autonomous chaplaincy departments should be to best achieve their purposes. Religious identities were more porous in Frankland's chaplaincy department compared to Full Sutton's because staff in the department (and the prison) created a space where prisoners could exercise agency comparatively free from institutional power. Power reconfigured what religious identity came to mean in the two prisons and how this identity was expressed. These ranged from identities of resistance in Full Sutton to personal meaning-making, exploration, and personal development in Frankland.

This chapter has sought to connect the rich tradition of prison chaplaincy studies and the sociology of religion in prisons, stimulated by Beckford and Gilliat's work, with the longstanding concerns of prison sociology around power, order, and the differences in the moral climates of prisons. The "management of religions," as Turner (2011) has described the wider problem facing Western liberal states following from anxieties over security and pluralism and multiculturalism, is seen in an intensified microcosm in the prison environment. Religion is no longer in the margins of prisoner social life or the prison's maintenance of order and control. It has come to feature in the day-to-day operations of prisons and in staff-prisoner interactions. This has wedded religious provision and faith recognition to longstanding concerns in prison sociology around power and order. The empirical reality of faith in prison today, and new security concerns around Islam, means that these two research domains can no longer be pursued independently.

Bibliography

Allen, Grahame, & Noel Dempsey. "Prison Population Statistics." *House of Commons Library* Briefing Paper Number SN/SG/04334, July 4, 2016.

Becci, Irene. "European Research on Religious Diversity as a Factor in the Rehabilitation of Prisoners: An Introduction." In Irene Becci & Olivier Roy (Eds.), *Religious diversity in European prisons: Challenges and implications for rehabilitation* (pp. 1–14). London: Springer, 2015.

Beckford, James, & Sophie Gilliat. *Religion in prison: Equal rites in a multi-faith society.* Cambridge: Cambridge University Press, 1998.

Beckford, James, Daniele Joy, & Farhad Khosrokhavar. *Muslims in prison: Challenges and change in Britain and France.* Basingstoke, England & New York: Palgrae MacMillan, 2005.

Bottoms, A. E., & R. Sparks. "How Is Order in Prisons Maintained?" In A. Liebling (Ed.), *Security, justice and order in prison: Developing perspectives. Cambridge: University of Cambridge, Institute of Criminology,* 1997.

Clemmer, Donald. *The prison community* (2nd ed.). New York: Holt, Rinehart and Winston, [1940] 1958.

Crewe, Ben. *The prisoner society: Power, adaptation, and social life in an English prison.* Oxford: Oxford University Press, 2009.

Crewe, Ben, Alison Liebling, & Susie Hulley. "Heavy–Light, Absent–Present: Rethinking the 'Weight' of Imprisonment." *The British Journal of Sociology* 65, no. 3 (2014): 387–410.

Hirschkind, Charles. *The ethical soundscape: Cassette sermons and Islamic counterpublics.* New York: Columbia University Press, 2006.

Jacobs, James B. *Stateville: The penitentiary in mass society.* London: University of Chicago Press, 1977.

Liebling, Alison. *Prisons and their moral performance.* Oxford: Oxford University Press, 2005.

Liebling, Alison. "'Legitimacy under Pressure' in High Security Prisons." In *Seeking legitimacy in criminal justice contexts* (pp. 206–226). Oxford: Oxford University Press, 2014.

Liebling, Alison, Ruth Armstrong, Ryan J. Williams, & Richard Bramwell. "Locating Trust in a Climate of Fear: Religion, Moral Status, Prisoner Leadership, and Risk in Maximum Security Prisons—Key Findings from an Innovative Study." Prisons Research Centre, Institute of Criminology: University of Cambridge, 2015.

Liebling, Alison, & Helen Arnold. "Social Relationships between Prisoners in a Maximum Security Prison Violence Faith and the Declining Nature of Trust." *Journal of Criminal Justice* 40 (2012): 413–424.

Liebling, Alison, Helen Arnold, & Christina Straub. *An exploration of staff-prisoner relationships at HMP Whitemoor: 12 years on.* Cambridge: Cambridge Institute of Criminology, Prisons Research Centre, 2011.

Liebling, Alison, David Price, & Charles Elliot. "Appreciative Inquiry and Relationships in Prison." *Punishment and Society* 1, no. 1 (1999): 71–98.

Liebling, Alison, David Price, & Guy Shefer. *The prison officer.* New York: Taylor & Francis, 2010.

Liebling, Alison, & Ryan J. Williams (in press). "The New Subversive Geranium: Some Notes on the Management of Additional Troubles in Maximum Security Prisons." *British Journal of Sociology.* doi:10.1111/1468-4446 .12310

Silke, Andrew. *Prisons, terrorism and extremism: Critical issues in managment, radicalisation and reform.* London: Routledge, 2014.

Sparks, J. R., & A. E. Bottoms. "Legitimacy and Order in Prisons." *The British Journal of Sociology* 46, no. 1 (1995): 45–62.

Sparks, R., & A. E. Bottoms. "Legitimacy and Imprisonment Revisited: Notes on the Problem of Order Ten Years After." In J. Byrne, F. Taxman, & D. Hummer (Eds.), *The culture of prison violence* (pp. 91–104). Boston: Allyn and Bacon, 2007.

Sparks, Richard, Anthony Bottoms, & Will Hay. *Prisons and the problem of order, Clarendon studies in criminology.* Oxford: Oxford University Press, 1996.

Sykes, Gresham M. *The society of captives: A study of a maximum security prison.* Princeton. NJ: Princeton University Press, [1958] 2003.

Turner, Bryan S. *Religion and modern society: Citizenship, secularisation, and the state.* Cambridge: Cambridge University Press, 2011.

CHAPTER FOURTEEN

Breaking the Prison-Jihadism Pipeline: Prison and Religious Extremism in the War on Terror

Gabriel Rubin

Recent terror attacks in Europe, in which 32 people were killed in Brussels and 130 in Paris along with hundreds injured, have led to increased attention on the psychological roots of terrorism. One thread that has gained increased attention (Mufson 2016), but that has not received enough systematic study, is that of jihadists radicalizing in prison (Bisserbe 2016; Hall 2016; Hickey 2016; Nawaz 2016). The FBI notes that prisoner radicalization that turns to terrorist violence, while not common, is a serious and recurring phenomenon (Ballas 2010). The media usually portray the issue as one of ordinary Muslims radicalized by "bad guys" in prison. But such a formulation is simplistic in that it ignores the outside forces that lead a prisoner to radicalize.

This chapter argues that jihadist prisoner radicalization is a symptom of tensions and conflicts going on in the world outside of the prison. Throughout history, prisoners have radicalized in ways that mirrored outside radical movements and that sought to address prisoner concerns about injustices both in the prison and in the wider society (Hamm 2013, 1). As Michael Welch notes, summarizing the work of Scharg and Clemmer, "the inmate social world is shaped by the personal characteristics that convicts import into prison" (Clemmer 1958; Schrag 1960; Sykes 1958; Welch 1995, 155). Muslim prisoners—and those who convert to Islam in prison—are part of societies that are in conflict with Muslims. These conflicts are exhibited by tense relations within civil society, intercommunal tensions, and even wars. For example, Muslims are more likely to radicalize in French prisons due to factors external to the prison such as being discriminated against and profiled in France (Haddad 2015; Sageman 2008). Europe in general has done a poorer job than America has of assimilating Muslim immigrants and, concomitantly, has seen greater tension between Muslims and the "native" populations (Sageman 2008). These tensions, naturally, spill over into prisons.

Although jihadist prison radicalization is a sign of events and movements occurring outside the penitentiary, jihadist prisoners are not qualitatively different than other prisoners. They turn to gangs or extremism for the same reasons. While reading the reasons that jihadist prisoners radicalize the world over, those acquainted with the literature on corrections and prison gangs will surely find much that is familiar. The fact is that prisoners who turn to jihad against the West are subject to the same prison conditions and overcrowding that push other prisoners into other extremist causes. In a recent report from the RAND Corporation, the authors concluded that radicalization of prisoners "is neither new nor unique" (Hanna, Clutterbuck, & Rubin 2008, x). To this end, the reason that these prisoners turn to jihadism rather than some other form of radicalization has to do with conflicts going on in the outside world that prisoners are familiar with and latch on to.

The chapter will be organized in the following fashion. First, the problem will be framed and radicalization will be defined. Second, the ways prisoners radicalize will be discussed. Third, the role of the outside world will be examined. Finally, the argument about why prisoners radicalize will be linked to how prisoner radicalization can be stopped—like the cause, the solution will be based on political factors.

Building on previous research, this chapter takes a critical criminological approach to explaining the incidence of jihadist radicalization in prisons. Drawing from Karl Marx's sociological approach, critical criminology examines power differentials and inequalities as a way of explaining crime (Lynch 2010; Welch 1995, 107; Welch 1996). As Michael Lynch avers, "critical criminology perspectives attempt to promote economic, social, and political equity to diminish the production of crime and disparities in the making and enforcement of law" (Lynch 2010). Critical criminology urges social scientists to look beyond the simple facts of the crime and instead, to explore the social contexts that lead to the crime. In this light, jihadist radicalization can be seen as a symptom of wider societal problems that include the treatment of Muslims outside of prisons.

Framing the Problem and Defining Radicalization

Although jihadist prisoner radicalization is a hot topic in the news, there is very little systematic academic research done on the phenomenon for a few valid reasons. First, it is difficult to access prisoners who are radicals or in the process of radicalization. Even if prisons grant researchers access to these sorts of prisoners, certainly not a given (see Hamm 2007 report, 37–38), jihadist inmates are not flocking to speak to researchers. Correctional officers and researchers, further, may not know *who* these prisoners are—and certainly extremists are not eager to reveal themselves. A second confounding factor is that current research on the phenomenon shows that the incidence of prisoners who actually radicalized in prison and went on to attack Western targets as jihadist terrorists is low. Mark Hamm calls these sorts of prisoners "the spectacular few," but his study of them unearthed only one strong case of an al Qaeda-like prison group in California. Patrick Dunleavy's *Fertile Soil of Jihad* unearths an additional network of radicalized prisoners in U.S. prisons. However, the people these authors study do not have much success in their proposed terrorist attacks, leaving the question open as to whether they were real threats that were snuffed out or instead just minor threats. As will be seen in later sections, there have been more cases of jihadist radicalization in Middle East and European prisons than in U.S. prisons, due to political and social conditions in those regions.

The low incidence of prisoners turning to jihadism in prison may be seen as a reason not to study the topic—after all, if it doesn't happen that much, should we really be concerned about it? Although such a view is certainly valid, one must recognize that the study of terrorism in general suffers from a lack of cases to study (Pinker 2011, Chapter 6). For instance, although billions of dollars have gone into counterterrorism since 9/11 (Sahadi 2015), the actual incidence of terrorism in the West, aside from the huge outlier of the September 11 attacks, has actually gone down over time (The Economist 2016).

As a recent RAND report notes: "Due to the lack of open sources and reluctance on the part of the authorities to discuss these issues, it is not currently possible to draw any definitive conclusions about the extent of violent jihadist radicalization and recruitment in European prisons. Although there is some evidence that a problem exists, without greater access to security and prison authorities and, perhaps, to the prisons themselves, it will remain impossible to quantify its extent (Hanna, Clutterbuck, & Rubin 2008, ix–x).

All this said, inmate jihadist radicalization remains a concern because of a few high-profile cases that cannot be easily dismissed. Further, terrorism operates on human fears. One successful terror attack can drive a society to panic and push resources toward security or even war (Pinker 2011; Rubin 2011). Understanding how people radicalize and why they might turn to jihadism due to the conditions in prisons can help subvert such potential problems, which while admittedly not common, are still important.

Defining Radicalization

Before delving into cases of jihadist radicalization, the definition of radicalization needs to be established. A key question that has not been settled in research on the subject is what prisoner radicalization means. Mulcahy, Merrington, and Bell note that the definition of radicalization, like that of terrorism, remains contentious and ill-defined not only in scholarly research but also among government agencies. Agencies within the same government will opt to define radicalization differently, making what's being studied a matter of debate (Mulcahy, Merrington, & Bell 2013, 5). Randy Borum concurs that radicalization is ill-defined in scholarly sources and adds that too many times radicalization or extremism are used as proxies for terrorist behavior when, in reality, there are many more radicals than terrorists (Borum 2011).

In many cases, prisoners that are examined in studies on radicalization were radicals before entering prison. For instance, Hamm spends a chapter discussing the prison "radicalization" of famous historical figures such as Adolf Hitler and Mahatma Gandhi—men who had strong political views well before their incarceration (Hamm 2013, Chapter 1; SpearIt 2014). In Israeli prisons, moreover, many Palestinians are inmates precisely because of their radical views (Merari 2010). In order to isolate the role of prison, radicalization must be defined as a process and the universe of cases must be trimmed to cut out those where prisoners were already radicals before entering prison.

There are real negative side effects of poor conceptualization of terms like radicalization. Some works, due to the difficulties of gathering information on this subject noted above, have suffered from selection bias due to authors wanting to include more cases to increase the "N" in their studies (Hamm 2013; Khosrokhavar 2013). The alternative approach taken by scholars of prisoner jihadist radicalization is to rely on anecdotal examples given the limited number of prisoners that have actually radicalized while incarcerated (Dunleavy 2011; Mulcahy, Merrington, & Bell 2013). This selection bias has watered down the definition of prisoner radicalization and minimized the role of prisons in the process.

This chapter will use Hanna, Clutterbuck, and Rubin's definition of radicalization as a "process whereby individuals transform their worldview over time from a range that society tends to consider to be normal into a range that society tends to consider to be extreme" (Hanna, Clutterbuck, & Rubin 2008, 2). This is a decidedly subjective definition that rests on the definer's knowledge of what mainstream and outside-the-norm views are. However, this definition will be used here precisely because it does not presuppose or prejudge what a radical will do. For instance, radicalization need not mean someone is committed to acting out violently or even that he or she believes in violence. As Jenkins argues, not all people who radicalize turn to violence. Instead, radicalization should be viewed as a process wherein some people "go all the way" and become violent extremists while others "drop out" at various points (Hanna, Clutterbuck, & Rubin 2008, 3; Jenkins 2007, 4).

In the next section some cases of prisoner radicalization will be covered to show why the problem is significant, which will be followed by a section on why and how prison radicalizes people. Following that, the argument that prisoners radicalize in the ways they do because they are products not just of the prison world they live in but of the world outside of the prison will be forwarded. The chapter will end with some proposed solutions.

Why Prisoner Jihadist Radicalization Is Significant

As stated in the previous section, one might argue that due to the small number of cases of prisoners actually becoming jihadist radicals in prison, the problem is not important. After all, Mark Hamm calls those who turn radical beliefs into terrorist action "only a tiny, infinitesimal fraction of prison converts to white supremacy faiths and Islam" (Hamm 2013, 18). Although, as previously argued, the actual number of these sorts of inmates is unknown due to limitations on research, the cases that are known are highly significant. Some of the men radicalized to become jihadists in prison carried out the worst terror attacks in modern times. This section will list a few of these cases in order to show the significance of the problem in the face of potential arguments that this is a low-incidence phenomenon that need not concern many people.

Abdelhamid Abaaoud was a relatively privileged Belgian immigrant educated at a prestigious, private Catholic high school. Yet, in Molenbeek, Belgium, the borough of Brussels now notorious for its mass of jihadis, the son of Moroccan immigrants fell into a crowd of petty criminals who committed minor crimes of theft and assault (Higgins & Freytas-Timuras 2015). In 2003, at the age of 16, his parents kicked him out of the house having had had enough of his wild behavior. By 2010, the young criminal was serving time in Belgian prisons where he met Ibrahim Abdeslam (Faiola & Mekhenet 2015). In 2013, Abaaoud visited Syria for the first time and by January 2014, he was bringing along his 13-year-old younger brother Younes to Syria to fight alongside the Islamic State (Dalton 2015). In Syria, Abdelhamid Abaaoud dragged the mutilated bodies of Islamic State's dead enemies from his truck (Higgins & Freytas-Timuras 2015). On November 13, 2015, Abdelhamid Abaaoud, Ibrahim Abdeslam, and nine others killed 129 innocent Parisians in a series of shootings and bombings. Abaaoud and Abdeslam, who had met in prison, shot up bars and restaurants together along with another man (BBC News 2016).

Abaaoud's own father credits the son's prison stay with his jump from petty criminal to "extremely professional commando" (CBS News 2015). There, Abaaoud found radical Islam and decided to fight for jihad. In a place where he was supposed to be rehabilitating—or at least kept segregated from the public for its safety—Abaaoud transmuted from a minor thug to one of Europe's most notorious terrorist masterminds. To be sure, his "commando" skills were learned under the Islamic State in Syria, not in prison, but prison was what got him believing in causes like the Islamic State in the first place.

Like Abaaoud, Abu Musab al-Zarqawi, the creator of al Qaeda in Iraq, which later became ISIS, began his criminal career with minor offenses. Zarqawi was born in a Palestinian refugee camp in Jordan. After his father died in 1984, Zarqawi, a 17-year-old at the time, "became a petty criminal and a thug." He was soon imprisoned for possession of drugs and sexual assault (Reidel 2010, 89). Like Abaaoud, Zarqawi became radicalized in prison. After a general amnesty released Zarqawi in 1988, he married and went to Afghanistan to join the mujahideen, who were fighting the Soviet Union there. However, Zarqawi was late to the fight and ended up spending his time in Peshawar, Pakistan, where he linked up with other jihadis (Reidel 2010, 90).

In 1992, Zarqawi, now fully indoctrinated in Wahhabi ideology, returned to Jordan to try to overthrow the Hashemite monarchy there. When Jordanian intelligence officers raided his home in March 1994, Zarqawi tried to shoot the officers and then tried to kill himself, but he failed in both attempts. At trial, Zarqawi called for the King of Jordan to be tried in his stead. The would-be revolutionary was found guilty of having illegal weapons and being part of an illegal organization and was sent to a desert prison for 15 years (Reidel 2010, 92).

In his second stint in Jordanian prison, Zarqawi was joined by his friend Mohamed al-Barqawi, otherwise known as al-Maqdisi. Maqdisi was another Palestinian who lived in Kuwait and studied in Iraq. After his studies, Maqdisi met Zarqawi in Pakistan. Maqdisi, along with other Palestinians, was kicked out of Kuwait after the first Gulf War in 1991, and came to the al Ruseifah refugee camp in Jordan—the same camp that Zarqawi had lived in (Reidel 2010, 92–93).

Maqdisi and Zarqawi formed a radical prison gang. Maqdisi, who wrote two books outlining his radical religious beliefs and advocating the overthrow of the Saudi royal family, was the spiritual leader of the group and Zarqawi was the enforcer. In prison, Zarqawi memorized the Qur'an, made sure other inmates in his gang followed religious law such as growing beards, and developed a brutal reputation for attacking inmates as well as guards (Reidel 2010, 93).

After Jordan's King Hussein died in February 1999, his son Abdullah II pardoned many of the father's political enemies thus releasing Maqdisi and Zarqawi from prison after they had served less than five years each. The idea was that pardoning one's enemies may change them, but Zarqawi set out to plan his next terrorist attack once he was out of prison (Reidel 2010, 93–94). He would go on to link up with al Qaeda and run an organization, al Qaeda in Mesopotomia, that was so brutal and wanton in its violence that even the leaders of al Qaeda sought to distance themselves from his actions (Reidel 2010, 100, 103–104). This group would eventually morph into ISIS, which today also goes by the moniker Islamic State. That the founder of such an important terrorist group radicalized while in prison speaks to the importance of the topic.

Although an anecdotal list of terrorists radicalized in prison can go on and on, the point is that many very important jihadists, such as convicted attempted shoe bomber Richard Reid, al Qaeda leader Ayman al-Zawahiri, Abdelhamid Abaaoud, and Abu Musab al-Zarqawi, adopted their cause in prison. Indeed, in a report for the RAND Corporation, Greg Hanna, Lindsay Clutterbuck, and Jennifer Rubin list multiple instances of radicalization in British prisons (Hanna, Clutterbuck, & Rubin 2008, 34–35). Ayman al Zawahiri, the current leader of al Qaeda, was arrested for plotting to topple the Egyptian regime after the assassination of Gamal abd al-Nasser. Zawahiri decried the use of torture against him including whippings, beatings, electric shocks, and "the use of wild dogs" (Till 2011; Wright 2007, 64). Brian Till writes in *The Atlantic* that, "Zawahiri is part of a lineage of giants in the modern jihadi movement who were further radicalized by their years in prison. There's also Sayyid Qutb, the critical thinker in the evolution of the Muslim Brotherhood's ideology [and] the blind sheik Omar Abdel-Rahman whose terror network Gamaat Islamiya killed scores, and who, years later, inspired the 1993 World Trade Center bombers in New York mosques" (Till 2011). More recently, terrorists like Abdelhamid Abaaoud and Salah Abdeslam, an alleged attacker who was captured in Brussels, met in a Belgian prison (Mufson 2016). While in France, Ahmed Coulibaly, who killed four hostages at a Parisian kosher grocery store in January 2015, served time with the mother of one his accomplices (Birnbaum 2015).

This section shows that jihadist radicalization in prisons is a significant topic for study. The anecdotal evidence presented above shows that none other than the biggest names in global jihadism became extremists while in prison. Some, like Zawahiri, had extreme views to begin with. But others, like Abaaoud and al-Zarqawi, did not and seem to have been radicalized purely while incarcerated. Now that the problem has been framed and its importance has been emphasized, it is time to turn to how prisoners are radicalized.

Factors That Lead to Radicalization: General Prison Conditions

In this section, the general prison conditions and related psychological factors that lead prisoners to radicalize will be examined. As previously discussed, these factors are common to all prisoners who join extremist groups whether those groups are jihadist or not. As Cilluffo, Cardash, and Whitehead note: "Historically prisons have served as incubators of extreme ideas, and jihadists would not be the first to infiltrate and recruit from prisons." The authors note that inmates are susceptible to radicalization due to the fact that they "form a captive audience" and can exhibit factors making them vulnerable to radicalizers such as "alienation, anti-social attitudes, cultural disillusionment, social isolation, and violent tendencies" (Cilluffo, Cardash, & Whitehead 2007, 114). The same factors that led to the importation of "street gangs" into prisons (Welch 1995, 156) lead to the spread of jihadist ideologies among inmates.

In 2005, then-FBI director Robert Mueller sounded the alarm on prisoner radicalization, declaring that "prisons are . . . fertile ground for extremists [and that] Inmates may be drawn to an extreme form of Islam because it may help justify their violent tendencies" (Hamm 2013, x). Later, Charles Allen, former chief intelligence officer for the Department of Homeland Security advised the U.S. Congress in 2009 that the U.S. prison population was susceptible to jihadist radicalization due to prison conditions coupled with social marginalization. These factors lead inmates to seek out groups to join and people with whom to bond—and given the incarceration of prominent jihadists, the groups and relationships inmates form could certainly lead them to Islamic extremism (Hamm 2013, x).

Penitentiaries since their inception have been intended to transform the incarcerated (Hamm 2013, 16, 19–20; Welch 1995). But the current era of mass incarceration has made prisons a more chaotic place where prisoners are more vulnerable to violence and more socially marginalized. These factors, according to intelligence expert Charles Allen, make prisons an ideal place for spreading terrorist beliefs (Hamm 2013, 16).

There are shared factors that lead prisoners to turn to extremist or radical beliefs of all kinds. These include that prisons are increasingly overcrowded (Hamm 2013, 51), that guards engage in "diesel therapy" by frequently moving prisoners from one prison to the next, and that inmates as a population are more likely than others to be disaffected by society due to their punishments and perhaps their crimes. Alienation and loneliness are additional factors that may lead the incarcerated to radicalize. As Cilluffo, Cardash, and Whitehead show, "[e]xtremist recruitment preys on alienation" (Cilluffo, Cardash, & Whitehead 2007, 120). Some studies further exhibit that prisoners desire to join extremist groups because of the loss of significance they feel (Dugas & Kruglanski 2014).

Environmental factors such as understaffed and overcrowded prisons lead prisoners to seek protection in groups. Group dynamics certainly play a role in radicalization since extremist organizations seek out individuals who have not found solace in existing religious views and, in turn, these groups "impart and anchor their ideology" to such people whose "ideological transformations are, in turn, reinforced and amplified by group dynamics" (Atran 2010; Rascoff 2012). So prison conditions lead to alienation and the need for protection, which in turn, lead some prisoners to adopt jihadist religious worldviews. At this point, the story will sound similar to that of prisoners joining gangs of any stripe while incarcerated. Subsequent sections—on the role of religion and the effects of the outside world on prisoners—will help explain why inmates turn to jihadism specifically.

Let's first go over prison conditions before turning to how the psychology of the prisoners and group dynamics lead inmates to radicalize. Khosrokhavar lists three important factors: "overcrowding, understaffing, and the high turnover of personnel and prisoners" that lead the incarcerated in France to turn to jihadist extremism (Khosrokhavar 2013, 284). Overcrowding, which, in France, has led to some cells meant for two prisoners holding three or four, reduces the ability of authorities to supervise inmate behavior. It also increases tension in the prison as guards are overburdened and prisoners are underserved. Khosrokhavar notes that guards frequently fail to bring registered prisoners to Muslim religious services, which is viewed by prisoners as a purposeful slight and by guards as a matter of prisoner choice (the guards say that the prisoners claim to be sick or want to do something else instead of going to religious services when called) (Khosrokhavar 2013, 294). Of course, overcrowding in prisons and the concomitant inability of guards to protect all inmates from each other leads prisoners to joining gangs all over the world. In the United States, the rise of prison populations, overcrowding, and the ascension of prison gangs are all connected (The Economist 2014).

Understaffing and turnover of guards and prisoners aggravate the problem. Guards do not have time to familiarize themselves with the inmates and their surroundings and are also overburdened with work. Guards that don't know the prisoners well are unable to pick up who is a radical, who is associating with whom, and so on (Khosrokhavar 2013, 294). Further, many guards do not know Arabic, so they suspect the worst when they see any Arabic script written by an inmate. These problems persist despite France emphasizing the monitoring and collecting of data on Islamic prisoner radicalization "at least a decade before other major western countries adopted the practice" (Khosrokhavar 2013, 295). Overcrowding, understaffing, and turnover explain why radicalization is allowed to happen but not how and why it happens.

Psychological factors work alongside prison conditions to lead inmates to radicalize. Michelle Dugas and Arie Kruglanski argue that prisoners who radicalize do so because they have felt a loss of significance in their life and seek to become a more significant person. This "quest for significance orients individuals toward an in-group in an effort to restore" their self-esteem (Dugas & Kruglanski 2014, 428). Prisoners are a classically humiliated, angry, and frustrated group of people who have been forcibly removed from society. The experience of imprisonment clearly can reduce one's feeling of significance in the world and lead individuals to seek out a new foundation for their life. This foundation, of course, does not have to embody extremism; many prisoners pursue journalism, education, or sports as ways to pass the time (Bell 2016). Suffice it to say, being imprisoned, and being dragged through the criminal justice system, is a humiliating, disempowering, and anxiety-ridden experience that leaves prisoners emotionally vulnerable (Dugas & Kruglanski 2014, 431).

Relatedly, Patrick Dunleavy in his book *The Fertile Soil of Jihad: Terrorism's Prison Connection* reinforces the fact that the psychology of inmates makes them ripe pickings for those seeking to recruit for terror organizations. Dunleavy cites a classified CIA study which found that, "Incarcerated individuals are probably particularly receptive to using violence against a government by which they feel they have been wronged" (Dunleavy 2011, 23). He further notes that an FBI report found that prisoners are particularly susceptible to radicalization as they feel discriminated against by the government and may feel hostile toward authority. The FBI report goes on to note that, in addition to the possibility of inmates having violent tendencies, they may also seek acceptance, power and influence, and desire to right the (perceived) wrongs committed against them (Dunleavy 2011, 23–24).

Psychological factors, such as alienation and disaffection, explain why prisoners seek out new groups or gangs to join while in prison. They join these gangs for social, psychological, and personal security reasons (The Economist 2014; Welch 1995, 156–158). As Clarke Jones and Resurrecion Morales note, "a prison gang's strict code of conduct and ideological influence may provide the circumstances for an inmate to adopt a new belief system, social identity, and pattern of behavior" (Jones & Morales 2012, 212). Prisoners who are not part of existing gangs or groups need to link up with others for protection as well as for social and psychological reasons. As Sune Haugbolle writes in a chapter on Syrian prisoners, "Imprisonment disfigures individuals through extended absence from the ones they love and leaves them with a sense of broken personal history, wasted time and emptiness" (Haugbolle 2010, 229). In the words of a federal prisoner housed in Terminal Island: "associating yourself with some clique in prison is very important because it gives you a sense of security and an alliance which you can build strong bonds with. The reality of prison is that you cannot survive without the help of others" (SpearIt 2013, 25).

These psychological factors are made worse by prison conditions such as overcrowding and understaffing. Further, guards, who may not speak the inmates' language, have become increasingly suspicious of potentially jihadist behavior. This makes life worse for all Muslim prisoners, but especially those who are not jihadists. These people are targeted for extra surveillance and scrutiny because of their religion.

Factors That Lead to Radicalization: The Role of Religion and What Might Be Special about Jihadists

In this section, the role of religion in jihadist radicalization will be explored. There are two important points to note: first, religions in general are sometimes afforded special protections in prison, giving inmates a way to connect and meet that they otherwise would not have had. Second, jihadist strains of Islam in particular are subject to special scrutiny in prison, making the recruitment and radicalization process both opaque for outsiders seeking to study jihadists and difficult for the jihadists themselves. Mark Hamm's research shows that White supremacist and jihadist groups radicalize prisoners "based on a prison gang model whereby inmates [go] through a process of one-on-one proselytizing by charismatic leaders" (Hamm 2013, 53). Khosrokhavar's research confirms these findings. He explains that radicalizers either seek out psychologically fragile individuals who have no knowledge of Islam or inmates who have some knowledge of Islam and are also in need of physical protection (Khosrokhavar 2013, 297–298). For both groups, "Becoming a Muslim automatically provides them with the protection of community members, particularly if they adhere (as they do in the majority of cases) to the Salafist or radical tenet of Islam" (Khosrokhavar 2013, 298). Obviously, the individuals discussed here seek out group membership in a certain religious group, but many social scientists that have studied Islamic radicalization seek to explain it away as either a political or strategic choice (Pape & Feldman 2010; Scheuer 2004). Although all terror groups have demands that they seek to reach through violent means (or the threat of violent means), jihadists' beliefs are not simply interchangeable with any other belief system. For instance, in order to truly understand the Islamic State group in Iraq and Syria, one must have a deep understanding of certain Islamic beliefs such as the coming of the apocalypse and the return of the Mahdi (basically, the Messiah) (McCants 2015).

As correctional officers have hemmed in jihadist activities the world over, those that seek to radicalize others have adjusted. Farhad Khosrokhavar, a sociologist at École des Hautes Études en Sciences-Sociales, has done extensive research on French prisons and prisoners in which he interviewed "160 inmates and many guards, doctors and social workers in four major facilities, some among the largest in Europe" (Khosrokhavar 2015). In a 2013 journal article, Khosrokhavar writes that radicalization in French prisons happens in small groups of typically two or three individuals to evade authority (Khosrokhavar 2013, 288). He notes in a 2015 *New York Times* piece that prison is an integral part of the "typical trajectory" of French jihadists. That trajectory begins with cultural alienation in France that leads to petty crime, prison, radicalization, and "an initiatory journey to a Muslim country like Syria, Afghanistan or Yemen to train for jihad" (Khosrokhavar 2015).

Religion plays a critical role in inmates' lives. Many of them find religion while incarcerated due to the stresses of prison life. As Dunleavy notes on this point: "there are no atheists in foxholes" (Dunleavy 2011, 22). Thomas and Zaitzow's research shows that inmates are more likely to convert religions in maximum security prisons than in medium or minimum security ones. To this end, the harshness of the prison conditions seems to be a factor in leading to religious conversion (Thomas & Zaitzow 2004, 242). Religious study and the solace that a religious worldview brings certainly helps an individual survive in prison. But religious gangs or groups in prison also have some important differences from other associations that prisoners join.

First and foremost, there are certain privileges and accommodations that are given to the various religious groups in prison. In New York State, prisoners cannot be denied access to clergy. In fact, "Any religious worker could demand to enter a prison in the New York system without restriction" (Dunleavy 2011, 61). Prisoners can also use the link to a prison chaplain to, for instance, send a package or a letter or even to bring in contraband (Allen & Costa 1981).

Patrick Dunleavy, a former deputy inspector general of the Criminal Intelligence Unit of the New York State Department of Correctional Services, developed intimate knowledge of how those who seek to radicalize others to the causes of jihadism operate in U.S. prisons through his involvement in Operation Hades, an investigation of radical Islamic recruitment inside and outside of U.S. prisons. Dunleavy follows the exploits of Abdel Nasser Zaben, a Palestinian jihadist who migrated to Brooklyn in the early 1990s to recruit others and carry out attacks. Despite his strict interpretation of Islam, Zaben was arrested and sent to Rikers Island after being arrested for a series of armed robberies and kidnappings (Dunleavy 2011, 16–21). In prison, Zaben not only linked up with other radicals such as Hamas fighter Rashid Baz, who was convicted for a 1994 shooting of Hasidic Jewish students on the Brooklyn Bridge, but also encountered psychologically pliable individuals whom he worked to radicalize (Dunleavy 2011, 25). Michael Lombard, a 55-year-old Italian American only child, certainly does not fit the profile that most people envision as a jihadist terrorist. But, alone in prison, without his codependent mother for the first time in his life, Lombard was converted to Islam by Zaben (Dunleavy 2011, 37). Remarkably, Lombard's mother also converted to Islam soon afterward (Dunleavy 2011, 40). Lombard's hatred of Jews (he was in prison for shooting a Jewish eye doctor who botched an eye procedure), feeling of isolation, and psychological vulnerability made him an easy mark for Zaben (Dunleavy 2011, 36). Wiretapped phone conversations between Lombard and his mother captured the two plotting attacks against prominent politicians (Dunleavy 2011, 40–42).

Abdel Zaben, Rashid Baz, and Edwin Lemmons, another one of Zaben's converts, all served as personal assistants to the Muslim chaplain at various times. Although the New York Department of Corrections had a committee for approving such appointments that was supposed to take into account the needs of the prison and security, in reality a chaplain's recommendation was good enough for a rubber-stamped approval (Dunleavy 2011, 52). In this way, inmates could access the chaplain's phone to communicate with operatives on the outside. In the case of Abdel Zaben, thousands of calls were made by the Muslim chaplain on Zaben's behalf to "radical Islamic organizations and associates of incarcerated terrorists in the United States, the Middle East, and North Africa." Procedures put in place to list why calls were made on an inmate's behalf, to list who was called, and to charge the inmate for the call were all not followed (Dunleavy 2011, 64–65).

From this example, we see that religious groups have important privileges in prisons. Religious services provide a meeting place for coreligionists that does not have the same protections around the world as other types of organizations in prison (Dunleavy 2011, 31–32). Further, religious clergy can serve as connectors linking the incarcerated to the outside world—for better or worse.

Another factor that differentiates religion, particularly radical Islam, from other types of associations prisoners could make, is the vicarious suffering felt by Islamic extremists worldwide. Marc Sageman writes that jihadists feel a sense of "moral outrage" and "vicarious humiliation" when they see their coreligionists suffer in wars and conflicts in sometimes-foreign lands. As Sageman explains: "The humiliation of friends can evoke strong anger. . . . Anger brings the desire to right a wrong, and this may lead to violence" (Sageman 2008, 72–73). Being part of a large group of coreligionists that are suffering at the hands of "world powers" or "the government," and whose suffering shows that they are on the side of justice, can be an especially attractive proposition for prisoners. As Khosrokhavar writes, "Radical preaching catches on because it offers young Muslim prisoners a way to escape their predicament and develop a fantasy of omnipotence by declaring death onto their oppressors" (Khosrokhavar 2015). He notes further that "international politics," specifically "the predicament of Muslims globally" that inmates follow daily on television, fuel "a radical version of Islam as the 'religion of the oppressed'" (Khosrokhavar 2013, 288–289). Religion, then, provides multiple psychic and social goods by giving inmates solace, a protective association, and a set of established grievances to fight against all while having the special status of a belief system that needs to be accommodated in many countries.

In the Middle East, this dynamic works a bit differently as fundamentalist religion is restricted by most regimes due to its connection to terrorism in the region, and due to its role as a potential regime destabilizer. Despite these restrictions, religion is the one means by which people are allowed to "protest" the regime in many Middle Eastern nations due to strictures on free speech and even freedom of association (Haugbolle 2010, 227). An emblematic case that exemplifies the religious-secular divide can be seen in Egypt where the Muslim Brotherhood has wrestled with the government ever since its 1928 inception during the times of King Farouk (Lapidus 1983). The long-standing organization of countergovernment religious associations explains the Muslim Brotherhood's national election victory in 2013, Hamas' national electoral victory in the Palestinian Territories in 2006, as well as the Islamic Salvation Front's short-lived victory in Algeria in 1991 (Kilpatrick 2012; Murphy 1991; Wilson 2006). Due to this connection between religion and opposition to government, religious prisoners are treated particularly poorly in many Middle Eastern and North African countries. Haugbolle notes that people in the Middle East additionally suffer from "the prison of living in a restrictive society" where religious freedoms are squashed and regime loyalty is paramount (Haugbolle 2010, 227).

Prison has played a prominent role in the radicalization of Middle Eastern Muslim figures since ibn Tamiya, one of the fathers of contemporary jihadism, died in prison in 1328. Later, Sayyid Qutb, one of Tamiya's recent and most prominent theological descendants, was tortured, abused and, in 1966, executed in Egypt for his radical beliefs and opposition to Gamal Abdel Nasser's government (Hanna, Clutterbuck, & Rubin 2008, 27). Current al Qaeda leader Ayman al-Zawahiri came to worldwide prominence after he was detained and tortured for allegedly being part of the plot to assassinate Egyptian president Anwar Sadat (Hanna, Clutterbuck, & Rubin 2008, 28).

In Muslim-majority countries, torture is a critical component of the experience of incarceration, and it seems to exacerbate the problem with radicalization. Although torture can get jihadists to turn on their compatriots, even Ayman al-Zawahiri is said to have "betrayed a comrade" after being tortured (Hanna, Clutterbuck, & Rubin 2008, 28); it also turns jihadists even further against the government. Torture at the hands of Americans at Abu Ghraib or Guantanamo, or at the hands of Egyptian, Libyan, Jordanian, or other security forces serves to unite jihadists and further alienate them from government forces. Jihadists even have produced instructions for each other on how to defend themselves at trial by pointing to human rights abuses by their captors (Hanna, Clutterbuck, & Rubin 2008, 69). Being tortured by their captors reinforces the jihadist view that their enemies are evil, irreligious, and immoral. To this end, although torture can help security forces glean information, it can also be a major component in the radicalization process. Torture can serve the same ends as vicarious humiliation by angering the inmate and giving him or her a group or entity to oppose.

Finally, the role of religion in prison is different from other forms of radicalization because religious study can be carried out in prison whereas other forms of extremist literature may be banned in detention facilities. Abu Musab al-Zarqawi is said to have memorized the Qur'an while in prison (Reidel 2010, 93). Further Abu Muhammad al-Maqdisi, one of the most important living jihadist thinkers, argues that prison is a place where the jihadist can solidify his faith. In an article entitled "Prison: Heavens and Fires" he wrote that in prison a religious extremist can focus on "obeying God, worshipping him, memorizing the Quran, seeking and spreading Da'wah [meaning: the proselytizing of Islam] and learning from the experience of those around him to become stronger for jihad" (Hanna, Clutterbuck, & Rubin 2008, 29).

As can now be seen, religion both protects and harms Muslim prisoners. It protects them when religious prisoners are given special time to meet and study, but it also harms them by exposing them to scrutiny all over the world. On the plus side, it not only helps prisoners by giving them the protection and social goods that come with joining an organization; it also has a special place in prison that makes religion a good cover for engaging in criminal activities. Moreover, religion links inmates to a wider group of people with whom the inmate can feel a sense of vicarious suffering. Yet the negatives of prison are also many for the jihadist prisoner; the torture that Muslim religious extremists face in prisons and detention centers reinforces their belief in a Manichaean world of evil Crusaders and corrupt Muslim governments fighting against true believers. As the potential for jihadist radicalization has been discovered the world over, radical Muslim prisoners have received increased scrutiny, which includes more solitary confinement and even torture (Ganor & Falk 2013; Haugbolle 2010; Khosrokhavar 2013). Similar arguments can be made of religious charities and how radical prisoners might exploit them to fund crime: while religious charities have special protections in some cases, Islamic religious charities in particular have been reserved for special scrutiny (Dunleavy 2011, 32).

Jihadist religious affiliation does have its drawbacks since those who run prisons the world over are today conscious of the potential for and effects of Islamic radicalization. To this end, jihadists today, as Khosrokhavar explains (Khosrokhavar 2013, 295), may need to work to hide their behavior in prison even more than other criminal enterprises do. This makes life in prison for jihadists perhaps similar to life outside of it where so-called taqfiris hide their religious affiliation in the modern world by, for example, not growing out their beards and by dressing in a secular fashion.

The Role of the Outside World

As discussed in the introduction, readers at this point may wonder why any given prisoner would turn to jihadism rather than Marxism, White supremacy, or any other ideology while in prison. In the previous section, the role religion plays in prison, both good and bad, vis-à-vis the incarcerated was discussed which provides a partial answer to the question. But one could still be curious about why prisoners choose jihadist interpretations of Islam over literally any other religion.

In this section, the role of the outside world will be brought in to help explain why prisoners turn to jihadist ideologies. As Mark Hamm emphasizes, prisoner radicalization "is a very old issue" that is "tempered and shaped by the prevailing events of the times in which it occurs" (Hamm 2013, 1). Hamm shows how social movements going on outside prisons affect the choices and perceptions of those inside prisons. For instance, in the 1960s, many Black prisoners sought out antiestablishment and Black nationalist groups due to movements like the Black Panthers becoming popular in the wider society (Hamm 2013, 34). The book *Soledad Brother* describes a similar process (Jackson 1994). As Stephen Rascoff notes, counterradicalization seeks to prevent violence by "shaping the ideational currents that are thought to underpin that violence" (Rascoff 2012, 127). Those currents come from both within the prison and from the outside world.

Critical criminologists seek to explain the incidence of crime, such as terrorism, by looking at power differentials in the wider society not just at the forensics of the crime itself. Without looking at the broader picture, the reason why some prisoners turn to jihadism cannot be landed on because the critic can always ask, "Why jihadism and not something else?" By looking at the outside world, we can explain, for instance, why a Palestinian prisoner turns to religious extremism after a stay in an Israeli detention facility. This fictive inmate latches on to ideologies that exist in the wider Palestinian society and turns to hate the Israelis for their occupation of his lands. Jihadism, then, is a routinized form of protest in the face of power differentials in the wider society.

Tensions between indigenous Europeans and late-generation Muslim immigrations have been enflamed throughout Europe. Examples of the failure of Muslim integration in Europe are plentiful including riots in Paris's *banlieu* (Chrisafis 2015), Switzerland's constitutional ban on new minarets on mosques (NBC News 2009), the banning of the veil in France and, potentially, Germany's ban of the burqa (Smale 2016), the Netherlands' ban on the export of halal meat (Lewis 2016) and the rise of far-right groups and Islamophobia across the continent (Walker & Taylor 2011). The flood of Muslim immigrants that came to Europe after World War II have, in sum, not been well assimilated into European society (Leiken 2005). Muslim unemployment in Molenbeek, the Belgian neighborhood described by media sources as an incubator for terror (Higgins & Freytas-Timuras 2015), is 30 percent (De Winter 2016). Although Europe and the United States have similar legal systems, the problem of jihadist radicalization is greater in Europe due to a larger proportion of Muslims there. The European Union has a 6 percent Muslim population while America is 1 percent Muslim (Hackett 2015; Mohamed 2016). Other factors that include the lower income of European Muslims as compared to American Muslims, European policing practices, and the lower assimilation rates of European Muslims as compared to American Muslims play a role in Muslim radicalization there. In Europe, concepts of community policing have not yet caught on so incidences of White police officers harassing immigrant Muslims are common (Sageman 2008).

Large disaffected minority groups are susceptible to turn to extremism due to their treatment by the majority. European Muslims radicalize whether in prison or outside of it due to the discrimination their people face in Europe. However, the question may be posed "Why Muslims?" Many people are ill-treated the world over, but few turn to terrorist behavior. The reason that Muslims turn to these belief systems is that they are available in the wider Muslim society. After the failure of Arab secular governments to defeat Israel or provide good lives for their people, an increasing number of Middle Eastern Muslims turned to religion as a way to challenge the existing structure and to attempt to make change (Martin 2016, 134). Emblematic of these changes was the rise of Hamas among the Palestinians, after the failure of the Palestinian Authority became increasingly perceived as ineffective and corrupt (Martin 2016, 134–135). Ayman Zawahiri, al Qaeda's leader, was part of the vanguard generation in Egypt that turned to the Muslim Brotherhood as a protest against their regime's peace deal with Israel. This wave of religious extremism was exacerbated by the successes of al Qaeda against the Soviet Union in Afghanistan and against America on 9/11 (Martin 2016). The existence of religious extremist groups in the Middle East fighting the establishment and the success of some of these groups explain why Muslims have lately turned to radical religious organizations more than other groups have.

Wars between the West and Muslim nations have also led Muslims to turn to extremist ideologies. These wars include Israel's invasion of Lebanon that created the radical Shia group Hezbollah and the second war in Iraq that created al Qaeda in Iraq—a group that later became ISIS. Drone strikes and wars in the Muslim world create grievances that can't be overstated. Hundreds of thousands of Iraqis have been killed since America's invasion in 2003 ("Iraq Body Count"). France's bombing of Mali and its treatment of Algerians during its time as colonizer there have also led to a rise in terrorism (Haddad 2015).

In the Middle East, of course, there are much higher Muslim populations than in the West and, in most cases, fewer rights. Prison stays also are more likely to involve torture (Khalili & Schwedler 2010; Till 2011). One of the main recruitment centers and organizing hubs for ISIS is prisons. As Weiss and Hassan report, "Whether by accident or design, jailhouses in the Middle East have served for years as virtual terror academies, where known extremists can congregate, plot, organize, and hone their leadership skills 'inside the wire,' and most ominously recruit a new generation of fighters" (Weiss & Hassan 2015, xv). For some Middle Eastern prisoners, incarceration led to popularity;

for instance, Ayman al Zawahiri gained "global notoriety" while detained (Weiss & Hassan 2015, 5). For other inmates, prison taught them how to fight the dictatorial regimes they opposed. Hassan and Weiss say that "Prison was [Abu Musab al-Zarqawi's] university" (Weiss & Hassan 2015, 9). Like with other criminals that join like-minded felons while behind bars, jihadists link up with one another in prison and radicalize each other, a process that happened in spades in Syria under the brutal rule of the Assad regime (Weiss & Hassan 2015, 145–146). The "outside world" in Iraq, where Sunni Muslim communities are existentially threatened by the majority Shia, has led Hassan and Weiss to report that "Sunnis are being radicalized at record proportions" (Weiss & Hassan 2015, 240). It is no wonder then that people like Abu Bakr al-Baghdadi, the current leader of ISIS, had such great luck in recruiting his fellow Iraqis to join jihadist causes and fight the Americans and the Shia while he was detained by U.S. forces (Weiss & Hassan 2015, 119).

In the Middle East prison conditions and political conditions merge to create an environment where prisoner radicalization flourishes. In such an environment, Boaz Ganor points out in his study of the Israeli case, what security forces and the government call "Islamic radicalization" is seen by the incarcerated as fighting for one's rights against an occupation government (Ganor & Falk 2013). To this end, strategies to quell radicalization need to involve both prisoner management and political policy changes. In the final section, strategies to stop prisoner jihadist radicalization will be explored with an eye toward solving the underlying political problems.

Solutions to the Jihadist Problem in Prison: Prison Management and Political Management

Now that the radicalization process has been elaborated upon, it is time to explore solutions to Islamic extremist radicalization in prison. Four main methods for dealing with radicalized prisoners will be examined: segregation, isolation, moving prisoners frequently, and deradicalization (also called rehabilitation). The first three methods, which are more prison management solutions, will be separated from rehabilitation, which can be seen as a political solution as well.

Segregation, Isolation, and Moving Prisoners Frequently

Many countries see the advantage of separating those convicted of terrorism from other inmates. Indeed, one of the underlying logics behind using prison as a punishment is to segregate convicts from the general population (Veldhuis & Lindenberg 2012, 425). In Saudi Arabia and Australia, separation is practiced alongside deradicalization programs (Jones & Morales 2012,

218). Segregating the most dangerous inmates surely removes the possibility of jihadists radicalizing other inmates. But it may be difficult to figure out who the jihadists are given that if authorities knew who the worst perpetrators were all the time, the prisoner radicalization issue would not exist. Further, grouping inmates of the same ilk together may "create even stronger radicalizing cells within the prisons" (Birnbaum 2015). Segregating radical Muslim prisoners is meant to prevent recruitment (Bouchaud 2014), but, for those with already radical tendencies, segregation of prisoners may intensify extremist patterns. As Haugbolle notes of prerevolution Syria, "Most prisons separate Islamist convicts from their secular inmates. Once released, former prisoners replicate those patterns of socialisation" (Haugbolle 2010, 237). Boaz Ganor and Ophir Falk find similar patterns in the Israeli case. There, they find that many prisoners had already been radicalized and organize themselves by association with revolutionary or political groups (Fatah, Hamas, Islamic Jihad, etc.) (Ganor & Falk 2013, 116–121). Moreover, even if segregation is a good solution in some cases, resource constraints prevent poorer countries like the Philippines from using this method effectively as a segregated prison population requires its own staff and sometimes its own facility (Jones & Morales 2012, 220).

Segregation alone may not provide a solution to recidivism. In examining the Dutch case, Veldhuis and Lindenberg note that after the 2004 killing of filmmaker Theo Van Gogh in Amsterdam, the Dutch government felt intense pressure to "do something" about radicalization in the Netherlands (Veldhuis & Lindenberg 2012, 434). In this case, the authors argue, short-term concerns won out as public demand for change made long government deliberation untenable. A terrorism wing was created to segregate radical inmates from the general prison population so as to reduce the likelihood of proselytization. "However," the authors observe. "No instruments [were] applied to rehabilitate or reintegrate the inmates, with the result that little [was] done to prevent recidivism or radicalization after inmates [were] released from the terrorism wing" (Demant & De Graaf 2010; Veldhuis & Lindenberg 2012, 437). As previously noted, recidivism is no small matter. Ganor, for instance, writes that, "historically, some of the most prominent Palestinian terrorists, responsible for the most horrific attacks against civilians, were released convicts" (Ganor & Falk 2013, 124).

A more extreme version of segregation is solitary confinement or isolation wherein the individual inmate is left alone for most or all of the day sometimes for the entire duration of his or her prison term. So-called "supermax" prisons, which are becoming the norm in the West for housing those convicted of terrorism, rely heavily on solitary confinement (Jones & Morales 2012, 218). Such isolation has been seen by human rights groups as well as psychologists as a form of abuse that can be tantamount to torture (Amnesty International 2014). As Jones and Morales note, solitary confinement has been shown to be psychologically damaging to inmates and "may act to reinforce the psychology of exclusivity and 'martyrdom'" among them (Jones & Morales 2012, 218). Although isolating prisoners has similar advantages to segregating them, it also has greater downsides. The human rights abuses inherent in solitary confinement can become a rallying cry for jihadists that are emboldened by the suffering of their peers at the hands of "infidel" forces. Further, isolating prisoners in places where inmates have no due process rights, and little, or no access to lawyers like Abu Ghraib Prison in Iraq, the Guantanamo Bay Detention Center in Cuba, and the many horrible prisons in places like Yemen, Syria, Libya, Egypt, and Iran, creates situations where guards face little or no penalty for abusing and torturing inmates. The Abu Ghraib abuse scandal is just the tip of the iceberg of prisoner abuse in situations when inmates are isolated from the outside world—and sometimes each other—and guards can act with impunity. It should also be noted here that jihadists have used the West's isolation and dehumanization of terrorist convicts as a recruiting tool and a symbol. Groups like ISIS make their Western hostages don the orange jumpsuits of Guantanamo detainees to show both moral equivalency and to exact revenge.

A third prisoner management solution is moving inmates between prison facilities frequently. The thought behind this management solution is to reduce the likelihood of prisoners' recruiting others to jihadist causes. Khosrokhavar writes that he encountered prisoners "who, in a decade, had been moved to as many as 30 prisons!" He notes, however, that this movement did not serve the intended ends of the French corrections services. Instead, many of these prisoners develop "anti-establishment views" (Khosrokhavar 2013, 302). One issue with moving prisoners is that the authorities move those that they know are problem cases and who have not responded to other punishments (Khosrokhavar 2013, 301). These prisoners are then allowed to germinate new connections in a new facility where staff may not be fully aware of the risks they pose. As Patrick Dunleavy writes, "frequent inmate movement as a management tool has long been a part of corrections" (Dunleavy 2011, 47). However, Abdel Zaben's movement to different prison facilities only allowed him to expose his views to new recruits and make more connections with jihadist elements in the prison system (Dunleavy 2011). Moving prisoners frequently, sometimes called "diesel therapy," can be seen as a form of segregation as the practice is meant to cut off inmates from the social connections they would otherwise make while incarcerated.

Rehabilitation

Deradicalization, a process by which counselors and religious figures try to change the worldviews of jihadist inmates and replace their violent tendencies with nonviolent ones, can be seen as a political solution to these prison problems since this strategy actually deals with the motivations for turning to jihadism both in prisons and in the outside world (Dugas & Kruglanski 2014, 433). Here deradicalization and rehabilitation will be used interchangeably. The deradicalization process is certainly a problematic one in countries where speech is protected and governments could be viewed as trying to squash a religious view that they find objectionable (Mufson 2016). Yet, while efforts to shift the terrorists' mindset are part of these programs, they are not the only piece. The best deradicalization programs also provide the inmates with the "opportunity to air grievances in a non-violent fashion," vocational training, new social opportunities, and also try to help the inmates reintegrate into the general public (Jones & Morales 2012, 217). These approaches have been implemented all over the world including in Sri Lanka, the Philippines, Saudi Arabia, Yemen, France, the United Kingdom, the Netherlands, Australia, Afghanistan, Indonesia, Malaysia, and Singapore, among other places.

With so many programs around the world, it is difficult to get a bead on whether deradicalization is an effective strategy or not. However, Dugas and Kruglanski's scientific study of Sri Lanka's deradicalization program for LTTE (Liberation Tigers of Tamil Eelam, a.k.a. Tamil Tiger) members found that the "rehabilitation program mattered in the changing attitudes" of the militants (Dugas & Kruglanski 2014, 436). Specifically, those LTTE members who were exposed to the deradicalization program saw a decline in their support for armed struggle while those that did not saw no change in their attitudes toward armed struggle (Dugas & Kruglanski 2014, 435).

In Israel, the deradicalization program is coupled with a carrot-and-stick approach. Compliance with the program brings more "family visits, telephone calls, canteen purchases . . . , preferred cooking facilities and accommodations, and leisure activities." Noncooperative prisoners receive a series of penalties (Ganor & Falk 2013, 125).

Ganor and Falk likewise contend that deradicalization programs are doomed to fail if prisoners are not "segregated from their peers, held in special prisons or separate sections within a prison, and their families provided with the necessary setting and protection by authorities" (Ganor & Falk 2013, 126). Still, the authors argue that deradicalizing Palestinian prisoners in Israel is an uphill battle even if everything is done according to best practices. This is because radical Palestinian prisoners have large networks in prison, family connections outside of prison, a deep opposition to their enemies (the Israelis) that is based in reality, and the knowledge that many Palestinian radicals have been released over the years, which reduces the need to change (Ganor & Falk 2013, 127–128).

Saudi Arabia's "Counseling Program" has received the most press for its purported high success rate. This program, like the others, seeks to challenge the jihadists' ideologies through dialogue with religious figures as well as psychological counseling (Jones & Morales 2012, 217). In the Philippines a more holistic approach is being used as well. Staff are being educated about radicalization, reforms meant to reduce corruption are taking place within prisons, and existing programs are being augmented with more vocational training and family involvement (Jones & Morales 2012, 215).

Marisa Porges has analyzed deradicalization programs all over the world and found that though they have not been a panacea, their overall effect has been positive. She notes that rehabilitating terror convicts is a risky business; given that letting even a small number of radical prisoners go, whose rehabilitation has not been successful, proves a massive risk even for countries that have extensive security capabilities (Porges 2011, 50). She notes that while deradicalization may not always achieve its objective, there are valuable secondary benefits to consider. Specifically, these programs can "forestall radicalization among vulnerable groups, including the friends and families of imprisoned terrorists." Further, rehabilitation programs aid in intelligence gathering (Porges 2011, 51).

Porges highlights that while the Saudi Counseling Program is normally lauded for its ability to counter jihadist beliefs with nonviolent ones, the Saudis have moved to a greater emphasis on changing jihadist behavior rather than ideology. As Porges observes, Saudi professors, psychologists, security officials, and religious scholars teach a range of classes to prisoners, but courses on psychology, sociology, art therapy, politics, and history now greatly outnumber lessons on religion, *sharia* law, and Islamic culture. The Saudis it seems have found vocational and "life skills" training to be vitally important in reintegrating prisoners into Saudi society (Porges 2011, 52). After all, a nonviolent ideology is nice to have, but a job can do wonders for one's social status and sense of worth. Singapore has a similarly balanced deradicalization program, and the United States has tried to mirror the Saudi program in their detention operations in Iraq and Afghanistan (Porges 2011, 52). Yemen, on the other hand, has focused solely on religious reprogramming, and their unsuccessful program was shuttered in 2005 after only three years (Porges 2011, 52–53). Of course, Saudi Arabia's infamous adoption of Wahhabist Islam and its export of this version of the religion confound the Gulf State's efforts at countering radicalism (Frontline 2016).

As previously seen in the Philippines case, family engagement is an integral part of rehabilitation. In Saudi Arabia, the government helps provide for jihadist prisoners' families as an incentive toward rehabilitation. In Iraq, Afghanistan, and Singapore, family visits are encouraged so as to give the prisoner social and psychological support and help in the reintegration effort. Many times "family members or respected representatives from a detainee's tribe or village are asked to take responsibility for a detainee after release" (Porges 2011, 53).

Moreover, Saudi Arabia and Singapore's rehabilitation programs focus heavily on reintegrating and helping the inmates successfully reenter society.

Saudi Arabia's focus on individually tailored programs complete with mentors has made replicating the Gulf nation's success in deradicalization difficult (Porges 2011, 54). Saudi officials, who held until January 2009 that their programs had a 100 percent success rate, now say that 80 to 90 percent of those who pass through their rehabilitation programs deradicalize. However, they are careful to note that these programs are not likely to turn "the most committed terrorists" (Porges 2011, 55).

Recidivism statistics are hard to come by for these programs as they rely on sometimes-confidential government and intelligence information. High-profile failures beg the question of whether even a low recidivism rate is good enough. After all, graduates of Yemen's rehabilitation program have gone to Iraq to fight against the American occupation and Ali al-Shihri, a former Guantanamo detainee who also graduated the Saudi program, rose to become the deputy commander of al Qaeda in the Arabian Peninsula (Porges 2011, 55). A recent *Washington Post* report detailed that a staggering 111 of the 532 Guantanamo detainees released as of March 2016 returned to terrorism. A Pentagon official confirmed in the report that Americans had died at the hands of these ex-detainees. Of the 111 released detainees, 57 are still alive and fighting—the rest were killed or captured (Lamothe 2016).

Of course, the Guantanamo detainees were not part of any Saudi-style rehabilitation program. Instead, they were subject to harsh treatment tantamount to torture (Wikileaks.org 2011). As previously argued, torture is certainly one method for managing terrorism suspects, but rehabilitation seems to provide better results for a variety of reasons. Torture rallies jihadists against the torturing country, demonizes the country that does the torturing among its friends as well as its enemies, makes attacks against the torturing country more justified in the eyes of extremists and perhaps others, and serves no rehabilitative purpose.

The most common methods for managing prisons so as to quell jihadism are summarized in Table 14.1.

Drones as an Alternative to Imprisonment?

Although perhaps seeming outside the scope of this chapter, drone strikes have been used by the United States, and increasingly other countries, as an alternative to imprisoning jihadists. Killing these people clearly limits their ability to proselytize, so to some drone strikes may be a simpler and better solution than imprisoning jihadists at all. With drone strikes, there is no worry that potential jihadists will radicalize or that terrorists will recidivate.

Like torture, drone strikes do not provide the same benefits to inmates and governments seeking public order that rehabilitation and other detention programs do. Although detention programs surely have their problems, and

Table 14.1 Prisoner Management Solutions to Jihadism

Country	Approach	Successful?
Saudi Arabia, Singapore, Philippines, and Sri Lanka	Deradicalization and reintegration into society	Saudis claim 80% to 90% success rate, *but* Saudi's exportation of official Wahhabist ideology foments radicalization; no data from Philippines; Singapore has seen anecdotal success; evidence of militants who went through rehabilitation programs in Sri Lanka reducing their support for armed struggle
Yemen	Deradicalization only (no reintegration program)	Program failed with militants returning to al Qaeda
Israel	Incentives and attempts at rehabilitation	Effectiveness confounded by ongoing conflict with Palestinians, which reduces inmates desire to change
France, the Netherlands, the United Kingdom, and Belgium, among others	Segregation of jihadist prisoners	Unclear due to lack of data and newness of policy in places like the United Kingdom, but problem clearly persists in Europe; segregated "terrorism wings" may be incubators for jihadist planning
United States	Isolation in solitary confinement (Guantanamo, Supermax, etc.)	High failure rate as 111 former Guantanamo detainees have returned to terrorism

abuses within detention facilities fan the flames of extremism, the opaque, extrajudicial killing of terror suspects has even more negatives than torture and has become a critical counterterrorism tool. After Israel was repeatedly condemned for its targeted killing campaign of Palestinians during the second intifada (Toensing & Urbina 2003), one would have thought that the world did not have the appetite for extrajudicial killings of terrorist suspects. However, the Barack Obama administration has made drone strikes an all-too-common element of their antiterrorism arsenal. The British Bureau of Investigative Journalism reports that two British nationals whose citizenship was revoked were soon after killed by U.S. drones (Macklin 2014, 8). The United States has even engaged in drone strikes against its own citizens. These included the targeted assassination of Anwar al-Awlaki and Sameer Khan in

Yemen, the killing of Jude Kenan Mohamed in Pakistan, and the assassination of Kemal Dawish and Abdulrahman al-Awlaki who were killed in separate strikes in Yemen. Another American, Warren Weinstein, was inadvertently killed by a drone strike. The U.S. government—in a 2011 secret memo—detailed their legal justifications for these strikes (Taylor 2015). This is despite an executive order prohibiting assassinations carried out by American personnel (Scahill 2016, 2).

As Jo Becker and Scott Shane observe, "Drones have replaced Guantánamo as the recruiting tool of choice for militants; in his 2010 guilty plea, Faisal Shahzad, who had tried to set off a car bomb in Times Square, justified targeting civilians by telling the judge, 'When the drones hit, they don't see children'" (Becker & Shane 2012). The United States has carried out more than 400 drone strikes in countries like Pakistan, Yemen, and Iraq, which has resulted in thousands of deaths many of which are innocent civilians. "The proliferating mistakes have given drones a sinister reputation in Pakistan and Yemen and have provoked a powerful anti-American backlash in the Muslim world. Part of the collateral damage in the strikes has been Mr. Obama's dream of restoring the United States' reputation with Muslims around the globe" (Shane 2015). Drone strikes and the killing of terrorist suspects certainly have their place—some terrorists may be impossible to neutralize otherwise and others may be too dangerous or difficult to capture. Still, the wanton use of targeted killings of terror suspects kills innocent civilians while providing a recruiting platform for jihadists. For these reasons, prison is the better option.

Political Solutions

Aside from prison management solutions, rehabilitation, and drone strikes, the political conditions that lead people to radicalize must be examined. Moving inmates from one cell block to another or isolating them in ever-more-elaborate prisons ignores the very real fact that these solutions deal with symptoms but not the root cause of the problem. People turn to jihadist groups for many reasons, some of which include decades of dictatorial government in the Middle East coupled with the quashing of religious expression. Conflicts in the region have further exacerbated the problem as the so-called Arab Spring and American military interventions have combined to leave chaotic regions full of internecine warfare where the countries Syria, Yemen, Iraq, and Libya once stood. As seen in the Israeli case, reprogramming Palestinian radicals would surely work better if they did not have very real grievances that pushed them toward radical ideologies. As Marisa Porges underlines, "relying on recidivism figures largely ignores the political and social context in which a deradicalization program operates and the security environment into which a program releases graduates" (Porges 2011, 55).

Although peace between warring parties and a more stable Middle East look unlikely in the near-term, short-term political solutions can include reforms in the Middle East and elsewhere that lead to better treatment of citizens, the enforcement of human rights for prisoners, and the eradication of torture. Saudi Arabia could also work to tone down some of the messages it spreads through its Wahhabist faith, such as those that are intolerant toward non-Muslims and Shi'as (Frontline 2016). Small steps towards liberalization, civil rights, and participatory politics in the Middle East and North Africa will also certainly help. So will greater integration and acceptance of Muslim immigrants in the West, especially given the historic immigrant waves coming to Europe from Afghanistan, Syria, Eritrea, and elsewhere.

Conclusion

Stopping terrorist radicalization has become a critical security issue in the 21st century. As many terrorists group together and radicalize in prison, breaking the prison-jihadism pipeline is an important piece of the counter-terrorism fight. Understanding how and why radicalization occurs in prison is important—as is understanding why people radicalize on the outside.

Examining the issue from the American perspective, a recent Institute for Social Policy and Understanding report provides some important insights, finding that "despite the existence of an estimated 350,000 Muslim prisoners, there is little evidence of widespread radicalization or successful foreign recruitment" in the American prison system (SpearIt 2013, 5). Despite Islam being the fastest growing religion in U.S. prisons, as 80 percent of prison conversions are conversions to the Muslim faith, the report holds that radicalization among the American Muslim prison population is rare and, even when it occurs, may not lead to violence (SpearIt 2013, 6, 9). It goes on to argue that Muslim inmates in the United States need better religious accommodations, such as more and better Islamic chaplains and better reentry programs (SpearIt 2013, 39–42). Finally, the report contends that religion is a net-positive for inmates and Muslim inmates are more likely to have their rights infringed on than to infringe on the rights of others (SpearIt 2013, 12, 14–15, 17).

Although it is true that we should never conflate Islam with radicalism or jihadism, and that the vast majority of Muslims are nonviolent people, the same conundrum faces security forces inside and outside of prison. Muslim radicals are viewed as a particularly noxious threat in many countries all over the world—be they Boko Haram in Nigeria, Al Shabaab in Somalia, Chechen separatists in Russia, or Islamic State operatives in France, Belgium, or Turkey. People the world over point to horrible attacks, some of which were carried out by people radicalized in prison, such as the 2015 attacks in Paris, the 2016 attacks in Brussels and Turkey, and similar recent attacks in Tunisia, Jordan, Iraq, Syria, Afghanistan, and elsewhere.

In many places, governments have sullied entire populations by accusing their people of harboring terrorists—a label that can lead to a person losing all of his or her rights including the right to life, due process, and citizenship (Ahmed 2013; Macklin 2014). Jihadist radicalization, such as what occurred in the cases of Abdel Zaben, Abdelhamid Abaaoud, Abu Musab al-Zarqawi, and many others, cannot be easily stopped in such a context where Muslims feel threatened and attacked. Political solutions are necessary in conjunction with using best practices in inmate management to quell the problem.

Holistic deradicalization programs that work to reintegrate, rather than reprogram, individuals seem to have the most promise for stopping the pipeline from prison to jihad. Other methods such as segregation of those convicted of terrorist crimes, and in extreme cases isolation, may be necessary in conjunction with rehabilitation plans. Belgium's approach, for instance, to radicalization in prison has been a mix of two elements: the first is to segregate the jihadist prisoners from the general population and the second is to improve prison conditions. Improvements include reducing overcrowding and providing more services, including religious, psychological, and educational, for Muslim prisoners (Mufson 2016). Torture, drone strikes, and the open-ended housing of jihadist inmates in detention centers cannot be recommended due to their heavy drawbacks.

Critical criminology shows us that social factors are the most important ones in determining whether or not people will turn to jihadism. To this end, political solutions, in the Middle East and in the Muslim diaspora, are necessary for giving Muslims hope and better life opportunities that will ultimately make jihadism appear to be an unwise path. As seen in the Saudi case, providing opportunities, such as jobs, is critical to eradicating jihadism as a belief system inside and outside of prisons. Better integrating Muslims into European societies is also a necessary component of any solution. Although prisons need to reduce overcrowding, provide all inmates with greater care, cater more to Muslim inmates, end prisoner abuse, and work to rehabilitate jihadists, prison management solutions alone are not going to stop jihadism from rising inside or outside of detention facilities. Political solutions that give young Muslims hope and employment that integrate Muslims into Western societies and that liberalize the Middle East will ultimately be the factors that break the prison-jihadism pipeline.

Bibliography

Ahmed, Akbar. *The Thistle and the Drone: How America's War on Terror Became a Global War on Tribal Islam*. Washington, DC: Brookings Institution Press, 2013.

Allen, Bud, & Diane Costa. *Games Criminals Play: How You Can Profit from Knowing Them*. Roseville, CA: Rae John, 1981.

Amnesty International. "Entombed: Isolation in the U.S. Federal Prison System," *Amnesty International Report,* July 2014, http://www.amnestyusa.org/sites/default/files/amr510402014en.pdf.

Atran, Scott. "The Romance of Terror," *The Guardian*, July 19, 2010, https://www.theguardian.com/commentisfree/belief/2010/jul/19/terrorism-radical-religion.

Ballas, Dennis. "FBI—Prisoner Radicalization," *FBI Law Enforcement Bulletin*, October 2010, https://leb.fbi.gov/2010/october/prisoner-radicalization.

BBC News. "Paris Attacks: Who Were the Attackers?" April 17, 2016, http://www.bbc.com/news/world-europe-34832512.

Becker, Jo, & Scott Shane. "Secret 'Kill List' Proves a Test of Obama's Principles and Will," *The New York Times*, May 29, 2012, http://www.nytimes.com/2012/05/29/world/obamas-leadership-in-war-on-al-qaeda.html.

Bell, W. Kamau. "United Shades of America: Behind the Bars of San Quentin," CNN video, April 26, 2016.

Birnbaum, Michael. "French Prisons, Long Hotbeds of Radical Islam, Get New Scrutiny after Paris Attacks," *The Washington Post*, January 28, 2015.

Bisserbe, Noemi. "European Prisons Fueling Spread of Islamic Radicalism," *The Wall Street Journal*, July 31, 2016, http://www.wsj.com/articles/european-prisons-fueling-spread-of-islamic-radicalism-1470001491.

Borum, Randy. "Radicalization into Violent Extremism I: A Review of Social Science Theories," *Journal of Strategic Security* 4, no. 4 (Winter 2011): 7–36.

Bouchaud, Melodie. "A French Jail Is Trying to Halt Radicalization by Isolating 'Radical Muslim' Prisoners Together," *Vice News*, November 14, 2014.

CBS News. "Alleged Paris Mastermind Transformed in Prison, Father Says," 1November 18, 2015, http://www.cbsnews.com/news/who-is-isis-paris-attacks-mastermind-abdelhamid-abaaoud.

Chrisafis, Angelique. " 'Nothing's Changed': 10 years after French Riots, Banlieus Remain in Crisis," *The Guardian*, October 22, 2015, https://www.theguardian.com/world/2015/oct/22/nothings-changed-10-years-after-french-riots-banlieues-remain-in-crisis.

Cilluffo, Frank, Sharon Cardash, & Andrew Whitehead. "Radicalization: Behind Bars and beyond Borders," *The Brown Journal of World Affairs* 13, no. 2 (Spring 2007): 113–122.

Clemmer, Donald. *The Prison Community*. New York: Holt, Rinehart and Winston, 1958.

Dalton, Matthew. "Abdelhamid Abaaoud Had Been Arrested Multiple Times in Belgium," *The Wall Street Journal*, November 17, 2015, http://www.wsj.com/articles/abaaoud-seemed-to-put-life-of-crime-behind-him-lawyer-says-1447965540.

Demant, Froukje, & Beatrice De Graaf. "How to Counter Radical Narratives: Dutch Deradicalization Policy in the Case of Moluccan and Islamic Radicals," *Studies in Conflict & Terrorism* 33, no. 5 (2010): 408–428.

De Winter, Leon. "Europe's Muslims Hate the West," *Politico*, March 29, 2016, http://www.politico.eu/article/brussels-attacks-terrorism-europe-muslims -brussels-attacks-airport-metro.

Dugas, Michelle, & Arie Kruglanski. "The Quest for Significance Model of Radi- calization: Implications for the Management of Terrorist Detainees," *Behav- ioral Sciences and Law* 32 (2014): 423–439.

Dunleavy, Patrick T. *The Fertile Soil of Jihad: Terrorism's Prison Connection*. Wash- ington, DC: Potomac Books, 2011.

The Economist, "Why Prisoners Join Gangs," *The Economist*, November 12, 2014, http://www.economist.com/blogs/economist-explains/2014/11/economist -explains-7.

The Economist, "Learning to Live with It," *The Economist*, September 3, 2016, http://www.economist.com/news/international/21706250-people-are -surprisingly-good-coping-repeated-terrorist-attacks-america-and.

Faiola, Anthony, & Souad Mekhenet. "The Islamic State Creates a New Type of Jihadist: Part Terrorist, Part Gangster," *The Washington Post*, December 20, 2015, https://www.washingtonpost.com/world/europe/the-islamic-state -creates-a-new-type-of-jihadist-part-terrorist-part-gangster/2015/12/20 /1a3d65da-9bae-11e5-aca6-1ae3be6f06d2_story.html.

Frontline. "Saudi Arabia Uncovered," PBS.org, March 29,- 2016, http://www.pbs .org/wgbh/frontline/film/saudi-arabia-uncovered.

Ganor, Boaz, & Ophir Falk. "De-Radicalization in Israel's Prison System," *Studies in Conflict and Terrorism* 36 (2013): 116–131.

Hackett, Conrad. "Five Facts about the Muslim Population in Europe," Pew Research Center, November 17, 2015, http://www.pewresearch.org/fact -tank/2015/11/17/5-facts-about-the-muslim-population-in-europe.

Haddad, Benjamin. "France's Forever War," *Foreign Policy*, November 17, 2015, http://foreignpolicy.com/2015/11/17/france-syria-isis-hollande-assad. Hall, Benjamin. "UK to Fight Prison Radicalization by Isolating Known Jihad- ists," *FoxNews.com*, September 3, 2016, http://www.foxnews.com/world /2016/09/03/uk-to-fight-prison-radicalization-by-isolating-known-jihadists .html.

Hamm, Mark. "Terrorist Recruitment in American Correctional Institutions: An Exploratory Study of Non-Traditional Faith Groups," National Institute of Justice Final Report, December 2007, https://www.ncjrs.gov/pdffiles1/nij /grants/220957.pdf.

Hamm, Mark. *The Spectacular Few: Prisoner Radicalization and the Evolving Terror- ist Threat*. New York: New York University Press, 2013.

Hanna, Greg, Lindsay Clutterbuck, & Jennifer Rubin. "Radicalization or Rehabilita- tion: Understanding the Challenge of Extremist and Radicalized Prisoners," RAND Europe: RAND Technical Report 2008, http://www.RAND.org /content/dam/RAND/pubs/technical_reports/2008/RAND_TR571.pdf.

Haugbolle, Sune. "The Victim's Tale in Syria: Imprisonment, Individualism and Liberalism." In Laleh Khalili& Jillian Schwedler (Eds.), *Policing and*

Prisons in the Middle East: Formations of Coercion (pp. 223–240). London: Hurst, 2010.

Hickey, Jennifer. "Ripe for Radicalization: Federal Prisons 'Breeding Grounds' for Terrorism, Say Experts," *FoxNews.com*, January 5, 2016, http://www .foxnews.com/us/2016/01/05/ripe-for-radicalization-federal-prisons -breeding-ground-for-terrorists-say-experts.html.

Higgins, Andrew, and Kimiko Freytas-Timuras. "An ISIS Militant from Belgium Whose Own Family Wanted Him Dead," *The New York Times*, November 17, 2015, http://www.nytimes.com/2015/11/18/world/europe/paris-attacks -abdelhamid-abaaoud-an-isis-militant-from-belgium-whose-own-family -wanted-him-dead.html.

"Iraq Body Count." Iraqbodycount.org, retrieved on November 11, 2016, https:// www.iraqbodycount.org.

Jackson, George. *Soledad Brother: The Prison Letters of George Jackson*. Chicago: Chicago Review Press, 1994.

Jenkins, Brian. "Building an Army of Believers: Jihadist Radicalization and Recruitment, Testimony to the House Homeland Security Committee," RAND Corporation, April 5, 2007, http://www.rand.org/content/dam/rand/pubs /testimonies/2007/RAND_CT278-1.pdf.

Jones, Clarke R., & Resurrecion S. Morales. "Integration versus Segregation: A Preliminary Examination of Philippine Correctional Facilities for De-Radicalization," *Studies in Conflict & Terrorism* 35 (2012): 211–228.

Khalili, Laleh, & Jillian Schwedler (Eds.). *Policing and Prisons in the Middle East: Formations of Coercion*. London: Hurst, 2010.

Kilpatrick, David. "Named Egypt's Winner, Islamist Makes History," *The New York Times*, June 24, 2012, http://www.nytimes.com/2012/06/25/world/middle east/mohamed-morsi-of-muslim-brotherhood-declared-as-egypts -president.html?_r=0.

Khosrokhavar, Farhad. "Radicalization in Prison: The French Case," *Politics, Religion & Ideology* 14, no. 2 (2013): 284–306.

Khosrokhavar, Farhad. "The Mill of Muslim Radicalism in France," *The New York Times*, January 26, 2015.

Lamothe, Dan. "Pentagon Official: Release of Guantanamo Detainees Has Led to American Deaths," *The Washington Post*, March 23, 2016, https://www .washingtonpost.com/news/checkpoint/wp/2016/03/23/pentagon-official -release-of-guantanamo-detainees-has-led-to-american-deaths.

Lapidus, Ira M. *Contemporary Islamic Movements in the Historical Perspective*. Policy Papers in International Affairs, Number 18. Berkeley, CA: University of California Press, 1983.

Leiken, Robert S. "Europe's Angry Muslims," *Foreign Affairs*, July/August 2005, http://www.cfr.org/religion/europes-angry-muslims/p8218.

Lewis, Kayleigh. "Netherlands Bans Export of Kosher and Halal Meat to 'Minimise' Negative Effects on Animal Welfare," *The Independent* (UK), February 18, 2016, http://www.independent.co.uk/news/world/europe/nether

lands-bans-export-of-kosher-and-halal-meat-to-minimise-negative-effects
-on-animal-welfare-a6881406.html.

Lynch, Michael J. "Critical Criminology," February 2010, Oxford Bibliographies, http://www.oxfordbibliographies.com/view/document/obo-97801953 96607/obo-9780195396607-0064.xml.

Macklin, Audrey. "Citizenship Revocation, the Privilege to Have Rights and the Production of the Alien," *Queen's Law Journal* 40, no. 1 (2014): 1–54.

Martin, Clarence Augustus (Gus Martin). *Essentials of Terrorism: Concepts and Controversies* (4th ed.). Thousand Oaks, CA: Sage, 2016.

McCants, William. *The ISIS Apocalypse: The History, Strategy and Doomsday Vision of the Islamic State.* New York: St. Martin's Press, 2015.

Merari, Ariel. *Driven to Death: Psychological and Social Aspects of Suicide Terrorism.* Oxford, UK: Oxford University Press, 2010.

Mohamed, Besheer. "A New Estimate of the US Muslim Population," Pew Research Center, January 6, 2016, http://www.pewresearch.org/fact-tank/2016/01 /06/a-new-estimate-of-the-u-s-muslim-population.

Mufson, Steven. "How Belgian Prisons Became a Breeding Ground for Islamic Extremism," *The Washington Post*, March 27, 2016.

Mulcahy, Elizabeth, Shannon Merrington, & Peter Bell. "The Radicalisation of Prison Inmates: Exploring Recruitment, Religion and Prisoner Vulnerability," *Journal of Human Security* 9, no. 1 (March 2013): 4–14.

Murphy, Kim. "Islamic Party Wins Power in Algeria," *The Los Angeles Times*, December 28, 1991, http://articles.latimes.com/1991-12-28/news/mn-810 _1_islamic-front.

Nawaz, Maajid. "It's High Time for Prisons within Prisons to Hold Jihadists," *The Daily Beast*, September 5, 2016, http://www.thedailybeast.com/articles /2016/09/05/it-s-high-time-for-prisons-within-prisons-to-hold-jihadists .html.

NBC News. "Swiss OK Ban on New Minarets," *NBC News*, November 29, 2009, http://www.nbcnews.com/id/34191036/ns/world_news-europe/t/swiss -approve-ban-new-minarets/#.WCYXti0rKpo.

Pape, Robert, & James Feldman. *Cutting the Fuse: The Explosion of Global Suicide Terrorism and How to Stop It.* Chicago: University of Chicago Press, 2010.

Pinker, Steven. *The Better Angels of Our Nature: Why Violence Has Declined.* New York: Penguin Books, 2011.

Porges, Marisa L. "Reform School for Radicals," *The American Interest* 6, no. 6 (2011): 50–56.

Rascoff, Samuel J. "Establishing Official Islam? The Law and Strategy of Counter-Radicalization," *Stanford Law Review* 64, no. 1 (February 2012): 125–190.

Reidel, Bruce. *The Search for Al Qaeda: The Leadership, Ideology and Future.* Washington, DC: Brookings Institution Press, 2010.

Rubin, Gabriel. *Freedom and Order: How Democratic Governments Restrict Civil Liberties after Terrorist Attacks—and Why Sometimes They Don't.* Lanham, MD: Lexington Books, 2011.

Sageman, Marc. *Leaderless Jihad: Terror Networks in the Twenty-First Century.* Philadelphia: University of Pennsylvania Press, 2008.

Sahadi, Jeanne. "The Cost of Fighting Terrorism," *CNN.com,* November 16, 2015, http://money.cnn.com/2015/11/16/news/economy/cost-of-fighting -terrorism.

Scahill, Jeremy. *The Assassination Complex: Inside the Government's Secret Drone Warfare Program.* New York: Simon & Schuster, 2016.

Scheuer, Michael. *Imperial Hubris: Why the West Is Losing the War on Terror.* Washington, DC: Potomac Books, 2004.

Schrag, Clarence. "Leadership among Prison Inmates," *American Sociological Review* 3 (Fall 1960): 11–16.

Shane, Scott. "Drone Strikes Reveal Uncomfortable Truth: U.S. Is Often Unsure about Who Will Die," *The New York Times,* April 24, 2015, http://www .nytimes.com/2015/04/24/world/asia/drone-strikes-reveal-uncomfortable -truth-us-is-often-unsure-about-who-will-die.html?_r=1.

Smale, Alison. "Germany, Like France, Questions Place of Veils in Its Society," *The New York Times,* August 19, 2016, http://www.nytimes.com/2016/08 /20/world/europe/germany-face-veils-burqa.html?_r=0.

Spearlt. "Facts and Fictions about Islam in Prison: Assessing Prisoner Radicalization in Post-9/11 America," Technical Report, Institute for Social Policy and Understanding, January 2013, http://www.ispu.org/pdfs/ISPU _Report_Prison_Spearlt_WEB.pdf.

Spearlt. "Spectacular or Specious? A Critical Review of *The Spectacular Few*: Prisoner Radicalization and the Evolving Terror Threat," *Thurgood Marshall Law Review* 39, no. 2 (2014): 225–244.

Sykes, Gresham. *The Society of Captives.* Princeton, NJ: Princeton University Press, 1958.

Taylor, Adam. "America Keeps Killing Citizens in Drone Strikes, Mostly by Accident," *Washington Post,* April 23, 2015, https://www.washingtonpost.com /news/worldviews/wp/2015/04/23/the-u-s-keeps-killing-americans-in -drone-strikes-mostly-by-accident.

Thomas, Jim, & Barbara Zaitzow. "Conning or Conversion? The Role of Religion in Prison Coping," *The Prison Journal* 86 (2004): 242–259.

Till, Brain, "A Note on Egyptian Torture," *The Atlantic,* February 1, 2011, http:// www.theatlantic.com/international/archive/2011/02/a-note-on-egyptian -torture/70476.

Toensing, Chris, & Ian Urbina. "Israel, the US and 'Targeted Killings,'" MERIP: Middle East Research and Information Project, February 17, 2003, http:// merip.org/mero/mero021703.

Veldhuis, Tinka M., & Siegwart Lindenberg. "Limits of Tolerance under Pressure: A Case Study of Dutch Terrorist Detention Policy," *Critical Studies on Terrorism* 5, no. 3 (2012): 425–443.

Walker, Peter, & Matthew Taylor. "Far Right on Rise in Europe, Says Report," *The Guardian,* 2011. Accessed on November 23, 2015, https://www.theguardian .com/world/2011/nov/06/far-right-rise-europe-report.

Weiss, Michael, & Hassan Hassan. *ISIS: Inside the Army of Terror.* New York: Regan Arts, 2015.

Welch, Michael. *Corrections: A Critical Approach.* New York: McGraw-Hill, 1995.

Welch, Michael. "Critical Criminology, Social Justice and an Alternative View to Incarceration," *Critical Criminology* 7, no. 2 (September 1996): 43–58.

Wikileaks.org. 2011. "The Guantanamo Files," https://wikileaks.org/gitmo.

Wilson, Scott, "Hamas Sweeps Palestinian Elections, Complicating Peace Efforts in Mideast," *The Washington Post*, January 26, 2006, http://www.washington post.com/wp-dyn/content/article/2006/01/26/AR2006012600372.html.

Wright, Lawrence. *The Looming Tower: Al Qaeda and the Road to 9/11.* New York: Vintage, 2007.

CHAPTER FIFTEEN

Orthodox Judaism as a Pathway to Desistance: A Study of Religion and Reentry in Israeli Prisons[†]

Elly Teman and Michal Morag

What tools does Judaism offer for prisoners on the pathway to desistance? What makes Jewish religious programs promote for the desistance of Israeli prisoners unique, and is there a core that can be extracted from this model that can be implemented toward other religious programs for the incarcerated? An extensive body of evidence has accumulated on religion-based programs within prisons and their effect on the reform of the incarcerated (Camp et al. 2008; Clear & Sumter 2002; Duwe & Johnson 2013; Johnson 2004; Mears et al. 2006; O'Connor & Perreyclear 2002;). Nevertheless, most of this scholarship focuses on prisons in the United States, with little attention

[†].**Acknowledgments:** The authors would like to thank first and foremost Rabbi Avinoam Cohen for his interest, support, and help with this project, as well as his staff at the TRP. We would also like to thank our three student research assistants: Tomer Poran, Mor Mutsafi, and Shlomit Tako. This project was made possible with the support of a faculty research grant from Ruppin Academic Center and the ethical approval of the research department of Israel's Prisoner Rehabilitation Authority.

devoted to faith-based prisoner rehabilitation programs in other countries. The scholarship primarily addresses the most popular religions in U.S. prisons—Evangelical Christianity and Islam—with little attention to religions that are less frequently represented (Hanley 2015). To date, only one researcher has explored the world of prisoner rehabilitation within the Jewish faith in Israel (Timor 1997, 1998; Timor & Landau 1998).

The research on religion in prison has revealed benefits of religiosity within the prison environment that are common beyond the specific characteristics of different religions (Aday et al. 2014; Clear et al. 2000; Dammer 2002; Hallett et al. 2016; Kerley & Copes 2009; Maruna et al. 2006; Santos & Lane 2013;). One of these benefits is the soothing and comforting effects of belief in a higher power and the feeling of purpose or meaning in life (Clear et al. 2000; Dammer 2002). Studies also suggest that religious involvement of prisoners can improve prisoner welfare by serving as a psychological coping mechanism, preventing dehumanization and devaluation, and fostering survival (Clear et al. 2000). Along these lines, the function of religious networks in prison has been compared to gang affiliations, as both are forms of subcultures that provide inmates with a way to deal with the emotional isolation of imprisonment and the feeling of being unsafe and at risk; both also enhance access to resources and promote a sense of solidarity and higher purpose (Thomas & Zaitzow 2006).

It has been suggested that religion in prison has intrinsic benefits: it can ease the process of an inmate's psychological adjustment to imprisonment, help to manage or reduce shame and guilt, help prisoners regain their dignity, improve self-esteem, and identify a positive horizon. It can also have extrinsic benefits such as enhanced safety, better access to material comforts, and increased access to visitors (Clear & Myhre 1995; Clear et al. 2000). Others suggest that religion in prison has social benefits that include strengthening prisoners' social networks and providing emotional support (Kerley et al. 2006; Kerley & Copes 2009). From an institutional standpoint, some of the research has concluded that religious practice within prison helps to control inmate behavior (Rowell et al. 1987).

In our study of Jewish faith-based rehabilitation in Israel, we found similar benefits to those outlined in the studies noted above. However, we also identified unique benefits of the rituals, symbols, theological doctrine, and structure of the Jewish religion that added to the men's positive process of desistance. In the following study, we focus on a religious program for promoting desistance that is based on a strict religious doctrine rather than spirituality in a general sense. As Sumter (2006, 524) notes, much of the scholarship on religion in prison does not distinguish between spirituality and religion, the multiple dimensions of religion nor the variety of aspects of religiousness beyond participation. Hallett and Johnson (2014) add that the scholarship does not look in depth at specific elements of religiosity and their connection to desistance.

Following this line of argument, the present chapter aims to discuss a formal religious program for prisoners and released convicts based on strict doctrine and the specific elements of Judaism that may promote desistance. First, we begin with a short introduction to Judaism and the particular tradition embraced within prison. Next, we discuss Jewish faith-based programs within the Israeli prison system and the religious reentry program administered by the Israeli Prisoner Rehabilitation Authority. Finally, we explore the elements of the religious program that our interviewees found meaningful. We believe that the Jewish-Israeli case provides an important comparative case to the Christian and Islamic cases of the American-focused scholarship, and may extend the scholarly discussions of the impact of religion on adjustment to prison and on criminal desistance following reentry.

A Note on Judaism and the Path of Religious Strengthening

In order to explore the world of Jewish tools for desistance in prison and upon reentry, it is important to explain first that Judaism is not a singular category. Orthodox Jewish society in Israel includes a plurality of communities, each with its own level of religious observance and influenced by the teachings of its own rabbis. Distinguished from the more liberally oriented Conservative and Reform branches of modern Jewry, orthodox Judaism follows a more strict interpretation of religious law and observance based on the five books of Moses (the Torah) and a broad spectrum of rabbinic literature, commentary, and rulings (Teman, Ivry, & Bernhardt 2011).

There are strong divisions within the orthodox world between "modern orthodox" and "ultra-orthodox" affiliations. In simplified terms, the former is more open to synthesizing their religious observance into the secular world, and the latter reject modern secular culture. Within the ultra-orthodox world, there are many different groups with differing theological orientations, including Hassidic communities that embrace Jewish mysticism, known as Kabala (Ivry, Teman, & Frumkin 2011). There are also strong differences between ultra-orthodox groups based on ethnic origin—Middle Eastern Sephardicversus Eastern European Ashkenazi communities—as well as political inclination, including openness to Israel's statehood, openness to secular knowledge, and willingness to integrate into modern society (Friedman 1991; Ivry et al. 2011).

The type of religion practiced within Israeli prisons cannot, however, be definitively placed among these categories. Rabbis who administer the religious programs within these institutions would probably define themselves as ultra-orthodox, but they are not all from the same sector nor are they homogenous in their religious affiliation. Moreover, prisoners who participate in religious programming often embrace religion without strictly defining themselves among these categories. However, they do seem to connect strongly to the teachings of the Breslav Hassidic sect, as we explain further on.

Becoming increasingly orthodox within the Jewish faith is regarded in the Israeli public sphere as "return" [*hazara betshuva*], largely referring to non-religious Jews becoming observant. It is also regarded as "religious strengthening" or "religious invigoration" [*hitchazkut*], referring to a strengthening in belief and intensification of performance of religious practices in daily life (Leon & Lavie 2013) in a less strictly observant way. These terms are often used alternately, but both are differentiated from the term for religious conversion [*giyur*], which infers converting to Judaism from a different religion.

To be recognized as an orthodox Jew one must adopt a fully committed lifestyle to fulfilling the 613 commandments, including 248 positive commandments (the dos) and 365 negative commandments (the don'ts) that direct observant Jews on every aspect of their daily lives. These commandments include, but are not limited to: diet (not to eat nonkosher foods or milk with meat, for instance), when to bathe, when to shave, when it is permitted to have sexual relations, and how to observe the Sabbath (not to use electricity, not to work, etc.). Moreover, religious Jews have a support network for making decisions; they rely on the guidance of rabbis, who themselves interpret rabbinical texts. Thus, there is always a source to ask any question and to direct one's actions in accordance with the religious rules. In this way, the burden of making decisions completely on one's own is replaced by the firm rules and external mechanisms of religious decision making (see, e.g., Ivry 2010).

Regarding embracing religion in prison, it is thus important to distinguish the path of return or religious strengthening from mere participation in religious programming. A Jewish prisoner can indeed participate in bible study classes and Jewish ethics discussions with rabbis and orthodox seminary students without adopting the identity of a "religious" man and thus without committing fully to observing these restrictions and commandments. Indeed, approximately one-fourth of Jewish Israeli prisoners currently participate in religious seminary study groups while incarcerated. The Torah study programs [*midrashiot*] have become so popular within the prison system that they have expanded threefold since 2007 and now teach approximately 1,200 out of 4,500 incarcerated Jewish men (Presentation at Dekel Prison, June 9, 2016).

Incarcerated Jewish men who wish to progress a step further in their commitment to a religious way of life can ask to be transferred to a special ward designed for religious prisoners who are committed to keeping the strict rules of religious observance and are willing to give up the benefits of living in a secular ward, such as watching television and turning on the lights on the

Sabbath and Jewish holidays. According to Timor (1998), special wards for religious prisoners have existed in Israel's prisons since the early 1980s. In recent years, these wards have become more popular, expanding from three to six wards in the past five years (2010–2015).

Just as there are different degrees of orthodoxy within the orthodox population at large, these wards include three that are less strictly orthodox, comprised mainly of inmates who have embraced a more religious lifestyle after incarceration—and three that are for strictly ultra-orthodox prisoners, who were religious before imprisonment. All of these wards have a social worker in charge of the therapeutic aspects of counseling prisoners as well as a rabbi in charge of the religious guidance of the inmates. The wards are all reportedly at full capacity and some even have waiting lists; additional wards have not resulted from a larger proportion of crimes being committed or reported in the ultra-orthodox population, but from the increasing number of prisoners who have embraced religion within prison (interview with two prison rabbis, May 3, 2015).

Prisoners who decide to commit to continuing a religious way of life upon release from prison can apply for admission to a Jewish religious rehabilitation program. The Torah Rehabilitation Program (TRP), established in 2004, is part of Israel's Prisoner Rehabilitation Authority. The program is administered under the direction of a staff of orthodox Jewish correctional officers, and its main purpose is to support and assist released religious prisoners during reentry to civilian life through Torah study alongside other rehabilitative efforts, such as occupational and educational programs. We discuss this program fully elsewhere (Morag & Teman n.d.). There is a close and consistent collaboration between the TRP and the religious staff within the prisons. They work together to decide who are suitable candidates for the TRP—those who are "sincere," in Dammer's (2002) terms, in their commitment to a religious way of life—and to structure a personal reentry plan for each participant.

Method

The present chapter is based on 30 qualitative, semistructured interviews, carried out between 2013 and 2014, with 29 men who had been released from prison between two months and five years earlier into the TRP (one man was interviewed twice, having requested to be interviewed again after nine months from the first interview). The men ranged in age from 22 to 50 with an average age of 30 years old. None of the men were religiously observant before their first incarceration. The men were incarcerated for a wide range of crimes, including manslaughter, robbery, membership in a gang, drug dealing, money laundering, and tax evasion. Further details of the methodology of this study and of the interview sample are published elsewhere (Morag & Teman n.d.).

The study was approved by the ethics committee of the Prisoner Rehabilitation Authority. The interviews were conducted by three student research assistants (one man and two women). All of the interviews were digitally recorded with the consent of the interviewee and transcribed. All interviews were coded using grounded theory by the two lead researchers. Applying a modified model of the grounded theory process outlined by Glaser and Strauss (1967), we coded the data for emergent themes through stages of this process until a theoretical framework emerged. In the following, we take an interpretive approach toward uncovering the unique tools the interviewees spoke of that the Jewish religion offers in promoting desistance. We also examine the effect of the rituals, symbols, language, and structure of Judaism on modifying the behavior, beliefs, and values of repentant prisoners within prison and upon reentry to society.

Religious Restrictions and Moral Framework in Judaism

The first aspect of Jewish faith-based programs in Israel that differentiates the Jewish path to desistance from other faith-based programs is that it instantly provides the repentant prisoner with a "rulebook" of strict and elaborate strictures for day-to-day life. As Clear and colleagues (2000) note, the major religions provide certainty to prisoners because they are like total systems for living. For our interviewees, becoming religious provided them with a structured, clear framework of rules for proper behavior. For these men, who expressed difficulty coping with free choice, religious rules are interpreted as a boundary within which they can contain themselves and that they voluntarily impose on themselves, as explained by Adam: "Religion forbids doing these things, and I know that religion forbids it. If I do them, then I'm breaking the rules. My mind takes me straight to religion, what is allowed, what is forbidden." As noted above, when there are 613 commandments that spell out exactly how an observant Jew should behave in daily life, then religious observance leaves minimal room for dilemma.

The choice to impose on themselves a series of restrictions is indeed limiting, but they perceive it as a source of relief because they are excused from the necessity of making independent decisions. For our interviewees, the guidance provided by religious life was especially important since they mistrusted themselves in knowing how to make the "right decisions" in daily life and how to self-regulate their behavior (Kerley & Copes 2009). Religion provided them with an answer to every question and a guideline for every deed. Abraham compared his path of religious strengthening in the prison's religious ward and his reentry through the TRP to the path of nonreligious inmates:

> We have restrictions here, what is allowed, and what is forbidden, so you can become more religious and leave here . . . They (his fellow men in the TRP) get along, because the Torah tells them what is allowed and what is

forbidden. (In the general rehabilitation program) there is no such thing. They can go to clubs and things like that, assimilation, a recipe for mayhem . . . here it is forbidden. (Life outside) has no law, its every man for himself in the cold jungle, and that's what I knew before I came here.

The interviewees frequently described the clear rules and prohibitions of religious observance like a dam that prevents them from falling back into crime, as expressed by Haim: "If you stray a bit, you start to give in a little, a little more, and you get drawn back into it (crime) . . . When you set yourself boundaries and give up your own comfort . . . shaving, hygiene . . . the rules (keep you grounded)." Jacob described the daily struggle with temptation:

It's a daily battle. I want to do something, but no, I don't do it. I say to myself "Go home, lay your head down, tomorrow you'll feel much better. You are fixing something in yourself" . . . I overcome it because I know I'll feel better the next day. It's actually conquering your desire . . . you restrain yourself; you set yourself boundaries, clear boundaries. Because what are we without boundaries? Animals.

Linked to this strict structure of rules and boundaries is the moral framework or compass with which they can navigate their way. Doubting their "inner compass," they find support not only in the "dos and don'ts," but also in a detailed map of right and wrong provided by the Jewish religious texts. Gideon explains that the Torah imparts the basic foundations of morality: "For me, religion was healing. I had (criminal) tendencies and behaviors . . . warped thinking where nothing went right. And with religion, I started studying morality; I began to realize that the way I behaved was wrong . . . It makes me a better person, more level-headed, calmer."

The interviewees reported that they had assimilated moral principles by reading Jewish ethics and morality texts, participating in religion classes, and group sessions both in prison and in the TRP. They primarily quoted Hassidic books, drawing eclectically from rabbinical teachings from different orthodox sectors; they especially embraced the teachings of Rabbi Nachman of Breslau, which they found easier to comprehend than other texts and which did not require prior Torah knowledge. About Rabbi Nachman's ethics books, Gideon said, "They are very lofty but very simple . . . they simply tell you the whole truth." Jacob referred to the Mishna tractate Chapters of the Fathers [Pirkei Avot] as a training manual for life: "If you read Pirkei Avot from beginning to end, it tells you how to behave." Simon emphasized the importance of religious morality texts also in planning long-term goals with the aim of achieving perfection: "It shows you your negative points and where you have to reach. It directs you toward goals." He spoke about the book Path of the Just [Mesillat Yesharim], and said, "The path leads you to perfection."

The religious programs in prison and in the TRP consist of individual sessions and group sessions, which often include study of the weekly Torah portion with relevant insights tying it to everyday life. The interviewees emphasized the importance of these analogies, since they taught them how to live a better life without repeating past mistakes that could cause them to relapse. The interpretation of Torah teachings to practical daily activities was perceived to be of extreme importance. It seems that lacking this mediation, they would find it difficult to translate the Torah's lessons into day-to-day actions.

New Metaphors and Idioms for Understanding the World

In his study of religious wards in Israeli prisons in the 1990s, Timor (1998; Timor & Landau 1998) found that the prisoners adopted a new dialect upon embracing religion. Clear and colleagues (2000) also found that Christian prisoners sometimes adopt a new scheme of metaphors when they become religious in prison, including the devil metaphor to explain the evil urges that led them down the path to incarceration. In our study, we found that the men were less likely to interpret their *past* through these metaphors, but instead called on metaphors and idioms to interpret the *present* challenges of everyday life. They used metaphors to increase their self-control by interpreting challenges as acts of God. Along these lines, interviewees embraced a cosmological order in which all good things that God sets in their path are seen as "miracles" [*nisim*] and all hardships, or pitfalls, as God-sent ordeals [*nisyonot*], "trials from above" or "tests of faith" sent by God to test the strength of their commitment. This terminology is common in the worldview of orthodox Jews more generally (Ivry et al. 2011).

An example of the "miracle" discourse is how Omer viewed his entry into the TRP: "Ever since I became religious, I've had many miracles happen to me, and Prisoner Rehabilitation is a miracle too." Some interviewees viewed the miracle of joining the TRP as saving them from their former life. Akiva said, "I think that God is the one who saved my life. Prisoner Rehabilitation was sent by Him. He really helped me settle down; He really performed miracles for me, God. Thank God. He comes first, before everyone else." Akiva illustrated these miracles through a story of an incidence in which he was saved from an attempted stabbing thanks to God's protection.

Conversely, when the interviewees spoke about "tests of faith," they related to the obstacles, temptations, and difficulties that came their way. They experienced these tests in prison, but even more so when they were released. On the outside, they experienced "God sent ordeals" even more frequently. Simon said about his life outside of prison, "Today I see that the tests are even harder." The common perception is that God sets these challenges before them in order to test their strength and to test the toolkit they use for solving problems.

In the past, when they mostly relied on themselves and failed to resist temptation, they only had to answer to themselves and to society; now, when the obligation is to God, there is no room for failure, because failing the test of faith is to revoke on one's debt to God. To fail is to personally disappoint Him. Some interviewees mentioned a sense of spiritual elevation resulting from these tests, as is validated by the head of the TRP: "I teach them that a test of faith is not necessarily a bad thing but that it is a good thing, because if you withstand the test, it can elevate you. When a person withstands a test—he ascends, and when he doesn't—he falls."

A majority of the "test of faith" stories revolved around the inmate's encounter with "real life" following release from prison, specifically in the work environment. Gideon told us about his difficulty in exercising self-restraint and delaying his gut reaction toward a coworker who had a tendency to curse frequently. Relating to his coworker's behavior as a God sent ordeal, he resolved, "God sent him. These are tests of faith . . . I manage to restrain myself, to feel myself, to put on the brakes." Levi added that despite his desire to spend time with friends that he had known before his incarceration, he turned down their invitation to a café, because he knew that as soon as the police saw him with them, he would be arrested again. Levi described this temptation in terms of a trial from above: "There are many temptations where I come from . . . When you get out, life is full of obstacles, full of tests . . ."

In addition to miracles and tests of faith, the men learned to reinterpret moments of relapse, sin, or criminal downfalls in terms of a "fall" [*nefila*] in their religious path or as temporarily "stepping away" [*hitrachkut*] from their religious path. These temporary slips were perceived as eventually followed by a "return" [*chazara*] or by "becoming closer to religion" (*hitkarvut*). Abraham described such a "fall," quoting a biblical verse from the Book of Ecclesiastes (12:8) in order to highlight the choice he must make between the futile pursuit of material wealth and possessions and the path of repentance: "I stepped astray and then I suddenly returned. I began to recognize God, to recognize all of the miracles that occurred. It is all vanity of vanities."

The path the men embrace stems directly from the concept of repentance in Judaism as it is formulated in the term *teshuva*. *Teshuva* does not refer to a wholly consuming rebirth or sudden transformation. Rather, it is a continuous process of internalizing repentance. Accordingly, the inmates in the religious seminaries and wards are taught by the rabbis that one of the basic messages of *teshuva* is that even a righteous person—a *tzadik*—can "fall" on the path of repentance. This is exemplified to the men through the repeated rehearsing of the biblical verse "For though the righteous person [*tzadik*] may fall seven times, he will rise up again" (Proverbs 24:16). This verse was widely used by our interviewees to discuss their path of two steps forward, one step back, in which they never stopped the process of repentance but simply had momentary strays.

Many times interviewees spoke of their "falls" as synchronized with periods of incarceration and release. When incarcerated they found it easier to move forward toward religiosity and upon release they found it difficult to keep all of the rules of the religious way of life and eventually "fell" from the religious path. Levi spoke of his pattern in terms of strengthening and weakening: "You stick your head out of the window, you can't keep the Sabbath . . . when I got out, I was weakened." Levi stresses the internal struggle observed in most of our interviews, where religious rituals are easier to keep while in prison because there are less temptations and opportunities for criminal activity. After release, however, it is more difficult to resist the temptation to commit a crime because of the financial pressures of supporting themselves and their families. In this way, a weakening in religiosity is also linked to falling into criminality.

The final concept that our interviewees used to conceptualize their new worldview is an idea of *tikkun*, drawn from Jewish mysticism [Kabbalah]. Interviewees spoke of their penance as a process of *tikkun* [mending, repair, or spiritual rectification (Samuel 2014)] in reaction to *kilkul* [destruction, or spiritual damage], citing the verse "If you believe you can break it [*likalkel*], believe you can fix it [*litaken*]." The kabalistic idea of *tikkun* is far too complex to address fully here, however, it is important to note that divine worship, fulfilling the commandments of the Torah [*mitzvot*] and studying Torah are human actions that are believed to repair spiritual damage and rectify the human soul and the world according to this belief system.

According to the interviewees, their criminal acts in the past were *kilkul* [spiritual damage] while religious penance enables them *tikkun* [spiritual rectification]. *Tikkun*, in their eyes, entails learning to be more patient, less greedy, and to be humble. The interviewees often remarked, as Samuel did, that "this was my amendment, my atonement." This sentiment also echoes the formal canon of the TRP that quotes the words of the renowned Rabbi Israel Salanter of the Musar movement—"as long as the candle is still burning you can amend."

Tikkun isn't perceived as a singular moment but as ongoing. For Jacob, tikkun is perceived as a lifelong process: "(I wish myself) penance [*tshuva*]. Because there are still things to amend. Always. Even when you reach the age of 80. There will still be things to amend." Some interviewees explained their return to prison as fated by their ongoing path of *tikkun*, since the prior *tikkun* was incomplete: "I came for another prison term. I guess it is hard for me to fix myself [*litaken*] . . . I wasn't religiously fortified [*lo hitchazakti*] enough after my first imprisonment. I came back home and didn't keep the Sabbath, so God sent me here again to become religiously stronger [*le'hitchazek*]" (Gideon).

Using Symbols as Safeguards against "Falling"

An additional unique component of the Jewish religious pathway to desistance is the involvement of material artifacts that serve as external reminders of the path of repentance and of how to behave. Becoming orthodox, as Tavory (2010) notes, is entering a world of signs. Several of these signs of belonging are worn by men on their bodies, beginning with the dress code of black hats and dark suits for men as well as a long beard; as men become increasingly religious within prison confines they may begin to adopt these identifiers, ceasing to shave and wearing the black hat and coat upon release.

Most, however, adopt the dress of modern orthodox men, who wear a skullcap, known as a yarmulke or *kippah*, but wear modern clothing. For our interviewees, the first step of religious strengthening [*hitchazkut*] involved wearing the kippah as an external characteristic that sends a message to those around them that they are "in the process." Another material reminder of their path worn on the body in view of others is the prayer shawl [*talit*] worn during prayer services and the *tzizit*, a smaller prayer garment worn under one's clothing throughout the day. This everyday undergarment has specially knotted ritual fringes or tassels attached to it and is worn to remind the religious man of his religious obligations. The knotted cords attached to the bottom of the shirt-length body piece hang down from under the shirt and thus can be observed by all.

Finally, as they became more religious, interviewees spoke of adorning phylacteries every weekday morning during prayer. Phylacteries are small leather boxes containing scrolls of parchment inscribed with verses from the Torah. For some, these external reminders of their connection with religion served as a constant reminder and they felt as though they were protected at all times. Jacob, for example, claimed, "When I put on phylacteries in the morning, I feel that my entire day is okay . . . even if it's not good, I manage . . . When I don't put on phylacteries in the morning, my entire day is really bad."

Among the religious symbols worn on the body, the symbol that was described as the most significant to life outside prison was the yarmulke [*kippah*]. The *kippah* was important not only in its religious aspect but also as an external physical artifact that reminded them of their choice to follow a new path. Samuel portrayed the *kippah* as a multivocal symbol, which signifies belonging and identification on one hand, and man's futility versus the divine spirit on the other hand: "I can say that for me the *kippah* is a symbol. It is not obligated by religion. It's a symbol that I'm Jewish, it safeguards my head . . . It's a symbol, it's belonging. It shows you're religious. If you're seen with a *kippah,* it's automatic—this is a religious person . . . It's on my head because . . . I respect the divine spirit, and I know that there is always someone above me . . . It's the boundary between us and God."

Most interviewees reported that the shape of the *kippah,* its color, and size did not matter much to them, other than the choice of a white *kippah* for Shabbat. We were surprised by the lack of importance attributed to the type of *kippah* in view of the importance of its form and even position on the head to the mapping of religious groups among various orthodox communities in

Israel, as it serves internally among orthodox groups to categorize one's affiliation and to denote many additional meanings regarding one's level of religious practice (Tavory 2010). It seems that the very act of wearing a *kippah* is the essential element here: it serves as an ongoing reminder of the need to observe commandments and avoid straying from the righteous path. Wearing a *kippah* in and of itself or the symbolism of removing it during certain periods is fundamental to their relationship with God and the message they are sending to their surroundings.

The interviewees emphasized that the *kippah* was a constant reminder that one is obligated to the Godly path and preserving Jewish laws, so that it is often depicted as a "gatekeeper" to guard against disobeying guidelines or commandments. Since it is an easily identifiable external characteristic, some saw its importance in how one is perceived by others. Some interviewees related to an additional role of the *kippah,* namely that its physical existence was a reminder to be good and prevented them from committing sins. Gabriel said, "The *kippah* gives you order. When you're not wearing it, you don't say a blessing over chewing gum. It reminds you to say a blessing." In this context, Gabriel added, "A *kippah* means you're committed to something. A religious person wears a *kippah* . . . committed to Jewish laws, to what the Creator of the Universe asks of us . . . Once you wear a *kippah* and *tzitzit* (four-cornered garment to which fringes are attached), and you look religious, you can't allow yourself to do whatever you want."

Evidence of the *kippah*'s role as a "gatekeeper" can be found in Gideon's statement, which pointed out that people who start to shed religious practices such as the *kippah* start to slide as they abandon religion: "First you remove the *kippah*. That's it, I took off the costume, but with time . . . religion weakens." Another interviewee emphasized the direct connection between removing the *kippah* and sliding back into criminal life. Jacob said that he stopped wearing a *kippah*, but kept it in his pocket: "That was during the period that I stopped with religion." Jacob emphasized that the "*kippah* removal ceremony" happened specifically "when I went back to crime"—as a crime was being committed. Jacob's *kippah* also came off in environments where religious people are not commonly present (like a coed swimming pool):

> (If) I respect the place, I put it on—synagogue, Torah lessons, Shabbat, Holy Days, everyday. If I'm at the swimming pool, I take it off, it's inappropriate. I wouldn't want someone to look at me and say, "There's a religious guy with a *kippah*." There are immodestly dressed people here and girls, it's forbidden anyway.

The interviewees underlined the *kippah*'s role in the ongoing communication with their environment. Adam talked about the *kippah*'s significance in his father's ability to gauge his son's lifestyle: "My father saw that I was into religion. He realized that I wasn't getting arrested anymore, realized I was healthy. Suddenly he sees me remove the *kippah*, remove it all, go to my friends. Then he understands. He says to me, 'Only religion for you, only religion will change you.'" In this context, Adam also said that the *kippah* could indicate to the interviewers—if they saw him in the future—about his lifestyle and the risk of him returning to crime:

> This is what can change my life . . . If I take it off, it's possible I will return to prison. And if I keep it on then . . . If you see me without a *kippah*, know that . . . it's possible that . . . if I don't learn everything I should here and you see me without a *kippah*, I will probably return to prison. I will go back to doing stupid things. But if you see me with a *kippah*, know that I'm on the right path . . . The *kippah* symbolizes that I'm a human being . . . that I'm on the straight and narrow . . . because I won't go stealing with a *kippah* when I know "Thou shalt not steal." So I take it off and don't wear it for a while . . . when I know I did something wrong in God's eyes. So like . . . it's hard for me to go back to it.

Rebirth as a Righteous Man: Status Preservation through Religion

To this point, we have discussed the rules, language, and symbolic artifacts that shape the repentant men's new worldview. In the following, we look at the gap between these behavioral aspects of religion and the spiritual benefit of religion. Although formal Jewish religious doctrine, as we have noted, is plural, and different rabbis have different views on what must be included in the path of repentance, our interviewees felt a strong connection to the views of the Breslav Hasidic sect that allows a man to repent without the necessity of introspection. This view has some characteristics that are similar to Evangelical Christianity, which also offers the repentant forgiveness for his sins (Clear et al. 2000). However, beyond the theme of rebirth and forgiveness, the doctrine our interviewees drew upon emphasized the possibility for retention, or even attaining, the status of a righteous man [*tzaddik*] by embracing religion.

Most of our interviewees were drawn particularly to the worldview of the Breslav Hassidic sect because they understood Breslav teachings as not requiring extensive prying into the past. The head of the TRP explained this phenomenon: "It is easier for a person not to confront the past." He spoke of an analogy that illustrates the purpose of this principle in Breslav teachings: "It is just like stirring water in a barrel. It might raise up the sand and muck from the bottom and turn the water murky so that you can't see through it." Later, he quoted part of a song that inmates in the religious ward often sing: "What was, is past, the important thing is to start from the beginning. Father, renew me completely, light up my soul."

Most interviewees viewed their intensifying religiosity as enabling their soul to be pure again, much like born-again Christians. Haim said: "It is as if I was sort of created anew, reborn. Yes, I am reborn. I see how things were created, Adam and Eve and all of that." It is not by chance that Haim describes his rebirth by referring to the biblical creation story of Adam and Eve. His use of this reference expresses a sense of returning to a place of naivety, where there is no background of sin, and the chance to be granted a "clean slate" in the eyes of God, the religious community, and subsequently for themselves, even though they cannot erase their criminal past.

Yet this reference goes beyond simple rebirth; it also expresses a sense of being special, of one who has been "chosen" by God, who is now closer to God than other members of humankind, and who is now privy to privileged knowledge about God's creation of the universe. Such a path of rebirth and of being chosen was perceived by all interviewees as a possible and reachable option for any man, even a murderer. There is a sense that there is no obstacle in the way of the potential repentant. Adam said: "There is the option of repentance [*teshuva*] for anyone. God tells us that even if you have murdered someone, you have penance. I believe theft is lesser than murder—so I believe He'll forgive me for theft. That's what I see in my mind. I want him to forgive me."

Interestingly, Adam's interpretation of repentance veers from most formal rabbinical debates, in which repentance must usually include the sinner recognizing his wrongdoings, feeling sincere remorse, and doing everything in his power to undo any damage that has been done. In such a case, a murderer cannot be on the path of *teshuva* because he cannot undo the damage, and a "clean slate" is impossible without remorse. Indeed, the formal ethos of the TRP envisions religious rehabilitation as beginning with introspection and remorse, writing in their brochure: "Religious rehabilitation is built on three stages: acknowledging the sin, remorse for the action and its consequences, and true commitment with a full heart not to repeat the action." However, it seems that this ethos is not the one that the prisoners are internalizing; from their standpoint, *teshuva* is open for all and does not necessarily involve remorse but instead involves a change in behavior from the moment one's new path begins.

In this way, the "clean slate" releases the penitent from the introspective examination of the roots of criminal tendencies that is encouraged in conventional psychotherapeutic methods used in prison. As Maruna (2001, 131) notes, this construction of a new self and social identity as devout "seems to contradict one of the fundamental tenets of rehabilitation practice—the need to "own up" to one's past." Maruna suggests that while therapeutic work in the prison context has historically focused on coercing the prisoner to confess and accept blame or responsibility for the prisoner's actions, contemporary rehabilitation also uses therapeutic shaming as a technique for breaking down a prisoner's excuses and defenses. Our interviewees explicitly described the conventional group and individual therapy that they had taken part in, as more difficult for them to relate to than the religious counseling and study groups because social workers using conventional therapeutic techniques expect them to "dig into" the past, take responsibility for previous actions, exhibit remorse, and feel shame.

Interviewees explicitly compared conventional therapy with prison social workers to the Torah study groups and religious counseling sessions in prison and in the TRP upon release, which they viewed as focusing on their behavior in the present and future without digging into the past, as well as teaching them the morality of right and wrong and the "dos and don'ts" of religious law that are applicable to daily life. In this way, the religious programming served as a mechanism for shame management (Maruna, Wilson, & Curran 2006); indeed, the men drew upon the Jewish religious prohibition on shaming and embarrassing others in public in order to protect themselves against therapeutic shaming.

The men's experience of the religious programs in prison and on reentry seemed to be heavily shaped by this prohibition of shaming others in public, which is discussed in the Babylonian Talmud as comparable to murder (Talmud Baba Metzia 59a). Interviewees described the prison rabbis and the TRP staff as exhibiting a less judgmental attitude toward them than social workers, and the dynamic between prisoners in the religious ward as helping one another to "save face" and retain their dignity. They compared this to conventional therapy groups where they perceived fellow rehabilitants as less careful, or more hurtful, in group sessions where peer confrontation, or "mirroring" critiques, were encouraged. Haim compared these frameworks, noting: "People can judge you and all that in regular therapy . . . in religion you have the values, you have to respect one another and not shame them in front of others."

In this way, the "clean slate" carries a halo effect. Our interviewees drew upon the famous Talmudic quote "In the place where penitents stand even the wholly righteous cannot stand" in order to explain that in the eyes of God, one who repents is more righteous than someone who was born religious and never strayed. Interestingly, none of the interviewees spoke of the source of this quote, which first appears in Jewish religious texts in the Talmud Bavli (Berachot 34b) in a debate between two rabbis: Rabbi Abbihu, whose words are extracted in the famous quote, and Rabbi Yochanan, who argues the opposite, that those born religious are more righteous than those who repent. In later religious texts, rabbinic scholars interpret and continue this debate; for our interviewees, the endorsement of Rabbi Abbihu's stance seemed to inspire a sense of righteousness.

For some, the idea that they are now righteous boosts their self-esteem and enables them to see themselves as a better person. Haim, for instance, spoke of the way he now believed in himself more and had become a model prisoner in the religious ward: "I was really an example for everyone there . . . I would never have thought I could do it." Akiva took this further, explaining how embracing religion put him on a path toward "perfection": "I'm not perfect, I'm far from being perfect, but I'm a lot closer to it than I used to be." For others, however, the halo effect led to a sense of superiority, as though their metaphoric rebirth made them better than others who had not embraced religion. Ironically, this sense of superiority was sometimes displayed during the interviews for this study, as interviewees "preached" to the secular student interviewers about the heavenly consequences awaiting them for not keeping the Sabbath. Ironically, this occurred in interviews with ex-prisoners who had serious past felonies, including murder.

For interviewees who formerly held status positions in the criminal world, the halo effect also allows them to retain their sense of status. Ezra, for instance, was a criminal kingpin before incarceration and had been sentenced for severe crimes. Speaking of his life before incarceration, he explained: "I wasn't willing to let anyone tell me what to do. Because unfortunately I was a gang leader, I would tell them what to do, nobody told me what do." Entering the religious ward in prison was the first time he submitted himself to external rules: "Suddenly you come to this structured framework: don't do it this way, pray, wake up in the morning and say the blessing, eat together."

The halo effect emanating from the "clean slate" enabled Ezra to maintain his sense of status even as he submitted to a "bigger boss," as he relays through an analogy between himself and a righteous scholar in the Talmud: "They say a man who repents is in a higher place than the most righteous person . . . The rabbi told me that I am like Rish Lakish, who was a famous head of a band of bandits and became a righteous leader of scholars. Ever since he has called me 'Rish Lakish.'" By calling him Rish Lakish, the rabbi "koshers" Ezra as a leader of the righteous, in line with his previous status as a gang leader, preserving his position and role, and legitimizing his transformation. Although the "clean slate" includes the avoidance of responsibility, as Maruna (2001, 144) suggests, such techniques also help to protect self-esteem in a way that may be an important part of the desistance process.

Conclusion

In the above, we have outlined the central aspects of the Jewish religion that the repentant ex-prisoners described as critical for their desistance from relapse criminal activity. Although religion in general has been discussed as a source for prisoners and ex-prisoners to draw from on the path to desistance (Hallett et al. 2016; Maruna, Wilson, & Curran 2006), we believe that there are specific ingredients of the Jewish religion that assisted our interviewees in the desistance process. First, the strict obedience to the large body of "dos and don'ts" of the Jewish religious doctrine were found to be a central tool for desistance. These religious rules set clear boundaries for day-to-day behavior, provided our interviewees with answers to almost any question or dilemma, and outlined a clear moral code they were expected to adhere to.

This emphasis in the Jewish religious programs for prisoners on strict obedience to a set of clear rules differs markedly from the approach that Hallett et al. (2016) observed in the Christian-oriented Angola Prison Seminary. Participants at the seminary, who are trained to be religious counselors and guides for fellow prisoners, are encouraged to take active responsibility for their choices and to "make the right choices for the right reasons" (205) as part of religious practice rather than avoid decision making through strict obedience. Nevertheless, even if strict obedience to the rules of religious observance may have allowed the men in our Israeli case study to avoid decision making, it should not be discounted as a tool for desistance. Strict obedience to a clear set of religious rules can reduce anxiety and give a person a compass to navigate everyday life.

Second, the specific metaphorical language of Orthodox Judaism emerged as an important tool for desistance. When the men embrace religion, they adopt these metaphors and the worldview that their pitfalls are not simply personal failures but part of a divine plan to test their faith and their strength. They begin to understand temporary slipups in terms of "falls" or "stepping away," thus enabling them to continue their path without fear of falter. What we found comforting for our interviewees was that in this worldview and with this new language they could explain everything that had happened in their lives, good or bad, as directed and orchestrated by a higher power that "knows better." They found comfort in being in the hands of God. As we have noted, this new worldview, that explicitly prohibits public shaming, may serve as a way of avoiding taking responsibility and blame for their past actions. Yet the "clean slate" of a newly repentant self also serves as a tool for shame management and for preserving self-esteem in a way that seems to promote their desistance.

Finally, we would like to suggest that the emphasis on symbolic artifacts in Jewish religious practice played an important role in desistance. The yarmulke, prayer shawl, and phylacteries serve as constant physical reminders of their chosen path and repentant self. Wearing the yarmulke can be viewed as inscribing this new path and the repentant self upon the body, serving both as a sign that the wearer himself is aware of but also that his environment can interpret as a sign of his chosen path. The artifacts serve as a visible boundary, much like an electric handcuff. For many of our interviewees, it seems that these behavioral aspects of religion had an effect even when they had not yet internalized a sincere belief system; instead, the practical aspects of religion served as a type of behavioral code.

Our findings suggest that religion has benefits beyond generating introspection and the internal change of the self; a man might be able to begin the path of desistance through changes in behavior before a change in self is secured. As Maruna (2011, 671) has noted, a significant percentage of prisoners "seem to harbor deep and passionate hatred for psychology and all things psychological." As a result, prisoners may feel that turning to the conventional therapeutic apparatus in prison does not answer their needs for nonjudgmental help and support in making positive change. Religious practice in prison and upon reentry, however, can provide a clear set of behavioral tools for desistance that may be able to reach those who cannot be reached through conventional psychological therapy by incorporating psychological behavioral tools within religious programs.

Indeed, we believe that the interviewees in our study accepted a therapeutic process through religion that they might have resisted if it had been framed as "psychology"; nevertheless, the religious program's emphasis on behavioral rules, on rewording experiences, and on employing symbolic artifacts as reminders of the path to desistance were indeed psychological tools in a religion-based formulation. The particular benefits offered by Judaism toward this goal—the strict dos and don'ts, the cosmological explanatory metaphors (*teshuva*, tests of faith, falls, and *tikkun*), and the symbolic material artifacts incorporated in ritual practice (kippah, prayer shawl, phylacteries) are unique to the Jewish faith. However, we believe that similar behavioral codes may be extracted from religious practice of other faiths to be used in promoting desistance through religion.

Bibliography

Aday, Ronald H., Jennifer J. Krabill, & Dayron Deaton-Owens. "Religion in the Lives of Older Women Serving Life in Prison." *Journal of Women & Aging* 26, no. 3 (2014): 238–256.

Camp, Scott D., Dawn M. Daggett, Okyun Kwon, & Jody Klein-Saffran. "The Effect of Faith Program Participation on Prison Misconduct: The Life Connections Program." *Journal of Criminal Justice* 36, no. 5 (2008): 389–395.

Clear, Todd R., P. L. Hardyman, B. Stout, K. Lucken, & H. R. Dammer. "The Value of Religion in Prison: An Inmate Perspective." *Journal of Contemporary Criminal Justice* 16, no. 1 (2000): 53–74.

Clear, Todd R., & Melvina T. Sumter. "Prisoners, Prison, and Religion." *Journal of Offender Rehabilitation* 35, no. 3–4 (2002): 125–156.

Clear, T. R., & M. Myhre. "A Study of Religion in Prison." *IARCA Journal on Community Corrections* 6, no. 6 (1995): 20–25.

Dammer, Harry R. "The Reasons for Religious Involvement in the Correctional Environment." *Journal of Offender Rehabilitation* 35, no. 3–4 (2002): 35–58.

Duwe, Grant, & Byron R. Johnson. "Estimating the Benefits of a Faith-Based Correctional Program" 20176 (2013): 227–239.

Friedman, Menachem. *The Haredi Ultra-Orthodox Society: Sources Trends and Processes.* Jerusalem: The Jerusalem Institute for Israel Studies, 1991.

Glaser, Barney G., & Anselm L. Strauss. *The Discovery of Grounded Theory: Strategies for Qualitative Research.* Chicago: Aldine, 1967.

Hallett, Michael, Joshua Hays, Byron R. Johnson, Sung Joon Jang, & Grant Duwe. *The Angola Prison Seminary: Effects of Faith-Based Ministry on Identity Transformation, Desistance, and Rehabilitation.* New York: Routledge, 2016.

Hallett, Michael, & Byron R. Johnson. "The Resurgence of Religion in America's Prisons." *Religions* 5, no. 3 (2014): 663–683.

Hanley, Natalia. "Interrogating Religion in Prison: Criminological Approaches." *iNtergraph Journal of Dialogic Anthropology* 4, no. 1 (2014).

Ivry, Tsipy. "Kosher Medicine and Medicalized Halacha: An Exploration of Triadic Relations among Israeli Rabbis, Doctors, and Infertility Patients." *American Ethnologist* 37, no. 4 (2010): 662–680.

Ivry, Tsipy, Elly Teman, & Ayala Frumkin. "God-Sent Ordeals and Their Discontents: Ultra-Orthodox Jewish Women Negotiate Prenatal Testing." *Social Science & Medicine* 72, no. 9 (2011): 1527–1533.

Johnson, Byron R. "Religious Programs and Recidivism among Former Inmates in Prison Fellowship Programs: A Long-Term Follow-Up Study." *Justice Quarterly* 21, no. 2 (2004): 329–354.

Kerley, Kent R., Marisa C. Allison, & Rachelle D. Graham. "Investigating the Impact of Religiosity on Emotional and Behavioral Coping in Prison." *Journal of Crime and Justice* 29, no. 2 (2006): 69–93.

Kerley, Kent R., & Heith Copes. "'Keepin' My Mind Right': Identity Maintenance and Religious Social Support in the Prison Context." *International Journal of Offender Therapy and Comparative Criminology* 53, no. 2 (2009): 228–244.

Leon, Nissim, & Aliza Lavie. "Hizuk—The Gender Track: Religious Invigoration and Women Motivators in Israel." *Contemporary Jewry* 33, no. 3 (2013): 193–215.

Maruna, Shadd. *Making Good: How Ex-Convicts Reform and Rebuild Their Lives.* Washington, DC: American Psychological Association, 2001.

Maruna, Shadd. "Why Do They Hate Us? Making Peace between Prisoners and Psychology." *International Journal of Offender Therapy and Comparative Criminology* 55, no. 5 (2011): 671–675.

Maruna, Shadd, Louise Wilson, & Kathryn Curran. "Why God Is Often Found behind Bars: Prison Conversions and the Crisis of Self-Narrative." *Research in Human Development* 3, no. 2 (2006): 161–184.

Mears, Daniel P., Caterina G. Roman, Ashley Wolff, & Janeen Buck. "Faith-Based Efforts to Improve Prisoner Reentry: Assessing the Logic and Evidence." *Journal of Criminal Justice* 34, no. 4 (2006): 351–367.

Morag, Michal, & Elly Teman. n.d. "The Watchful Eye of God: A Qualitative Study of Religious Rehabilitation through Judaism." *International Journal of Offender Therapy and Comparative Criminology.*

O'Connor, Thomas P., & Michael Perreyclear. "Prison Religion in Action and Its Influence on Offender Rehabilitation." *Journal of Offender Rehabilitation* 35, no. 3–4 (2002): 11–33.

Rowell, John, Americo Rodriguez, & Harry S. Dammer. "Religion in Prison." *Encyclopedia of Prisons & Correctional Facilities*, 1–7. Thousand Oaks, CA: Sage, 1987.

Samuel, Gabriella. *Kabbalah Handbook: A Concise Encyclopedia of Terms and Concepts in Jewish Mysticism*. New York: Jeremy P. Tarcher, 2014.

Santos, Saskia Daniele, & Jodi Lane. "Expanding Clear et Al.'s Value of Religion Ideas: Former Inmates' Perspectives." *Deviant Behavior* 35, no. 2 (2013): 116–132.

Sumter, Melvina. "Faith-Based Prison Programs." *Criminology & Public Policy* 5, no. 3 (2006): 523–528.

Tavory, Iddo. "Of Yarmulkes and Categories: Delegating Boundaries and the Phenomenology of Interactional Expectation." *Theory and Society* 39, no. 1 (2010): 49–68.

Teman, E., T. Ivry, & B. A. Bernhardt. "Pregnancy as a Proclamation of Faith: Ultra-Orthodox Jewish Women Navigating the Uncertainty of Pregnancy and Prenatal Diagnosis." *American Journal of Medical Genetics, Part A* 155, no. 1 (2011): 69–80.

Thomas, Jim, & Barbara H. Zaitzow. "Conning or Conversion? The Role of Religion in Prison Coping." *The Prison Journal* 86, no. 2 (2006): 242–259.

Timor, Uri. "Coping with the Criminal Past of Ex-Delinquents Undergoing Rehabilitation in Yeshivas for Repentents." *Megamot* 15, no. 1 (1997): 30–47.

Timor, Uri. "Constructing a Rehabilitative Reality in Special Religious Wards in Israeli Prisons." *International Journal of Offender Therapy and Comparative Criminology* 42, no. 4 (1998): 340–359.

Timor, Uri, & Rachel Landau. "Discourse Characteristics in the Sociolect of Repentant Criminals." *Discourse and Society* 9, no. 3 (1998): 363–386.

CHAPTER SIXTEEN

Religious Diversity in Swiss and Italian Prisons: Combining Institutional and Inmate Perspectives

*Irene Becci, Mohammed Khalid Rhazzali,
and Valentina Schiavinato*

In the European context, prisons have historically arisen as secular institutions integrating religion. A Christian blueprint is visible in their main functions— reeducation, punishment, and rehabilitation—and are played out. Currently, emerging religious and spiritual practices and discourses are transforming the current conceptions of punishment, imprisonment, and rehabilitation. The religious change that most European correctional facilities have witnessed in recent years has primarily concerned the inmates. Compared to a couple of decades ago, the religious affiliations, discourses, and practices of inmates have greatly diversified. Moreover, there has been a change in the wider discourse

Note: This manuscript was translated by Irene Becci and Muriel Bruttin, and is a slightly modified version of a text first published as: Becci Irene, Khalid Rhazzali Mohammed, & Schiavinato Valentina, "Appréhension et expérience de la pluralité religieuse dans les prisons en Suisse et en Italie: une approche par l'ethnographie," *Critique internationale* 3/2016 (N° 72), p. 73–90 © Presses de Sciences Po.

connecting issues of religion to prison. From the Anglo-Saxon world, Europe has received echoes of the idea of letting religion, in particular religious communities, play an active role in the rehabilitation of criminals. As a consequence, religion—sometimes under the heading of spirituality—seems to find a new setting in the world of prisons.

In Switzerland and Italy, the right to religious freedom and freedom of consciousness is nowadays considered a human right that also applies to prisoners: their religious practice is hence free and every prisoner can ask, individually, to benefit from any religious service that is not offered by the institution or managed by the local chaplaincy. The chaplaincy is under the responsibility of the two established churches, the Protestant and the Catholic Churches (Becci 2012). Only very recently, in some local contexts, new religious representatives—such as Orthodox, Muslim, or Evangelical—have started to be a part of it.

This development is a soft response to a larger process that penitentiary institutions have been facing in the last 20 years or so: religious pluralization. This situation had not really been foreseen as it was assumed instead that the change affecting religion was mainly secularization. Now, the pluralization of religion is observable on multiple levels: it concerns both a larger variety of religious traditions and groups as well as individual practices and beliefs.

This new religious landscape is one of the consequences of the process of cultural globalization and the complexities of migration linked to large conflicts that are often connected to religious issues. In Europe, social scientific research on religion in prison has strongly developed in the last 20 years, beginning with James Beckford and Sophie Gilliat's research on religious diversity in prisons (1998) in the 1990s in England and Wales. Until the publication of Gilliat and Beckford's study, the only churches involved in prison work and prison chaplaincy were the Anglican Church and the Roman Catholic Church. The results of the study convinced the authorities to open chaplaincy first to Muslims and then to other faiths.[1]

Gilliat and Beckford's study, similar to many of the subsequent studies on the subject of religion and prisons, was concerned mainly with chaplaincy and spiritual care based on statistical data about inmates' religious belonging. A few years later, first in France, then in Italy, countries in which such data cannot be gathered legally, scholars inquired instead into the subjective religious experience of persons under conditions of imprisonment, in particular among Muslim inmates whose numbers in penitentiaries were increasing greatly (Khosrokhavar 2004; Rhazzali 2010). Although biographical or topic-related interviews were the main methodological tools of these pioneer surveys, methodological approaches have since become more complex and integrate comparisons with increasingly qualitative ethnographic work (Béraud, Galembert, & Rostaing 2016). This development reflects an increased sensitivity of researchers working on religion. As a matter of fact, the notion of religion is quite ambiguous, which can be seen in the various ways penitentiary institutions employ it.

In this chapter we propose, first, to investigate on the one hand, the different ways in which the variable "religion" is treated by prison authorities, and on the other hand, how inmates experience and live religion in this context. In both cases, we will be able to link our observations to larger social processes concerning religions. Second, we present some methodological aspects of our research and discuss the current religious plurality as it appears through quantitative data. Third, we present and analyze some interview material we collected among prisoners about their relation to religion. Connecting quantitative data to ethnographic fieldwork data will allow us to show the complex relations that exist between the category of "religious belonging" and lived religion. To conclude, we will elaborate on the importance of applying critical and reflexive methodology.

Methodological Premises

From an ideal-type point of view, religious plurality is visible in differences among theological doctrines, ritual practices, or transmission systems of religious belonging. From a socioanthropological perspective, on the contrary, the categories established through such differences are considered to be variable and can fluctuate according to geographic location, epochs, juridical structures, and their embeddedness into actual social relations. The methodological approach adopted in our research on religious plurality in prison follows the observation made by Le Caisne. She states that it is only through a true personal implication, which lasts in time and invests itself into the totality of the institution, that a reciprocal familiarization between the researcher and the persons met can be established, and through these relationships it is possible to discover the unobservable (Le Caisne 2015).

Here we present some of the results of two sets of studies, one conducted in Swiss prisons and one conducted in Italian prisons. These research projects follow in the footsteps of the pioneering 1990s study of England and Wales by the sociologists James Beckford and Sophie Gilliat. Their main question concerned equality of treatment of Christian and other inmates by the prison chaplaincy. In England and Wales, data on religious affiliations are gathered by state authorities on the basis of self-declarations. Beckford and Gilliat relied on this data to analyze what they called "religious needs," that is, the need to live according to the commonly shared understanding of one's religion, which implies most importantly the respect of rituals. The Beckford and Gilliat study, however, did not include the voice of inmates nor their personal perspectives (1998). A few years later, and unlike Beckford and Gilliat, sociologist Farhad Khosrokhavar concentrated on inmates' perspectives. His study is another source of inspiration for our research. His main focus was on Muslim inmates' subjectivity and religious experience in France. Through the combination of these two methodologies, an innovative approach to religion in prison has emerged. This approach combines the diversity of perspectives that can be found in the field with findings regarding institutional structures and the cultural context. At the methodological level, one of the main issues is to adopt an ethnographic approach that includes an epistemological sensitivity to situational plurality, that is, which discerns the situations in which social actors are involved.

As far as Italy is concerned, it is worth mentioning the pioneering research by Khalid Rhazzali on Muslims in prison (Rhazzali 2014), as well as the study done by Paolo Di Motoli (2013) on the regions of Piedmont and Aosta Valley. However, Di Motoli's study was not done within a prison, as he could not enter the prisons and only interviewed ex-inmates and spiritual caregivers. In fact, the only study that considers religious diversity inside prisons is Valeria Fabretti and Massimo Rosati's research in the Latium region (2012; Fabretti 2014). Our research in Italy started in 2005 and continues to this day, in 2016, mainly around three projects: Rhazzali's doctoral dissertation on Islam in prisons (2005–2009), the survey on "Islamic Radicalism in prisons" (2010–2012),[2] and the research project "Cultural and religious diversity in a total institution. Actors, social spaces and prayer in Italian prisons" (2013 to today).[3] Extracts 1, 2, 3, and 5 presented near the end of this chapter are taken from interviews found in Rhazzali's doctoral dissertation. His work can be qualified as qualitative[4] research and focused on three Italian prisons that were chosen for being representative of the organization of Muslim religious practice. In one detention center—where prisoners have been tried—collective rituals were allowed only during the annual celebrations. The other two prisons were jails (for inmates awaiting trial).[5] In one of them, an imam was regularly present on Fridays to lead the prayer and to offer spiritual and religious care. In the other jail, a self-proclaimed "imam inmate" led the prayer in a section of the prison where Muslim inmates made up the majority of the inmate population.

In Switzerland, religion in prison has traditionally been studied from a rather juridical or practical theological perspective (Buser 2007). The first sociological research started in 2007 with a three-year grant by the Swiss National Science Foundation (Becci, Bovay, Kuhn, Purdie, Knobel, & Vuille 2011). This study also contained a juridical aspect, but it articulated the question of religious freedom with a sociological approach to religious diversity. At a quantitative level, data from the 2000 federal census was analyzed, and a questionnaire was distributed to all chaplain members of the Swiss Prison Chaplaincy Association. In this questionnaire, the chaplains were asked about their activities in prison and the conditions of their mandate. At a qualitative level, we used a more ethnographic approach in three prisons that differed in a number of ways: one was a jail, and two were prisons for tried inmates. One was a women's prison, one a men's prison, and one held both men and women. They were also in different geographic locations (two were in the French-speaking region of Switzerland, and one was in the German-speaking region), and finally, the cantons in which they found themselves were ruled in different ways as far as church-state relations were concerned.[6] In every prison, we had informal ethnographic conversations as well as recorded interviews (one of which was a group discussion) with members of the direction, of the chaplaincy, of the surveillance and security staff as well as with inmates. We also observed and participated in various religious events, such as Christmas celebrations and evangelical group meetings. We also contacted a number of religious minority communities in Switzerland to ask them whether they had activities in prison.[7] The gathered data are regularly updated.

In Europe, the impact of social and cultural globalization of recent decades has strongly diversified the religious landscape: more and more religions (movements and groups) have appeared in the European context. Moreover, people's increased mobility has complicated the relation between religious belonging and identification. As Grace Davie writes, the Western world tends to believe that religious belonging and the religious tradition from which one comes from no longer determine one's religious practices and even less one's religious beliefs. These beliefs and practices are thought, on the contrary, to be linked to many other biographical factors and result also from choices (1993). However, if we look at the discourses of migrants' relation to religion, the tendency is to be opposite: the "other's" (Kilani 2011) religion is often considered to completely determine their identity. This tendency has been well studied and concerns in particular persons identified (Belhoul, Leuenberger, & Tunger-Zanetti 2013) as Muslims on the basis of their name, their appearance, or their language. Often, the (assumed) religious belonging is used as a key element in the interpretation of the person's conduct: one imagines that all members of a religion adhere to the same values, that all Muslims all over the world have the same practices. Islam in particular is considered as a monolithic and immutable tradition that completely determines individuals and generates what we call the *homo islamicus*. This way of apprehending this religion needs of course to be linked to what happens more largely in the context of international conflicts, often interpreted in terms of civilizational clashes (Huntington 1997). Within this imaginary, belonging to one religion might be seen as threat to the social order (see De Giorgi 2000). One of the implications of this construction of "religious difference" is the necessity, in order to maintain such a social order, to better control religion.

It is within this discursive context that Beckford and Gilliat published their 1998 study in which they denounced the unequal treatment of demands made by Anglican inmates compared to demands by inmates of other religions. The accommodation of the latter's claims and requests often seemed to be difficult for and disturbing to the daily functioning of the institution, whether at the level of the organization of work or of daily meals. Beckford and Gilliat's publication has sparked important public debate about this issue, and prison administrations have started to integrate members of other religions into the chaplaincy. After the attacks on the World Trade Center in New York on September 11, 2001, the prevention argument about "violent extremism" (Todd 2015) linked to Islam (Becci & Roy 2015) has accelerated this process. The interpretations of the results of the studies on religion in prison are hence strongly inscribed within this context of tense political relations.

It is very important, we contend, to always consider the larger geopolitical context in which a social scientific research is conducted on prisons since the context influences the framing of the core questions of the research.

The Institutional Understanding of the Variable "Religious Belonging" in Prison

The significance of a religious category (e.g., belonging or identification to Catholicism) varies with regard to a number of sociopersonal factors—such as gender, nationality, migratory status, economic capital, age, insertion within one's milieu, the social and administrative status that one holds in society, and language spoken—and to a person's biographical situation. Religious plurality—or "super-diversity" (Vertovec 2007)—results from the multiple intersections of these factors.

Prisons in particular are touched by this phenomenon and by each person's representations of their own religion and the religion of the "other." It is therefore important to bring together these different sources of information to put them into perspective. Tables 16.1 and 16.2 expose some of the tendencies of the religious super-diversity in prisons.

In Switzerland, in 1997,[8] 42 percent of prisoners were foreign nationals; eight years later, in 2005, they represented 70 percent of prisoners (OFS 2007). This increase can be explained by the increase in immigration in this country and by the larger exposure that foreign nationals have to the risk of imprisonment (Acherman & Hostettler 2004, 2007). This percentage diminishes by about one-third if we exclude nonresidents in Switzerland.[9] Taking into account age and gender brings further complexities to the picture. The proportion of young men, who are statistically more exposed to criminality than older men or women (Jaquier & Vuille 2008), is much higher among foreign nationals than among Swiss nationals (; Schwarzenegger & Studer 2013; Vuille & Kuhn 2010). All these factors have an effect on the category of religion. According to these studies, for young Muslims, religion assumes greater importance than for other youths (Morgenthaler et al. 2011).

In prison, the proportion of inmates that consider themselves Muslim has been rather stable in the last 10 years, but their national origin varies. At the beginning of the 2000s, Muslims in detention often came from Balkan countries, while in 2011, in western Switzerland, the principal place of origin was the Maghreb (Schneuwly Purdie 2011). This configuration changes in the German-speaking part of Switzerland, where persons from the Maghreb are a minority among the Muslim inmates. The majority of female inmates, on the other hand, tend to declare belonging to Christianity. See Table 16.1 for percentages of inmates from various religions in different types of prisons.

The modalities through which census data are gathered regarding a person's religious affiliation vary greatly between prison institutions and between regions. Sometimes, atheists are distinguished from those that do not respond to the census, but not always. None of the institutions differentiate between the different traditions or orientations within Islam, while everywhere we can count at least four different categories for Christianity. Often, these numbers

Table 16.1 Religious Belonging in a Few Swiss Prisons, 2010, 2012, and 2014

Religious belonging (census)	Prison institutions by type or region		
	Canton Vaud, %[1]	Women, %[2]	Men, Zurich, %[3]
Roman Catholic	25	42	25.1
Reformed Evangelical	6	31	12.5
Orthodox Christian	11	6	10
No affiliation	6	10	10.9
Muslim	45	5	28.3
Other Christian religion	3	—	17.7
No information/atheist	1	6	<1
Buddhist	<1	—	1.61
Total	<98	100	100

[1]Data for 2012, obtained through auto-declaration of inmates and provided by the chief of the Prison Service of medicine and psychiatry, Bruno Gravier, at the symposium "Spiritualité et religion dans les modèles de rétablissement en institution: accompagnement et régulation dans la diversité?," University of Lausanne, May 2014.

[2]Verbal information received in 2010. Considering the national origins and languages spoken according to the 2014 report from the prison of Bern, these figures should not have changed much (http://www.pom.be.ch/pom/de/index/freiheitsentzug-betreuung /vollzugseinrichtungen_erwachsene/anstalten_hindelbank/portrait.assetref/dam /documents/POM/FB/de/AnstaltenHindelbank/Jahresstatistik_2014_deutsch.pdf).

[3]Annual report of 2014 from the main prison of Zurich (http://www.justizvollzug.zh.ch /internet/justiz_inneres/juv/de/ueber_uns/veroeffentlichungen/jahresberichte/_jcr _content/contentPar/publication_0/publicationitems/titel_wird_aus_dam_e_3/download .spooler.download.1438592746537.pdf/Jahresbericht+2014.pdf) (accessed October 12, 2016).

are obtained through "self-declaration" of the individuals when they enter into the detention institution or just a little while later, when they are invested in a strategy of identity affirmation or when they are in the pursuit of pragmatic goals, such as gaining access to particular meals. The religious practice, therefore, does not follow mechanically from the declared religious affiliation. In general, research regarding Switzerland has shown that just over one-tenth of persons belonging to a religion have a recurring practice (Monnot 2013). More specifically, research on the experience of confinement showed that the vulnerability of detained persons, which has a strong impact on their relationship to religion, varies during their sentence and "career" in prison (Goffman 1968/2000).

Prison administrations aim for simple classifications to function effectively, for example, for meal planning, the distribution of inmates in cells, or the distribution of spaces for religious activities. According to information gathered during our fieldwork in western Switzerland, it is not uncommon for prison officers to place prisoners in the same cell if they are assumed to share the same religious beliefs. These assumptions are often based solely on the associations made between national origin or name and religious affiliation. Although these choices may come from benevolent intentions, such as allowing for better communication between inmates, they tend to contribute to the reification of collective representations about religion. We observed this dynamic with the case of Islam in particular, as it was considered by the officers we interviewed and by some detainees, especially non-Muslim detainees, as the majority religion of the institution, some estimating it to include up to 80 percent of the detainees, which is clearly different from the information provided in Table 16.1 (Schneuwly Purdie 2013).

In Italy, the proportion of foreign prisoners is smaller than in Switzerland, but it was in almost constant progression from 1997 (22.3 percent) to 2008 (37.5 percent) and has fallen in 2014 to the same proportions as 2005 (32.6 percent).[10] Within the total prison population (62,536), the percentage of young adults (18 to 34) was 38.6 percent at the end of 2014, and within this category the percentage of foreigners was 52.1 percent.[11] In Italy, the categorization of prisoners on the basis of their religion is forbidden by the Constitution. Yet a reduction of "the religious" to "religious affiliation" still exists within prisons.

The information in Table 16.2, provided by the Ministry of Justice of Italy, is based on data from the "transparency sheets on the prison."[12] Unlike the case of Switzerland, the data do not refer to the number of inmates declaring themselves as belonging to a religion, because the Constitution does not permit to sort detainees by their religious affiliation. Instead, the data for Italy are collected on the basis of the records kept in each prison of the visits of religious representatives (other than Roman Catholics) to detainees who have requested it, or, in the case of Muslims, during the celebrations of collective

Table 16.2   Presence of Religious Assistants Other Than
Roman Catholicism in Prisons in Italy

Religious affiliation	Number of prisons
Jehovah's Witnesses	53
Muslims	33
Orthodox Christians	19
Evangelicals	16
Buddhists	14
Jewish	5
Adventists	3
Christian Catholic Apostolic	2
Evangelical Pentecostal	2
Assembly of God in Italy	1
Waldesians	1
Other (not specified)	14

Source: Ministry of Justice of Italy, data updated in 2014, from 190 of the 199 prisons.

prayer (Barone 2014; Rhazzali & Vianello 2014). In Italian prisons, religious preferences for Islam can therefore be estimated on the basis of the criteria of the Pew Research Center (2009), counting the numbers of detainees coming from countries where Islam is the main religion or a significant presence. The proportion of Muslims, now fairly stable, appears to include about 50 percent of foreign prisoners (Rhazzali 2015).

Finally, Tables 16.3 and 16.4 reflect the administrative organization of the penitentiary institution but tell us little about its actual practices. A portion of religious life in prison is organized by the chaplaincy, which is run by the churches: the Catholic and Protestant Churches in Switzerland, and the Catholic Church in Italy. Beyond the chaplaincy, the administration can record specific requests for religious accommodations. However, as we noted above, religion is strongly related to other social factors and can be experienced in very different ways by inmates. The literature that defends the hypothesis of a specific "culture" (see Sykes 1958) particular to prisons also notes the existence of a gap between what is intended in the institution's formal plans and what inmates experience in prison. This culture can emerge when religious practices occur spontaneously, leaving no administrative traces, for example, when they occur outside of the time (on Sunday) or place (the chapel) that the institution had intended for religious practice.

Table 16.3   Estimate of Muslim Detainees Based on National Origin (April 30, 2016)

Countries	Women	Men	Total
Albania	32	1.954	1.986
Algeria	0	399	399
Bangladesh	0	46	46
Bosnia e Herzegovina	19	56	75
Egypt	2	539	541
Gambia	2	199	201
Libya	1	78	79
Morocco	43	3.042	3.085
Pakistan	2	187	189
Senegal	3	422	425
Somalia	2	94	96
Mali	0	52	52
Tunisia	11	1.978	1.989
Turkey	1	64	65
Other countries	7	317	324
Total	125	9.427	9.552

Source: Data elaborated from statistics of the Ministry of Justice. https://www.giustizia.it/giustizia/it/mg_1_14_1.page?facetNode_1=1_5_33&facetNode_2=1_5_33_9&contentId=SST1232347&previsiousPage=mg_1_14 (accessed September 15, 2016).

Table 16.4   Prison Population Present (April 30, 2016)

Region of detention	Number of prisons	Present detainees		Of which foreigners
		Total	Women	
National total	193	53.725	2.213	18.074

Source: Ministry of Justice. https://www.giustizia.it/giustizia/it/mg_1_14_1.page?facetNode_1=1_5_33&facetNode_2=1_5_33_9&contentId=SST1232346&previsiousPage=mg_1_14 (consulted September 15, 2016).

The fact that prisons work with the categories of religious belonging and provide services of religious and spiritual assistance reflects their attempt to regulate the religious plurality of the population of detainees, while respecting individual freedom of conscience and choice. However, this framework has changed little in form mainly due to the increased migration of people of different faiths, and prison employees have to face novel religious practices that are very fluid and mobile.

Religion Lived behind Bars: The Perspective of Inmates

Due to the new type of religious plurality observed in prisons, which requires questioning the boundaries between the religious and the nonreligious, field observations today must take into account prison life in its entirety and not be limited to religious and spiritual assistance. This implies a methodology of ethnographic inspiration, which does not classify in advance the object of observation as religious or nonreligious, and which is not limited to the description of the organizational aspects or institutional sources of religion (such as access or requests for meetings with religious representatives, presence and organization of spaces, and times officially and formally dedicated to religious services).

We indeed observed that detainees mobilize religion in multiple ways: frequenting the chaplaincy can be a form of resistance to the power of the institution (Becci 2010). A particular ritual practice can be very private, sometimes hidden, it can be inserted during "free" time, or it can become the subject of formal requests. Spiritual practices can be located on the margins of institutional religion, can be cultural-worship hybrids, and can take place in the cell, in the yard during work hours, during interpersonal exchanges between prisoners, and through personal readings. Inmates who participate in religious rituals are not necessarily those who declared to belong to the religions in question. In addition, some detainees that appear to belong to all sorts of religious backgrounds participate in prison practices such as yoga, Tai Chi, or Voodoo, which are subjectively regarded as spiritual, but which do not appear as such in the administrative classifications. It is also by identifying the books borrowed from the library of a prison in western Switzerland that we came to realize the prisoners' interests for esoteric topics such as astrology.

The perspective of the sociologist ethnographer can encompass, for example, the ways in which religious experiences, which are constructed and redefined in the practices and in the daily meetings of prisoners, emerge as a response to needs and desires that come forth in relationships, despite or perhaps because of the institutionally restrictive nature of the prison as a space of separation and control. For some detainees, the prison setting can provide an opportunity to explore or (re)construct a personal or community dimension to religion, an opportunity which can be a real challenge in the prison context. In this sense, we observed the ways in which detainees speak about religion, as well as the meaning and role it has in their prison experience. The interviews we conducted with inmates, in Switzerland and Italy, brought forth two aspects: the relational dimension of the development of religious experience in everyday life, particularly in the space of the cell, and processes of identity definition through the attribution of membership and recognition of religious practice.

The detainees interviewed in the Italian prison (Rhazzali 2010) narrate the role of fellow inmates in the rediscovery of a religious dimension previously abandoned and in the learning or relearning of the ritual of prayer. The testimony of Maati[13] illustrates this process well.

Extract 1

In a very intelligent way and without warning me, when we were together, in my or his cell, he asked me to stay silent and he started doing *Tajweed*. His voice was beautiful and hearing him, I started to cry but in a way that was less and less desperate and more and more aware that God exists and that we can address ourselves to him. I began gradually to communicate with God. And so I began to be curious and to ask lots of questions to my friend. I also started to remember that as a child I lived in a village where there was a *Tijania* brotherhood. He taught me how to do ablution and prayers. It's not that I do not know how to do them, but I made many mistakes. And so we remained friends until now on this path.

(*Maati, 39, Moroccan prisoner convicted for drug trafficking, got three years and six months in prison, detention center, Italy.*)

Here, Maati is talking about a Senegalese fellow prisoner who belongs to a Sufi brotherhood. The contact with the other, within a small space which makes the other inmate's figure immediately visible and his voice (the song) strongly present, can serve to bring back one's self-consciousness, one's own historical memory, remote in time (the memory of a Tijania brotherhood in the Moroccan inmate's past), and to rebuild a self around a new image within the current time of the prison experience, an image which takes shape in the learning process of the rituality of the religious experience (Becci 2012).

It is on the spaces, times, people, and objects of the sacred that the researcher focuses. In the prison context the Qur'an takes on the function of an "object," in the sense Tobias Nathan (2001) understood it as an object that heals:

Extract 2

Especially in prison many *Shayaateen* circulate. If you are in contact with many people some of them could get to you messages of *Shaytan*. And, myself, I don't have problems about how to beat the *Shaytan*. It is sufficient to put the Qur'an between me and him and he flees. While with human beings, even if you protect yourself with the Qur'an, they do not disappear.

(*Habib, 31, convicted of drug trafficking, got three years and six months imprisonment, house arrest, Italy.*)

Extract 3

At night here, it's hard. At night, if I do not take the sleeping pill, it is a suffering, a *Jahannam* [Hell]. God appears to me at night and questions me about my whole life. I acknowledge all my sins. I ask for forgiveness. But in a situation of anguish and fear. I started reading the *Fatiha* [The Opener, the first chapter of the Qur'an] in the hope that God gives me the opportunity to live again and not go to hell. But during the day I do nothing and I do not hold the promise to pray and stand on the right path.

(*Fouad, 39, convicted for drug trafficking, got three years and six months in prison, detention center for convicted persons, Italy.*)

The Qur'an is physically held near one's self, under the pillow or at the least in the private space of one's own cell, as a therapeutic "object." It is credited with the ability to protect from the devious attacks of *Shaitan* (Satan) (Habib, extract 2), which seeps through one's contact and relationships with others. It also brings comfort and eases torment (Fouad, extract 3), suffering and anguish, which, in the suspended time of the night, are conveyed by hesitant thoughts on life, on one's own conduct and on the future that awaits us.

The Bible as an object is also present in prison, and its omnipresence triggers reactions from some of the detainees, including David, a 40-year-old Swiss inmate educated in Catholicism.

Extract 4

So I have great debates with all the people walking around with Bibles in their hands . . . who will tell you: "God is great, the Eternal is my Lord" when they come to open the door. I try to read them the Bible, because they have it but they do not understand it, they have never studied it. They will tell you great theories on words they do not understand.

(*David, 40, several convictions—for traffic offenses—in total 10 years in jail, prison, Switzerland.*)

This desire to explore religious questions is to be understood within the experience of confinement, which focuses one's attention and intensifies sensations through deprivation, including sensory deprivation (Clemmer 1940). Objects provide anchor points and, due to their rarity in the universe of the prison, have an amplified value (Rostaing, de Galambert, & Béraud 2014).

The universe of the prison also amplifies the total or totalizing discourse on Islam (Belhoul 2009), which imposes itself as common sense, whether inside or outside the prison. As shown by Rhazzali in his study of Islam in prisons in Italy, such a representation also comes to compose the interpretative repertoires of Muslim detainees who give in to this temptation and mobilize it in their speeches about themselves and about their own relationship to religion. Extract 5, from the interaction between the interviewer (I) and prisoner (A), illustrates this attitude.

Extract 5

I: Well, I'm interested in your experience, especially your religious experience. Can you tell me a little bit about it?

A: Ah, ah . . . You're Muslim?

I: Yes.

A: It's the same. There is no difference. It's the same.

I: Yes, it's probably the same for the principles we believe in, but I'm interested in how you live your religion, to hear you tell it by yourself.

A: Yes, but it's the same, there is no difference.

I: I understand. Then can you talk about how we as Muslims are the same?

A: We Muslims, we are all the same and have the same relationship to God. It is not our experience which changes God, He stays the same. I'm locked up in here, it's not God's fault . . . God has nothing to do with my story. This is my fault only. I arrived in prison not because God wanted it, but for what I did . . . And in here it's like outside, there is the same God. And there is the same behavior.

I: And what sense is there in praying?

A: Because we all, Muslims, we pray. All must pray. Same for all.

(Amadou, 38, sentenced for attempted murder to 11 years imprisonment, detention center for convicted persons, Italy.)

Asked about his religious experience, Amadou responds with a question that aims for mutual recognition in terms of identity ("You're Muslim?") as the condition of the negation of experience and subjectivity of lived experience ("it's the same there is no difference"). Amadou seems to put in play, in the interaction with the interviewer, a total identity positioning, which is projected onto a normative dimension that is constructed and shared socially (the repeated use of "we" and "all"). This "Islamic self" in the words of Rhazzali (2010) leads not only to ignoring and excluding other possible positions, but also denies to the self any allocation of subjectivity and agency. This attitude can be illustrated by many empirical examples: a stereotype under which individuals suffer becomes the center around which they condense a very limited and limiting self-definition. The interviewer tries to question this equation while also answering the question about his Muslim identity, and in turn attempts to defy the self-attribution given by Amadou in the interaction by following his initial concession ("Yes," "Yes, it's probably the same," "I understand") with oppositional formulations ("but," "then"). He offers the interviewee, by proposing further questions, the opportunity to explore other dimensions of identity ("can you talk about how we as Muslims are the same?") and lived religious experience ("I'm interested in how you live your religion, to hear you tell it by yourself"). The nuances of this "Islamic self" stand out when compared to how local prisoners, who can be described as secular Christians, answered questions about their own religious identity:

Extract 6

I: We'll start by talking a little about your childhood, of religious questions during your childhood. Were you educated in a religion?

D: I do not really understand the meaning.

I: Did you receive a religious education?

D: Uh.

I: Did your parents pass on a religious education?

D: Well I've been to Sunday school . . . and I did my first communion. So yeah. After I just kind of stopped there.

I: But were your parents church-goers, believers?

D: Believers yeah, church-goers I don't know (.).

I: And what religion do they belong to?

D: I think they are Catholic, but I'm not sure (laughs) . . .

I: And later, when you became an adult, did religion play a role for you?

D: Actually I was all the time in somewhat bizarre trips. Back then I did not pay too much attention to that. It's only when I arrived here that I started taking out the Bible, actually.

(Bruno, 21 years old, father of one, six-year sentence extendable according to psychic state, penitentiary, Switzerland.)

This excerpt shows the difficulty of the inmate, Bruno, in identifying with a well-defined religious education: he responds only to the third reformulation of the question, after having indirectly requested clarification and after some hesitation ("Uh," "Well"). It is only after a subsequent question that he reveals the religious affiliation of his own family, Catholic, and expresses, again, doubts so as to distance himself from these affirmations. Unlike Amadou, who proposed a total and simplistic identification to his own religion, Bruno presents religion as an aspect that is neither central nor immediately recognizable in the identity definition of the person or the family. The contrast posed by these two extracts demonstrates the importance of the contextualization of a person's relationship to religion.

Conclusion

The study of religious diversity in prisons poses a real challenge to research in social sciences. It requires sociologists of religion to go beyond the normative views adopted by the prison institutions. Administrative data on memberships or religious practices that prisons make public are indeed indicators that need to be deconstructed and contextualized. The prison institution has planned a specific place for religion at the level of its regulations, its spaces, and its employees, thus promoting a normative vision of religion. However, the religious and spiritual assistance schemes and the spaces allocated for collective prayer are only two of the many aspects of religion in prison. Social science can highlight the categorical reductions of religion operated by the penitentiary institutions, but also the ways in which religion becomes the locus of new practices and gives rise to new meanings. These reductions are the product of a Eurocentric historicity as they nourish a vision of self and others that impoverishes possible social relations. Ethnography, however, can show the wealth and creative value that religion can endorse in prison. Asking prisoners about their personal relationship with religion, for example, allows us to recognize the ways in which religious experience is constructed day after day, in the experience of the cell, in the relationship with other inmates, and with the "objects" that inhabit the prison (e.g., the Qur'an).

The interview excerpts presented here highlight the different ways in which religion becomes significant for prisoners: they may challenge a particular religious belonging or, conversely, assume a "total" identity, as in the case of the adoption of the "Islamic self" (see Schiavinato, Cottone, & Mantovani 2007). The ethnographic approach allows the sociologist to adopt an active role in this process by participating in the interview (see Alby & Fatigante 2014) and by intervening in the positioning process in which the interviewee leads. By adopting a critical and reflexive ethnographic approach, the researcher commits to observing the dynamics and outcomes of these dialogues. The challenge for research in correctional institutions is to show the weight of the institution, its power of categorization, without neglecting the agency of the different actors.

Notes

1. The details on this case are in Beckford's chapter following the introduction.

2. This research takes place within the framework of the European project "BEFORE—Building Experiences in Opposing Violent Radicalisation in Europe," sponsored by the ministry of Justice (Italy) and the FEI fund, University of Turin–University of Padua.

3. Project financed by the University of Padua.

4. To collect data, we primarily used participant observation (six months), in depth interviews (54 interviews with Muslim inmates), and ethnographic conversations (230 conversations, of which 200 were with Muslim inmates and 30 were with prison operators of all three prisons).

5. In both cases, only the inmates who were definitively convicted were taken into consideration.

6. Considering the small number of institutions in Switzerland that correspond to these characteristics, and to guarantee the protection of the identity of the people we interviewed, we have not added any additional details.

7. Starting from the database of the Centre intercantonal d'information sur les croyances (www.cic-info.ch) (accessed on May 10, 2015).

8. Press release of the federal office of statistics (Office fédéral de la statistique, OFS), *Privation de liberté: moins d'incarcérations, mais davantage de détenus avec de longues peines*, n° 110, December 5, 1997. Cf. http://www.bfs.admin.ch/bfs/portal/fr/index/themen/19/22/press.html (accessed on October, 11 2016).

9. Website of Groupe Infoprisons (http://www.infoprisons.ch/titre_3/article_23.htm) (accessed on October 11, 2016).

10. Dipartimento dell'amministration penitenziaria, Ufficio per lo sviluppo e la gestione del sistema informativo automatizzato, section statistique (http://www.giustizia.it/giustizia/it/mg_1_14_1.wp?facetNode_1=1_5_30&previsiousPage=mg_1_14&contentId=SST165666) (accessed May 2, 2015).

11. Dipartimento dell'amministrazione penitenziaria, Ufficio per lo sviluppo e la gestione del sistema informativo automatizzato, sezione statistica (http://www.giustizia.it/giustizia/it/mg_1_14_1.wp?facetNode_1=1_5_30&previsiousPage=mg_1_14&contentId=SST978359) (accessed May 2, 2015).

12. The "transparency sheets" (schede trasparenza) of prisons contain the information provided by prison directions on the structure and history of each institution and on the services, sports, cultural and work initiatives, rules, and useful information for communication with inmates. They are available online on the website of the Ministry of Justice of Italy (https://www.giustizia.it/giustizia/it/mg_2_3_2.wp) (accessed June 8, 2015).

13. For the purpose of confidentiality, pseudonyms have been attributed to the interviewees. Interviews 1, 2, and 3 were conducted in a mixture of North African–Italian languages and number 5 in French and Italian; the extracts were then all translated into English (by Irene Becci and Muriel Bruttin).

Bibliography

Abdel-Malek, Anouar. *La dialectique sociale*, Paris, Le Seuil, 1972.

Achermann, Christin, & Ueli Hostettler. *"Ausländerinnen* und Ausländer im *geschlossenen Strafvollzug:* eine ethnologische Gefängnisstudie," *Tsantsa* 9 (2004): 105–108.

Achermann, Christin, & Ueli Hostettler. "Femmes et hommes en milieu pénitentiaire fermé en Suisse: réflexions sur les questions de genre et de migrations," *Nouvelles Questions Féministes* 26, no.1 (2007): 70–88.

Alby, Francesca, & Marilena Fatigante. "Preserving the Respondent's Standpoint in a Research Interview: Different Strategies of 'Doing' the Interviewer," *Human Studies* 37, no. 2 (2014): 239–256.

Annual report of 2014 from the main prison of Zurich. (http://www.justizvollzug .zh.ch/internet/justiz_inneres/juv/de/ueber_uns/veroeffentlichungen /jahresberichte/_jcr_content/contentPar/publication_0/publicationitems /titel_wird_aus_dam_e_3/download.spooler.download.1438592746537 .pdf/Jahresbericht+2014.pdf) (accessed October 12, 2016).

Babès, Leïla. *L'islam positif: La religion des jeunes musulmans de France*, Paris, L'Atelier, 1997.

Barone, Antonella. "Assistenza religiosa in carcere: un diritto in cerca di nuove tutele," *Coscienza e Libertà* 48 (2014): 56–61.

Becci, Irene. "Tactiques religieuses dans les espaces carcéraux d'Allemagne de l'Est," *Revue d'histoire des sciences humaines* 23 (2010): 141–156.

Becci, Irene. *Imprisoned Religion. Transformations of Religion during and after Imprisonment in Eastern Germany*, Ashgate, Aldershot (2012): chap. 3.

Becci, Irene, Claude Bovay, André Kuhn, Mallory Schneuwly Purdie, Brigitte Knobel, & Joëlle Vuille. *Enjeux sociologiques de la pluralité religieuse dans les prisons suisses*, rapport final, PNR 58 "Religions, the State and Society," École d'études sociales et pédagogiques, Lausanne/Haute École de travail social et de la santé, Vaud, January 20, 2011.

Becci, Irene, & O. Roy (eds.). *Religious Diversity in European Prisons*, chaps. 3 and 4, 2015.

Beckford, J. A., & S. Gilliat. *Religion in Prison: Equal Rites in a Multi-Faith Society.* Cambridge: Cambridge University Press, 1998.

Belhoul, Samuel Martin. *"Discours total. Le débat sur l'islam en Suisse et le positionnement de l'islam comme religion publique,"* in Mallory Schneuwly Purdie, Gianni Matteo, & Jenny Magali (dir.), *Musulmans d'aujourd'hui: Identités plurielles en Suisse*, Genève, Labor et Fides, 2009.

Belhoul, Samuel Martin, Susanne Leuenberger, & Andreas Tunger-Zanetti (eds.). *Debating Islam: Negotiating Religion, Europe, and the Self*, Bielefeld, Transcript, 2013.

Béraud, Céline, Claire de Galembert, & Corrine Rostaing. *De la religion en prison*, Rennes, Presses universitaires de Rennes, 2016.

Buser, Samuel. *Psychotherapie und Seelsorge im Strafvollzug: Unterschiede und Gemeinsamkeiten*, Berne, Peter Lang, 2007.

Clemmer, Donald. *The Prison Community*, Boston, Christopher, 1940.

Davie, Grace. Believing without Belonging. A Liverpool Case Study," *Archives de sciences sociales des religions* 81 (1993): 79–89.

De Giorgi, Alessandro. *Zero Tolleranza: Strategie e pratiche della società di controllo*, Rome, Derive Approdi, 2000.

Di Motoli, Paolo. "I musulmani in carcere. Teorie, soggetti, pratiche," *Studi sulla questione criminale* 2 (2013): 75–98.

Dipartimento dell'amministration penitenziaria, Ufficio per lo sviluppo e la gestione del sistema informativo automatizzato, section statistique (http://www.giustizia.it/giustizia/it/mg_1_14_1.wp?facetNode_1=1_5_30&previsiousPage=mg_1_14&contentId=SST165666) (accessed May 2, 2015).

Dipartimento dell'amministrazione penitenziaria, Ufficio per lo sviluppo e la gestione del sistema informativo automatizzato, sezione statistica (http://www.giustizia.it/giustizia/it/mg_1_14_1.wp?facetNode_1=1_5_30&previsiousPage=mg_1_14&contentId=SST978359) (accessed May 2, 2015).

Fabretti, Valeria. *"Addressing Religious Differences in Italian Prisons: A Postsecular Perspective,"* in I. Becci & O. Roy (eds.), *Religious Diversity in European Prisons*, 101–116, 2015.

Fabretti, Valeria. *Le differenze religiose in carcere. Culture e pratiche negli istituti di pena alla prova del pluralismo*, Roma, UniversItalia, 2014.

Fabretti, Valeria, & Massimo Rosati. *L'assistenza religiosa in carcere. Diritti e diritto al culto negli istituti di pena del Lazio*, Centro Studi e Documentazione su Religioni e Istituzioni Politiche nella Società Postsecolare (CSPS), 2012 (http://csps.uniroma2.it/about-us).

Goffman, Erving. *Asiles*, Paris, Éditions de Minuit, 1968. Voir également Léonore Le Caisne, *Prison. Une ethnologue en centrale*, Paris, Odile Jacob, 2000.

Gravier, Bruno. "Spiritualité et religion dans les modèles de rétablissement en institution: accompagnement et régulation dans la diversité?," symposium, University of Lausanne, May 2014.

Hunt, Stephen. "Testing Chaplaincy Reforms in England and Wales," *Archives de sciences sociales des religions* 153 (2011): 43–64.

Huntington, Samuel P. *The Clash of Civilizations? Foreign Affairs* 72, no. 3 (1993): 22–49.

Huntington, Samuel P. *The Clash of Civilizations and the Remaking of World Order*, New York, Simon & Schuster, 1996.

Huntington, Samuel P. *Le choc des civilisations*, Paris, Éditions Odile Jacob, 1997.

Jaquier, Véronique, & Joëlle Vuille. *Les femmes: jamais criminelles, toujours victimes?* Grolley, Éditions de L'Hèbe, 2008.

Khosrokhavar, Fahrad. *L'islam dans les prisons*, Paris, Balland, 2004.

Kilani, Mondher. "La religion dans la sphère civile. Une critique du 'désenchantement.'" *ESPRIT* 372 (2011): 91–111.

Le Caisne, Léonore. "La condition carcérale: points d'ombre d'une ethnographie," recension de Fassin, Didier. *L'ombre du monde. Une anthropologie de la condition carcérale*, Paris, Le Seuil (2015), in *Métropolitiques*, May 22, 2015, 5 (http://www.metropolitiques.eu/La-condition-carcerale-pointsd.html).

Monnot, Cristophe. *Croire ensemble. Analyse institutionnelle du paysage religieux en Suisse*, Zurich, Seismo, 2013.

Morgenthaler, Cristoph, et al. *Wertorientierungen und Religiosität—Ihre Bedeutung für die Identitätsentwicklung und psychische Gesundheit Adoleszenter. The VROID-MHAP-Study: Values, Religious Orientations, Identity Development and Mental Health Adolescents' Perspectives*, Bern, University of Bern, 2011 (http://www.nfp58.ch/files/downloads/Schlussbericht_Morgenthaler_Kaeppler.pdf) (accessed October 11, 2016).

Nathan, Tobie. *Nous ne sommes pas seuls au monde*, Paris, Les Empêcheurs de Penser en Rond, 2001.

OFS, *Enquête sur la privation de liberté, Détention préventive: fortes différences dans les pratiques cantonales*, press release, February 27, 2007: 5.

Pew Research Center, *Mapping the Global Muslim Population: A Report on the Size and Distribution of the World's Muslim Population,* 2009, http://www .pewforum.org/ 2009/10/07/mapping-the-global-muslim-population/#map2 (accessed September 15, 2015).

Rhazzali, Mohammed Khalid. *L'islam in carcere. L'esperienza dei giovani musulmani nelle prigioni italiane*, Milano, Franco Angeli, 2010.

Rhazzali, Mohammed Khalid. "I musulmani e i loro cappellani. Soggettività, organizzazione della preghiera e assistenza religiosa nelle carceri italiane," in Antonio Angelucci, Maria Bombardieri, & Davide Tacchini (eds.), *Islam e integrazione in Italia*, Venise, Marsilio Editore, 2014.

Rhazzali, Mohammed Khalid. "Religious Care in the Reinvented European Imamate Muslims and Their Guides in Italian Prisons," in Irene Becci & Olivier Roy (eds.), *Religious Diversity in European Prisons*, New York, Springer, 2015.

Rhazzali, Mohammed Khalid, & V. Schiavinato, "Islam of the Cell. Sacralisation processes and everyday life in prison," *Etnografia e ricerca qualitativa,* 2, maggio-agosto (2016).

Rhazzali, Mohammed Khalid, & Francesca Vianello, "Riconoscimento e pratiche del pluralismo religioso nelle carceri italiane," *Coscienza e Libertà* 48 (2014): 62–76.

Rostaing, C., C. de Galembert, & C. Béraud. "Des Dieux, des hommes et des objets en prison. Apports heuristiques d'une analyse de la religion par les objets," *Champ pénal/Penal Field,* "Objets et enfermements," XI (2014): 8868 (https://champpenal.revues.org/8868?lang=en).

Schiavinato, Valentina, Paolo Cottone, & Giuseppe Mantovani. "Self-Positioning in Contesti Interculturali," in Alessandra Talamo & Fabio Roma (eds.), *La pluralità inevitabile*, Milan, Apogeo, 2007.

Schneuwly Purdie, M. "'Silence . . . Nous sommes en direct avec Allah.' Réflexions sur l'émergence d'intervenants musulmans en contexte carcéral," *Archives de sciences sociales des religions* 153 (2011): 105–121.

Schneuwly Purdie, M. "Formating Islam versus Mobilizing Islam in Prison: Evidence from the Swiss Case," in S. M. Belhoul, S. Leuenberger, & A. Tunger-Zanetti (eds.), *Debating Islam: Negotiating Religion, Europe, and the Self*, Transcript-Verlag (2013): 99–118.

Schwarzenegger, Christian, & David Studer. "Kriminalstatistiken und ihre Interpretation," *Neue Zürcher Zeitung*, April 5 (2013).

Sykes, Gresham. *The Society of Captives: A Study of a Maximum Security Prison*, Princeton, Princeton University Press, 1958.

Todd, Andrew J. "Religion, Security, Rights, the Individual and Rates of Exchange: Religion in Negotiation with British Public Policy in Prisons and the Military," *International Journal of Politics, Culture, and Society* 28 (2015): 37–50.

Vertovec, Steven. "Super-Diversity and Its Implications," *Ethnic and Racial Studies* 30, no. 6 (2007): 1024–1054.

Vuille, J., & A. Kuhn. "L'exercice de la liberté de conscience et de croyance dans les établissements de privation de liberté en Suisse," *Jusletter*, April 12 (2010).

CHAPTER SEVENTEEN

Incarcerated Child Sexual Offenders and the Reinvention of Self through Religious and Spiritual Affiliation‡

Stephanie Kewley, Michael Larkin,
Leigh Harkins, and Anthony Beech

The stigmatization of those imprisoned for sexual offending is great. For their own safety, prisons tend to segregate those with sexual convictions into dedicated wings or facilities. Contact with other prisoners is kept to a minimum by separating them away from the main prison population. Likened to that of the "food chain" (Schwaebe 2005), only the strongest and most powerful reap social, physical, and emotional rewards in prison. Such social organization and hierarchy (Sykes 1958) is shaped in part by the *prisoner* or *convict code*, and dictates the attitudes and behaviors of incarcerated communities (Ricciardelli 2014; Trammell 2012). In particular, the convict code casts a moral judgment on people convicted of certain types of offenses (Ricciardelli &

---

‡This chapter is developed from Stephanie Kewley, "How Might Religion and Spirituality Help to Reintegrate Those Convicted of Sexual Offending and How Do Practitioners Respond?" PhD dissertation, University of Birmingham, 2015.

Moir 2013), and those with sexual convictions are treated as the most reviled subgroup within the prison community (West 1985).

Notwithstanding these unwritten codes and hierarchies, Western prisoners are further subjected to poor and harsh living conditions. A range of factors contributes to these challenging conditions. One explanation is the dramatic increase in prison populations. This increase has been experienced by institutions in both the United States and the United Kingdom over recent decades and has resulted in the inevitable overcrowding of many institutions (Cavadino, Digan, & Mair 2013). In addition to the current economic climate that has seen efficiency savings and cuts to public services, the effects of prison overcrowding are great; prisoner health and safety are compromised, privacy is limited, the prison regime is regularly interrupted and regardless of the best intentions of staff, retaining some sense of dignity and respect is often unachievable (Haney 2012). These conditions extend beyond prisoners too, as prison officers and staff experience occupational stress (Martin et al. 2012), and when prison visits are canceled family and friends are refused contact, which disrupts important social bonds.

Other significant issues mean prison living conditions are dangerous as both staff and prisoners face threats of physical violence. Across almost all male prisons in England and Wales during 2015 and 2016 the rate of violent incidents and serious assaults against staff and prisoners increased (HM Chief Inspector of Prisons for England and Wales Annual Report 2015–16). Likewise, the rate of sexual violence is said to have increased also (Stevens 2015), with particular groups, such as the young, lower educated prisoners and those with mental health conditions being more vulnerable to targets of sexual assault (Morash et al. 2012). The true prevalence of sexual violence is, however, unknown; indeed rates are assumed to be far greater than reports suggest, as sexual violence in prison is often a hidden and greatly underreported crime (Fowler et al. 2010).

The consequences of these harsh and hostile conditions include the spreading of sexually transmitted infections, exposure to disease through drug misuse, increased anxiety, depression, sleep deprivation, feelings of hopelessness (Liebling & Maruna 2005), physical injury (Sung 2010), a greater risk of suicide (Jenkins et al. 2005), and homicide (HM Chief Inspector of Prisons for England and Wales Annual Report 2015–16). Conditions for those with sexual convictions are perhaps greater still, given the rules of the prison code set by the general offending population (West 1985). Therefore, prisoners attempt to keep their sexual convictions a secret, trying not to draw attention to themselves in an effort to prevent bullying, violence (Schwaebe 2005), and sexual assault (Edgar & O'Donnell 1998). This means they often purposefully exclude themselves from social interaction, engaging with interventions or are excluded by others in the prison. As well as the social rejection inside prison, many find themselves displaced and disconnected from family and friends on the outside (Levenson, D'Amora, & Hern 2007). Accessing any type of support therefore becomes a significant problem (Burchfield & Mingus 2008). Indeed, the rate of suicide for those convicted of sex crimes is notably greater than that of the general offending population (Jeglic, Spada, & Mercado 2013). Given this harsh and unforgiving environment, it is of interest to understand if and how people with sexual offenses cope or gain relief and solace while existing in these conditions.

Although scarcely researched, religious or spiritual conversion in prison is said to bring several benefits and comforts to those incarcerated (Maruna, Wilson, & Curran 2006). *Conversion* is the rejuvenation of religious or spiritual belief, or the orientation of new ones, followed by the transformation of relationships, behaviors, thoughts, and emotions (Mahoney & Pargament 2004). Indeed, use of religion and spirituality as a means of coping is not an uncommon idea. The religion and spirituality literature indicates religious involvement as being positively associated with improved mental (Bonelli & Koenig 2013) and physical (Powell, Shahabi, & Thoresen 2003) health and well-being. In a prison context, people engaged in religion or spirituality have been found to be able to better define personal crisis, manage feelings of shame, build new identities, develop a sense of purpose and empowerment, feel forgiven, have peace of mind and a sense of hope (Dammer 2002; Maruna et al. 2006); cope with the psychological adjustment of the prison environment (Clear & Sumter 2002); and it has even been found to contribute to the rehabilitation process on release (Jensen & Gibbons 2002). Yet, despite these important findings, to date, no study has specifically examined the meaning and role of religion and spirituality for those convicted of sexual offending. This is surprising given that this particular subgroup faces additional pressures of segregation, violence, rejection, and humiliation by peers and officers while in prison.

The Present Study

This chapter presents the findings of a study aimed to begin to address this gap. Through in-depth interviews of nine men, all incarcerated for sex offenses, the present study explores the meaning made of religion and spirituality while in prison. Because of the subjective nature of religion and spirituality a phenomenological approach was used, enabling exploration of the idiosyncratic and personal experiences of participants.

Method

To best understand the "real world" and meaning made by participants, interpretative phenomenological analysis (IPA) was deemed an appropriate approach. IPA is theoretically grounded in phenomenology, hermeneutics, and idiography (Smith, Flowers, & Larkin 2009). It is a method used to understand how, from first-person experience, a person makes sense of a particular phenomenon, while presented from a third-person perspective. In contrast to a more nomothetic approach to studying human phenomenon, IPA enables the exploration of unique and idiosyncratic experiences of smaller populations.

Context

The prison where participants were incarcerated was a relativity small one, holding a maximum of 523 inmates. At the time of the interview, its purpose was to accommodate vulnerable prisoners (VP). VPs are essentially prisoners at risk; they are segregated from the general prison population for their own safety. VPs may be at risk of being bullied by other inmates, or have a mental health condition that makes coping in prison a greater challenge. Most people convicted of sexual offending are identified as a VP. This is because the nature of their offending places them at greater risk of harm from other inmates. In the establishment where my participants were drawn from, the majority of prisoners had committed a sexual offense. Therefore, there was no segregation wing or unit for the purpose of housing prisoners based on their offense alone.

The establishment also specialized in the delivery of accredited sexual offending behavior programs, such as the Core Sexual Offender Treatment Programme (SOTP) or its adapted version, for people with social or learning impairments. Additionally, the prison provided other programs, which aim to target generalized thinking associated with offending behavior, such as, Enhanced Thinking Skills (ETS) or A to Z motivation life course, and offered one-to-one programs where group work was deemed inappropriate. Men in this establishment had either completed a program, were midway through treatment, waiting to start, or to be assessed by the psychology department, for their suitability to attend a sexual offender behavior program. Completion of a program was central to many prisoners' sentence planning.

Although multifaith provisions, services, and events were available to men at this prison, only Christian ministers were resident staff members as part of the prison chaplaincy. Imams, Buddhist teachers, and other faith ministers visited when necessary.

Sampling

Participants were recruited from one prison in England and Wales. Purposive sampling was used to select participants. Purposive sampling allows participants to be selected with specific characteristics (Teddlie & Yu 2007). By doing this, the likelihood of collecting rich data from a homogenous sample was maximized. Participants self-selected to participate in the study by responding to posters and flyers located around the prison detailing the study. Participants were required to register their interest with a nominated staff member, and the sample was then selected based on the criteria of having a conviction of at least one sexual offense, and a current or previous experience of practicing or engaging with religion or spirituality. Purposive sampling was critical as it ensured those selected were able to provide information relevant to the research questions—this being a fundamental aspect to IPA.

Data Collection Procedures

As noted by Smith et al. (2009), the nature of IPA interviews is best described as conversational. They require a flexible and natural approach, which allows participants to tell their story. Although a semistructured interview schedule was developed, it was used as a prompt and guide during each interview. The schedule consisted of general introductory questions with the aim of putting the participant at ease. These then moved to open and prompting questions about participants' religious or spiritual affiliation and what this means or meant to them, how they experience(d) religion or spirituality, what role religion or spiritual communities play(ed) during periods of nonoffending, offending, detection and (where appropriate) while in custody, and while living in the community. All interviews ended with questions about how participants viewed their future. All one-to-one interviews were conducted inside of the prison by the first author (SK), and no other person was present in the private interview room. Interviews lasted between 60 and 90 minutes and were digitally recorded. Interviews were later transcribed verbatim and copies sent to participants.

The Sample

Although not prescriptive, between 4 and 10 interviews are advised for an IPA study (Smith et al. 2009). The sample in this study consists of nine adult males, all incarcerated for sexual offending and either at the point of interview or previously practicing a religion. Of the nine interview transcripts, only seven were analyzed in full; two participants (Ben and Mark) were only partially analyzed. This was because not all of their interviews were directly relevant to the phenomenon in question; instead part of their interview drifted away from the central topic.

At the point of interview, the mean age of participants was 58 years (range 29–80 years, SD 16.8). At the point of offending the mean age was 34 years (range 9–50 years, SD 11.7). Five participants had no previous offending history, two had previous general offending convictions, and two had prior convictions for sexual offending. The sample consisted mainly of people convicted for sexual offenses against children. Victims were both male and female children, and previous offenses included indecent assault; possession, distribution, and making of indecent images; rape; detaining a child; gross indecency; incest; and buggery. The various religious denominations with which participants identified included Buddhism, Christianity, Mormonism, and Paganism. A demographic overview of each participant is provided in Table 17.1. To ensure anonymity, participants' real names are not used. Instead random male names have been assigned to each participant.

Data Analysis Procedures

The analytical process as detailed by Osborn and Smith (1998) was followed by the first author (SK). To ensure the validity and rigor of the analysis, regular audit checks were undertaken by the second author (ML). Analysis was complete when all data had been included and developed into a relevant cluster and then theme. It is also worth noting in light of the methodological approach chosen that no specific definitions between religion and spirituality were prescribed. Instead, meaning from the subjects' own interpretation of their experiences of religion and spirituality was examined.

Findings

Although participants' stories are unique, many similarities and shared experiences were uncovered between the nine participants. Through the application of IPA, a range of important themes emerged. Due to the word limitations of this current chapter only three themes will be discussed. Each of the superordinate and subordinate themes is detailed in Table 17.2.

The first theme—*managing the conflict between religion or spirituality and sexual offending*—considers the extent to which participants managed the internal conflict they felt between their past behaviors of sexual offending and current and past religious engagement. More than half of the sample are described as being actively religiously engaged at their time of offending and so how they managed to function and reconcile what are argued to be conflicting experiences is of particular interest. Likewise, the second theme—*use of religious analogies*—details the use participants made of religious stories to help them both explain sexual offending and also help describe the transition they had made from one of an "offender" to a more religious or spiritual individual. The final theme—*experiencing religious or spiritual affiliation in prison and the community aids a sense of community, support, and improved status*—provides some important insight as to how participants drew on religious and spiritual communities as a resource of social capital. In particular, an interesting observation is made in relation to how inmates use religious

Table 17.1 Description of Sample

Participant	Age at point of interview	Approximate age at start of offending	Offense	Previous offending history	Religion as identified by participants
Evan	46	42	Sexual activity with a child Making indecent photographs	None	Baptist
Ben	61	31	Indecent assault	None	Buddhist
Mark	29	23	Rape of female 14 years old	Criminal damage, burglary with intent to steal, attempt to obtain property by deception	Pagan
Andrew	69	38	Meeting a child following sexual grooming Possession of indecent images Failing to comply with notification requirements	Rape, buggery, incest, gross indecency and indecent assault	Baptist
Anthony	80	36	Indecent assault, making, distributing, and possessing indecent images of children	None	Christian
Nicholas	49	9	Indecent assault Making, distributing, and possessing indecent images of children	None	Mormon
Greg	72	35	Gross indecency with a male child Sexual assault of a female child	Sexual assault	Christian
Tim	42	38	Detaining of a child without lawful authority Having sex with a child	Driving a motor vehicle with excess alcohol	Buddhist
Robert	70	50	Indecent assault, possession of indecent images	None	Christian/ Salvation Army

Table 17.2   Superordinate and Subordinate Themes

Superordinate themes	Subordinate themes
Managing the conflict between religion or spirituality and sexual offending	• Compartmentalized identities and incongruent behaviors
	• The process of forgiveness and feeling forgiven by God
Use of religious analogies	• Used to articulate experience
	• Used for identity transformation
Experiencing religious or spiritual affiliation in prison and the community aids a sense of community, support, and improved status	• Belonging to a faith group brings intimacy as experienced by family belongingStatus is gained by belonging to the in-group

belonging to aid their sense of status while in prison. Social identity theory is used to assist in the interpretation of findings but is discussed in more detail in the discussion section of this chapter. It is also worth noting that the ordering of these themes does not suggest an order of importance, as most participants experienced aspects of each of these themes, to some degree.

Managing the Conflict between Religion or Spirituality and Sexual Offending

This first theme focuses on five of the nine participants (Evan, Andrew, Anthony, Greg, and Robert) who all sexually offended during periods of active participation with their church. They described holding positions of authority within their church including youth leaders, lay preachers, or organizers of church activities. It is therefore important to explore how these five participants experienced being active in the church, while sexually offending. Two subordinate themes emerged: "compartmentalized identities and incongruent behaviors" and "the process of forgiveness and feeling forgiven by God"; each will be considered and detailed in turn here.

Compartmentalized Identities and Incongruent Behaviors

This theme outlines the extent to which participants presented themselves and framed their behaviors in a socially and morally acceptable way. In order for participants to rationalize what appear to be incongruent behaviors (i.e., sexual offending and practicing a faith), they presented two separate and distinct identities—one being their core forgiven nonoffending-self and the other a temporary and historic offending-self. Identities were separate and participants did not recognize offending behavior as associated with their core selves. Rather, offending was a fleeting anomaly to their central, core, and true-self. They were able to present their nonoffending identities with confidence, because central to their transformed self was the belief of being forgiven by God.

Participants made concerted efforts to communicate their core being and true-selves as decent, virtuous, and honest. Greg, for example, stated "I don't swear at all I don't blaspheme"; likewise Andrew has "never sworn I don't drink and I don't smoke" and Evan has "never had as much as parking tickets or a speeding fine or anything like that in a whole 46 years on this planet." They did not perceive themselves to be like a typical prisoner, who were inhumane and "animals" (Robert). Indeed, Andrew perceived himself to be far more intellectual: "a little bit more dare I say intelligent and have a better background than most of the people in here." Although participants perceived themselves to be superior to other inmates, they were not sanctimonious, in the sense that they recognized they too were imperfect: "I do try not that I am sinlessly perfect I don't think that is possible" (Anthony).

On some level, all participants experienced conflict between their offending behavior and their engagement with religion or spirituality; they had an acute awareness that their offending behavior was wrong. Andrew, with hindsight, viewed his behavior as insincere: "it was totally hypocritical of me. . . . I was a total hypocrite you know I knew what was right and what is wrong." At the time of offending, he developed strategies to support the view that his offending-self and religious-self were distinct and different: "I think I managed to compartmentalize my faith and what I was doing at other times (right okay), which is why I said totally hypocritical."

Andrew held the belief that sexual offending was wrong; the stereotyped schema he held about "sexual offenders" was one of a violent and callous stranger. Thus, his schema was not conflicted by his own behavior, as he believed his sexually abusive behavior was mutual, consenting, and loving. By maintaining this belief, he preserved his self-schema and identity, confirming he was not a real "sexual offender": "It weren't someone off the street . . . it was basically in the family . . . mutual masturbation with the boy and heavy petting and touching with the girl. . . . I was madly in love with her." Yet, when Andrew began to accept he had sexually abused his daughter, he was shocked and appalled at his behavior. The conflict he experienced can be observed in his narrative, as he attempted to wrangle with the idea of his core-self being associated with sexually abusive acts:

> I just can't even understand why at the moment I made these children [pause] . . . and you know I just [pause] I'm just appalled by it . . . it was possible to say I will of ruined their lives . . . I had created victims.

Andrew was able to sooth himself of this pain because he believed he would be forgiven: "God knows that I am truly sorry for what I have done."

Several of the participants' crimes went unreported for decades. This helped to some degree manage any conflict they felt in relation to their offending-self and their true-self, by simply ignoring the offending. Anthony, for example, viewed his behaviors as historic and contextualized within an isolated period of time. He therefore did not need to reconcile his religious identity with his offending one, because he believed his offending was the result of exceptional historic circumstances. The passage of time resolved any conflict. In addition, Anthony used justifications to help maintain his self-schema, by minimizing the abusive behaviors and taking little responsibility for the sexual assaults. He explained his offending behavior as having been a result of his lifestyle: "it was just one of the many things in my life because I lived a busy life," and being less mature "I was younger . . . I was in my 50s, I was still pretty young at heart." Not only does he believe that his youthfulness meant he was free spirited, but he convinced himself that his behaviors were innocent, harmless, and mutually consenting:

> I never took [her] anywhere except counselled her after church and dropped her home and gave her a cuddle in the car, and that's it basically, and then she started to chase me, she her car was found outside my college where I was lecturing, waiting for me and she would follow me home . . . there was no assault on her, she was cooperative in everything.

Greg also reported spending many years not thinking about his offending, thereby keeping his offending-self separate from his core-self. Following his recovery from cancer, Greg put everything, including his offending, behind him: "I came through cancer eventually got back and picked up life again." He too satisfied the conflict of his abusive behaviors with justifications that his offending was harmless, quick, and gentle: "I just slipped my hand in . . . I just stroked her I didn't grope her . . . took my hand away and nothing was said not thinking what effect it would have upon her . . . just one incident two minutes." This allowed him to believe he was not a bad person. His actions, he believed, were not carried out as a result of some calculated and predatory intention; rather he was an upstanding and moral Christian, who made one mistake: "because I am a practicing Christian . . . doesn't mean to say that I am perfect." It is also feasible to interpret these comments as Greg forming a cognitive distortion to support his offending behavior. Many child sexual offenders often use such distortions when developing offending narratives.

The ability to ignore, minimize, or contextualize offending or deviant behavior was not experienced by all participants. Robert found it difficult to manage his two identities. On the one hand, his nonoffending identity was a public and open entity, but his offending-self was secretive, private, and something that preoccupied him for many years: "it was always something that was in private that because it was so shameful . . . it was almost a Jekyll and Hyde." Indeed, as much as Robert tried to put his offending behavior to the back of his mind, he was unable to: "it had been on my mind all those years and I suppose I'd had tried to however ashamed of it I was, I tried not to think." Robert attempted to separate his offending-self with his core-self by blaming external and supernatural powers: "daemonic . . . evil forces at work in me." This was, in the long term however unattainable, and is reflected in his experiences of feeling unfulfilled with his life. He asks himself soul-searching questions: "I've got practically everything I could want, er we had recently bought a new car, and I was walking back from church thinking, I am not happy what is wrong, what is missing." It appears that only when the offenses officially came to light that Robert was able to begin to accept and address his offending-self.

Evan was unusual to the group in that, although he maintained two separate identities, his offending identity was, in part, fueled by his experiences with the church. Evan experienced a number of challenges in his life such as a marriage breakdown, bereavement, and financial problems. Unable to cope, Evan sought emotional and sexual comfort from his stepdaughter. Parallel to his offending, Evan gained support and comfort from his local church: he "became this big person in the church respected and everything was so good," he received positive and warm fellowship from his church peers and "was always being blessed . . . and it was the first time I started to feel happier." He believed God was rewarding him, he "felt like it was God you know in a sense saying it's okay," rather than punishing him for offending: "I should be being punished for what I've done . . . but instead I'm getting fellowship." Evan was able to reconcile and continue both offending and attending church by believing God endorsed his behavior. He felt: "it was almost as if God was saying to me this is the right this is the way." Evan's justifications and distorted use of his environment enabled him to offend while retaining a nonoffending view of himself.

The Process of Forgiveness and Feeling Forgiven by God

Another important mechanism that allowed participants to move on from their crimes and develop new nonoffender identities was through the process of seeking and receiving forgiveness. The importance of feeling forgiven was essential. Participants were acutely aware of both the stigma attached to having committed sexual offenses, for example, "if you mentioned the word sex offender people run a mile" (Robert), while also having to face rejection from their own family. In Greg's case "my family have chosen at the moment not to forgive me which is their choice." But it was not until they experienced forgiveness that they could reject the stigma and begin to deal with their social isolation.

Feeling forgiven had significant dramatic effects on participants' self-esteem. It enabled them to process their offending behavior to such an extent that they believed they were completely restored to a position of non-guilt, and therefore an equal member of society once again. For example, Anthony reconciled his offending behavior because he was forgiven; he "had to come to terms with it and say God has forgiven me and God has forgiven me and accepted me." Not only was Anthony able to come to terms with his offending behavior, but he believed he had also returned to the position of nonguilt, prior to his offending, because God's forgiveness had completely eradicated the whole incident from his life: "God has wiped it out I've wiped it out." Anthony believed that God forgave him and more importantly accepted him, enabling him to move forward with his life: "it is . . . not going to exist in a way that it conquers me and controls me," raising his levels of esteem. However, it is also possible that this process might also have enabled him to disassociate from having to take responsibility for his offending behavior.

Likewise, Greg was also able to move on with his life following God's forgiveness. Greg was not held back or wracked with guilt about his offending behavior: "I'm not screwed up by it." Indeed, even while those around him disowned him, Greg described having a great sense of peace: "I really do I get a great sense of peace . . . I have got quiet confidence." A belief in God's acceptance meant that both Anthony and Greg felt they were not alone, were no longer guilty for their crimes, and although were serving out their punishment, they had hope for a positive future.

Perceiving oneself to be forgiven by God did not automatically restore all participants' sense of self-worth; rather it was a process that took time. Robert, for example, could not comprehend how God could forgive those who sexually offended; he perceived his own crime to be of the worst kind: "I couldn't understand how God could forgive someone . . . the slime at the bottom of the pond." Initially, he was unable to fully restore his sense of self-worth as he was unable to forgive himself and continued to hold onto the shame of his offending history: "I couldn't forgive myself and it's taken two years I hadn't forgiven the sin I hadn't forgiven what I did." So although Robert accepted God had forgiven him, the shame he felt about his behavior prevented him from moving on. It took him almost two years to begin to deal with his feelings of shame and forgive himself: "I hadn't forgiven what I did but, I'd been able to forgive myself."

Forgiveness, for some participants was immediate; Andrew claimed "you only have to ask once." For Nicolas, "forgiveness is eternal." Yet for others, forgiving oneself was less straightforward, and required time. Forgiveness, on the whole, however, allowed participants to be restored and free to move beyond their past offenses, feeling able to release themselves from shame and guilt.

This theme developed from participants' conflicting experiences of engaging in religious or spiritual activities while also offending and moving away from offending. In order for them to achieve this, they appeared to develop separate identities. Their true and core nonoffending-self was nondeviant, virtuous, honest, kind, and hardworking. Their offending identities on the other hand were historic, deviant, temporary, a result of external forces, but importantly now forgiven. It is possible that by presenting change and a return to an upstanding and moral self, while also believing that God had forgiven them, participants created distance between an offending identity and their current nonoffending identities. By presenting the flawed and problematic identity, as one which was historic and one in which even God has moved on from, participants did not need to engage in excuses or justifications for their true-selves. Their renewed identities were fully repaired and restored. However, this was only one way in which participants articulated their experiences. Emerging in the second theme, we report how participants relied heavily on the use of religious analogies to help present their changed self.

Use of Religious Analogies

This second theme details the extent to which religious analogies were used by participants during the presentation of their experiences. Analogies are generally used to provide a mechanism to help explain a situation or point. Religious analogies themselves are often stories or lessons used to convey a particular spiritual or moral message to followers of the faith. In the case of the participants in this study, they used religious analogies in two very interesting ways: first, they used them as a mechanism to help articulate a painful and shameful experience, through the lens of their faith. Second, these concepts were used to convey the meaning of transition from one of "offender" salience to spiritual salience. Although five participants used analogies, Nicolas and Tim used them most readily and will therefore be used here to demonstrate this theme.

One such example is the "journey" analogy. Participants used this to help describe how they moved through a particular process, describing the hurdles, barriers, and challenges they faced along the way. In the case of Nicolas, he used the journey analogy to help describe his choices, to both offend and not offend, while attempting to follow Jehovah Witness and Mormon instruction and law. Nicolas described becoming disengaged with his religion when he became sexually interested in an adult female outside of his church congregation. After the relationship was over (his only sexual encounter with an adult), Nicolas began to access adult pornography through the Internet. He soon began to routinely access, download, and collect indecent images of children and engage in chat room discussions about child sexual abuse.

The use of the journey analogy enabled Nicolas to communicate his understanding and beliefs around the ideas of autonomy and predestination. Although free to make moral choices, he believed his life was predestined. He believed it was mapped out by a number of routes, each of which was determined by the choices he made. When he made decisions against scriptural instruction, he understood these to be poor choices that could lead to offending. Likewise, this analogy enabled Nicholas to explain how he came to live a life free from crime; by abiding by scriptural instruction he would be taking the alternative nonoffending route: "all I have to do is be good . . . and if I follow a path that has been laid down."

Nicolas's experience continued with the idea of a journey to help recollect and describe the periods in which he began to offend. He recalled how at first, when he began to detach from the church, he sensed falling or slipping:

> I started missing the meetings (okay) and started slipping away from the church and once you start missing one meeting you sort of, it doesn't really matter, I'll miss the next one and all this sort of thing, so . . . I started sliding away from the church.

The use of a "slip" or "fall" by Nicolas is an interesting one. To some degree it allows him to present his offending role as blameless. To slip, slide, or fall is an unwanted and unintentional occurrence; it represents being momentarily out of control. To Nicolas however, the idea of slipping represents more than being out of control for one moment, and means more than a one off incident. It represents the beginning of his offending process; the analogy enabled him to describe how he began to offend, for example: "if you are starting to slip . . . that's what starts the slippery slope again." Nicolas described how his disengagement from the church and God took the inevitable downward trajectory: "I started sliding away from the church . . . I let myself slide away from God."

Nicolas chose not to intervene or stop himself from sliding away from the church, but presents how he unintentionally began to access images of younger children; he "somehow slipped into . . . younger, in inverted commas, models." The term "slipping" is used by Nicolas to suggest his passive role. It is possible that analogies used in this way might also be mechanisms to avoid having to take full responsibility for one's actions.

Likewise, Tim also used the journey analogy. Tim became a Buddhist during his time in prison (previously Agnostic). He used the analogy not only to describe his experiences with Buddhism but also his journey through life, the destructive nature of his alcoholism, right through to his recovery. Tim's first period of sobriety was experienced during the first 18 months of his current prison sentence. At the pinnacle of his alcoholism, his life became chaotic and destructive. He regularly sought out women for casual sex and on one such occasion met a 15-year-old girl; he took her home and had sex with her.

Tim recalled the poor choices he made in life or the difficult times he faced and described going down a slope or spiraling downward; his "life had gone really really downhill." Tim appeared to use this analogy to describe the meaning of life experience in a temporal sense, rather than as a form of justification. He reflected that experiencing Buddhism and moving through life was itself an ongoing journey, that: "it's all about your . . . your journey through life."

The journey analogy comes into the fore for Tim when he described his process of recovery. He recounted how he began to tentatively rebuild his life following years of alcohol abuse. Tim had to prepare himself for the changes he had to make; he "got ready for the journey" and Buddhism was a platform that enabled him to find his old self; it was a "stepping stone for me finding myself." He was only able to begin to recover when he wanted to stop drinking: "you actually turn that corner where you want to stop being an alcoholic." The use of the analogy to describe recovery and not justify offending is perhaps not unsurprising as Tim only came to Buddhism at the point of sobriety.

The journey analogy appeared to help Tim retell his life story and explain how he arrived at each point in time; it allowed him to both communicate and develop a new identity. Tim talked about turning the corner, moving away from alcoholism, and reconnecting with the person he once was. Tim's true identity was immobilized during his time as an alcoholic; it was only when he desisted from alcohol that he recognized this: "when you've been an alcoholic for a long time and you stop drinking and . . . it actually you actually turn that corner . . . you're back to where you were, so for me . . . it's like I'm a teenager again and I'm discovering things again."

Tim recognized that the alcoholic and offending behaviors of his past were not the behaviors of the person he now identified with. Indeed, when he reflected on the destructive periods of his life journey, he recalled how his true-self would have rejected such behaviors: "I've really stepped over the mark, you know, this is something that 20 years ago I would have been appalled."

Buddhism enabled Tim to begin to see this true-self: "made me open my eyes more . . . especially to myself." His journey of self-discovery was motivated by him wanting to address the issues in his life and take the positive and intended route of his life journey: "I wanted to get my life back on track."

In simple terms, the use of analogies, as presented by participants, appears to be a useful linguistic tool, which enabled participants to articulate their experiences to others. Although examples here are from Tim and Nicholas, they were typical of the remaining participants. They too used analogies not only to convey their story in a more palatable manner but it enabled them to distance themselves from their offending selves. The use of these analogies

appears to have a secondary purpose; they appear to have enabled participants to engage in a greater reflective and validation process. The use of analogies assisted participants to make sense of their identity transition from a
salient "offender" identity to one more religiously or spiritually prominent.
This appeared important to participants, as it enabled them to make sense of
both painful and shameful experiences, as well as experiences of recovery and
restoration. This verbalization of religious stories helped internally rationalize past behavior while also conveying change to others. Demonstrating
change to others was an important feature for participants, and having the
opportunity to symbolically demonstrate change was seen by participants
attaching themselves to religious groups in prison. The importance of religious affiliation while in prison is discussed now in this final theme.

Experiencing Religious or Spiritual Affiliation in Prison and the Community Aids a Sense of Community, Support, and Improved Status

This final theme begins to document the importance of human connection,
belonging, and social identity. All participants had experienced rejection as a
result of their offending or incarceration. Indeed, feelings of loneliness, isolation, and a sense of despair all dissipated when participants made connections
with faith groups in prison. However, an unexpected finding emerged from
this theme; participants' perceived sense of social status and standing in the
prison hierarchy also improved. This perception brought about greater
feelings of self-worth and purpose for many participants. This final theme is
divided into two subordinate themes: "belonging to a faith group brings intimacy as experienced by family belonging" and "status is gained by belonging
to the in-group." Each are considered here in turn.

Belonging to a Faith Group Brings Intimacy as Experienced by Family Belonging

As a consequence of a sexual offending history, participants reported experiencing rejection both by others in prison and by family and friends. Among this
group, feelings of social and emotional isolation were great. Importance was
therefore placed on being affiliated with their religious community. Participants
described others who were religiously associated or affiliated to their church as
being like their family. Indeed, for most, the only people who maintained contact during their incarceration were people from a religious community.

This was highlighted most by Andrew's case, who was serving his third
prison sentence. He recalled the only people who maintained support
throughout each prison sentence were the people from his church: "I feel part
of the Christian family since in fact since the people who have stood by me
when I came out of prison in 85' it was a Baptist church." Indeed, his church

affiliates remained the only source of care and compassion who he viewed as his only family.

Like Andrew, others experienced the corrosion of emotional support from family and friends but an increase in support from religious peers. This tolerance and acceptance by religious associates came as a surprise to Nicolas. While on police bail he attempted to reject church friends by telling them of his sexual offending history and pending criminal charges. He was surprised, but also pleased, when they insisted on continued contact: "I told them of my offence . . . thinking they'd run away . . . they were still friendly towards me." For Nicolas this acceptance was extremely important—it validated his self-worth—he was able to begin to believe he was worthy of being part of a community, in spite of his sexual offending history.

Robert experienced a similar experience while in prison. When welcomed into a church, he was shocked by the acceptance of a fellow worshiper: "he said come to my church . . . we will accept you for what you are not for what you have done, and I was . . . gobsmacked." Robert had been rejected by every member of his family; he had been moved away from his friends and was extremely isolated in prison. Being accepted in this way meant he could consider a future and a chance to become part of a community once again.

Religious support networks, although developed in prison, were not limited to periods of incarceration. Relationships extended beyond their prison sentence and were anticipated to play a role in participants' lives, postprison. This is demonstrated in the recollection of Greg's experience. His religious support network was not only expecting his return but were ready to embrace him: "they know I will be going back there and I know I am welcome back." Assistance from religious affiliates featured strongly in participants' release and rehabilitation plans, helping Robert with practical issues; "the Salvation Army captain . . . said . . . I'm going to find you accommodation now," or Andrew with emotional support; "they will do anything to help me on release and they will be mentors and friends with no questions," and for Nicholas's risk management network "when I get out I will be able to . . . ring up one of the bishops . . . and say look can you come and chat to me pray with me . . . just to help me get my focus." Participants were reassured therefore with the notion that their church community would help, support, and guide them on release.

Prisons were not always able to accommodate all of participants' religious and spiritual needs, or at least, meet their expectations at all times. However, participants acknowledged that there were likely to be a range of explanations for this including a lack of funding, limited resources, security, prison regime, personal expectations, and so on. In saying this, where expectations and needs were met, the benefits experienced by participants were great. They were able to feel part of the wider supportive community; for many this was experienced to the same intimacy levels of a family and relationships extended beyond the prison walls, providing emotional and practical support, beyond release.

Unlike family, however, these relationships offered some additional security in terms of safeguarding practices.

Status Is Gained by Belonging to the In-Group

Just belonging to a particular religion was, for several participants, insufficient. Proactive engagement was also important; it was important because of the social status this brought. In the community, while affiliation aided feelings of belonging, being seen to be an active member in the church also aided a sense of status, purpose, and authority. This is evidenced most in Evan's narrative. He had been deeply engaged in a religious group for most of his adult life, and offended while actively practicing as a Christian. Evan believed that being involved in church activities such as organizing music, youth plays, and fundraising activities was part of this duty as a Christian: "I got involved with music there tried to help with all the plays try to help with everything any fundraising . . . did everything I could I worked hard." Playing a lead role in the organization of church activities improved Evan's sense of self-worth; he earned the respect from others within the community, which in turn made him feel important, needed, and of value: "I became this big person in the church respected and everything was so good." This was particularly important to Evan's sense of self-worth because within his own family "no matter what I did I wasn't ever allowed to really be a parent I was never really allowed to have . . . any input on any decision-making"; thus he felt powerless and redundant.

Equality, status, responsibility, and power for Anthony were recurring themes throughout his life. For many years, he was a preacher: "I would go out preaching in the X town go to X area all over I was pretty well known there as a preacher." Of importance was his position of power. Being the leader of a council, mixing with famous people he "used to meet with royalty I met with David Cameron with politicians I have had tea and dinner with them living the high life." Anthony also believed he had had a lasting influence on many people's lives: "ask them whoever they are, did you meet Anthony, and was he important in your life." His narrative and sense of worth appeared to fuel his sense of importance and entitlement. Both sexual offenses were commissioned during his employment as leader of a council and as an elder in his local church.

In custody, however, status was not achieved in the same way, yet it was as equally important to participants' identities and feelings of worth. Although opportunities to take a religious lead role or organize activities were not readily available, status and a perceived sense of superiority were achieved by just being associated with a religious group. Indeed, presenting oneself as devoutly religious further increased one's status. As already noted, participants were aware of the prisoner hierarchy within the prison; they knew they were, for example, at "the bottom of the feeding chain" (Robert). Yet this subgroup differentiated themselves further, by presenting the idea that when compared to nonreligious others, belonging to a religious group (according to the prison hierarchy) was superior. This was found to be the case with Andrew, Anthony, Greg, and Robert. They categorically opposed the idea that they were like other prisoners. Instead they presented others as immoral, inferior, and unintelligent: "all they want to talk about is sex . . . I'm not like that" (Andrew), "they were just animals" (Robert), "the walls are plastered up with half naked over virtually naked women" (Greg), and "prison has been an eye-opener really because some of them very simpleminded" (Anthony).

Being affiliated to a religious group in prison appeared to give participants permission to present themselves as superior to others. This seems to have occurred in light of the view that they perceived their religious group to be virtuous, moral, and superior when compared to nonbelieving prisoners. Although this appears from an interpersonal perspective to be a somewhat callous outlook, it is plausible that this is a process by which participants attempt to distinguish themselves from the "slime at the bottom of the pond." By viewing others of a nonreligious denomination in this way, participants are able to perceive themselves as more socially accepted and even socially elevated, thus distancing themselves from the social stigma associated with incarceration and indeed, sexual offending.

This final theme provides an interesting perspective in terms of how participants benefit from being affiliated with a faith community while in prison. First, they develop a greater sense of belonging, association, and togetherness; indeed, the religious community to some extent replaces the participants' families, thus providing an essential social bond. It also helps participants' social standing within the prison hierarchy. This perceived elevation of status helped restore participants' sense of dignity and self-worth.

Discussion

Although there is a great deal of literature highlighting some of the benefits of engaging in religious or spiritual activity, no research to date examines this perspective solely from those convicted and incarcerated for sexual offending. Through the analysis of in-depth interviews, a number of themes help to explain the unique experiences and meanings made from those engaged in religious or spiritual activities during incarceration. Participants were able to draw on religious and spiritual language and concepts, helping to articulate experiences of offending and making sense of their transformation of identities from one of "offender" to "nonoffender." In addition, participants developed social bonds with others, improving a sense of belonging, and social status. Consequentially, participants viewed their new selves as repaired and restored, bringing a sense of optimism, hope, and efficacy for their future, even during incarceration. These were important experiences and might be best understood through the lens of social identity theory.

Social identity theory is concerned with an "individuals' self-concept which derives from their knowledge of their membership of a social group (or groups) together with the value and emotional significance attached to that membership" (Tajfel 1981, 255). Tajfel and Turner (1979) argue that through the affiliation of particular social groups, people are able to define and make sense of themselves and others through their social status and identity in society. Yet because social groups are value laden, the social ranking of a group is determined by society's positive or negative perspective on the groups' attributes or characteristics. Indeed, people within groups compare their own group's attributions and characteristics to those of others. This, in turn, impacts on members of the group whose sense of self becomes shaped on the social status of the group. Thus, when social identity is unsatisfactory, because the affiliated group is of a lower social status, individuals attempt to either improve their group or join another more prestigious one (Tajfel & Turner 1979).

These experiences were reported by the participants in this study. They found themselves affiliated with two very low social status groups, and to some extent were doubly stigmatized first by the label "offender" and second by derogatory terms such as "nonce," "paedo," and "monster" (Hanvey, Wilson, & Philpot 2011; Marshall 1996). Such labels are steeped in stereotypical and typically disproportionate notions (Dabney, Dugan, Topalli, & Hollinger 2006; Haegerich, Salerno, & Bottoms 2013; Nee & Witt 2013). Values associated with these stereotypes include the idea that "sex offenders" are inevitable recidivists (Levenson, Brannon, Fortney, & Baker 2007) and are unreformable, depraved, and deviant (Pickett, Mancini, & Mears 2013). In an effort to distance themselves away from such stereotyping it was observed that through affiliation with the positive features of a religious or spiritual group, participants were able to adopt the positive characteristics of the group.

Social identity theory supposes that humans strive to achieve a positive sense of self and are therefore motivated to improve or at least maintain levels of self-esteem. It is perhaps unsurprising then that participants made such effort to affiliate with social groups in which they perceived themselves more akin to. Affiliation to nonoffending groups enables people to begin to develop and generate new narratives that support reformed identities (Maruna 2001). These new identities serve to provide distance between the reformed-self and the old offending-self. Participants' eagerness to convey this change was observed throughout the study. As a result of religious or spiritual affiliation, not only did participants develop a new sense of self, but this was corroborated by their disassociation with lower status "offender" out-groups. This was noted most when participants referred to other nonreligious prisoners, in derogatory terms such as "simpleminded animals." Identifying with a more socially prestigious religious and spiritual in-group, participants perceived themselves to share the in-groups' positive attributes and characteristics. Such internal change meant participants perceived themselves to be reformed, no longer deviant, and had absorbed the positive and prosocial traits of the new in-group.

These initial findings are encouraging because social identity theory tells us that members of an in-group will ultimately take on the behaviors and attitudes of their preferred group. Although the participants in this study presented adoption of in-group behaviors in an undesirable way, this needs to be understood within the complexity of the prison code. Participants accepted the low ranked status of their offense category, that is, nonsexual offending groups are more superior to groups of people convicted of sexual offending (Ricciardelli & Moir 2013), yet they reinterpreted this code by classifying those with a lack of morality or etiquette, a limited education or a lower socio-economic status as being inferior to them. Although presenting hostile attitudes toward other inmates is perhaps an undesirable characteristic, in the light of social identity theory, it is perhaps understandable. Indeed, participants with very strong religious affiliations appeared to rid themselves of the social stigma and affiliation of a "sex offender" out-group, with ease. Through the motivation to improve their sense of self and become affiliated to an in-group, participants in this study were able to classify themselves, not according to their crimes, but according to their religious or spiritual affiliation.

This use of religious and spiritual affiliation to operate as a platform to change social status and identity is potentially important, not only in terms of it supporting a person to cope during periods of incarceration but it might also have the potential to support a process of desistance (Giordano, Cernkovich, & Rudolph 2002; Maruna 2001; Paternoster & Bushway 2009). Indeed, an understanding of how the shift in one's identity occurs as a result of affiliating with religious and spiritual groups has been somewhat overlooked in the literature (Ysseldyk, Matheson, & Anisman 2010).

Although participants did not use the term "identity transformation," they frequently expressed the notion of internal change, personal reform, or the reconnecting with the true-self. Participants appeared to achieve identity transformation in three ways. First, their newfound religious or spiritual affiliation provided them a new socially accepted group with which to attach to (Stryker 1968). Presenting oneself as belonging to a particular group is as much a signal to others about social identity as is belonging to the group. Second, religious or spiritual affiliation provided participants access to analogies, symbols, and language that enabled them to better communicate their identity transformation to others (Marranci 2009). Third, through affiliation with a religious or spiritual group, participants were not only able to develop new nonoffending identities or narratives (Giordano et al. 2002; Maruna 2001; Paternoster & Bushway 2009) but could justify their transformed self. They did this by claiming their capacity to change was not only a result of their own doing, but a result of God's intervention and sanction. Their change was because God had redeemed them. This use of external corroboration is echoed in Maruna's (2001) redemption scripts. However, participants here had no external outlet to provide a validation of change. Absent of such support, their testimony came from a higher power.

The findings in this study are of importance in that they provide some preliminary insight into the potential role religious and spiritual communities might play for those convicted of sexual offending. This role is likely to be complex, but has the potential to assist people to break away from the stigma attached to their offending histories and therefore elevate their social status.

As with all research, there are limitations to this study. Among them is the small sample size and subjective approach used in IPA, which can be perceived to be a fundamental weakness of empirical research. Indeed, such criticism is central to decades of debates regarding nomothetic and idiographic approaches (Hermans 1988). Essentially, critics argue that small sample sizes fail to generalize findings and cannot establish any general scientific principle, therefore rendering it immaterial (Eysenck 1954). However, the establishment of new laws or generalization of findings is of course not the purpose of IPA. Instead, as in the case here, small sample sizes assist researchers to examine and explore in detail, the unique and idiosyncratic experiences of participants, thus giving a "voice to the concerns of participants" (Larkin, Watts, & Clifton 2006, 102). Likewise, Guest, Bunce, and Johnson (2006) found that thematic saturation from qualitative research can appear at as little as six interviews.

Findings of this study also reveal some important opportunities for penal policy makers. First, it demonstrates that by providing prisoners with greater opportunities to engage and affiliate themselves with religious communities, health and well-being outcomes are likely to improve. For example, by providing inmates with as many opportunities to engage in faith interventions, religious services, faith group discussions, access to prayer meetings, religious text study, and so on, the need for medical intervention or prescription drugs for conditions such as depression, anxiety, and sleep disorders might be reduced. Thus, improved mental and physical health will also help prisoner's behavior in terms of increasing motivation to change, engagement in education, work, and accredited programs, as well as reduce the likelihood of disorder and violence. Finally, by strengthening external social bonds, the opportunities available to develop robust formal risk management plans, when preparing to release prisoners back into the community, are far greater. Instead of relying heavily on statutory services to support the reintegration of socially isolated clients, correctional officers can draw on the support of community members to help with this important process, thus returning people back to the community in a safe, controlled, and dignified manner.

Conclusion

This study has provided some preliminary yet important insights into the experiences of those incarcerated for sexual offending while engaged in a religious or spiritual community. There are, of course, far more questions that need answering; indeed this research possibly unearths more questions than provides answers. What is clear from this study, however, is that the religious and spiritual experiences of those incarcerated helped them to feel forgiven, develop an improved sense of self-efficacy, and feel hope for their future.

Bibliography

Bonelli, R. M., & Koenig, H. G. Mental disorders, religion and spirituality 1990 to 2010: A systematic evidence-based review. *Journal of Religion and Health* 52, no. 2 (2013): 657–673.

Burchfield, K. B., & Mingus, W. Not in my neighborhood: Assessing registered sex offenders' experiences with local social capital and social control. *Criminal Justice and Behavior* 35, no. 3 (2008): 356–374.

Cavadino, M., Dignan, J., & Mair, G. *The penal system: An introduction* (5th ed.). London: Sage, 2013.

Clear, T. R., & Sumter, M. T. Prisoners, prison, and religion: Religion and adjustment to prison. *Journal of Offender Rehabilitation* 35, no. 3–4 (2002): 125–156.

Dabney, D. A., Dugan, L., Topalli, V., & Hollinger, R. C. The impact of implicit stereotyping on offender profiling: Unexpected results from an observational study of shoplifting. *Criminal Justice and Behavior* 33, no. 5 (2006): 646–674.

Dammer, H. R. The reasons for religious involvement in the correctional environment. *Journal of Offender Rehabilitation* 35, no. 3–4 (2002): 35–58.

Edgar, K., & O'Donnell, I. Assault in prison the 'victim's' contribution. *British Journal of Criminology* 38, no. 4 (1998): 635–650.

Eysenck, H. J. The science of personality: Nomothetic. *Psychological Review* 61, no. 5 (1954): 339–342.

Fowler, S. K., Blackburn, A. G., Marquart, J. W., & Mullings, J. L. Would they officially report an in-prison sexual assault? An examination of inmate perceptions. *The Prison Journal* 90, no. 2 (2010): 220–243.

Giordano, P. C., Cernkovich, S. A., & Rudolph, J. L. Gender, crime, and desistance: Toward a theory of cognitive transformation. *American Journal of Sociology* 107, no. 4 (2002): 990–1064.

Guest, G., Bunce, A., & Johnson, L. How many interviews are enough? An experiment with data saturation and variability. *Field Methods* 18, no. 1 (2006): 59–82.

Haegerich, T. M., Salerno, J. M., & Bottoms, B. L. Are the effects of juvenile offender stereotypes maximized or minimized by jury deliberation? *Psychology, Public Policy, and Law* 19, no. 1 (2013): 81–97.

Haney, C. Prison effects in the era of mass incarceration. *The Prison Journal*, 2012.

Hanvey, S., Wilson, C., & Philpot, T. *A community-based approach to the reduction of sexual reoffending: Circles of support and accountability.* London: Jessica Kingsley, 2011.

Hermans, H. J. M. On the integration of nomothetic and idiographic research methods in the study of personal meaning. *Journal of Personality* 56, no. 4 (1988): 785–812.

HM Chief Inspector of Prisons for England and Wales Annual Report 2015–16. London. https://www.gov.uk/government/uploads/system/uploads/attach ment_data/file/540513/hmip-annual-report-print.pdf

Jeglic, E. L., Spada, A., & Mercado, C. C. An examination of suicide attempts among incarcerated sex offenders. *Sexual Abuse: A Journal of Research and Treatment* 25, no. 1 (2013): 21–40.

Jenkins, R., Bhugra, D., Meltzer, H., Singleton, N., Bebbington, P., Brugha, T., Coid, J., Farrell, M., Lewis, G., & Paton, J. Psychiatric and social aspects of suicidal behaviour in prisons. *Psychological Medicine* 35, no. 2 (2005): 257–269.

Jensen, K. D., & Gibbons, S. G. Shame and religion as factors in the rehabilitation of serious offenders. *Journal of Offender Rehabilitation* 35, no. 3 (2002): 209–224.

Jones, S. *Criminology* (4th ed.). New York: Oxford University Press, 2009.

Kewley, S., Beech, A. R., & Harkins, L. Examining the role of faith community groups with sexual offenders: A systematic review. *Aggression and Violent Behavior* 25 (2015): 142–149.

Larkin, M., Watts, S., & Clifton, E. Giving voice and making sense in Interpretative Phenomenological Analysis. *Qualitative Research in Psychology* 3, no. 2 (2006): 102–120.

Levenson, J., Brannon, Y., Fortney, T., & Baker, J. Public perceptions about sex offenders and community protection policies. *Analyses of Social Issues and Public Policy* 7, no. 1 (2007): 137–161.

Levenson, J., D'Amora, D., & Hern, A. Megan's Law and its impact on community re-entry for sex offenders. *Behavioral Sciences & the Law* 25, no. 4 (2007): 587–602.

Liebling, A., & Maruna, S. *The effects of imprisonment.* London: Routledge, 2005.

Mahoney, A., & Pargament, K. I. Sacred changes: Spiritual conversion and transformation. *Journal of Clinical Psychology* 60, no. 5 (2004): 481–492.

Marranci, G. *Faith, ideology and fear Muslim identities within and beyond prisons.* London: Continuum International, 2009.

Marshall, W. L. The sexual offender: Monster, victim, or everyman? *Sexual Abuse: A Journal of Research and Treatment* 8, no. 4 (1996): 317–335.

Martin, J. L., Lichtenstein, B., Jenkot, R. B., & Forde, D. R. "They can take us over any time they want": Correctional officers' responses to prison crowding. *The Prison Journal* 92, no. 1 (2012): 88–105.

Maruna, S. *Making good: How ex-offenders reform and reclaim their lives.* Washington, DC: American Psychological Association, 2001.

Maruna, S., Wilson, L., & Curran, K. Why God is often found behind bars: Prison conversions and the crisis of self-narrative. *Research in Human Development* 3, no. 2–3 (2006): 161–184.

Morash, M., Jeong, S., Bohmert, M. N., & Bush, D. R. Men's vulnerability to prisoner-on-prisoner sexual violence: A state correctional system case study. *The Prison Journal* 92, no. 2 (2012): 290–311.

Nee, C., & Witt, C. Public perceptions of risk in criminality: The effects of mental illness and social disadvantage. *Psychiatry Research* 209, no. 3 (2013): 675–683.

Osborn, M., & Smith, J. A. The personal experience of chronic benign lower back pain: An Interpretative Phenomenological Analysis. *British Journal of Health Psychology* 3, no. 1 (1998): 65–83.

Paternoster, R., & Bushway, S. Desistance and the "feared self": Toward an identity theory of criminal desistance. *The Journal of Criminal Law and Criminology* 99, no. 4 (2009): 1103–1156.

Pickett, J. T., Mancini, C., & Mears, D. P. Vulnerable victims, monstrous offenders, and unmanageable risk: Explaining public opinion on the social control of sex crime. *Criminology* 51, no. 3 (2013): 729–759.

Powell, L. H., Shahabi, L., & Thoresen, C. E. Religion and spirituality: Linkages to physical health. *American Psychologist* 58, no.1 (2003): 36–52.

Ricciardelli, R. An examination of the inmate code in Canadian penitentiaries. *Journal of Crime and Justice* 37, no. 2 (2014): 234–255.

Ricciardelli, R., & Moir, M. Stigmatized among the stigmatized: Sex offenders in Canadian penitentiaries. *Canadian Journal of Criminology and Criminal Justice* 55, no. 3 (2013): 353–386.

Schwaebe, C. Learning to pass: Sex offenders' strategies for establishing a viable identity in the prison general population. *International Journal of Offender Therapy and Comparative Criminology* 49, no. 6 (2005): 614–625.

Smith, J. A., Flowers, P., & Larkin, M. *Interpretative Phenomenological Analysis: Theory, method and research.* London: Sage, 2009.

Stevens, A. Sex in prison: Experiences of former prisoners. Technical Report. Commission on Sex in Prison (2015). Howard League for Penal Reform.

Stryker, S. Identity salience and role performance: The relevance of symbolic interaction theory for family research. *Journal of Marriage and Family* 30, no. 4 (1968), 558–564.

Sung, H.-E. Nonfatal violence-related and accident-related injuries among jail inmates in the United States. *The Prison Journal* 90, no. 3 (2010): 353–368.

Sykes, G. *The society of captives: A study of a maximum security prison.* Princeton, NJ: Princeton University Press, 1958.

Tajfel, H. *Human groups and social categories: Studies in social psychology.* New York: Cambridge University Press, 1981. http://books.google.co.uk/books

Tajfel, H., & Turner, J. C. An integrative theory of intergroup conflict. In W. G. Austin & S. Worchel (Eds.), *The social psychology of intergroup relations* (pp. 33–47). Monterey, CA: Brooks-Cole, 1979.

Teddlie, C., & Yu, F. Mixed methods sampling a typology with examples. *Journal of Mixed Methods Research* 1, no. 1 (2007): 77–100.

Trammell, R. *Enforcing the convict code: Violence and prison culture.* Boulder, CO: Lynne Rienner, 2012. https://www.rienner.com/uploads/4ec29d8a8c6c2 .pdf

West, D. J. Helping imprisoned sex offenders: Discussion paper. *Journal of the Royal Society of Medicine* 78, no. 11 (1985): 928–932.

Ysseldyk, R., Matheson, K., & Anisman, H. Religiosity as identity: Toward an understanding of religion from a social identity perspective. *Personality and Social Psychology Review* 14, no. 1 (2010): 60–71.

PART 4

Conclusion

CHAPTER EIGHTEEN

Assessing the Past, Present, and Future of Research on Religion in Prison

Kent R. Kerley

In trying to craft a conclusion for this project, it became clear right away that the breadth and depth of these chapters make it difficult to identify a unifying theme other than the one reflected already in the title: the role of religion in prison life. Indeed, the chapters presented here represent remarkable advances in the religion and crime literature during the last two decades. What was a fairly homogenous and limited literature is now exceptionally diverse. This diversity is reflected in the study of multiple faith traditions, use of rigorous research methodologies, and growth of international studies. What these papers have in common is a focus on scientific discovery, regardless of the results.

I close by recounting one of my favorite conversations from nearly 20 years of conducting research on religion in correctional contexts. I was at the University of Alabama at Birmingham at the time, and was meeting with the local director of programs touted as "community and faith-based alternatives to prison." He was also pastor of a local interdenominational congregation and had recently converted the kitchen and one large section of his church building into a restaurant open to the public. We were discussing faith-based prison programs and lamenting the political debates surrounding them. We observed that one side argued that religion was the only effective way to rehabilitate inmates and reduce recidivism, while the other side argued that religious programs should never be used in prison because they are inherently coercive and unconstitutional. There was little empirical evidence to support either side, and there were very few voices in the middle. I expressed my goal of studying the topic from a dispassionate scientific perspective, and to do so as neither advocate nor dissident. As best I can remember, he summarized his view this way, "My view is not that faith-based programs should be the featured entrée in prison, but they should be on the menu." His observation captured perfectly the convergence of his tripartite career as criminal justice professional, pastor, and restaurateur.

My goal for this volume was to showcase current high-level empirical and conceptual work on religion in correctional contexts. My view is not that religion is the most important topic for understanding crime and the criminal justice system, but it should be a book in the series.

About the Editor and Contributors

The Editor

Kent R. Kerley, PhD, is Professor and Chair in the Department of Criminology and Criminal Justice at The University of Texas at Arlington. His primary research interests include corrections, religiosity, and drug careers. He is author of the research monograph *Religious Faith in Correctional Contexts* (2014). His research has appeared in many top journals, including *Aggression and Violent Behavior, Journal for the Scientific Study of Religion, Justice Quarterly, Social Forces,* and *Social Problems.* He is Principal Investigator for two National Science Foundation Research Experiences for Undergraduates (REU) grants (NSF Award # 1261322 and 1004953).

The Contributors

Irene Becci, PhD, is a sociologist and anthropologist who was trained in Switzerland, Italy, Germany, and the United States where she also taught and conducted research. In 2012 she was appointed Professor at the Faculty of Theology and Religious Studies at the University of Lausanne. Her main research areas concern religious diversity in public institutions in particular in prisons and hospitals, in urban contexts, and processes of the spiritualization of ecological issues. She has recently published articles in *Current Sociology, Journal for the Scientific Study of Religion, Women's Studies,* and *New Diversities.* She has recently coedited a book with Olivier Roy, *Religious Diversity in European Prisons: Challenges and Implications for Rehabilitation* (2015).

Kristen Benedini is a doctoral student in the Department of Sociology and Criminology & Law at the University of Florida. Her research interests include gender differences in offending and victimization and intervention programs for justice system–involved juveniles. Anthony Beech is Head of the Centre for Forensic and Criminological Psychology at the University of Birmingham, UK. Professor Beech has authored over 180 peer-reviewed articles, 50 book chapters, and six books in the area of forensic science/criminal justice. In 2009 he received the Significant Achievement Award from the Association for the Treatment of Sexual Abusers in Dallas, and the Senior Award from the Division of Forensic Psychology, British Psychological Society. His particular areas of research interests are risk assessment, the neurobiological bases of offending, reducing online exploitation of children, and increasing psychotherapeutic effectiveness of the treatment given to offenders. His recent research has examined Internet offending, new approaches to treatment of offenders, and the neurobiological basis of offending.

Nicholas Blagden, PhD, is a Senior Lecturer in Forensic Psychology at Nottingham Trent University and a Chartered Psychologist. He has worked and researched within the criminal justice system and HM Prison Service extensively. He has taught undergraduate and postgraduate courses in psychology, forensic psychology, and criminology. His work has been funded by the Ministry of Justice, BIAL, and the National Offender Management Service, and he is currently engaged in numerous collaborative forensic psychology projects. Current projects include understanding deviant sexual interest in pedophiles, prison circles of support and accountability, rehabilitative prison climates, religiosity in sexual offenders, and denial in sexual offenders. He has published articles in international journals and disseminated research at international conferences. He is a trustee of the Safer Living Foundation—a charity set up in collaboration with HMP Whatton, Nottingham Police and Probation Trust, to offer prison-based CoSA for elderly and intellectually disabled high-risk sex offenders.

Riane M. Bolin earned her PhD in criminology and criminal justice at the University of South Carolina. She is an Assistant Professor in the Department of Criminal Justice at Radford University. Her primary research interests include issues related to juvenile justice and corrections.

Megan R. Bookstaver is a Graduate Teaching Assistant at the University of North Florida. She received her BS in criminal justice and BA in political science (international relations and comparative politics track) from the University of Central Florida.

Andrew S. Denney, PhD, is an Assistant Professor in the Department of Criminology and Criminal Justice at the University of West Florida. His research focuses on institutional corrections, offender reentry, faith-based programing, sex offenses and offenders, and sexual deviance. He also currently serves on the Northwest Florida Human Trafficking Task Force. His most recent publications have appeared in *Corrections: Policy, Practice and Research, Children and Youth Services Review*, and *Criminal Justice Review*.

Grant Duwe is the Director of Research and Evaluation for the Minnesota Department of Corrections, where he evaluates correctional programs, develops risk assessment instruments, and forecasts the state's prison population. His recent work has been published in *Criminology & Public Policy, Criminal Justice Policy Review, The Prison Journal, The Journal of Offender Rehabilitation*, and *International Journal of Offender Therapy and Comparative Criminology*. He is a nonresident Senior Fellow with Baylor University's Institute for Studies of Religion and, along with Michael Hallett, Joshua Hays, Byron Johnson, and Sung Joon Jang, a coauthor of the book, *The Angola Prison Seminary: Effects of Faith-Based Ministry on Identity Transformation, Desistance and Rehabilitation* (2017).

Erin Grant, PhD, is an Assistant Professor of Criminal Justice at Washburn University. She teaches courses in communication, research, and the role of gender in the criminal justice system. Dr. Grant also serves as faculty mentor for the Criminal Justice clubs on campus. Prior to her time at Washburn, Erin worked as a Research Specialist for Travis County Criminal Justice Planning, engaging in program evaluation, program creation, and focusing much on reentry efforts. Her interest in reentry and program evaluation continue as part of her research at Washburn, as well as environmental causes of crime and experiential learning in higher education internships.

Michael Hallett, PhD, is a Professor in the Department of Criminology & Criminal Justice at the University of North Florida. Dr. Hallett just finished his fourth book and has published research appearing in numerous additional books and journals including *Punishment & Society, Journal of Offender Rehabilitation, Critical Criminology*, and others. Dr. Hallett's focus is corrections and social inequality, punishment and society, and religion and crime. Most recently, Dr. Hallett led a three-year study at America's largest maximum security prison, "Angola" (aka Louisiana State Penitentiary), exploring the religious lives of long-term inmates titled *The Angola Prison Seminary: Effects of Faith-Based Ministry on Identity Transformation, Desistance, and Rehabilitation* (2016).

Leigh Harkins, PhD, is an Assistant Professor in forensic psychology at the University of Ontario Institute of Technology. Leigh has authored a number of articles, chapters, and an edited book on sexual offending. Her research interests include understanding sexual aggression, improving treatment effectiveness with sexual offenders, and multiple perpetrator offending. She also has experience working in forensic practice settings in the UK and Canada.

This has included experience working with sex offender groups at the Centre for Addiction and Mental Health and with the Correctional Service of Canada. She has also been involved in offender assessment work in the UK.

Joshua Hays is a Research Associate at Baylor University's Institute for Studies of Religion and coauthor of *The Angola Prison Seminary: Effects of Faith-Based Ministry on Identity Transformation, Desistance, and Rehabilitation* (2016).

Byron R. Johnson, PhD, is Distinguished Professor of the Social Sciences at Baylor University. He is the founding director of the Baylor Institute for Studies of Religion (ISR) as well as director of the Program on Prosocial Behavior. Johnson recently published a series of studies on the role of religion in addressing homelessness, crime reduction, drug and alcohol addiction, prosocial youth behavior, and rehabilitation of inmates in maximum security prisons. He has served as a member of the Advisory Board of the National Institute on Corrections and a member of the Coordinating Council for Juvenile Justice and Delinquency Prevention (presidential appointment).

Jason Jolicoeur, PhD, is an Assistant Professor of Criminal Justice in the Criminal Justice and Legal Studies Department at Washburn University. He earned his PhD in education from the University of Missouri–St. Louis and his MA and BS in criminal justice from Wichita State University. He has previously published in a variety of professional journals, and his current research interests focus on the relationship between personal religious orientation and deviant human behavior, criminal justice training and education practices, and the scholarship of teaching and learning in criminal justice higher education programs.

Sung Joon Jang, PhD, is Research Professor of Criminology and Co-director of Program on Prosocial Behavior at the Institute for Studies of Religion at Baylor University. His research focuses on the effects of religion, family, school, and peers on crime and delinquency, and he has been published in various journals in the fields of sociology, criminology, psychology, and social work. Jang is leading a series of studies examining the process of identity transformation among inmates participating in a prison-based seminary, and is coauthor of the new book *The Angola Prison Seminary: Effects of Faith-Based Ministry on Identity Transformation, Desistance, and Rehabilitation.*

Stephanie Kewley, PhD, is the Programme Director for the Masters in Criminology at Birmingham City University. She teaches on both undergraduate and masters programs and is a member of the Centre for Applied Criminology. Dr. Kewley's particular expertise and research interests are in the exploration and application of strengths-based approaches for those working with clients with a history of sexual offending. She is experienced in both qualitative and quantitative methods, and translates research into practice-based training, development programs, and workshops. Dr. Kewley has published articles and book chapters in relation to strengths-based approaches, desistance theories, risk assessment, and risk management planning processes.

Mohammed Khalid Rhazzali, PhD, is Lecturer of the Sociology of Religion and the Sociology of Politics at the University of Padua, where he codirects the Master in Studies of European Islam, and the Interuniversity Center F.I.D.R. (International Forum for Religions and Democracy). His main research interests are religious diversity in public institutions (schools, prisons, hospitals); communication and intercultural mediation in institutional settings and in everyday interactions; and religious experience in the context of migration. He recently published articles in *Annual Review of the Sociology of Religion, Etnografia e Ricerca Qualitativa, Critique Internationale, Journal of Intercultural Communication, Italian Journal of Sociology of Education,* and a book entitled *Intercultural Communication and Public Sphere: Diversity and Mediation within Institutions* (2015).

Jodi Lane earned her PhD at the University of California, Irvine. She worked at RAND Corporation before moving to the University of Florida in 1999. She primarily teaches courses on the criminal and juvenile justice systems, evaluation research, and professional development for graduate students. Her research interests are in fear of crime and attitudes as well as juvenile justice and corrections policy.

Lonn Lanza-Kaduce earned his JD and PhD at the University of Iowa. For the last 35 years he has been at the University of Florida and has served as a Center Director, Department Chair, and Undergraduate Coordinator. He teaches courses on law and society, juvenile law, and criminal law and procedure. His research interests in the areas of juvenile justice, policing, and substance use often have a policy focus. Some of his grant work and publications have dealt with the transfer of juveniles to criminal court, faith-based juvenile corrections, the exclusionary rule, and social control in the aftermath of a hurricane. He is currently working on the interplay between race factors and correctional policy preferences.

Michael Larkin, PhD, is a Senior Lecturer in Psychology at the University of Birmingham, UK. Michael's main roles involve teaching, supporting and supervising research on the clinical psychology doctorate, and organizing the masters research clinical psychology course. Michael also supervises PhD students using qualitative research methods to explore experiences of psychological distress, recovery, relatedness, and caring. Research interests are in these same areas.

Judith A. Leary, PhD, serves as Program Coordinator of the Criminal Justice program at Maranatha Baptist University and as Assistant Director of Great Lakes Bible Institute. She received her master of ministry from Piedmont International University in 2007, her master of science in criminal justice from Bowling Green State University in 2014, and her doctorate of philosophy in higher education administration, also from Bowling Green, in 2015. Her 13-year law enforcement career includes emergency dispatching and adult and juvenile corrections. Her research interests include the intersections of criminal justice, theological higher education, and prisoner reentry.

Matthew T. Lee, PhD, is Professor of Sociology at the University of Akron, where he teaches classes such as "Love in Action" and "The Meaning of Life." His research on topics such as crime, substance abuse, immigration, altruism/compassion, and spirituality has been published in such journals as *Criminology, Social Psychology Quarterly, Social Problems,* and *Youth & Society.* He serves as Vice President of the Institute for Research on Unlimited Love and is a Program Facilitator for Heart to Heart Communications. His latest coauthored book is titled *The Heart of Religion: Spiritual Empowerment, Benevolence, and the Experience of God's Love.*

Alison Liebling is Professor of Criminology and Criminal Justice at the University of Cambridge and the Director of the Institute of Criminology's Prisons Research Centre. Her most recent research explores the moral quality of prison life, and the changing nature of staff-prisoner and prisoner-prisoner relationships in high-security prisons. She was awarded an ESRC-funded Transforming Social Science research contract in 2012–2014 to explore the location and building of trust in high-security settings and is currently writing up that work, with Ryan J. Williams and colleagues. Her books include *Prisons and their Moral Performance, The Effects of Imprisonment, Legitimacy and Criminal Justice,* and *The Prison Officer.* She is a coeditor of Punishment and Society and the Oxford Clarendon Series on Criminology.

Benjamin Meade earned his PhD in criminology and criminal justice at the University of South Carolina. He is an Assistant Professor of Justice Studies at James Madison University.

Michal Morag, PhD, is a Clinical and Forensic Psychologist specializing in the interdisciplinary field between psychology, criminal behavior, and law. She has accumulated field experience on the psychological aspects characterizing specific populations-at-risk such as prisoners and gang members, as well as undercover agents, intelligence informants, and whistleblowers. She has published material on the development of actuarial risk assessment tools and is currently involved in research on the social construction of trust/distrust in Israeli criminal organizations and cults.

Janet Moreno, MA, completed a graduate degree in criminology and criminal justice at the University of Texas at Arlington in 2016.

Christine Norman, PhD, is a Senior Lecturer in psychology and a member of the Sexual Offences, Crime and Misconduct Research Unit at Nottingham Trent University. Her teaching interests are in the areas of forensic psychology, psychology of religion, and mental health. Her doctoral research concerned the role of dopamine in schizophrenia, and current research includes the relationship between religion and mental health, religion and offending, and the role of sexual addiction and preoccupation in sexual offenders.

Maria E. Pagano, PhD, is Professor of Psychiatry and Biostatistics, and Research Director of the Addiction Psychiatry Training Program at Case Western Reserve University School of Medicine. She has been Principal Investigator or Co-Investigator on more than 15 NIH- and foundation-funded investigations, including the Service to Others in Sobriety (SOS) study with 200 juvenile offenders court-referred to addiction treatment. For the past decade, she has led investigations that elucidate how helping others in the 12-step program helps the helper stay sober, find faith, shifts self-centering thinking at the root of addiction, dispels isolation, the drink-trouble cycle, and the perception of not fitting in.

Christian Perrin, PhD, is a Lecturer at the University of Liverpool, UK. His teaching currently centers around the topic of persistence and desistance in offending behavior. Christian's doctoral research explored the impact of peer-support programs in prisons across the UK, and how prisoners can generate meaning and purpose through prisoner-led interventions such as the Listener scheme. More recently, Christian has published in the areas of therapeutic community, rehabilitative climate in prisons, sexual offender treatment, and the role of religiosity in the desistance process.

Stephen G. Post, PhD, is Professor of Family, Population and Preventive Medicine; Division Head of Medicine in Society; Founding Director of the Center for Medical Humanities, Compassionate Care & Bioethics at Stony Brook University School of Medicine. He is Founder and President of the Institute for Research on Unlimited Love (www.unlimitedloveinstitute.org). His 300 articles have appeared in the *New England Journal of Medicine,* the *Journal of the American Medical Association, Lancet, Nature, Science,* the *Journal of Religion,* the *Journal of the American Academy of Religion,* and the *Journal of Social Philosophy.*

Malcolm L. Rigsby is an attorney and faculty member in the Department of Sociology, Human Services and Criminal Justice at Henderson State University, Arkansas. Rigsby is an Associate Professor and Coordinator of criminal justice and conducts research in prisoner conversion experiences and transformations in identity. His research provides an interdisciplinary approach employing outcomes-based measures for lowering recidivism rates and helping prisoners experience greater likelihood of desistance from crime, antisocial, and radical outcomes. He is active in publication peer review, public speaking, documentary film review, and consulting. Interests include human rights worldwide. He has been interviewed in both domestic and international circuits.

Gabriel Rubin, PhD, is an Associate Professor of Justice Studies at Montclair State University. He is the author of *Freedom and Order: How Democratic Governments Restrict Civil Liberties after Terrorist Attacks—and Why Sometimes They Don't* (2011) and has published articles and chapters on terrorism and global justice. His current book project explores today's exploding number of migrants and refugees, exposing how the current nation-state system created the problem and how global coordination and a human rights approach are needed to solve it.

Valentina Schiavinato earned her PhD in social and personality psychology and specialized in clinical and community psychology. She teaches social psychology and community psychology at the University of Padua, where she also coordinated the master in studies on European Islam. Her main research interests are cultural and religious pluralism, communication and intercultural mediation in institutional settings and in everyday interactions, and construction of identities and positioning practices. She is specialized in qualitative methods of social research and in discourse and conversation analysis. She is a member of Interaction & Culture Lab (University of Padova) and FIDR (International Forum for Religions and Democracy—Interuniversity Center Culture, Religions and Law). She recently published articles in *Etnografia e Ricerca Qualitativa, Critique Internationale,* and *Journal of Intercultural Communication.*

Andrew Skotnicki, PhD, teaches Christian ethics at Manhattan College in New York City. He is the author of *Religion and the Development of the American Penal System, Criminal Justice and the Catholic Church, The Last Judgment: Christian Ethics in a Legal Culture,* and numerous articles on the moral and religious implications of criminal justice.

Elly Teman, PhD, is a cultural anthropologist specializing in the anthropology of the body, medical anthropology, the anthropology of reproduction, life stories, and Jewish folklore. She has published ethnographic articles on

Ultra-orthodox Jewish women's decision making during pregnancy, as well as many articles on surrogate motherhood in Israel. Her ethnography, *Birthing a Mother: The Surrogate Body and the Pregnant Self*, was published in 2010.

Ryan J. Williams, PhD, is a Research Associate with the Centre of Islamic Studies in Cambridge and jointly an associate member in the Prisons Research Centre at the Institute of Criminology. He has held fellowships in Canada and at Cambridge and recently served as Co-Investigator for an ESRC-funded study on faith identity and trust in two high-security English prisons. His current research focuses on lived experiences of citizenship among Muslims through the criminal justice system. He has published in the areas of interfaith dialogue, the sociology of religion, and religion and health, and has ongoing interests around faith identity, ethics, and multiculturalism.

Belinda Winder, PhD, is a Professor in Forensic Psychology and Head of the Sexual Offences, Crime and Misconduct Research Unit, in the Division of Psychology at Nottingham Trent University. She is also part-based at HMP Whatton, one of Europe's largest sex offender prisons, and works closely with the senior management, psychology, and health care departments there to conduct mixed method research and evaluations that make a significant and practical contribution to our understanding of sex offenders and sexual crime. Belinda is also a trustee and cofounder of the Safer Living Foundation, a charity set up to promote the rehabilitation of sex offenders and the prevention of further victims of sexual crime. Belinda's research interests focus on sexual crime, but also more broadly on desistance and rehabilitation. In addition, Belinda maintains a strong interest in religion and spirituality (in forensic and nonforensic settings) and is undertaking a mixed method program of research exploring the psychology of religion.

Index

Note: Page numbers in *italics* refer to tables.